Constitutional Dialogues

Constitutional Dialogues
Interpretation as Political Process

Louis Fisher

Princeton University Press
Princeton, New Jersey

Library of Congress Cataloging-in-Publication Data:
Fisher, Louis.
Constitutional dialogues : interpretation as political process / Louis
Fisher.
p. cm.
Bibliography: p.
Includes index.
ISBN 0-691-07780-0 (alk. paper). ISBN 0-691-02287-9 (pbk.)
1. United States—Constitutional law—Interpretation and
construction.   2. Judicial review—United States.   I. Title.
KF4550.F57   1988   342.73′024—dc19   [347.30224]   88-9629

This book has been composed in Linotron Baskerville

Clothbound editions of Princeton University Press books
are printed on acid-free paper, and binding materials are
chosen for strength and durability. Paperbacks, although satisfactory
for personal collections, are not usually suitable for library rebinding

Printed in the United States of America
by Princeton University Press,
Princeton, New Jersey

Portions of the first six chapters of this book are taken from the author's forthcoming *American Constitutional Law* and are reproduced by
permission of the publisher, Random House, Inc.

To Herman C. Pritchett,
*for enriching and gracing
the lives of students and friends*

Contents

Acknowledgments

The theme of this book results in large part from a fifteen-year dialogue between myself, a political scientist, and Morton Rosenberg, an attorney. As colleagues in the Congressional Research Service, we have worked jointly on a number of projects, shared materials and discoveries, and critiqued each other's writings and ideas. These exchanges produced a deeper understanding of how constitutional law develops. I am also indebted to Phillip J. Cooper of the State University of New York at Albany. Attracted to his studies in public law, I struck up another dialogue and benefited greatly from his friendship and encouragement. His views were particularly helpful and instructive with Chapters two and three. Finally, I want to thank Judith Rabinowitz, a trial attorney with the Department of Justice. Her reading of the manuscript provided valuable insights from someone who works at the ground level, and sometimes in the trenches, with the practice and theory of law.

A number of other people helped sharpen my ideas. In particular, I want to thank Paul Brest of the Stanford Law School, U.S. Judge Frank M. Coffin of the First Circuit, Neal Devins of the William and Mary Law School, U.S. Judge Ruth Bader Ginsburg of the D.C. Circuit, Robert A. Katzmann of the Brookings Institution, U.S. Judge Abner J. Mikva of the D.C. Circuit, W. Michael Reisman of the Yale Law School, and C. C. Torbert, Jr., Chief Justice of Alabama.

With regard to my publishers, I first want to thank Bertrand W. Lummus of Random House for allowing me to use, for this book, portions of a much larger study in process on American constitutional law. I am also very pleased to work again with Sanford G. Thatcher of Princeton University Press. This is my third book with Princeton and with Sandy. From what might otherwise be a rather solitary regimen of research and writing, it is a pleasure to maintain his association and support. Brian R. MacDonald copyedited the manuscript and offered many helpful suggestions for clarity and style.

Some of the material in this book originally appeared as articles in the following journals: *Cumberland Law Review, Georgia Law Review, Journal of Political Science, North Carolina Law Review,* and *Public Administration Review.* I also presented papers and addresses at conferences sponsored by the American Political Science Association, Cumberland Law School, Dickinson College, George Mason University, Kennesaw College, Northwestern University, Princeton University, the University of Cincinnati, the University of Dallas, the U.S. District Court for the Northern District of California, Wake Forest University, the Law School at Melbourne University in Australia, the Philippine Bar Association in Manila, and the Hebrew University in Jerusalem.

Constitutional Dialogues

Introduction

The purpose of this book is to show that constitutional law is not a monopoly of the judiciary. It is a process in which all three branches converge and interact with their separate interpretations. Important contributions also come from the states and the general public.

The theme itself is not new. In *The Least Dangerous Branch* (1962), Alexander Bickel said that the courts find themselves engaged in a "continuing colloquy" with political institutions and society at large, a process in which constitutional principle is "evolved conversationally not perfected unilaterally." Recent studies by John Agresto, Sotirios Barber, and Walter Murphy emphasize the contributions by institutions outside the courts.[1] In previous works, I have explored this larger framework of constitutional law.[2]

This book demonstrates, with very concrete examples, the kind of colloquy Bickel had in mind. Constitutional law is a complicated, subtle process—far removed from the simple and beguiling model of the Supreme Court issuing the "final word." Most of my illustrations come directly from the judiciary, either from caselaw or the outside writings of judges. In its more candid moments, if the reader will take the time to tease out the underlying message, the Court readily acknowledges that it is not the sole agency in deciding constitutional questions.

Unfortunately, most of the major textbooks on constitutional law promote the idea of judicial supremacy. The subject is treated as the discipline of interpreting the text of a document and the gloss placed

[1]John Agresto, The Supreme Court and Constitutional Democracy (1984); Sotirios Barber, On What the Constitution Means (1984); Walter F. Murphy, "Who Shall Interpret? The Quest for the Ultimate Constitutional Interpreter," 48 Rev. Pol. 401 (1986).

[2]Constitutional Conflicts between Congress and the President (1985); "Constitutional Interpretation by Members of Congress," 63 N.C. L. Rev. 707 (1985); "Congress and the Fourth Amendment," 21 Ga. L. Rev. 107 (1986); "Social Influences on Constitutional Law," 15 J. Pol. Sci. 7 (1987).

upon it by judicial rulings. In a provocative comment, Professor Michael Reisman recently described the method used in law schools:

> Constitutional law in American law schools is identified as the work of the Supreme Court in supervising the discharge of what is decided are the "constitutional functions" performed by all other authorized agencies in the national community. But the Constitution is not a document; it is an institution, as Llewellyn put it. As such, it involves a process in which many other formal and informal, authoritative and functional actors participate. These, alas, are never studied under the rubric of constitutional law. In this respect, there is no comprehensive course on constitutional law in any meaningful sense in American law schools.[3]

The intersections between law and politics are given inadequate attention for a number of reasons. In part we want to believe that law is unsullied by politics, despite rather abundant information that comes to us year after year demonstrating beyond doubt various linkages and interactions. We remain of two minds. As Robert Dahl noted three decades ago, Americans are not quite willing to accept the fact that the Supreme Court "*is* a political institution and not quite capable of denying it; so that frequently we take both positions at once. This is confusing to foreigners, amusing to logicians, and rewarding to ordinary Americans who thus manage to retain the best of both worlds."[4]

A purely technical approach to the law misses the constant, creative interplay between the judiciary and the political system. Adjudication is one of many methods in government for resolving politi-

---

[3]W. Michael Reisman, "International Incidents: Introduction to a New Genre in the Study of International Law," 10 Yale J. Int'l L. 1, 8 n.13 (1984). A few legal textbooks include sections on congressional and presidential participation: Paul Brest, Processes of Constitutional Decisionmaking 15–31 (1975), and Gerald Gunther, Constitutional Law 21–29 (11th ed. 1985). The section in Brest is omitted from his second edition, coauthored in 1983 with Sanford Levinson, but the second edition devotes an entire chapter to the allocation of constitutional decisionmaking authority between Congress and the judiciary (pp. 903–1015). See also Laurence H. Tribe, American Constitutional Law (1978). Tribe does not regard the rulings of the Supreme Court "as synonymous with constitutional truth" (p. iv) and he recognizes a process "which on various occasions gives the Supreme Court, Congress, the President, or the states, the last word in constitutional debate."

[4]Robert A. Dahl, "Decision-Making in a Democracy: The Supreme Court as a National Policy-Maker," 6 J. Pub. L. 279 (1957). Emphasis in original.

cal conflict. Private individuals and public agencies, joined by a growing number of interest groups, come before the courts to settle their disputes. These cases may begin as a personal grievance, but they contain issues of broad sociopolitical dimensions. Basic questions of political philosophy and individual rights are at stake, requiring a dialogue not just among jurists but among all sectors of society.

The customary identification of the Supreme Court as the exclusive source of constitutional law is far too limiting. The Supreme Court is not the sole or even dominant agency in deciding constitutional questions. Congress and the President have an obligation to decide constitutional questions. For members of Congress to shy away from these issues, claiming that the Court must make the ultimate determination, is tempting but irresponsible. Constitutional issues generally turn not so much on technical legal analysis of particular provisions but rather on a choice between competing sections that contain conflicting political and social values. The Court needs the conscientious guidance and participation of the legislative and executive branches. Equally important are the judgments of state courts and the general public.

The Constitution undergoes constant interpretation and reinterpretation by legislators and executive officials. Constitutional questions are considered when Congress debates legislation and when Presidents decide to sign or veto bills presented to them. The Attorney General and the Comptroller General analyze (and resolve) many constitutional questions, as do general counsels in the agencies. Actions by the political branches, over the course of years, help determine the direction and result of a Supreme Court decision. Often constitutional issues are hammered out without the need for litigation.

Charles Evans Hughes, in a widely quoted epigram, said that "We are under the Constitution, but the Constitution is what the judges say it is."[5] The Supreme Court nevertheless recognizes that each branch of government, in the performance of its duties, must initially interpret the Constitution.[6] Those interpretations are given great weight by the Court; sometimes they are the controlling factor.[7] When courts

[5]Charles Evans Hughes, Addresses and Papers 139 (1908).
[6]United States v. Nixon, 418 U.S. 683, 703 (1974).
[7]Rostker v. Goldberg, 453 U.S. 57 (1981), concerning male-only registration for military service.

5

decide to duck a case by using threshold devices of standing and other techniques, the political branches have the first and last word on constitutional issues. Indeed, they have the only word.

To explain the process that shapes our fundamental law, this book is divided into seven chapters. The contributions of Congress and the President must be placed within a broad setting, for all three branches are constantly buffeted by political, historical, and social forces. Just as it is a mistake to study constitutional law solely from the standpoint of court decisions, so would it be misleading to treat constitutional interpretation as simply the interactions between the judiciary and the other branches. Government operates within a political culture that presses its own brand of constitutional law.

Chapter One lays the groundwork for this broad context. It covers litigation as a political process, the intervention of interest groups, the Executive's role in court, congressional duties, and the judge as lawmaker and administrator. A number of institutional questions are addressed. To what extent does the Solicitor General divide his duties between the President and the judiciary? How are the House and the Senate organized to protect the interests of Congress? How do Congress and the President fit into the complex picture of institutional and interest-group pressures?

Chapter Two examines the doctrine of judicial review. Unless we understand the unsettled nature of the Court's authority to review actions by other branches, we are unable to see why the door is deliberately left open for congressional and executive participation. It is one thing to concede the Supreme Court's duty to review state actions but quite another to accept judicial review of coordinate bodies, Congress and the President. Important constraints operate on the second type of judicial review; this reality allows the executive and legislative branches to authoritatively advance their own doctrines of constitutional law.

Because of the shaky foundation of judicial review, the Court consciously circumscribes its activities and invites other branches to participate. Chapter Three analyzes the threshold requirements used by the Court to restrain its power: the case-or-controversy test, standing, mootness, ripeness, and political questions. The courts employ these thresholds to minimize collisions with the other branches of government. A number of issues never reach the courts because of these self-limiting conditions imposed by judges. This spirit of give-

and-take and mutual respect allows an unelected Court to function and survive in a democratic society.

Thresholds raise important questions. How much can Congress determine who has standing to sue without encroaching on the judiciary's right to decide what is a case or controversy? How do courts issue "advisory opinions" that telegraph helpful hints to legislatures? How did Congress, by authorizing declaratory judgments, supply the Court with a middle ground between the previous rule on case or controversy and the forbidden advisory opinion? When does the Court invoke issues of ripeness because Congress is unwilling to challenge presidential actions?

To appreciate other connections between the judiciary and the political branches, Chapter Four examines questions of judicial organization: how Congress set up the court system, how Congress created "legislative courts" that in time became full-fledged constitutional courts, and how the Senate and the House are involved in appointments to the courts. In addition to appointments, Congress also handles the sensitive matter of removing or disciplining federal judges by working through the judicial councils, which are themselves creatures of Congress. Other aspects of organization concern congressional determinations of judicial compensation and how the courts lobby Congress.

Constitutional dialogues include the decisionmaking process within the courts. Chapter Five covers the mechanics of how the judiciary reaches a decision, the boundaries of jurisdiction for courts, and the choice between striving for unanimity or allowing concurrences and dissents. Unanimity is often important to assure compliance with controversial rulings, as in the desegregation case of 1954 and the Watergate tapes case of 1974. Concurrences and dissents permit the courts to ventilate disagreements and prepare the way for future adjustments of judicial doctrines. Chapter Five concludes with a discussion on the role of the lower courts.

Chapter Six analyzes the methods used by Congress and the President to curb the judiciary when it overreaches or is out of step with political sentiments. By using the amendment process to reverse judicial decisions, overturning decisions that concern statutory construction, resorting to court packing, and threatening to withdraw jurisdiction, the political branches are able to keep the judiciary within bounds. Moreover, when the Supreme Court decides a question, its ruling must be translated into action by lower courts, executive agencies, Congress, and local government. Those bodies can avoid compliance through a variety of more or less subtle means. Compliance is often made difficult because of ambiguities in the Court's decision, producing broad choices of interpretation and implementation.

The final chapter on coordinate construction examines specific instances in which the three branches shape constitutional law. In some cases Congress and the President take the initiative in determining the meaning of a constitutional provision. Congressional and executive practices over a number of years can be instrumental in fixing the meaning of the Constitution. If their actions are challenged in the judicial arena, courts may affirm or invalidate, but even in the latter case the colloquy between the branches continues. Congress can rewrite the statute, preparing it for another round of litigation, or may decide to present essentially the same statute in later years to a court with a changed composition. At times the judiciary invites Congress to pass legislation that challenges previous decisions. Judicial rulings rest undisturbed only to the extent that Congress, the President, and the general public find the decisions convincing, reasonable, and acceptable. Otherwise, the debate goes on.

Preoccupation with the Supreme Court as the principal and final arbiter of constitutional questions fosters a misleading impression. A dominant business of the Court is statutory construction, and through that function it interacts with other branches of government in a process that refines the meaning of the Constitution. Judges share with the Legislature and the Executive the duty of defining political values, resolving political conflict, and protecting the integrity and effectiveness of the political process. Constitutional law is a process that operates both inside and outside the judicial arena, challenging the judgment and conscience of all three political branches at the national level, the state governments, and the public at large.

1. Public Law and Politics

For those who teach constitutional law, the relationship between the judiciary and politics remains an awkward topic. Technical details of a decision have a way of driving out the political events that generate a case and influence its disposition. To infuse law with dignity, majesty, and perhaps a touch of mystery, it is tempting to separate the courts from the rest of government and make unrealistic claims of judicial independence.

Legal scholars who explored this relationship early in the twentieth century were discouraged by traditional leaders of the legal profession. To speak the truth, or even search for it, threatened judicial symbols and concepts of long standing. In 1914, when Morris Raphael Cohen began describing how judges make law, he encountered strong objections from his colleagues. The deans of major law schools advised him that his findings, although unquestionably correct, might invite even greater recourse to "judicial legislation."

Undeterred by these warnings, Cohen had "an abiding conviction that to recognize the truth and adjust oneself to it is in the end the easiest and most advisable course." He denied that the law is a "closed, independent system having nothing to do with economic, political, social, or philosophical science." If courts were in fact constantly making and remaking the law, it became "of the utmost social importance that the law should be made in accordance with the best available information, which it is the object of science to supply."[1]

For more than a century, the legal profession claimed that judges "found" the law rather than made it. This doctrine of mechanical jurisprudence, joined with the supposed nonpolitical nature of the judiciary, provided convenient reasons for separating courts from the rest of government. In a perceptive essay, C. Herman Pritchett noted that the disciplines of law and political science drifted apart for semantic, philosophical, and practical reasons: "Law is a presti-

---

[1]Morris R. Cohen, Law and the Social Order 380–81 n.86 (1933).

gious symbol, whereas politics tends to be a dirty word. Law is stability; politics is chaos. Law is impersonal; politics is personal. Law is given; politics is free choice. Law is reason; politics is prejudice and self-interest. Law is justice; politics is who gets there first with the most."[2]

Chief Justice Warren believed that law could be distinguished from politics. Progress in politics "could be made and most often was made by compromising and taking half a loaf where a whole loaf could not be obtained." He insisted that the "opposite is true so far as the judicial process was concerned." Through the judicial process, "and particularly in the Supreme Court, the basic ingredient of decision is principle, and it should not be compromised and parceled out a little in one case, a little more in another, until eventually someone receives the full benefit."[3]

Yet the piecemeal approach fits the judicial process quite well. The Supreme Court prefers to avoid general rules that exceed the necessities of a particular case. Especially in the realm of constitutional law it recognizes the "embarrassment which is likely to result from an alleged attempt to formulate rules or decide questions beyond the necessities of the immediate issue." The Court prefers to follow a "gradual approach to the general by a systematically guarded application and extension of constitutional principles to particular cases as they arise, rather than by out of hand attempts to establish general rules to which future cases must be fitted."[4]

Compromise, expediency, and ad hoc action are no less a part of the process by which a multimember court gropes incrementally toward a consensus and decision. The desegregation case of 1954 was preceded by two decades of halting progress toward the eventual abandonment of the "separate but equal" doctrine enunciated in 1896. After he left the Court, Potter Stewart reflected on the decision to exclude from the courtroom evidence that had been illegally seized: "Looking back, the exclusionary rule seems a bit jerry-built—like a roller coaster track constructed while the roller coaster sped along. Each new piece of track was attached hastily and imperfectly to the one before it, just in time to prevent the roller coaster from crashing,

---

[2]C. Herman Pritchett, "The Development of Judicial Research," in Joel B. Grossman and Joseph Tanenhaus, eds., Frontiers of Judicial Research 31 (1969).
[3]Earl Warren, The Memoirs of Earl Warren 6 (1977).
[4]Euclid v. Ambler Co., 272 U.S. 365, 397 (1926).

but without an opportunity to measure the curves and dips preceding it or to contemplate the twists and turns that inevitably lay ahead."[5]

The desegregation case plunged the Court into a political maelstrom that pitted blacks against whites, the North against the South, and states righters against advocates of national action. Justice Jackson, viewing the briefs as sociology rather than law, was reluctant to rule segregation as unconstitutional. When he finally decided to join the majority, he said that the case was basically a question of politics: "I don't know how to justify the abolition of segregation as a judicial act. Our problem is to make a judicial decision out of a political conclusion. . . ."[6]

The Social Environment

Constitutions do not govern by text alone, even as interpreted by a supreme body of judges. Constitutions draw their life from forces outside the law: from ideas, customs, society, and the constant dialogue among political institutions. In *South Carolina* v. *United States* (1905), the Supreme Court stated that the Constitution "is a written instrument. As such its meaning does not alter. That which it meant when adopted it means now." Having announced the conventional formula, the Court immediately noted: "Being a grant of powers to a government its language is general, and as changes come in social and political life it embraces in its grasp all new conditions which are within the scope of the powers in terms conferred."[7]

Just as the Supreme Court leaves its mark on American society, so do social forces influence constitutional law. The Court, regarded as a nonpolitical and independent branch of government, is very much a product of its times. Justice Cardozo remarked that the "great tides and currents which engulf the rest of men do not turn aside in their course and pass the judges by."[8] Courts are obviously buffeted by social pressures. To what extent is difficult to say. We see the final

[5]Potter Stewart, "The Road to Mapp v. Ohio and Beyond: The Origins, Development and Future of the Exclusionary Rule in Search-and-Seizure Cases," 83 Colum. L. Rev. 1366 (1983).
[6]Bernard Schwartz, Super Chief 89 (1983).
[7]199 U.S. 437, 448 (1905).
[8]Benjamin N. Cardozo, The Nature of the Judicial Process 168 (1921).

result in a decision but must speculate how the court got there. The link between social cause and judicial effect cannot be measured with scientific accuracy, or anything approaching it, but we can make reasonable and informed judgments about social influences on constitutional law.

For their own institutional protection, courts must take account of social movements and public opinion. It is too flippant to accept Mr. Dooley's pronouncement that the Supreme Court follows the election returns, but careful studies by Robert Dahl, David Adamany, and Richard Funston show that the Court generally stays within the political boundaries of its times.[9] When it strays outside and opposes the policy of elected leaders, it does so at substantial risk to its legitimacy and effectiveness. The Court maintains its strength by steering a course that fits within the permissible limits of public opinion. This reality does not make it a political body in the same sense as Congress and the President, but pragmatism and statesmanship must temper abstract legal analysis. De Tocqueville noted in the 1840s that the power of the Supreme Court "is enormous, but it is the power of public opinion. They are all-powerful as long as the people respect the law; but they would be impotent against popular neglect or contempt of the law." Federal judges, he said, "must be statesmen, wise to discern the signs of the times, not afraid to brave the obstacles that can be subdued, nor slow to turn away from the current when it threatens to sweep them off. . . ."[10]

The responsiveness of courts to the social community is even more immediate at the local level. District courts reflect public opinion on such matters as civil rights, labor relations, and sentencing of Vietnam resisters.[11] A conference of federal judges in 1961 agreed that public opinion "should not materially affect sentences" and that the judiciary "must stand firm against undue public opinion." Note that the courts are to resist only *undue* public opinion. The judges cau-

---

[9]Robert A. Dahl, "Decision-Making in a Democracy: The Supreme Court as a National Policy-maker," 6 J. Pub. L. 279 (1957); David Adamany, "Legitimacy, Realigning Elections, and the Supreme Court," 1973 Wisc. L. Rev. 790 (1973); Richard Funston, "The Supreme Court and Critical Elections," 69 Am. Pol. Sci. Rev. 795 (1975).

[10]Alexis de Tocqueville, Democracy in America (Bradley ed.) Vol. i, pp. 151–52.

[11]E.g., Dianne Bennett Graebner, "Judicial Activity and Public Attitude: A Quantitative Study of Selective Service Sentencing in the Vietnam War Period," 23 Buff. L. Rev. 465 (1974); Beverly B. Cook, "Public Opinion and Federal Judicial Policy," 21 Am J. Pol. Sci. 567 (1977); Herbert M. Kritzer, "Federal Judges and Their Political Environments: The Influence of Public Opinion," 23 Am J. Pol. Sci. 194 (1979); Beverly B. Cook, "Judicial Policy: Change Over Time," 23 Am. J. Pol. Sci. 208 (1979).

tioned that resistance to public opinion "should not mean that the community's attitude must be completely ignored in sentencing; although judges should be leaders of public opinion, they must never get so far out in front that the public loses sight of them."[12]

Social forces affect the process by which the courts function. In such areas as civil rights, sex discrimination, church and state, and criminal procedure, the Supreme Court moves with a series of half steps, disposing of the particular issue at hand while preparing for the next case. Through installments it lays the groundwork for a more comprehensive solution, always sensitive to the response of society and the institutions of government that must enforce judicial rulings. This social and political framework sets the boundaries for judicial activity and helps influence the substance of specific decisions—if not immediately, then within a few years.

By recognizing the force of social movements and public opinion, do we reduce the judiciary to just another political body responding to majoritarian pressures? Not necessarily. If the Court succumbs to social needs in such areas as economic regulation, so are there examples—school prayer, school busing, abortion—where the Court can be steadfast in the teeth of intense opposition. In one of the most majestic paragraphs in Supreme Court history, Justice Jackson in 1943 struck down a mandatory flag salute and declared that the "very purpose of a Bill of Rights was to withdraw certain subjects from the vicissitudes of political controversy, to place them beyond the reach of majorities and officials and to establish them as legal principles to be applied by the courts. One's right to life, liberty, and property, to free speech, a free press, freedom of worship and assembly, and other fundamental rights may not be submitted to vote; they depend on the outcome of no elections."[13]

Nonetheless, constitutional rights depend to a substantial extent on contemporary standards and majority opinion. Jackson could write what he did in 1943 partly because Frankfurter's decision in 1940, upholding a mandatory flag salute, had aroused almost uniform opposition throughout the country.[14] Frankfurter, writing for an 8-to-1 Court, concluded that states could force children of Jehovah's Wit-

[12]35 F.R.D. 398 (1964).

[13]West Virginia Board of Education v. Barnette, 319 U.S. 624, 638 (1943).

[14]For reference to critical responses to Minersville School District v. Gobitis, 310 U.S. 586 (1940), see West Virginia Board of Education v. Barnette, 319 U.S. at 635 n.15.

13

nesses to salute the flag in grade school exercises. The Witnesses claimed that saluting a secular symbol violated their religious beliefs. In examining the response to the 1940 decision, one study was unable "to locate a single clearly approving statement in any of the accessible law reviews."[15] Newspapers and weeklies were virtually unanimous in denouncing the decision.[16] This same study explains the 1940 decision as a reaction to the war hysteria that developed after the German army raced across northern France and fears mounted of a "Fifth Column" developing within the United States. After these fears subsided and the country regained respect for religious freedom, the changed climate allowed the Court to reverse itself in 1943.

On such subjects as obscenity, law enforcement, and the death penalty, the Supreme Court attempts to determine "contemporary standards" and "evolving standards of decency."[17] Justice Frankfurter, in a death penalty case, felt obliged to follow "that consensus of society's opinion which, for purposes of due process, is the standard enjoined by the Constitution."[18] When legislatures passed death sentences for certain crimes, jurors often refused to return guilty verdicts. This response forced legislatures to permit discretionary jury sentencing.[19]

To say that constitutional rights merely reflect contemporary values would be misleading. If that were the case, we could dispense with the Constitution and simply legislate all constitutional questions. The Constitution is revered because it represents enduring values and a consensus of broad moral and political ideas. The fundamental principle that people cannot be governed without their consent created an inherent conflict between the Declaration of Independence and the Constitution, which sanctioned, at least for a time, the institution of slavery. This basic incompatibility between natural rights and the Constitution had to be redressed, if not by the courts and Congress then by civil war.

[15]Francis H. Heller, "A Turning Point for Religious Liberty," 29 Va. L Rev. 440, 451 (1943).

[16]Id. at 452–53.

[17]Woodson v. North Carolina, 428 U.S. 280, 288, 293 (1976) (death penalty). See also Miller v. California, 413 U.S. 15, 30 (1973) (obscenity) and Rochin v. California, 342 U.S. 165, 169, 173 (1952) (law enforcement).

[18]Francis v. Resweber, 329 U.S. 459, 471 (1947).

[19]McGautha v. California, 402 U.S. 183, 198–203 (1971).

Two cases in 1986 illustrate the Court's sensitivity to social attitudes. *California* v. *Ciraolo* concerned flights by police officers over a backyard to discover marijuana plants. The Court claimed that the grower's "expectation that his garden was protected from such observation is unreasonable and is not an expectation that society is prepared to honor."[20] How the Court divined society's judgment it declined to say. In *Bowers* v. *Hardwick*, the Court by a 5-to-4 margin upheld a state law that made consensual sodomy among homosexuals a criminal offense. The Court rejected the argument that the law should be struck down because it merely reflects the "presumed belief of a majority of the electorate in Georgia that homosexual sodomy is immoral and unacceptable." The Court noted that the law "is constantly based on notions of morality."[21] Justice Stevens, dissenting, pointed out that the fact the majority in Georgia views sodomy as immoral "is not a sufficient reason for upholding a law prohibiting the practice; neither history nor tradition could save a law prohibiting miscegenation from constitutional attack."[22]

Constitutional law is constantly shaped by people operating through the executive and legislative branches. Through this rich and dynamic political process, the Constitution is regularly adapted to seek a harmony between legal principles and the needs of a changing society.

Litigation as a Political Process

The decision of many political scientists in recent decades to ignore the substance of Supreme Court opinions came at a most peculiar time. The Supreme Court had moved from narrow nineteenth-century questions of private law (estates, trusts, admiralty, real property, contracts, and commercial law) to contemporary issues of public law (federal regulation, criminal law, immigration, equal protection, and federal taxation).[23] The period after World War II is generally considered a high-water mark in judicial policymaking. Decisions with

[20]106 S.Ct. 1809, 1813 (1986).

[21]Id. at 2841, 2846.

[22]Id. at 2857.

[23]Felix Frankfurter, "The Supreme Court in the Mirror of Justices," 105 U. Pa. L. Rev. 781, 792–93 (1957).

15

nationwide impact were handed down, affecting desegregation in 1954, reapportionment and school prayers in 1962, criminal justice in the 1960s, and abortion in 1973.

Although members of Congress complain about "judicial activism," they do their part to encourage judicial policymaking. Congress passes statutes that give standing to litigants, provides fees for attorneys, and establishes separate agencies (such as the Legal Services Corporation) to bring suit on broad public issues. Class-action suits open the doors of the courts even wider. Instead of merely resolving private disputes between private individuals, courts develop and articulate public values on major social, economic, and political questions. Their decisions are increasingly prospective rather than retrospective. Judges become active participants in negotiating a resolution and maintain their involvement after issuing an initial decree.[24] This activist role by the courts has been criticized by those who believe that federal judges lack both the legitimacy and the capacity to decide questions of broad social policy.[25]

Justices of the Supreme Court have encouraged the belief that a gulf does indeed separate law from politics. Chief Justice John Marshall, in *Marbury* v. *Madison* (1803), insisted that "Questions in their nature political . . . can never be made in this court."[26] In that very same decision, however, he established a precedent of far-reaching political importance: the right of the judiciary to review and overturn the actions of Congress and the Executive. As noted by one scholar, Marshall "more closely associated the art of judging with the positive qualities of impartiality and disinterestedness, and yet he had made his office a vehicle for the expression of his views about the proper foundations of American government."[27]

During his days as law school professor, Felix Frankfurter referred to constitutional law as "applied politics."[28] "The simple truth of the matter," he said, "is that decisions of the Court denying or sanctioning the exercise of federal power, as in the first child labor case, largely involve a judgment about practical matters, and not at all any

[24]Abram Chayes, "Public Law Litigation and the Burger Court," 96 Harv. L. Rev. 4 (1982).

[25]Donald L. Horowitz, The Courts and Social Policy (1977).

[26]5 U.S. (1 Cr.) 137, 170.

[27]G. Edward White, The American Judicial Tradition 35 (1976).

[28]Felix Frankfurter, "The Zeitgeist and the Judiciary," a 1912 address reprinted in Archibald MacLeish and E. F. Prichard, eds., Law and Politics 6 (1962).

esoteric knowledge of the Constitution."[29] He regarded courts as "less than ever technical expounders of technical provisions of the Constitution. They are arbiters of the economic and social life of vast regions and at times of the whole country."[30]

Once on the bench, however, he did his part to perpetuate the law–politics dichotomy. Refusing to take a reapportionment case in 1946, he said it was "hostile to a democratic system to involve the judiciary in the politics of the people."[31] In 1962 the Supreme Court liberated itself from this narrow holding[32] and has demonstrated throughout its history a keen sense of the political system in which it operates daily. Writing in 1921, Justice Cardozo dismissed the idea that judges "stand aloof on these chill and distant heights; and we shall not help the cause of truth by acting and speaking as if they do."[33] Although the Supreme Court is an independent branch, it is subject to the same social winds that press upon the executive and legislative branches, even if it does not respond in precisely the same way. It does not, and cannot, operate in a vacuum.

From the late nineteenth century to the 1930s, the courts struck down a number of federal and state efforts to ameliorate industrial conditions. Laws that established maximum hours or minimum wages were declared an unconstitutional interference with the "liberty of contract." Lawyers from the corporate sector helped translate the philosophy of laissez-faire into legal terms and constitutional doctrine.[34] These judicial rulings were so spiced with conservative business attitudes that Justice Holmes in *Lochner* (1904) protested that the case was "decided upon an economic theory which a large part of the country does not entertain." He chided his brethren: "The Fourteenth Amendment does not enact Mr. Herbert Spencer's Social Statics."[35] When it was evident that the country would no longer tolerate interference by the courts, the judiciary backed off. After retiring from the Court, Justice Roberts commented on the expansion of national power over economic conditions: "Looking back, it

[29]Id. at 12 (1924 unsigned editorial on "The Red Terror of Judicial Reform").
[30]Felix Frankfurter and James M. Landis, The Business of the Supreme Court 173 (1928). Footnote omitted.
[31]Colegrove v. Green, 328 U.S. 549, 553–54 (1946).
[32]Baker v. Carr, 369 U.S. 186 (1962).
[33]Cardozo, The Nature of the Judicial Process 168.
[34]Benjamin R. Twiss, Lawyers and the Constitution (1942).
[35]Lochner v. New York, 198 U.S. 45, 75 (1904).

17

is difficult to see how the Court could have resisted the popular urge for uniform standards throughout the country—for what in effect was a unified economy."[36]

In *Buck* v. *Bell* (1927), the Supreme Court upheld Virginia's compulsory sterilization law.[37] The decision was handed down in the midst of the eugenics movement, which sanctioned efforts to prevent reproduction of the "unfit." In the hands of reformers and progressives, eugenics became a respected argument for opposing miscegenation and excluding "lower stock" immigrants from the Mediterranean countries, Eastern Europe, and Russia.[38] After odious efforts in Nazi Germany to conduct biological experiments and exterminate millions of Jews, Poles, gypsies, and other groups to produce a "master race," the eugenics movement had run its course.

A combination of racism in totalitarian countries and the emergence of the United States as a world leader after World War II helped set the stage for the desegregation decision of 1954. America could not fight world communism and appeal to dark-skinned peoples in foreign lands if it maintained racial segregation in its own school system. The executive branch made the Court mindful of these realities. The federal government prepared an amicus brief that explained in great detail the harmful effects of American segregation on the foreign policy of the executive branch. Racial discrimination within the District of Columbia, the nation's capital, operated in full view of foreign officials, who were often mistaken for American blacks and refused food, lodging, and entertainment. The problem of racial discrimination, said the brief, had to be viewed within the context of the world struggle between freedom and tyranny: "Racial discrimination furnishes grist for the Communist propaganda mills, and it raises doubts even among friendly nations as to the intensity of our devotion to the democratic faith."[39]

On the foundation of court cases that established rights for black Americans, the feminist movement pressed for fundamental changes

[36]Owen J. Roberts, The Court and the Constitution 61 (1951).

[37]274 U.S. 200 (1927).

[38]Louis Fisher, "Social Influences on Constitutional Law," 15 J. Pol. Sci. 7, 11–15 (1987); Clement E. Vose, Constitutional Change: Amendment Politics and Supreme Court Litigation Since 1900 5–20 (1972). *Buck* was substantially weakened by Skinner v. Oklahoma, 316 U.S. 535 (1942).

[39]49 P. Kurland and G. Casper, eds., Landmark Briefs and Arguments of the Supreme Court of the United States: Constitutional Law 121 (1975).

in women's rights. From the stereotype in *Bradwell* v. *State* (1873), which viewed women as too timid and delicate for work outside the home,[40] women made important gains in occupations and professions. Statutory protections came in the form of the Equal Pay Act of 1963 and the Civil Rights Act of 1964, which prohibited discrimination based on sex and created the Equal Employment Opportunity Commission to investigate cases of discrimination. The Equal Rights Amendment passed Congress by overwhelming margins, but the Supreme Court's abortion decision in 1973 split the women's movement and polarized the country, making ratification of the amendment impossible. Throughout the 1970s, however, it appeared that most of the goals of the amendment could be accomplished by legislative action and judicial decisions.[41]

To associate litigation with social forces is not meant to demean the courts or reduce adjudication to just another form of politics. Judges make policy, but not in the same manner as legislators and executives. Unlike the elected branches, the judiciary is not expected to satisfy the needs of the majority or respond to electoral pressures; instead, it has a special responsibility to protect minority interests and constitutional rights. Although judges have an opportunity to engage in their own form of lobbying, they are not supposed to debate a pending issue publicly or participate in *ex parte* meetings that are open to only one party—privileges routinely exercised by legislators and administrators. Most lobbying by the executive and legislative branches is open and direct; lobbying by the judiciary is filtered through legal briefs, professional meetings, and law review articles.

The executive and legislative branches have elaborate mechanisms for handling public relations, self-promotion, and contacts with the press. For the most part, judges release their opinions and remain silent. If executive officials and legislators are criticized in the press, they can respond in kind. Judges, with rare exceptions, take their lumps without retaliation.

Judges must wait for a case to present itself. They cannot initiate policy with the same ease as members of the political branches. As Judge David Bazelon once remarked, a federal judge "can't wake up one morning and simply decide to give a helpful little push to a

[40]Bradwell v. State, 16 Wall. (83 U.S.) 130 (1873).

[41]Gilbert Y. Steiner, Constitutional Inequality: The Political Fortunes of the Equal Rights Amendment (1985); Jane J. Mansbridge, Why We Lost the ERA (1986).

19

school system, a mental hospital, or the local housing agency."[42] Furthermore, judges cannot be as willful as legislators and executives. They are expected to base their decisions on reason and precedent. Courts may overrule themselves, and frequently do, but they must explain (or attempt to explain) why it is necessary to break with a prior holding.

Even so, the operations of the judiciary are often difficult to distinguish from Congress and the Executive. In reviewing the work of federal courts in tax matters, Judge Charles E. Wyzanski witnessed the constant interaction between the judiciary and Congress. The disputes generally were "not about a fundamental value but about the choice of insistent interests or pressing policies to be preferred. In short, here again we have an emphasis on those aspects of the law which relate to bargain and compromise, not to 'absolutes' and not even to principles or 'standards.' "[43]

The operations of the political branches can resemble those of the courts. Although responsive to majoritarian pressures, Congress and the President are sensitive to minority rights. Since the days of President Franklin D. Roosevelt, executive orders and congressional statutes have advanced the cause of civil rights. Although the political branches are more at liberty to engage in ad hoc actions, they usually follow general principles and precedents of their own and feel an obligation to present a reasoned explanation for their decisions.

Lobbying the Courts

Private organizations do not hesitate to treat litigation as a political process. They regularly conclude that their interests will be better served through court action than through the legislative and executive branches. Many of the major labor-management struggles were fought out in the courts, with unions and employers hiring counsel to represent their interests. In 1963 Justice Brennan called litigation "a form of political expression." Groups unable to achieve their objectives through the electoral process often turn to the judiciary: "under the conditions of modern government, litigation may well be the

[42]David L. Bazelon, "The Impact of the Courts on Public Administration," 52 Ind. L. J. 101, 103 (1976).
[43]Charles E. Wyzanski, Jr., "History and Law," 26 U. Chi. L. Rev. 237, 242 (1959).

20

sole practicable avenue open to a minority to petition for redress of grievances."[44] For groups such as the National Association for the Advancement of Colored People (NAACP) and the American Civil Liberties Union (ACLU), litigation is not merely a technique for resolving private differences. It is a form of political expression and association.[45]

The use of litigation in the 1940s and 1950s to shape social policy led to broader public participation and produced fundamental changes in the amicus curiae (friend of the court) brief. Originally such briefs permitted third parties, without any direct interest in the case, to bring certain facts to the attention of the court to avoid judicial error. Over the years it lost this innocent quality and became an instrument used by private groups to advance their cause. The amicus curiae brief moved "from neutrality to partisanship, from friendship to advocacy."[46] The briefs are now regularly used as part of the interest-group struggle in the courts.

The number of amicus briefs increased so rapidly that the Supreme Court adopted a rule in November 1949 to discourage their filing. With the exception of government units, all parties must consent to the filing of an amicus brief. If a party objects, the applicant must submit to the Court a motion for leave to file.[47] The value of an amicus brief is sometimes sharply questioned by Justices. In a 1947 case, Justice Jackson noted that an amicus brief filed by the American Newspaper Publishers Association failed to cite "a single authority that was not available to counsel for the publisher involved, and does not tell us a single new fact" except the large number of publishers who belonged to the association. Objecting to this kind of lobbying, Jackson thought that the case "might be a good occasion to demonstrate the fortitude of the judiciary."[48]

The political nature of litigation is underscored by many familiar

[44]NAACP v. Button, 371 U.S. 415, 429–30 (1963). See also United Transportation Union v. Michigan Bar, 401 U.S. 576, 585–86 (1971).

[45]In re Primus, 436 U.S. 412, 428 (1978).

[46]Samuel Krislov, "The Amicus Curiae Brief: From Friendship to Advocacy," 72 Yale L. J. 694 (1963). See Lucius J. Barker, "Third Parties in Litigation: A Systemic View of the Judicial Function," 29 J. Pol. 41 (1967).

[47]Fowler V. Harper and Edwin D. Etherington, "Lobbyists Before the Court," 101 U. Pa. L. Rev. 1172, 1173–74 (1953). The procedures are currently governed by Rule 36 of the U.S. Supreme Court.

[48]Craig v. Harney, 331 U.S. 367, 397 (1947) (Jackson, J., dissenting).

examples. Through dozens of court actions, the Jehovah's Witnesses secured for themselves such rights as the refusal to salute or pledge allegiance to the American flag, the right to solicit from house to house, and the right to preach in the streets without a license. Those objectives were not available from legislatures responsive to majoritarian pressures. The NAACP created a Legal Defense and Educational Fund to pursue rights denied blacks by Congress and state legislatures. A series of victories in the courts established basic rights for blacks in voting, housing, education, and jury service. The National Consumers' League channeled its resources into litigation and won important protections for factory workers. The American Liberty League, organized by conservative businessmen, turned to litigation in an effort to prevent the enactment of economic regulation by Congress.[49]

Political motivations dominated each dispute. Encouraged by Congress and the courts, private groups decided that the judiciary was the best arena to further their interests. When the Reagan administration appeared to have made an inadequate commitment to environmental protection, private organizations responded with more lawsuits. A senior staff attorney for the Natural Resources Defense Council protested in 1981 that the administration was "massively disobeying these laws because they don't like them. In this context, the only mechanism we have for enforcement is the courts."[50] To call this activity "legal" rather than "political" would take these attorneys by surprise.

Through the publication of articles, books, and commission reports, authors hope to influence a future court decision. Reliance on this body of literature has been of deep concern to many legislators who fear that the judiciary indiscriminately considers "unknown, unrecognized and nonauthoritative text books, law review articles, and other writings of propaganda artists and lobbyists."[51] The author of this statement, Congressman Wright Patman, complained in 1957 that the Supreme Court had turned increasingly for guidance to private publications and studies promoted by the administration. The

[49]Clement E. Vose, "Litigation as a Form of Pressure Group Activity," 319 The Annals 20 (1958). See Lee Epstein, Conservatives in Court (1985).

[50]Lawrence Mosher, "Environmentalists Sue to Put an End to 'Regulatory Massive Resistance,'" National Journal, December 19, 1981, at 2233.

[51]103 Cong. Rec. 16160 (1957).

research was designed, he said, not to study an issue objectively but to advance the particular views of private interests trying, through the medium of publication, to influence the judiciary's disposition of public policy questions. Experts have pointed out that the members of these study committees and commissions are aware that lawyers will cite the reports in their briefs "and that the real impact of this might very well be in the decisions made by courts and administrative agencies."[52]

The practice of citing professional journals goes back at least to Justice Brandeis in the 1920s. Other Justices, like Cardozo and Stone, adopted this technique as a way of keeping law current with changes in American society. Brandeis's opinions introduced a new meaning to the word "authority." He believed that an opinion "derives its authority, just as law derives its existence, from all the facts of life. The judge is free to draw upon these facts wherever he can find them, if only they are helpful."[53]

Congress and the White House are accustomed to seeing individuals and groups outside carrying placards and signs designed to lobby for or against a particular issue. These tactics are considered inappropriate for the courts. In 1983, however, the Supreme Court unanimously struck down as unconstitutional a statute that prohibited the display of any flag, banner, or device in the Supreme Court or on its grounds "to bring into public notice any party, organization, or movement." Part of the purpose of the statute was to insulate the Court from direct lobbying, but the Court held that distributing leaflets and carrying picket signs on the public sidewalk around the building was protected by the First Amendment.[54]

The courts are political institutions operating within a political climate. Their decisions determine the ongoing struggle between individual rights and the state, between the national and state governments, and between the three branches of the federal government. The courts are part of this system and respond to it. Sharp protests from Congress, including the threat to withdraw appellate jurisdic-

---

[52]Id. at 16167 (Professor Louis B. Schwartz). Senator James O. Eastland made a similar complaint about the Supreme Court's desegregation decision in 1954; 101 Cong. Rec. 7119–23 (1955). See Chester A. Newland, "Legal Periodicals and the United States Supreme Court," 3 Midwest J. Pol. Sci. 58 (1959).

[53]Chester A. Newland, "The Supreme Court and Legal Writing: Learned Journals as Vehicles of an Anti-Antitrust Lobby?," 48 Geo. L. J. 105, 140 (1959).

[54]United States v. Grace, 461 U.S. 171 (1983).

tion or to take other court-curbing actions, change the climate for future judicial decisions. Professional associations, business and labor groups, consumer and environmental associations, law reviews and scholars all organize their time and talents to influence future court decisions. The following sections describe how the three branches of government intersect in their legal activities: the executive in court, congressional duties, and judge as lawmaker and administrator.

The Executive in Court

The Judiciary Act of 1789 established an Attorney General to prosecute and conduct all suits in the Supreme Court concerning the Government. He represented Congress as well as the President. Despite some ambiguity in the original statute as to whether the Attorney General was an executive officer in the same sense as the department heads of State, Treasury, and War, the first Attorney General (Edmund Randolph) attended Cabinet meetings and was identified early on as an administrative official.

Unlike the heads of the executive departments, who received full-time salaries, the Attorney General received a nominal sum and was expected to maintain a private practice to supplement his income. Randolph complained that he was "sort of a mongrel between the State and the U.S.; called an officer of some rank here under the latter, and yet thrust out to get a livelihood in the former, —perhaps in a petty mayor's or county court."[55] The staff of the Attorney General was so small that outside counsel had to be hired to conduct the Government's business in court. Partly to do away with this expense, in 1870 Congress established a Department of Justice and created the office of Solicitor General to assist the Attorney General. To the Solicitor General fell the primary responsibility of representing the federal government in court.[56]

Contemporary duties of the Solicitor General are broad ranging. After consulting agency officials, the Solicitor General conducts (or assigns and supervises) Supreme Court cases, including appeals, pe-

[55]Leonard D. White, The Federalists 164–65 (1948).

[56]See Thomas D. Thacher, "Genesis and Present Duties of Office of Solicitor General," 17 A.B.A.J. 519 (1931); Charles Fahy, "The Office of Solicitor General," 28 A.B.A.J. 20 (1942).

titions regarding certiorari, and the preparation of briefs and arguments; authorizes or declines to authorize appeals by the federal government to appellate courts; authorizes the filing of amicus briefs by the government in all appellate courts; and may, in consultation with each agency, authorize intervention by the government in cases involving the constitutionality of acts of Congress.[57] When only private interests are at stake, the Solicitor General may still intervene to advise the Court to accept or deny a case.[58]

The cases that flow through the office of Solicitor General raise complex and specialized issues, but, as a former Solicitor General remarked, the incumbent "must try to discover the social tensions, the reverberations of strife and passion, the political issues, the clashes of interest that are dressed up in technical legal forms."[59] To carry out this responsibility the Solicitor General juggles several conflicting assignments. As the federal government's lawyer, he is an advocate. However, he is also positioned to play a somewhat detached role, similar to that of an appellate judge. By entering only at the appellate level, he does not begin with the same emotional attachment as the original parties in district court (including agency attorneys). He must also decide which cases, out of a multitude requested by the agencies, deserve the attention of the Supreme Court.[60]

Because the Solicitor General appears before the Supreme Court with such frequency, he has been characterized as the Court's "ninth-and-a-half" member.[61] He serves many functions for the Court:

> The Supreme Court's frequent invitation to the Solicitor General to participate as amicus in constitutional cases is one indication of his useful role. The Solicitor General and his staff have unparalleled experience in constitutional litigation. Their access to and knowledge of the government apparatus not only enable them to inform the Court of factors unknown to private parties, but also to proffer statutory grounds for a decision

[57]28 C.F.R. §0.20–0.21 (1981).

[58]Karen O'Connor, "The Amicus Curiae Role of the U.S. Solicitor General in Supreme Court Litigation," 66 Judicature 256 (1983).

[59]Simon E. Sobeloff, "Attorney for the Government: The Work of the Solicitor General," 41 A.B.A.J. 229, 279 (1955).

[60]Archibald Cox, "The Government in the Supreme Court," 44 Chi. B. Rec. 221 (1963).

[61]Kathryn Mickle Werdeger, "The Solicitor General and Administrative Due Process: A Quarter-Century of Advocacy," 26 G.W. L. Rev. 481, 482 (1968).

avoiding the constitutional issues raised. The Solicitor General may indicate the relationship of the case to others pending on the docket, or the particular infirmities or strengths of the case for resolving constitutional or statutory issues. Knowing the Justices' proclivities, the Solicitor General may be able to offer a compromise solution that can gain a majority vote of the Court. The Supreme Court, lacking an extensive staff of its own, often benefits from the Solicitor General's impartial and sophisticated analysis of such constitutional cases.[62]

The long-term and "impartial" objectives of the Solicitor General compete with, and are sometimes subordinated to, the particular and immediate needs of the President. This relationship is especially common in the field of national security. In arguing cases involving the discharge of federal employees, exclusion and deportation of aliens, and conscientious objectors, Solicitors General in the past have shown little sympathy for fundamental notions of due process.[63]

Attorneys General and Solicitors General are legal officers, sometimes operating as members of the bar and therefore officers of the court. But they are also executive officials responsible to the President.[64] Even in state constitutions that locate Attorneys General within the judicial branch, courts recognize that as a practical matter the Attorney General functions as a member of the executive branch: "the posture of the Attorney General is always that of an advocate, never the stance of an arbiter."[65]

As underscored by the actions against Japanese-Americans during World War II, Justice Department attorneys at times swallow their doubts and defend government actions that seem to them not merely unwise but unconstitutional. Under these conditions, constitutional issues are subordinated to the task of behaving as the "President's lawyers."[66] Rex Lee, Solicitor General during the Reagan administration, said that one of his duties is "to represent his client, the presi-

[62]Note, "Government Litigation in the Supreme Court: The Roles of the Solicitor General," 78 Yale L. J. 1442, 1480 (1969). Footnotes omitted.

[63]Werdeger, "The Solicitor General," 26 G.W. L. Rev. at 482.

[64]See Luther A. Huston, Arthur Selwyn Miller, Samuel Krislov, and Robert G. Dixon, Jr., Roles of the Attorney General of the United States (1968), and Daniel J. Meador, The President, the Attorney General, and the Department of Justice (1980).

[65]State ex rel. Turner v. Iowa State Highway Com'n, 186 N.W.2d 141, 144–45 (Iowa 1971).

[66]Peter Irons, Justice at War 350–51, 356–58, 359–60 (1983).

dent of the United States. One of the ways to implement the president's policies is through positions taken in court. When I have that opportunity, I'm going to take it."[67] But if a Solicitor General becomes too partisan, he risks losing the trust and confidence of the Supreme Court.

During the Carter presidency, Attorney General Griffin Bell complained about White House interference in litigation that involved questions of church-state separation, affirmative action, and civil rights. Vice President Walter Mondale, his aide Bert Carp, domestic adviser Stuart Eizenstat, and other White House officials treated many of these matters as broad policy questions rather than technical legal issues. In one case, after the Justice Department had taken a position on a church-state question, President Carter responded to political considerations and personally intervened to overrule the decision.[68]

Carter behaved like most Presidents, deferring to some Court decisions and opposing others. When he was asked how he, as a professed Christian, could accept the Court's abortion decision, he replied that he was personally opposed to abortion but "as President I have taken an oath to uphold the laws of the United States as interpreted by the Supreme Court of the United States. So, if the Supreme Court should rule, as they have, on abortion and other sensitive issues contrary to my own personal beliefs, I have to carry out, in accordance with my solemn oath and my duties as President, the ruling of the Supreme Court."[69] But when the Court decided that the needs of law enforcement could override the First Amendment interest of newspapers to be free of searches and seizures, Carter gave active support to legislation that reversed the Court's ruling.[70]

Part of the lesson supposedly learned from the Watergate affair was the need to keep the Justice Department independent from White House pressures. After Attorney General John Mitchell was convicted and sent to prison, there was broad agreement that never again should a close personal friend of the President be appointed to that office. Nevertheless, President Carter selected Griffin Bell, a personal friend, to head the Justice Department. Bell appeared to make

[67]John A. Jenkins, "The Solicitor General's Winning Ways," 69 A.B.A.J. 734, 736 (1983).

[68]Griffin B. Bell, Taking Care of the Law 24–45 (1982).

[69]3 Public Papers of the Presidents, 1980–1981, at 2354.

[70]2 Public Papers of the Presidents, 1978, at 1591, 2234; 1 Public Papers of the Presidents, 1979, at 585; 3 Public Papers of the Presidents, 1980–1981, at 2218.

a concerted effort to resist White House pressures, but the line between the White House and the Justice Department narrowed again when President Reagan chose William French Smith, a friend and legal adviser for many years, to be Attorney General. In 1983 Smith announced that he was leaving the Justice Department to help Reagan's reelection effort. To replace Smith, Reagan nominated Edwin Meese III, another close friend.

Efforts to subordinate constitutional principles to political tactics can backfire against the President. Faced with a nationwide strike in 1952, President Truman decided to attack the steel companies and work informally with the labor unions rather than invoke the Taft-Hartley Act, which he had vetoed. When that tactic failed, he seized the steel mills and claimed that he could act "for whatever is for the best of the country."[71] Realizing that his definition of presidential authority had sent shock waves across the country, raising questions about his power to seize the press and the radio, he later explained that his powers were derived from the Constitution and that individual rights were protected.[72]

In district court, however, the Justice Department told Judge Pine that "there is no power in the Courts to restrain the President." There were only two limitations on the executive power: "One is the ballot box and the other is impeachment."[73] This audacious and ill-advised presentation may have provoked the judiciary to act boldly to reject a sweeping and dangerous theory of inherent executive authority.[74] The political climate invited a rebuff to presidential power. As Chief Justice Rehnquist noted in 1987, the Steel Seizure Case was "one of those celebrated constitutional issues where what might be called the tide of public opinion suddenly began to run against the government, for a number of reasons, and that this tide of public opinion had a considerable influence on the Court."[75]

The Justice Department urged the Supreme Court to adopt an expansive interpretation of presidential power. It supported this thesis by citing statements that Attorney General Robert Jackson had made while serving for the Franklin D. Roosevelt administration.

[71]Public Papers of the Presidents, 1952, at 273 (April 17, 1952).
[72]Id. at 301 (April 27, 1952). See also pp. 290–91.
[73]Reprinted in H. Doc. No. 534—Part 1, 82d Cong., 2d Sess. 362, 371 (1952).
[74]Youngstown Co. v. Sawyer, 343 U.S. 579, 587–89 (1952); Youngstown Co. v. Sawyer, 103 F.Supp. 569, 577 (D.D.C. 1952).
[75]William H. Rehnquist, The Supreme Court 95 (1987).

28

Jackson, by now a member of the Court, found the reference to his earlier pronouncements unconvincing: "While it is not surprising that counsel should grasp support from such unadjudicated claims of power, a judge cannot accept self-serving press statements of the attorney for one of the interested parties as authority in answering a constitutional question, even if the advocate was himself."[76]

The Justice Department has made a concerted effort to retain exclusive control over agency litigation policy. Loss of authority to the agencies can produce an incoherent and ineffective strategy in court. Some of the legal setbacks of the New Deal can be traced to the splintering of litigating authority in the Roosevelt administration. The Justice Department had to compete with autonomous and unsuccessful efforts by the Interior Department and other agencies.[77]

The tremendous growth of litigation since the 1930s, coupled with a decision by Congress to restrict the number of attorneys in the Justice Department, has made decentralization inevitable. Congress has given several agencies independent litigating authority. In addition, the Justice Department enters into special agreements called Memoranda of Understanding, which allow agencies to litigate certain types of cases at the district and appellate levels.[78]

An unusual situation occurred during the Reagan administration when the Supreme Court appointed a special counsel to argue against the Justice Department. Since 1970 the Internal Revenue Service had denied tax exemptions to private schools that practiced racial discrimination. In January 1982 the Reagan administration announced that it was abandoning this decade-old policy (on the ground that it lacked statutory authority) and would move to dismiss two cases brought by the Bob Jones University and Goldsboro Christian School. The Acting Solicitor General, Lawrence G. Wallace, had previously stated the Justice Department's position that the Internal Revenue Service (IRS) possessed statutory authority to deny the two schools tax-exempt status. Having already announced that position in a September 1981 brief and in a draft brief of early January 1982, which had been circulated to two congressional committees, Wallace felt an

---

[76]Youngstown Co. v. Sawyer, 343 U.S. at 647.

[77]Peter H. Irons, The New Deal Lawyers (1982).

[78]See Susan M. Olson, "Agency Litigating Authority as a Factor in Court Policy Making," a paper presented at the 1983 Annual Meeting of the American Political Science Association.

obligation to call the Court's attention to this change and to dissociate himself from the administration's new position.[79]

The Supreme Court appointed William T. Coleman, Jr., former law clerk to Justice Frankfurter and Secretary of Transportation during the Ford administration, to defend the IRS policy. In 1983 the Supreme Court decided in favor of the IRS and against the Reagan administration. Tax exemption could not be granted to institutions that discriminate on the basis of race.[80]

Congressional Duties

During the nineteenth century it was not unusual for members of Congress to maintain a flourishing business in the federal courts. Daniel Webster is the most prominent illustration of a Congressman with a dual career as lawyer and legislator. While serving in Congress as a Representative and a Senator, he delivered forceful arguments in major cases before the Supreme Court, which at that time was located in a chamber beneath the Senate. Congressmen supplemented their income by "duck[ing] into the lower chamber, so to speak, for a lucrative hour or two. After all, should not those who made laws help interpret them?"[81]

Although Congress depends on the Justice Department to protect its interests, members of Congress may intervene on an individual basis. In *Myers* v. *United States* (1926), which involved the President's power to remove executive officials, the Supreme Court invited Senator George Wharton Pepper to serve as amicus curiae. His oral argument and an extract of his brief, together with those of the appellant and the Solicitor General, are printed immediately before the Court's opinion.[82]

During the impoundment disputes of the Nixon administration, members of Congress submitted an amicus brief on behalf of the

[79]136 P. Kurland and G. Casper, eds., Landmark Briefs and Arguments of the Supreme Court of the United States: Constitutional Law 95 (asterisked material) (1984).

[80]Bob Jones University v. United States, 461 U.S. 574 (1983). For the complex involvement of all three branches in the tax-exempt status of private schools, see Neal Devins, "*Bob Jones University* v. *United States*: A Political Analysis," 1 J. Law & Pol. 403 (1984).

[81]Maurice G. Baxter, Daniel Webster & the Supreme Court 31 (1966).

[82]272 U.S. 52, 65–88 (1926).

plaintiff suing the administration.[83] In the abortion case eventually decided by the Supreme Court in 1980, the district court permitted Senator James L. Buckley, Senator Jesse A. Helms, and Congressman Henry J. Hyde to intervene as defendants.[84] The Ninth Circuit invited both the House and the Senate to submit briefs concerning a legislative veto used by Congress in deportation cases. When the case reached the Supreme Court, both houses of Congress had intervened to protect their interests and fully participated before the Court during oral argument.[85] The attorneys for Congress defended the legislative veto, but in a separate brief nine members of the House of Representatives urged the Supreme Court to declare the legislative veto unconstitutional.[86]

A striking development over the past decade is the frequency with which members of Congress take issues directly to the courts for resolution. Senator Edward M. Kennedy was successful at both the district court and appellate court levels in challenging Nixon's attempt to use the "pocket veto" during brief recesses of the House and Senate.[87] As a result of those lower court decisions, the Ford administration announced that it would use the pocket veto only during the final adjournment at the end of a Congress.[88] The Carter administration honored that agreement. President Reagan, however, reopened the issue by using a pocket veto in December 1981 between the first and second sessions of the 97th Congress and again, two years later, between the first and second sessions of the 98th Congress. A political agreement, forced by earlier lower court decisions, was now pushed back into the judicial arena. In 1985 an appeals court decided in favor of Congress and the matter was taken to the Supreme Court for a final determination, but the Court held the case moot because the bill in question had expired.[89]

[83]State Highway Commission of Missouri v. Volpe, 479 F.2d 1099 n.1 (8th Cir. 1973).

[84]Harris v. McRae, 448 U.S. 297, 303 (1980).

[85]Chadha v. INS, 634 F.2d 408, 411 (9th Cir. 1980).

[86]"Motion for Leave to File and Brief of Certain Members of the United States House of Representatives, amicus curiae," INS v. Chadha, Docket Nos. 80-1832, 80-2170, 80-2171, U.S. Supreme Court (January 8, 1982).

[87]Kennedy v. Sampson, 364 F.Supp. 1075 (D.D.C. 1973); Kennedy v. Sampson, 511 F.2d 430 (D.C. Cir. 1974).

[88]Louis Fisher, Constitutional Conflicts between Congress and the President 151–52 (1985).

[89]Barnes v. Kline, 759 F.2d 21 (D.C. Cir. 1985); Burke v. Barnes, 107 S.Ct. 734 (1987).

31

Senator Kennedy was successful because his prerogative to vote (to override a presidential veto) had been denied by the pocket veto. Other members of Congress have been unsuccessful when they have tried to achieve political goals from the courts that are available through the regular legislative process. In such cases the members have been told by the courts that they lack standing to sue, the issue is not ripe for adjudication, or the matter is a "political question" to be decided by Congress and the President.[90] A legislator must overcome the standing hurdles (faced by any litigant) by showing that he has suffered injury, the interests are within the zone protected by the statute or constitutional provision, the injury is caused by the challenged action, and the injury can be redressed by a favorable court decision. But legislators face an additional obstacle. If they suffer from an injury that can be redressed by colleagues acting through the regular legislative process, a court may exercise "equitable discretion" to dismiss the action.[91]

Throughout these cases there is a general wariness on the part of judges that the controversy is really not between Congress and the Executive. Rather, it is one group of legislators pitted against another. Federal judges may suspect that members of Congress turn to the courts because they have been unable to attract sufficient votes from colleagues to pass a bill. When legislators fail to make use of remedies available within Congress, they have been denied standing to resolve the issue in court.[92]

A typical example is a case decided in 1982. Twenty-nine members of the House of Representatives charged that President Reagan had violated the War Powers Resolution of 1973 by sending fifty-six military personnel to El Salvador. Sixteen Senators and thirteen Representatives promptly intervened on the other side, warning the court not to interfere with a political issue that should be resolved through

[90]Note, "Congressional Access to the Federal Courts," 90 Harv. L. Rev. 1632 (1977). Also on Congressmen as plaintiffs, see Note, "Congress Versus the Executive: The Role of the Courts," 11 Harv. J. on Legis. 352 (1974).

[91]Riegle v. Federal Open Market Committee, 656 F.2d 873 (D.C. Cir. 1981), cert. denied, 454 U.S. 1082 (1981); Harrington v. Bush, 553 F.2d 190, 204–05 (D.C. Cir. 1977); Goldwater v. Carter, 481 F.Supp. 949, 951 (D.D.C. 1979).

[92]E.g., Public Citizen v. Sampson, 379 F.Supp. 662 (D.D.C. 1974); Harrington v. Schlesinger, 528 F.2d 455 (4th Cir. 1975); Metcalf v. National Petroleum Council, 553 F.2d 176 (D.C. Cir. 1977); Reuss v. Balles, 584 F.2d 461, 468 (D.C. Cir. 1978), cert. denied, 439 U.S. 997 (1978). See Carl McGowan "Congressmen in Court: The New Plaintiffs," 15 Ga. L. Rev. 241 (1981).

the regular legislative process. A federal district judge dismissed the lawsuit in 1982. The factfinding necessary to establish whether U.S. forces had been introduced into hostilities was appropriate for Congress, not the courts. Only if the President disregarded a congressional resolution to report under the War Powers Resolution, or to withdraw forces, would there be a constitutional impasse appropriate for judicial resolution.[93]

The Legislative Reorganization Act of 1970 explicitly recognized the need within Congress for a more systematic and continuing review of court decisions that affect legislative prerogatives. Congress had been represented in court by the Department of Justice, and sometimes through appearances of Senators, Congressmen, and attorneys acting as amicus curiae, but these ad hoc remedies were unsatisfactory to Congress. A Senate committee concluded in 1966 that the effect on Congress of court decisions "should be a matter of continuous concern for which some agency of the Congress should take responsibility."[94]

The 1970 statute created a Joint Committee on Congressional Operations and made it responsible for identifying "any court proceeding or action which, in the opinion of the Joint Committee, is of vital interest to the Congress, or to either House of the Congress, as a constitutionally established institution of the Federal Government. . . ." Congress directed the Joint Committee to make periodic reports and recommendations to the Senate and House.[95]

Starting in 1971, the Joint Committee on Congressional Operations began publishing a series of reports on legal proceedings of interest to Congress. After the Joint Committee expired in 1977, the task of publishing the report fell to a newly created House Select Committee on Congressional Operations, working in conjunction with the Senate Committee on Rules and Administration. When the House decided to discontinue the Select Committee, the House Judiciary Committee inherited the responsibility for producing the reports on legal proceedings. Moreover, Senate Rule XXV charges the Senate Committee on Rules and Administration with the duty of identifying "any court proceeding or action which, in the opinion of the com-

---

[93]Crockett v. Reagan, 558 F.Supp. 893 (D.D.C. 1982), aff'd, 720 F.2d 1355 (D.C. Cir. 1983), cert. denied, 467 U.S. 1251 (1984).
[94]S. Rept. No. 1414, 89th Cong., 2d Sess. 47 (1966).
[95]84 Stat. 1187, §402 (1970).

mittee, is of vital interest to the Congress as a constitutionally established institution of the Federal Government and call such proceeding or action to the attention of the Senate."

In recent years members of Congress have become concerned about the refusal of the Justice Department to defend the constitutionality of certain statutory provisions. Sometimes the Department took this position after deciding that a statute infringed on presidential power or was so patently unconstitutional that it could not be defended, as in the bill of attainder case in 1946.[96] As a result of language placed in authorization acts for the Justice Department, the Attorney General must now report to Congress whenever the Department does not intend to defend the constitutionality of a law passed by Congress. These reports specify the statutory provision and contain a detailed explanation by the Department for calling the provision unconstitutional.

Congress has always been able to hire private counsel to defend itself, as it did in the civil action brought against it by Congressman Adam Clayton Powell in the 1960s. Yet there was no established procedure for Congress to defend its statutes when the Justice Department chose not to. The institutional interests of Congress, as noted by the Senate Committee on Governmental Affairs in 1977, made it "inappropriate as a matter of principle and of the constitutional separation of powers for the legislative branch to rely upon and entrust the defense of its vital constitutional powers to the advocate for the executive branch, the Attorney General."[97] The committee recalled that in *Doe* v. *McMillan* and in *Eastland* v. *United States Servicemen's Fund,* both cases involving the power of Congress to investigate, the Justice Department withdrew its representation of Congress just as the litigation reached the Supreme Court, after having represented Congress in the district and appellate courts.[98]

As part of the Ethics in Government Act of 1978, the Senate established for itself an Office of Senate Legal Counsel. The Senate Legal Counsel and the Deputy Legal Counsel are appointed by the President pro tempore of the Senate from among recommendations

[96]United States v. Lovett, 328 U.S. 303 (1946). See "Representation of Congress and Congressional Interests in Court," hearings before the Senate Committee on the Judiciary, 94th Cong., 2d Sess. 6 (1976).

[97]S. Rept. No. 170, 95th Cong., 1st Sess. 11 (1977).

[98]Id. at 12.

submitted by the majority and minority leaders of the Senate. Appointments become effective upon approval by resolution of the Senate.

The principal duty of the Counsel is to defend the Senate or a committee, subcommittee, member, officer, or employee of the Senate when directed by two-thirds of the members of the Joint Leadership Group or by the adoption of a Senate resolution. The Joint Leadership Group consists of the majority and minority leaders, the President pro tempore, and the chairmen and ranking minority members of the Committees on the Judiciary and on Rules and Administration. When directed by Senate resolution, the Counsel brings a civil action to enforce a subpoena issued by the Senate, or by a Senate committee or subcommittee, and intervenes or appears as amicus curiae in cases involving the powers and responsibilities of Congress. Individual Senators may initiate suits on their own. In the House of Representatives, the office of the Clerk of the House handles litigation that involves members, House officers, and staff. Decisions to go to court are made by a bypartisan leadership committee.

Legislative precedents in the House and the Senate do not permit the Speaker or the Chair to rule on questions of constitutionality. Points of order, raising the issue of unconstitutional provisions, are referred to the full chamber for decision. A fascinating example of this practice occurred in 1984 after Senator Mack Mattingly offered an amendment to give the President item-veto authority over appropriations, subject to an override vote of a majority of each House rather than the two-thirds required by the Constitution. After Senator Lawton Chiles expressed concern about "rewriting the Constitution" with a statute, Senator Alan J. Dixon admitted that as a lawyer he had some difficulty on the constitutionality of the amendment, but concluded that "it is for the courts, not the Senate," to dispose of the issue.[99]

Other Senators, including Pete V. Domenici, John Stennis, and Howard Baker, said that it is wrong to pass a provision that the Senate thinks is unconstitutional, pushing the dispute into the courts for resolution.[100] Senator Chiles then raised a point of order "that the bill is legislation which changes the Constitution of the United States." Before the question could be debated, Mattingly moved to table the

[99] 130 Cong. Rec. S5297–305 (daily ed. May 3, 1984).
[100] Id. at S5310–12.

point of order, hoping to avoid the substantive question through a procedural maneuver. That tactic failed by the vote of 45 to 46.[101] During debate on the point of order, Senator Slade Gorton found the arguments in favor of the amendment "profoundly disturbing" because none of the proponents seemed to believe that the proposal was constitutional. Members could not, he said, "hide behind the fact that the Supreme Court has final authority on constitutional questions. You cannot hide behind that proposition to ignore your own duty properly to interpret the Constitution, which you have inherited after 200 years of history. It is your duty to make a judgment as to whether or not this amendment is constitutional."[102] The Senate voted 56 to 34 to support Chiles's point of order, thereby rejecting the Mattingly amendment.[103]

When there is substantial doubt within Congress concerning the constitutionality of a bill, it is increasingly the habit to place within the bill a procedure for expedited review by the courts. Examples include the Federal Election Campaign Act Amendments of 1974, which led to *Buckley* v. *Valeo* two years later, and the Gramm-Rudman-Hollings Act of 1985, resulting in *Bowsher* v. *Synar* the following year.[104]

Judge as Lawmaker

From the common law of England to the decisions of American courts, judge-made law has been a fact of life. Lawmaking by legislature was a late development in our history, and one that judges opposed because of its blunt and imprecise quality.[105] It is an act of dissembling to say that judges "find" the law rather than "make" it. Jeremiah Smith, who taught at Harvard after a career on the New Hampshire Supreme Court, was refreshingly candid on this point. When asked

[101]Id. at S5312.
[102]Id. at S5313.
[103]Id. at S5323.
[104]86 Stat. 1285, § 315 (1974); Buckley v. Valeo, 424 U.S. 1 (1976); 99 Stat. 1098, § 274 (1985); Bowsher v. Synar, 106 S.Ct. 3181 (1986).
[105]Lawrence M. Friedman, A History of American Law 316 (1973); Roscoe Pound, The Formative Era of American Law 45, 59–72 (1938).

"Do judges make law?" he responded: " 'Course they do. Made some myself."[106]

Throughout its history the federal judiciary has been accused of engaging in "judicial legislation." Few statutes or constitutional provisions are clear in meaning. Judicial interpretation, broadly exercised, becomes a substitute for legislation. Because judges fill in the "interstices" of law, Holmes said he recognized "without hesitation that judges do and must legislate."[107]

There have been periods when judicial interpretations seemed so flagrant and arbitrary that they provoked biting criticism. At the end of the nineteenth century, after legislative attempts to regulate the economy were frustrated by Supreme Court decisions, certain members of the Court condemned what they regarded as a judicial assumption of power. When the Court in 1890 decided that the judiciary, not the legislature, was the final arbiter in regulating railroad fares, freight rates, and other charges on the public, Justice Bradley's dissent considered this an arrogation of authority the Court had no right to make.[108] In the Income Tax Case of 1895, Justice White's dissent accused his brethren of amending the Constitution by judicial fiat. For more than a century, the federal government and constitutional scholars had confined the definition of direct tax to capitation and land taxes. The Court decided to add a third category—the income tax. White said that the Constitution should have been amended directly rather than by the judiciary.[109] It took a constitutional amendment—the Sixteenth—to override the Court.

Dissenting in a 1904 case, Justice Harlan charged that the Court "entrenches upon the domain of the legislative department. . . . It has made, not declared, law."[110] In an antitrust decision in 1911 he assailed the Court for converting the formula of the Sherman Act from restraint of trade to "rule of reason." Borrowing language from an earlier decision, he charged that the Court had read into the Act *"by way of judicial legislation an exception that is not placed there by the lawmaking branch of the Government,* and this is to be done upon the

---

[106]Paul Freund, The Supreme Court of the United States 28 (1961).

[107]Southern Pacific Co. v. Jensen, 244 U.S. 205, 221 (1917).

[108]Chicago, Milwaukee & St. Paul R.R. Co. v. Minnesota, 134 U.S. 418, 462–63 (1890).

[109]Pollock v. Farmers' Home & Trust Co., 157 U.S. 429, 639 (1895).

[110]Schick v. United States, 195 U.S. 65, 99 (1904).

theory that the impolicy of such legislation is so clear that it cannot be supposed Congress intended the natural import of the language it used. This *we cannot and ought not to do. . . .*" By mere interpretation, he said, the Court had modified an act of Congress and deprived it of its force in combating monopoly practices. The most ominous part of the decision for Harlan was "the usurpation by the judicial branch of the Government of the functions of the legislative department."[111]

Judges answer that they must make law because of general language in the Constitution and because of gaps and inadequacies in the statutes enacted by Congress.[112] Even Justice Rehnquist, who objects to loose notions of a "living Constitution" that allow judges to adapt it constantly for contemporary needs, recognizes that the framers spoke in general language and "left to succeeding generations the task of applying that language to the unceasingly changing environment in which they would live."[113] Ironically, judges are more likely to confine their lawmaking if they are conscious of their role and the need to transcend bias and prejudice. Lawmaking may be more pronounced by judges who believe that they adhere to judicial objectivity and follow neutral formulas.[114]

Although the Supreme Court no longer substitutes its judgment for what Congress considers necessary in economic legislation, or at least not to the degree that the judiciary interfered up to the 1930s, courts still play an active legislative role by interpreting such general concepts as "equal protection" and "due process." Other opportunities are available for judicial legislation. In 1966 the Supreme Court interpreted a congressional statute, passed in 1865, to prohibit not merely obscene materials but those in which the publisher "pandered" (deliberately appealed to the customer's erotic interests). In his dissent, Justice Harlan said he feared that what the Court "has done today is in effect to write a new statute, but without the sharply focused definitions and standards necessary in such a sensitive area.

---

[111]Standard Oil v. United States, 221 U.S. 1, 88, 99, 103 (1911).

[112]Jack G. Day, "Why Judges Must Make Law," 26 Case West. Res. L. Rev. 563 (1976); Henry J. Friendly, "The Gap in Lawmaking—Judges Who Can't and Legislators Who Won't," 63 Colum. L. Rev. 787 (1963).

[113]William H. Rehnquist, "The Notion of a Living Constitution," 54 Tex. L. Rev. 693, 694 (1976).

[114]Charles E. Clark and David M. Trubek, "The Creative Role of the Judge: Restraint and Freedom in the Common Law Tradition," 71 Yale L. J. 255, 270 (1961).

Casting such a dubious gloss over a straightforward 101-year-old statute . . . is for me an astonishing piece of judicial improvisation."[115]

The abortion decisions in 1973 represent for many scholars a spectacular example of judicial legislation. Writing for the majority, Justice Blackmun declared that during the first trimester of pregnancy a physician, after consulting with the woman, is free to perform an abortion without interference by the state. During the second trimester, the state may regulate and even prevent abortion except where it is necessary to preserve the life or health of the mother. The state's interest increases even more during the third trimester.[116] In one of the two dissents, Justice Rehnquist said that the Court's "conscious weighing of competing factors . . . is far more appropriate to a legislative judgment than to a judicial one."[117]

If the weighing of competing factors constitutes an act of lawmaking, the courts do little else. Questions of federalism and the commerce power turn on the competing interests of the federal government and the states. The courts regularly balance the government's national security interests against the rights of individual freedom. The needs of law enforcement collide with the rights to privacy. A judge's decision to close a trial conflicts with the right of the press and the public to attend. The power of Congress to investigate the executive branch must be weighed against the President's privilege to withhold information.

In addition to this level of involvement, federal judges act on issues that are within the jurisdiction of Congress and could have been addressed through the regular legislative process. Justice Powell remarked that much of the expanded role of the Warren Court "was a reaction to the sluggishness of the legislative branch in addressing urgent needs for reform."[118] There are other pressures on judges to legislate. If one section or provision of a statute is unconstitutional, courts may decide to "sever" that portion while retaining the balance of the statute. Such decisions require that courts make judgments that the altered statute, as redesigned by the judiciary, is consistent

[115]Ginsburg v. United States, 383 U.S. 463, 494–95 (1966).

[116]Roe v. Wade, 410 U.S. 113, 162–65 (1973); Doe v. Bolton, 410 U.S. 179, 195, 199 (1973).

[117]Roe v. Wade, 410 U.S. at 173.

[118]Justice Lewis F. Powell, Jr., "What the Justices Are Saying . . . ," 62 A.B.A.J. 1454, 1455 (1976).

with legislative objectives. Judicial rewriting can provoke comments from colleagues that the author of a majority opinion has erred by "simply deleting the crucial statutory language and using the words that remain as the raw materials for a new statute of his own making."[119] Justice Harlan once complained that the Court, in the name of interpreting the will of Congress, had resorted to "judicial surgery" to remove an offending section, so transforming the statute that the Court performed "a lobotomy."[120]

If a statute is unconstitutional because it excludes a legitimate party or group, the courts may prefer to include the party rather than declare the entire statute invalid, even if the effect is to rewrite the law. Still more controversial is judicial rewriting that creates an additional charge on the public purse. If legislators dislike the judiciary's handiwork, they can rewrite the statute along constitutional lines. Until they do, the judicially amended statute continues in force.[121]

Judge as Administrator

Judicial lawmaking is a venerable and long-debated topic. A more contemporary issue, linked to the public law litigation explosion, concerns judges who actually *administer* a political system to protect legal rights. Attorney General William French Smith offered this criticism in 1981:

> . . . federal courts have attempted to restructure entire school systems in desegregation cases—and to maintain continuing review over basic administrative decisions. They have asserted similar control over entire prison systems and public housing projects. They have restructured the employment criteria to be used by American business and government—even to the extent of mandating numerical results based upon race or gender. No area seems immune from judicial administration. At least one federal judge even attempted to administer a local sewer system.[122]

[119]Regan v. Time, Inc., 468 U.S. 641, 673 (1984) (Brennan, J.).
[120]Welsh v. United States, 398 U.S. 333, 351 (1970).
[121]Ruth Bader Ginsburg, "Some Thoughts on Judicial Authority to Repair Unconstitutional Legislation," 28 Cleveland State L. Rev. 301 (1979).
[122]William French Smith, "Federal Courts Have Gone Beyond Their Abilities," 21

Involvement in administrative affairs is not a totally new phenomenon for the courts. Nineteenth-century judges reviewed dismissals of federal employees, ordered administrators to carry out "ministerial" (nondiscretionary) duties, and decided questions about the liability of federal officials subjected to lawsuits. With the rise of federal regulatory commissions toward the end of the nineteenth century and the early decades of the twentieth, federal courts became involved in reviewing agency rulemaking and adjudication.

The Administrative Procedure Act of 1946 provides that any person suffering legal wrong because of agency action is entitled to judicial review. The reviewing court "shall decide all relevant questions of law, interpret constitutional and statutory provisions, and determine the meaning or applicability of the terms of any agency action." Courts shall hold unlawful and set aside agency actions found to be arbitrary, capricious, an abuse of discretion, or contrary to law; contrary to constitutional right, power, privilege, or immunity; or unsupported by substantial evidence in cases subject to formal rulemaking. Although courts have a doctrine of deferring to agency expertise and judgment, granting a presumption of regularity in favor of the federal government, judges have required agencies to take a "hard look" at the decisions entrusted to their jurisdiction and have insisted on adequate documentation to support the agency's determinations.[123]

The breadth of judicial administration is reflected in the efforts of District Judge W. Arthur Garrity, Jr., to desegregate the Boston school system. In 1975 he placed South Boston High School in temporary receivership under a supervisor appointed by him. His ruling came after more than a decade of racial discrimination by the local school board.[124] Another federal judge, seeking to promote school desegregation in Wilmington, Delaware, "set a tax rate for the school district, ordered state payments to the district, required new training programs for teachers and administrators, mandated specific curricular offerings, ordered the reassignment of staff and

---

The Judges' Journal 4, 7 (Winter 1982). Adopted from his speech to the Federal Legal Counsel, October 29, 1981.

[123]Richard B. Stewart, "The Reformation of American Constitutional Law," 88 Harv. L. Rev. 1667 (1975).

[124]Barry Stuart Roberts, "The Extent of Federal Judicial Equitable Power: Receivership of South Boston High School," 12 N.E.L. Rev. 55 (1976).

called for the development of an 'appropriate human relations program.' "[125]

District Judge Frank M. Johnson, Jr., was deeply involved for more than a decade in administering certain institutions in Alabama. "The history of Alabama," he explained, "is replete with instances of state officials who could have chosen one of any number of courses to alleviate unconstitutional conditions but who chose instead to do nothing but punt the problem to the courts."[126] Because of the failure of state officials to correct shocking deficiencies in state prisons, mental hospitals, and institutions for the retarded, Johnson repeatedly found violations of the Eighth and Fourteenth Amendments. He graphically described the conditions: "the evidence reflected that one resident was scalded to death when a fellow resident hosed water from one of the bath facilities on him; another died as a result of the insertion of a running water hose into his rectum by a working resident who was cleaning him; one died when soapy water was forced into his mouth; another died of a self-administered overdose of inadequately stored drugs; and authorities restrained another resident in a straightjacket for *nine years* to prevent him from sucking his hands and fingers."[127]

Rather than devise specific steps to improve conditions, Johnson at first directed the state to design its own plan for upgrading the system to meet constitutional standards. After two deadlines passed without acceptable progress, Johnson intervened to define the minimal constitutional standards. The story suggests a solitary judge pitted against the state, but other parties intervened in the suit, including the Department of Justice, the American Psychological Association, the American Orthopsychiatric Association, and the ACLU.[128] Johnson was able to forge an effective alliance of state officials and private

[125]Terry W. Hartle, "The Law, the Courts, Education and Public Administration," 41 Pub. Adm. Rev. 595, 599 (1981). For the Supreme Court's involvement in school discipline, see J. Harvie Wilkinson, III, "Goss v. Lopez: The Supreme Court as School Superintendent," 1975 Sup. Ct. Rev. 25.

[126]Steven Brill, "The Real Governor of Alabama," New York Magazine, April 26, 1976, at 38.

[127]Frank M. Johnson, "The Constitution and the Federal District Judge," 54 Tex. L. Rev. 903, 909 (1976). Emphasis in original.

[128]Wyatt v. Stickney, 334 F.Supp. 1341 (M.D. Ala. 1971). See also Wyatt v. Stickney, 344 F. Supp. 373, 387 (M.D. Ala. 1972).

citizens to bring pressure on the legislature and the governor.[129] A case of "judicial activism"? It is difficult to reach that judgment when the attorney for the state of Alabama admitted in open court that every prisoner in the state system was subjected to cruel and inhuman treatment within the meaning of the Eighth Amendment.[130]

Supreme Court decisions have also put pressure on states to upgrade conditions in their prison systems. In 1978 the Court upheld a lower court's ruling that placed a maximum limit of thirty days for confinement in isolation cells, which were windowless cells, eight by ten feet, containing an average of four and sometimes as many as ten or eleven prisoners held for an indeterminate period of time. The Court also upheld the award of attorney fees to the plaintiffs, to be paid out of state funds.[131]

These vignettes from the three branches of government show the extent to which the line between law and politics blurs and becomes indistinct. Subsequent chapters explore the effort of the judiciary to maintain its legitimacy and strength against the other, popularly elected, branches. The posture is not always adversary, for the courts often combine forces with one branch to restrain another.

[129] Tinsley E. Yarbrough, "The Judge as Manager: The Case of Judge Frank Johnson," 1 J. Policy Anal. & Mgt. 386 (1982).

[130] Pugh v. Locke, 406 F.Supp. 318, 322, 329 & n.13 (M.D. Ala. 1976).

[131] Hutto v. Finney, 437 U.S. 678 (1978).

2. The Doctrine of Judicial Review

Judicial review in America has managed to survive a number of nagging, unresolved questions. By what right do life-tenured judges invalidate policies adopted by popularly elected officials? If judicial review is of such crucial importance for a written Constitution, why did the framers omit it? Why is it based on implied, rather than explicit, power? If judicial review is essential for a constitutional democracy, how do other nations preserve their constitutions without judicial review?

At some point judicial review assumes the characteristics of lawmaking. Constitutional interpretation is more than a technical exercise or display of judicial erudition. The power to interpret the law is the power to make the law. Judicial review can be another name for judicial legislation. As Bishop Hoadley announced in 1717: "Whosoever hath an absolute authority to interpret any written or spoken laws, it is he who is truly the lawgiver, to all intents and purposes, and not the person who first wrote or spoke them."[1]

Courts may overturn a government action, find support for it, or refuse to rule at all. Judicial review applies not only to Congress but to the chief executive, administrative agencies, state legislatures, and rulings of state courts. Although the holding of the Supreme Court is of utmost importance, it often serves as but one stage of an ongoing constitutional process shared with lower courts, the executive branch, and legislators.

Sources of Judicial Review Authority

When legislators or the chief executive make unpopular decisions, the voters may remove them at the next election. The ballot box

[1] James Bradley Thayer, "The Origin and Scope of the American Doctrine of Constitutional Law," 7 Harv. L. Rev. 129, 152 (1893).

represents a periodic test of the legitimacy of elected officers, a reaffirmation of authority they are quite happy to cite. The federal judiciary, however, cannot draw legitimacy from elections. When judges announce an unpopular decision, citizens want to know on what authority courts may overturn the judgments of elected officials who also take an oath to uphold the Constitution. Judges must be able to identify persuasive and authoritative sources: constitutional language, pre-*Marbury* precedents, principles announced by the Marshall Court, and convincing evidence that has accumulated since that time.

Constitutional Language. Article III, Section 1 of the Constitution provides that "The judicial Power of the United States, shall be vested in one Supreme Court, and in such inferior Courts as the Congress may from time to time ordain and establish. . . ." Section 2 extends the judicial power to various cases and controversies, but there is no specific grant of power to declare an act of Congress, the President, or state government unconstitutional. The absence of an explicit grant is not conclusive. An implied power may exist. For example, although the Constitution provides no authority for the President to assert executive privilege, remove appointees from office, issue executive orders with the force of law, or enter into international agreements without the advice and consent of the Senate, the Supreme Court has considered those powers implicit in Article II.[2] Similarly, the Court has found an implied power for Congress to investigate, issue subpoenas, and exercise the power of contempt.[3]

The power of judicial review can be implied from two sources. Under Article III, Section 2, the judicial power extends to all cases "arising under this Constitution, the Laws of the United States, and Treaties made." Moreover, the Supremacy Clause in Article VI provides that the Constitution, federal laws "made in Pursuance thereof," and all treaties shall be the supreme law of the land, "and the Judges

[2]United States v. Nixon, 418 U.S. 683 (1974) (executive privilege); Myers v. United States, 272 U.S. 52 (1926) (removal power); Contractors Ass'n of Eastern Pa. v. Secretary of Labor, 442 F.2d 159 (3d Cir. 1971), cert. denied, 404 U.S. 854 (1971) (executive orders); and Dames & Moore v. Regan, 453 U.S. 654 (1981) (executive agreements).

[3]McGrain v. Daugherty, 273 U.S. 135 (1927) (investigations); Eastland v. United States Servicemen's Fund, 421 U.S. 491, 505 (1975) (subpoenas); Anderson v. Dunn, 19 U.S. (6 Wheat.) 204, 228 (1821) (contempt power).

in every State shall be bound thereby, any Thing in the Constitution or Laws of any State to the Contrary notwithstanding." This language requires federal courts to review the actions of state governments and might invite review of congressional statutes that are not "in pursuance" of the Constitution. However, judicial review over presidential and congressional acts raises a wholly different dimension—the relations between coordinate branches of the national government. Justice Holmes once remarked: "I do not think the United States would come to an end if [the Supreme Court] lost [its] power to declare an act of Congress void. I do think the Union would be imperiled if we could not make that declaration as to the laws of the several States."[4]

The Pre-Marbury Precedents. A number of precedents for judicial review before *Marbury* prepared the way for Marshall's famous opinion in 1803. British efforts in the 1760s to reestablish control over America provoked accusations by colonists that the laws of Parliament had violated the "common law" and the "law of reason" and were therefore void. These charges became important ingredients in the case presented to a "candid world" in 1776.

The best-known American challenge to an act of Parliament came in 1761 when James Otis argued the Writs of Assistance Case in Boston. He claimed that British customs officials were not empowered by Parliament to use general search warrants. Even if Parliament had authorized the writs of assistance, Otis said that the statute would be "against the constitution," "against natural equity," and therefore void.[5] In 1766 a Virginia court held the Stamp Act unconstitutional. On the eve of the Declaration of Independence, a Massachusetts judge instructed the jury that it should treat acts of Parliament in violation of fundamental law as "void" and "inoperative."[6]

The proposition that courts could void an act of Parliament appears in Chief Justice Coke's opinion in *Dr. Bonham's Case* (1610). He said that when an act of Parliament "is against common right and reason, or repugnant, or impossible to be performed, the common law will controul it, and adjudge such Act to be void."[7] A few British

---

[4]Collected Legal Papers 295–96 (1920).
[5]Edward S. Corwin, The Doctrine of Judicial Review 30 (1914).
[6]Id. at 32.
[7]77 Eng. Rep. 646, 652 (1610).

46

judges in the seventeenth and eighteenth centuries cited Coke's argument, but the principle of judicial review never took root in English soil.[8] In 1884 the Supreme Court noted: "notwithstanding what was attributed to Lord Coke in *Bonham's Case* . . . the omnipotence of Parliament over the common law was absolute, even against common right and reason."[9]

For their understanding of British law, the framers relied mainly on Blackstone's *Commentaries,* which states the case for parliamentary supremacy with singular clarity. For those who believed that acts of Parliament contrary to reason were void, he offered this advice:

> But if the parliament will positively enact a thing to be done which is unreasonable, I know of no power that can control it: and the examples usually alleged in support of this sense of the rule do none of them prove, that, where the main object of a statute is unreasonable, the judges are at liberty to reject it; for that were to set the judicial power above that of the legislature, which would be subversive of all government.[10]

Although *Dr. Bonham's Case* provides inadequate support for the American concept of judicial review, it was accepted as good law and precedent by those who wanted to break with England. Intellectual justifications were needed to neutralize the appearance of impetuous and impulsive behavior. But "voiding" the acts of Parliament did not automatically deliver the power of judicial review to American courts, especially those at the national level.

From independence to the framing of the Constitution, some of the state judges challenged the acts of their legislatures. Although scholars disagree on the strength of those precedents, decisions providing support for the theory of judicial review were handed down by judges in Virginia, New Jersey, New York, Connecticut, Rhode Island, and North Carolina. The language used by judges in holding state laws invalid was often more bold than the results they achieved.[11]

---

[8]Day v. Savadge, 80 Eng. Rep. 235, 237 (1614) and The City of London v. Wood, 88 Eng. Rep. 1592, 1602 (1702).

[9]Hurtado v. California, 110 U.S. 516, 531 (1884).

[10]William Blackstone, Commentaries on the Laws of England, Book One, §3, p. 91 (Oxford 1775).

[11]Charles Grove Haines, The American Doctrine of Judicial Supremacy 88–120 (1932).

The Framers' Intent

By the time of the convention, some of the framers expected judicial review to be part of the new government. In reading their statements at the convention and during the ratification debates, it is important to keep their thoughts in context and recognize conflicting statements. The framers did not have a clear or fully developed theory of judicial review.

The framers wanted to replace the Articles of Confederation to make the central government more effective, resolve disputes among the states over legal and monetary systems, and limit legislative abuses. Each goal would be affected by the structure and power of the federal judiciary. Instead of the legislative supremacy that prevailed under the Articles of Confederation, the new Congress would be only one of three coordinate and coequal branches. Both the Virginia Plan presented by Edmund Randolph and the New Jersey Plan advocated by William Paterson called for the creation of an independent judiciary headed by a Supreme Court. Although the new judicial article left undecided such questions as lower federal courts and the status of state courts, it did grant broad authority to the Supreme Court.

The framers were worried that thirteen sets of state courts would announce contradictory rulings on matters of national concern. In Federalist 80, Hamilton said that thirteen independent courts of final jurisdiction "over the same causes, arising upon the same laws, is a hydra in government from which nothing but contradiction and confusion can proceed." The convention resolved that problem by adopting the Supremacy Clause. Judicial review over presidential and congressional actions, however, was a subject of much greater delicacy. By 1787 the framers had become alarmed about legislative overreaching. In Federalist 48, Madison wrote that the "legislative department is everywhere extending the sphere of its activity and drawing all power into its impetuous vortex." Several delegates to the Philadelphia Convention expressed the same concern.[12] But giv-

---

[12] 1 Max Farrand, ed., *Records of the Federal Convention* 254 (Wilson) and 2 Farrand 35 (Madison), 110 (Madison), and 288 (Mercer) (1937) (hereafter Farrand).

ing the courts the final say over congressional acts was an extremely radical notion.

A common pastime of constitutional scholars is counting the heads of framers who favored judicial review. Depending on which year he wrote, Edward S. Corwin vacillated on the statistics, ranging from a high of seventeen framers to a low of five or six.[13] Other studies were also flavored by a crusading spirit, either to "prove" the legitimacy of judicial review[14] or to chop away at its foundations.[15] The issue remains unsettled; this very ambiguity adds an inhibiting force to judicial activism.

Judicial review was discussed at the convention as a means of checking Congress and the states. The most important debate was over the veto of legislation passed by Congress. Randolph proposed a Council of Revision consisting of the "Executive and a convenient number of the National Judiciary . . . with authority to examine every act of the National Legislature before it shall operate, & every act of a particular Legislature before a Negative thereon shall be final; and that the dissent of the said Council shall amount to a rejection, unless the Act of the National Legislature be again passed. . . ."[16] Some commentators accept the elimination of the revisionary council as proof that the framers rejected judicial review. However, one of the arguments against the Council was the *availability* of judicial review. As reported by Madison: "Mr. [Elbridge] Gerry doubts whether the Judiciary ought to form a part of it, as they will have a sufficient check agst. encroachments on their own department by their exposition of the laws, which involved a power of deciding on their Constitutionality. In some States the Judges had ⟨actually⟩ set aside laws as being agst. the Constitution. This was done too with general approbation."[17] Rufus King supported Gerry's argument after observing that the Justices of the Supreme Court "ought to be able to expound the law as it should come before them, free from the bias of having participated in its formation." This comment provides

[13]Leonard W. Levy, ed., Judicial Review and the Supreme Court 3–4 (1967).

[14]Charles A. Beard, The Supreme Court and the Constitution (1912), and Raoul Berger, Congress v. The Supreme Court (1969).

[15]Louis B. Boudin, Government by Judiciary (1932), and William W. Crosskey, Politics and the Constitution (1953).

[16]1 Farrand 21.

[17]Id. at 97.

broad support for judicial review, whereas Gerry appeared to restrict it to legislative encroachments.

Also debated was the need for a congressional veto over proposed state legislation. That idea was rejected for two reasons. The addition of the Supremacy Clause would presumably handle any conflicts between national law and state legislation. Moreover, the state courts could exercise judicial review to control legislative excesses. They "would not consider as valid any law contravening the Authority of the Union," and if such laws were not set aside by the judiciary they "may be repealed by a Nationl. law."[18] Madison later said that "A law violating a constitution established by the people themselves, would be considered by the Judges as null & void."[19] These statements were clearly limited to judicial review at the *state,* not the national, level. A year later, writing to Jefferson, Madison denied that the Constitution empowered the Court to strike down acts of Congress, for that would have made the judiciary "paramount in fact to the Legislature, which was never intended and can never be proper."[20]

James Wilson, soon to be a member of the Supreme Court, defended the concept of judicial review at the Pennsylvania ratification convention. He said the legislature would be "kept within its prescribed bounds" by the judiciary.[21] At the Connecticut ratifying convention, Oliver Ellsworth (destined to be the third Chief Justice of the Supreme Court) expected federal judges to void any legislative acts that were contrary to the Constitution.[22] At the Virginia ratifying convention, John Marshall anticipated that the federal judiciary would strike down unconstitutional legislative acts.[23] The context of these remarks suggests that the availability of judicial review was used to reassure the states that national power would be held in check.

The *Federalist Papers* include several essays that speak strongly for judicial review. The principal essay, Hamilton's Federalist 78, is designed partly to allay state fears about the power of the central government, but certainly he articulates a lucid case for judicial review. The restrictions that the Constitution places on the legislative au-

[18] 2 Farrand 27–28 (Sherman and Morris).

[19] Id. at 93.

[20] 5 Writings of James Madison 294 (Hunt ed. 1904).

[21] 2 Jonathan Elliot, ed., Debates in the Several State Constitutions on the Adoption of the Federal Constitution 445 (1836) (hereafter Elliot).

[22] Id. at 196. See also Samuel Adams's comments in Massachusetts; id. at 131.

[23] 3 Elliot 553. See also George Nicholas, id. at 443.

thority, such as the prohibition on bills of attainder and ex post facto laws, "can be preserved in practice no other way than through the medium of courts and justice, whose duty it must be to declare all acts contrary to the manifest tenor of the Constitution void. Without this, all the reservations of particular rights or privileges would amount to nothing."

Hamilton denied that this power would "imply a superiority of the judiciary to the legislative power." His basic principle is that no authority can act in a manner contrary to the power delegated to it, for this would affirm "that the deputy is greater than his principal; that the servant is above his master; that the representatives of the people are superior to the people themselves; that men acting by virtue of powers, may do not only what their powers do not authorize, but what they forbid." To allow Congress to be the judge of its own powers would enable "the representatives of the people to substitute their *will* to that of their constituents." Hamilton dismissed the possibility that judges would abuse their powers and "substitute their own pleasure to the constitutional intentions of the legislature." As he noted earlier in the essay, the courts "may truly be said to have neither FORCE nor WILL, but merely judgment."

Hamilton's reasoning is not without its limitations. If Congress could not go beyond the power delegated to it without affirming that "the deputy is greater than the principal," how could the courts exercise the power of judicial review, which is not, at least expressly, delegated to it? If it is impermissable to let Congress be the judge of its own powers, for fears that the representatives will substitute "their *will* to that of their constituents," how can the courts be kept in check? Why should they be entrusted to be the judge of *their* powers? Is it realistic to expect courts to exercise only judgment and never will?

The arguments in Federalist 78 were later borrowed by John Marshall to buttress his *Marbury* opinion. Hamilton's enthusiasm is somewhat suspect; he appears to be a late convert to the cause of judicial review. His plan of government presented to the 1787 convention did not grant this power to the judiciary.[24] State laws contrary to the Constitution would be "utterly void," but he did not identify the judiciary as the voiding agency.[25]

In the years between ratification and *Marbury* v. *Madison*, the issue

[24] 1 Farrand 282–93, 302–11; 3 Farrand 617–30.
[25] 1 Farrand 293.

of judicial review was debated often in Congress, but not with any consistency. When Madison introduced the Bill of Rights in the House of Representatives, he predicted that once they were incorporated into the Constitution, "independent tribunals of justice will consider themselves in a peculiar manner the guardians of those rights; they will be an impenetrable bulwark against every assumption of power in the Legislative or Executive."[26] But nine days later, during debate on the President's removal power, he denied that Congress should defer to the courts on this constitutional issue. He begged to know on what principle could it be contended "that any one department draws from the Constitution greater powers than another, in marking out the limits of the powers of the several departments?" If questions arose on the boundaries between the branches, he did not see "that any one of these independent departments has more right than another to declare their sentiments on that point."[27] In 1791, when proponents of a national bank cited judicial review as a possible check on unconstitutional legislation, Madison was unpersuaded and voted against the bank.[28]

The Road to *Marbury*

Federal courts reviewed both national and state legislation prior to *Marbury*. In *Hayburn's Case* (1792), three circuit courts held divergent views on an act of Congress that appointed federal judges to serve as commissioners for claims settlement. Their decisions could be set aside by the Secretary of War. One of the courts agreed to serve. The other two believed that the statute was "unwarranted" because it required federal judges to perform nonjudicial duties and to render what was essentially an advisory opinion. The Supreme Court postponed decision until the next term, and by that time Congress had repealed the offending sections and removed the Secretary's authority to veto decisions rendered by judges.[29] In 1794, a year after Congress repaired the statute, the Supreme Court decided that the original statute would have been unconstitutional if it sought to place

[26] 1 Annals of Congress 439 (June 8, 1789).
[27] Id. at 500 (June 17, 1789).
[28] 3 Annals of Congress 1978–79 (February 4, 1791), 2011 (February 9, 1791).
[29] 2 Dall. 409 (1792); see 1 Stat. 243 (1792) and 1 Stat. 324 (1793).

nonjudicial powers on the circuit courts. Interestingly, this decision was not published until 1851.[30] The use of this 1794 case as a precedent for judicial review is rendered suspect by the fact that the statutory provision no longer existed.[31]

Between 1791 and 1799, federal courts began to challenge and strike down a number of state laws.[32] With regard to national legislation, in *Hylton* v. *United States* (1796) the Supreme Court upheld the constitutionality of a congressional statute that imposed a tax on carriages. If the Court had authority to uphold an act of Congress, presumably it had authority to strike one down. Otherwise, it would be engaged in a frivolous and idle enterprise. Justice Chase said it was unnecessary "*at this time,* for me to determine, whether this court, *constitutionally* possesses the power to declare an act of Congress *void* . . . but if the court have such power, I am free to declare, that I will never exercise it, *but in a very clear case.*"[33] Two years later the Court upheld the constitutionality of another congressional act, this time involving the process of constitutional amendment.[34]

Three other cases between 1795 and 1800 explored the authority of federal judges to declare state acts unconstitutional. In the first case, a circuit court decided that a Pennsylvania law was unconstitutional and void.[35] In the second, Supreme Court Justices offered differing views on the existence and scope of judicial review.[36] In the third, Justice Chase said that even if it were agreed that a statute contrary to the constitution would be void, "it still remains a question, where the power resides to declare it void?" The "general opinion," he said, is that the Supreme Court could declare an act of Congress unconstitutional, "but there is no adjudication of the Supreme Court itself upon the point."[37]

From 1789 to 1802, eleven state judiciaries exercised judicial review over state statutes.[38] The assertion of power by the national judiciary was much more sensitive, and yet even the Jeffersonian

[30]United States v. Yale Todd, 13 How. 51 (1794).
[31]1 Charles Warren, The Supreme Court in United States History 80–82 (1937).
[32]Id. at 65–69.
[33]3 Dall. 171, 175 (1796) (emphases in original).
[34]Hollingsworth v. Virginia, 3 Dall. 378 (1798).
[35]Vanhorne's Lessee v. Dorrance, 2 Dall. 304 (1795).
[36]Calder v. Bull, 3 Dall. 386 (1798).
[37]Cooper v. Telfair, 4 Dall. 14, 19 (1800).
[38]Haines, American Doctrine, at 148–64.

Republicans rebuked the federal courts for not striking down the repressive Alien and Sedition Acts of 1798.[39] In that same year Jefferson looked to the courts to protect basic rights: "the laws of the land, administered by upright judges, would protect you from any exercise of power unauthorized by the Constitution of the United States."[40]

Marshall Court Foundations. By 1801 the Supreme Court had yet to solidify its position as a coequal branch of government. It had upheld the constitutionality of a congressional statute. In a series of dicta, it gingerly explored the theory that it could hold one unconstitutional. In four decisions from 1803 to 1821, the Court held that it had the power to determine the constitutionality of statutes passed by Congress and state legislatures, as well as authority to review judgments by state courts in cases raising federal questions.

The election of 1800 marked a pivotal point for the nation. Although formally neutral between Britain and France, America was rapidly dividing into two warring camps. The Federalist party was pro-British, whereas the Jeffersonian Republicans supported the French. Efforts by the Adams administration to limit Republican criticism led to the Alien and Sedition Acts, further exacerbating partisan strife. When the Jeffersonians swept the elections of 1800, the Federalists looked for ways to salvage their dwindling political power.

Early in 1801, with a few weeks remaining for the Federalist Congress, two bills were passed to create a number of federal judges and District of Columbia justices of the peace.[41] Within a matter of days President Adams nominated Federalists to the new posts, much to the outrage of Republicans. John Marshall was at that point serving as Secretary of State, although he had already been appointed to the Supreme Court for the next term. The commissions of office were processed, sent to the Senate, and confirmed. Some of the commissions, William Marbury's among them, were never delivered.

Upon assuming the presidency, Jefferson ordered that the commissions he withheld. The administration also urged Congress to repeal the Circuit Court Act (with its additional judgeships) and to

[39] 1 Warren, The Supreme Court, at 215.
[40] 10 Writings of Thomas Jefferson 61 (Memorial ed. 1903). Letter to A. H. Rowan, September 26, 1798.
[41] 2 Stat. 89, 103 (1801).

block the anticipated 1802 term of the Supreme Court. Congress complied.[42] Partisan bitterness increased in the spring of 1801 when two Federalist judges instructed a district attorney to prosecute a newspaper that had published an attack on the judiciary. The jury refused to indict, but the Republicans saw this as additional evidence that the Federalists were engaged in a national conspiracy.[43] As part of a counterattack, the House of Representatives impeached District Judge John Pickering (a Federalist), contemplated the removal of Justice Chase from the Supreme Court, and planned the removal of other Federalist judges, including John Marshall.[44]

In this tense political climate, William Marbury and his colleagues appealed to the former Attorney General, Charles Lee, for legal assistance. Lee brought the action directly to the Supreme Court under Section 13 of the Judiciary Act of 1789, which empowered the Court to issue writs of mandamus "in cases warranted by the principles and usages of law, to any courts appointed, or persons holding office, under the authority of the United States."[45] Lee argued that the Court had jurisdiction under Section 13 because Madison was a person holding office (Secretary of State) under the authority of the United States. He asked the Court to issue a writ of mandamus, ordering Madison to deliver the commissions.

Marshall's options were circumscribed by one overpowering fact: whatever technical ground he used to rule against the administration, any order directing Madison to deliver the commissions was sure to be ignored. If the Court's order could be dismissed with impunity, the judiciary's power and prestige would suffer greatly. As Chief Justice Burger has noted: "The Court could stand hard blows, but not ridicule, and the ale house would rock with hilarious laughter" had Marshall issued a mandamus ignored by Jefferson.[46] Marshall chose a tactic he used in future years. He would appear to absorb a short-term defeat in exchange for a long-term victory. The

[42]Id. at 132, 156 (1802).

[43]George Lee Haskins and Herbert A. Johnson, 2 History of the Supreme Court of the United States: Foundations of Power: John Marshall 161–62 (1981).

[44]Jerry W. Knudson, "The Jeffersonian Assault on the Federalist Judiciary, 1802–1805; Political Forces and Press Reaction," 14 Am. J. Leg. Hist. 55 (1970).

[45]1 Stat. 81 (1789).

[46]Warren E. Burger, "The Doctrine of Judicial Review: Mr. Marshall, Mr. Jefferson, and Mr. Marbury," in Mark W. Cannon and David M. O'Brien, eds. Views From the Bench 14 (1985).

decision has been called "a masterwork of indirection, a brilliant example of Marshall's capacity to sidestep danger while seeking to court it, to advance in one direction while his opponents are looking in another."[47]

The opinion acknowledged the merits of Marbury's case but denied that the Court had power to issue the mandamus. Through a strained reading, Marshall concluded that Section 13 expanded the original jurisdiction of the Court and thereby violated Article III of the Constitution. He maintained that Congress could alter the boundaries only of appellate jurisdiction. Announcing that the statute conflicted with the Constitution and that judges take an oath of office to support the Constitution, Marshall claimed that the power of constitutional interpretation was vested exclusively in the judiciary.[48]

The decision has its share of shortcomings. Marshall's analysis of original and appellate jurisdiction is less than compelling. He could have read Section 13 to connect mandamus action to appellate jurisdiction. Even if he related it to original jurisdiction, the Constitution did not explicitly prohibit Congress from adding to original jurisdiction. And if the Court did indeed lack jurisdiction, why did Marshall reach further and explore the merits of Marbury's claim and expound on novel questions of judicial authority? Finally, given his previous involvement in the case, there was strong reason for Marshall to disqualify himself.[49]

Encircled by hostile political forces, Marshall decided that it was time to strike boldly for judicial independence. Instead of citing historical and legal precedents, all of which could have been challenged and picked apart by his opponents, Marshall reached to a higher plane and grounded his case on what appeared to be self-evident, universal principles. His decision seems to march logically and inexorably toward the only possible conclusion.

Developments After Marbury. The power to strike down unconstitutional actions by coordinate branches of government was not

[47]Robert G. McCloskey, The American Supreme Court 40 (1960). For the evolution of judicial review prior to Marbury, see Julius Goebel, Jr., 1 History of the Supreme Court of the United States: Antecedents and Beginnings to 1801 (1971).

[48]5 U.S. (1 Cr.) 137 (1803).

[49]See William W. Van Alstyne, "A Critical Guide to Marbury v. Madison," 1969 Duke L. J. 1 (1969).

used again until 1857, in *Dred Scott* v. *Sandford*.[50] Judicial review of state actions, however, was more frequent. In two sets of decisions, the Court established its authority to review state statutes and state judicial decisions.

United States v. *Peters* (1809) and *Fletcher* v. *Peck* (1810) were decided in a difficult political period. Some states, reacting against the growth of national power, threatened secession and nullification. Richard Peters, a federal judge in Pennsylvania, was unable to compel state officials to obey a decree he had issued. The state legislature passed a law declaring the decree a usurpation of power and ordered the Governor to resist any attempt to enforce it. Marshall then issued a mandamus ordering enforcement on the ground that state legislatures cannot interfere with the operation of the federal judicial process.[51] The Governor called out the militia to prevent a federal marshal from executing the court order. He also sought President Madison's assistance, but the state's resistance collapsed when Madison replied that the President "is not only unauthorized to prevent the execution of a decree sanctioned by the Supreme Court of the United States, but is expressly enjoined, by statute, to carry into effect any such decree where opposition may be made to it."[52]

In *Fletcher* v. *Peck*, the Court struck down an act of a state legislature as unconstitutional. Several land companies had obtained a huge land grant at a bargain price from the Georgia legislature, offering bribes to a number of legislators. After elections, the new legislature revoked the land grant. In the meantime, innocent third parties had bought property from the corrupt land companies. Some of the purchasers challenged the revocation, claiming impairment of the obligations of a contract protected by Article I, Section 10 of the Constitution. Justice Marshall, recognizing the delicate task of reviewing state legislation, concluded that the revocation did constitute a violation of the impairments clause.[53]

A second pair of cases was decided after the War of 1812, following a substantial change in the Supreme Court's membership. The most important addition was Joseph Story. Though appointed by Madison, he became as ardent a defender of national interests as

[50]60 U.S. (19 How.) 393 (1857).
[51]9 U.S. (5 Cr.) 115 (1809).
[52]Annals of Congress, 11th Cong. 2269. See 1 Warren, The Supreme Court, at 382.
[53]10 U.S. (6 Cr.) 87, 136–39 (1810).

Marshall. He wrote the decision in *Martin* v. *Hunter's Lessee* (1816), establishing the Court's authority to review state court decisions involving federal questions.[54] The dispute in *Martin* was between two private parties. In *Cohens* v. *Virginia* (1821), with a state one of the parties, Marshall solidified the relationship of the Court to state courts and breathed new life into the Supremacy Clause.[55]

Constraints on Judicial Review

By the time of his visit to America in the 1830s, Alexis de Tocqueville could write of judicial review: "I am aware that a similar right has been sometimes claimed, but claimed in vain, by courts of justice in other countries, but in America it is recognized by all the authorities; and not a party, not so much as an individual, is found to contest it."[56] In fact, judicial review was resisted at every level of government. State courts and state legislatures regularly challenged the jurisdiction of the Supreme Court, not only up to the Civil War but afterwards as well.[57]

Justice Gibson's dissent in *Eakin* v. *Raub* (1825) represents a trenchant rebuttal of Marshall's position on judicial review. Gibson, a Pennsylvania judge, conceded that the Supremacy Clause required judges to strike down state laws in conflict with the federal constitution, but he rejected judicial review as a means of policing Congress and the President. Although a constitution was superior to a statute, that fact alone did not elevate judges to be the sole interpreter. The oath to support the Constitution was not unique to judges. The political branches had an equal right to put a construction on the Constitution. If a legislature were to abuse its powers and overstep the boundaries established by the Constitution, Gibson preferred that correction come at the hands of the people. Judicial errors were more difficult to correct, for they required constitutional amendment. In

[54] 1 Wheat. 304 (1816).

[55] 6 Wheat. 264 (1821).

[56] 1 Alexis de Tocqueville, Democracy in America 100 (Bradley ed. 1951).

[57] Charles Warren, "Legislative and Judicial Attacks on the Supreme Court of the United States—A History of the Twenty-Fifth Section of the Judiciary Act," 47 Am. L. Rev. 1, 161 (1913).

subsequent years, Gibson resigned himself to a more generous definition of judicial review.[58]

President Jackson, who inherited some of the Jeffersonian distrust toward the judiciary, disagreed sharply with John Marshall on both personal and policy grounds. Every public officer, he said in 1832, took an oath to support the Constitution "as he understands it, and not as it is understood by others." The opinion of judges "has no more authority over Congress than the opinion of Congress has over the judges, and on that point the President is independent of both."[59] But Jackson appreciated the value of judicial independence. He saw the courts as natural allies in his fight against the Nullifiers, who wanted to release the states from judgments of federal courts.[60]

Concern about judicial overreaching prompted some judges to advocate a philosophy of self-restraint. To temper criticism, they offered to presume the validity of government actions and to uphold the legislature in doubtful cases.[61] Similar guidelines were issued when reviewing lower court decisions. For judges who felt comfortable with the legitimacy of judicial review, the power was wielded actively and aggressively.

A major challenge to judicial review arose late in the nineteenth century when federal judges began to impose their own philosophies of economic laissez-faire. Repeatedly the courts struck down state and federal statutes designed to relieve economic hardship. Legislative efforts to deal with monopoly, prices, minimum wages, maximum work hours, and organized labor were either rejected by the courts or severely restricted.[62] The philosophy of judicial restraint, the presumption of legislative validity, and avoidance of decisions

[58]Eakin v. Raub, 12 S.& R. 330, 343 (Pa. 1825); Norris v. Clymer, 2 Pa. 277, 281 (1845). Gibson's comment in the latter case was not in his decision but in response to an attorney's argument.

[59]3 James D. Richardson, ed., Messages and Papers of the Presidents 1145 (July 10, 1832).

[60]Richard P. Longaker, "Andrew Jackson and the Judiciary," 71 Pol. Sci. Q. 341, 358–61 (1956). For Lincoln's arguments on the limits of judicial supremacy, see Gary J. Jacobsohn, "Abraham Lincoln 'On This Question of Judicial Authority': The Theory of Constitutional Aspiration," 36 West. Pol. Q. 52 (1983).

[61]Fletcher v. Peck, 10 U.S. at 128; Dartmouth College v. Woodward, 17 U.S. (4 Wheat.) 517, 625 (1819).

[62]Robert G. McCloskey, "Economic Due Process and the Supreme Court: An Exhumation and Reburial," 1962 Sup. Ct. Rev. 34.

based on the wisdom of government action seemed virtually abandoned.

The judges reached outside the Constitution to discover a "liberty of contract" and read narrowly the scope of interstate commerce and the taxing power. These decisions stood in the path of progressive legislation and threatened effective government. Justice Stone lectured his colleagues in 1936 that courts "are not the only agency of government that must be assumed to have capacity to govern."[63]

Changes in the composition of the Supreme Court after 1937 removed the judicial impediment to economic regulation. The era of "substantive due process" appeared to be over. But the Warren Court sparked another round of debate over judicial review, this time raising the claim that courts had tilted in a liberal direction. The opinions outlawing desegregation, requiring legislative reapportionment, providing right of counsel, and announcing novel constitutional rights of association and privacy, all supported the weak and politically disfranchised.

Critics who had called for judicial self-restraint during the 1930s now found themselves applauding the substantive results of the activist Warren Court. Others warned that the Court risked losing popular support by issuing broad decisions in social and political areas. Reacting against Judge Learned Hand's plea in 1958 for judicial restraint, Herbert Wechsler maintained that the issue was not whether judges possessed judicial review but rather how they exercised that authority. He objected to what he regarded as idiosyncratic, ad hoc, and poorly reasoned decisions and urged the courts to follow principled rules, deciding on grounds of "adequate neutrality and generality, tested not only by the instant application but by others that the principles imply."[64]

Many scholars agree that the Warren Court opinions should have been better crafted to clarify statements of principles. If a majority opinion simply announced a result without adequately explaining the underlying argument, the courts would rule by fiat and decree.[65] However, the concept of "neutral principles" has remained elusive and confusing. It appears to run counter to Holmes's dictum that

---

[63]United States v. Butler, 297 U.S. 1, 87 (1936) (dissenting opinion).

[64]Herbert Wechsler, "Toward Neutral Principles of Constitutional Law," 73 Harv. L. Rev. 1, 15 (1959). See Learned Hand, The Bill of Rights (1958).

[65]Howard Ball, Judicial Craftsmanship or Fiat? (1978).

"The life of the law has not been logic: it has been experience."[66] Elsewhere Holmes said: "Behind the logical form lies a judgment as to the relative worth and importance of competing legislative grounds, often an inarticulate and unconscious judgment, it is true, and yet the very root and nerve of the whole proceeding."[67]

In such areas as separation of church and state or search-and-seizure operations, it is difficult to discover general principles that guide the Court. The process has been characterized by starts and stops, direction and redirection, trial and error. Some have pointed out that an insistence on principled decisions might prevent judges from discovering novel responses for unprecedented conditions.[68] Strict adherence to fixed principles would prevent the tactical use of threshold arguments (such as standing, mootness, and ripeness) needed to protect the Court's prestige and effectiveness.

The years after the Warren Court were marked by continued controversy over the scope of judicial decisions. Presidents used rulings on such contentious issues as school desegregation, the death penalty, criminal procedures, and birth control as political rallying points. Courts were accused of deciding too many cases and overtaxing their institutional capacity. They were urged to use their power to control court access to divert issues from the courthouse to the legislative arena.

Despite President Nixon's vow to nominate "strict constructionists" to the bench, the Burger Court continued to play an activist role. It created a constitutional right of "commercial free speech"[69], struck down death-penalty statutes, initiated busing to overcome segregation in schools, began the process of eradicating sex discrimination, and authored the abortion decision. Many commentators view the abortion decision as a revival of the era of "substantive due process" that prevailed before 1937.[70] The Court's decision against the legislative veto in 1983, Justice White noted, struck down in "one fell

[66]Oliver Wendell Holmes, The Common Law 1 (1881).

[67]Oliver Wendell Holmes, Collected Legal Papers 181 (1920).

[68]Charles E. Clark, "A Plea for the Unprincipled Decision," 49 Va. L. Rev. 660, 665 (1963).

[69]Virginia State Board of Pharmacy v. Virginia Citizens Consumer Council, 425 U.S. 748 (1976); First National Bank of Boston v. Bellotti, 435 U.S. 765 (1978).

[70]Richard A. Epstein, "Substantive Due Process By Any Other Name: The Abortion Cases," 1973 Sup. Ct. Rev. 159.

swoop provisions in more laws enacted by Congress than the Court has cumulatively invalidated in its history."[71]

The conditions that encourage judges to play an activist role were discussed by Justice Powell in a revealing interview in 1979. He admitted that judicial independence "does give the Court a freedom to make decisions that perhaps are necessary for our society, decisions that the legislative branch may be reluctant to make." An example he gave was the desegregation case of 1954. Although Congress had the authority to enact legislation to meet the problem of segregated schools, "it was the Supreme Court that finally decided in 1954 that segregation in our society must come to an end."[72] The problem of segregated schools, however, proved too intractable for a single opinion from the Supreme Court.

Some critics of contemporary courts argue that the main objection to judicial review is that it runs counter to American democratic values. John Hart Ely advised judges to limit their work to supporting broad participation in the democratic process and protecting minority rights.[73] In another influential study, Jesse Choper endorsed judicial review for protecting individual rights, but proposed that the courts withdraw from almost all areas of federalism and separation of powers.[74]

To call judicial review antidemocratic is tempting, but misleading. The Constitution establishes a limited republic, not a direct or pure democracy. Popular sentiment is filtered through a system of representation. Majority vote is limited by various restrictions in the Constitution: candidates must be a certain age, Presidents may not serve a third term—regardless of what the people want. Although states range in population from less than a million to more than twenty million, each state receives the same number of Senators. Filibusters conducted by a minority of Senators can prevent the Senate from acting. Majority rule is further constrained by checks and balances, separation of powers, federalism, a bicameral legislature, and the Bill of Rights.

To the extent that the judiciary protects constitutional principles,

---

[71] INS v. Chadha, 462 U.S. 919, 1002 (1983) (dissenting opinion).

[72] "Constitutional interpretation: An interview with Justice Lewis Powell," Kenyon College Alumni Bulletin, Summer 1979, at 15.

[73] John Hart Ely, Democracy and Distrust (1980).

[74] Jesse H. Choper, Judicial Review and the National Political Process (1980).

including minority rights, it upholds the values of the people who drafted and ratified the Constitution. Throughout much of its history the judiciary gave little support to civil liberties or civil rights. The record does not support the assertion that judicial review has been a force for protecting individual liberties.[75] But in a number of decisions over the past few decades affecting reapportionment, the right of association, and the "White Primary" cases, the Supreme Court opened the door to broader public participation in the political process. In many ways the contemporary judiciary has helped strengthen democracy. Through its decisions it performs an "informing function" previously associated with legislative bodies.[76]

The judiciary performs other positive, legitimizing functions. Actions by executive and legislative officials are contested and brought before the courts for review. When upheld, citizens can see some standard at work other than the power of majorities and the raw force of politics. Alexander Bickel wrote: "The Court's prestige, the spell it casts as a symbol, enable it to entrench and solidify measures that may have been tentative in the conception or that are on the verge of abandonment in the execution."[77] But what happens when the Court faces a repressive executive or legislative action? If judges lend their support, as in the curfew and imprisonment of Japanese-Americans during World War II, the reputation of the judiciary as the guarantor of constitutional liberties is tarnished. Yet if courts refuse to take such a case, they risk communicating the message that might is right and no independent judicial check exists.

If the judiciary behaves in ways intolerable to the public, there are many methods available to legislators and executives to invoke court-curbing pressures. Presidential appointments and Senate confirmations supply a steady stream of influence by popularly elected public officials. Court decisions can be overturned by constitutional amendment, a process that is directly controlled by national and state legislatures. Short of such drastic remedies, judges remain sensitive and responsive to public opinion, notwithstanding traditional claims of judicial isolation from political forces. Nonetheless, as witnessed by

[75] Henry W. Edgerton, "The Incidence of Judicial Control over Congress," 22 Corn. L. Q. 299 (1937).

[76] Aryeh Neier, Only Judgment 238–39 (1982).

[77] "Foreword: The Passive Virtues; The Supreme Court 1960 Term," 75 Harv. L. Rev. 40, 48 (1961). See also Charles L. Black, Jr., The People and the Court (1960) for further comment on the legitimizing function.

the "court packing" effort of 1937 (discussed in Chapter Six), there exists within the public a strong reservoir of support for the independence of the judiciary and the exercise of judicial review.

Methods of Constitutional Interpretation

In a 1985 article, Attorney General Edwin Meese III proposed a "Jurisprudence of Original Intention." He said that the framers expected federal judges to guard the Constitution and "resist any political effort to depart from the literal provisions of the Constitution. The text of the document and the original intention of those who framed it would be the judicial standard in giving effect to the Constitution."[78] He pledged that in the cases filed by the Reagan administration, as well as those in which the administration joined as amicus, "we will endeavor to resurrect the original meaning of constitutional provisions and statutes as the only reliable guide for judgment."[79]

The framers' intent is an important but inadequate method of interpreting the Constitution. Although understanding original intent is "necessary and proper," it is rarely sufficient for adjudication. Terry Eastland, Director of Public Affairs at the Justice Department, claimed that "those who reject a jurisprudence of original intention still admire judicial power."[80] I am no more an admirer of judicial power than of congressional or presidential power. Like any other branch of government, the judiciary must operate within limits. Freewheeling judicial activism should be indefensible from any quarter, liberal or conservative.

The doctrine of original intent is an impractical remedy for judicial activism; an activist judiciary can flourish under the banner of strict constructionism, a doctrine that can be, and often is, synonymous with judicial activism. The Jurisprudence of Original Intention suffers from other limitations. It suggests that constitutional inter-

[78]Edwin Meese III, "The Attorney General's View of the Supreme Court: Toward a Jurisprudence of Original Intention," 45 Pub. Adm. Rev. 701 (Special Issue, November 1985).

[79]Id. at 704.

[80]Terry Eastland, "Proper Interpretation of the Constitution," N.Y. Times, January 9, 1986, at A23.

pretation is merely the search for textual and contextual meanings, whereas constitutional law is constantly shaped, and properly so, by fundamental social and economic changes and by the interactions among all three branches of government.

Justice Jackson once remarked that "Nothing has more perplexed generations of conscientious judges than the search in juridical science, philosophy and practice for objective and impersonal criteria for solution of politico-legal questions put to our courts."[81] No completely satisfactory guide to judicial review has ever been fashioned, although different techniques are available, including reliance on literalism, natural law, historical development, and eclecticism.

Literalism. Advocates of strict constructionism, or what some scholars call "interpretivism," argue that judges should enforce only those norms that are stated or clearly implicit in the Constitution. Judges who offer interpretations that cannot be discovered within the "four corners" of the Constitution are considered activists or noninterpretivists. Most judges try to interpret the Constitution in accordance with the framers' intent, so far as that is possible, and yet even if they restricted themselves to that task the results would not be uniform. Judges hear conflicting evidence and reach different conclusions. They differ on whether the framers intended the Constitution to be interpreted statically or dynamically.[82] Judge Irving R. Kaufman of the Second Circuit has said that on most issues "to look for a collective intention held by either drafters or ratifiers is to hunt for a chimera."[83]

Justice Black was the principal exponent of literalism. He believed that this approach would curb the appetite of judges to go outside the Constitution and impose their own preferences, dressed up either as natural law or due process. With regard to the First Amendment, he insisted that the words mean precisely what they say. Allowing no exceptions, he accused his brethren of rewriting the Constitution to produce a new amendment: "Congress shall pass no law abridging

[81]Robert H. Jackson, "Maintaining Our Freedoms: The Role of the Judiciary," delivered to the American Bar Association, Boston, Massachusetts, August 24, 1953; reprinted in Vital Speeches, No. 24, Vol. xix, p. 759 (October 1, 1953).

[82]Arthur J. Goldberg, Equal Justice 38 (1971).

[83]Irving R. Kaufman, "What Did the Founding Fathers Intend?," N.Y. Times Magazine, February 23, 1986, at 59.

freedom of speech, press, assembly, and petition, unless Congress and the Supreme Court reach the joint conclusion that on balance the interests of the government in stifling these freedoms is greater than the interest of the people in having them exercised."[84]

Black did not want judges deciding on such vague grounds as what is fair, reasonable, fundamental, or decent. He urged us "to follow what our Constitution says, not what judges think it should have said."[85] But the Constitution "says" nothing about an indigent's right to counsel, segregated housing, segregated schools, or many other issues that Black agreed to decide. He accepted an individual's right of association as implied by the First Amendment.[86] Although he spoke the language of a literalist, at the same time he fought vigorously for the incorporation doctrine, which now applies most of the national Bill of Rights to the states. Like other judges, Black looked outside the Constitution for guidance. He said that the religion clauses "had the same objective and were intended to provide the same protection against governmental intrusion on religious liberty" as the Virginia Statute of Establishing Religious Freedom.[87] Black went beyond the literal text to consider fundamental values. He regarded prosecution of individuals by the federal government and a state for the same offense as "contrary to the spirit of our free country."[88]

Although literalism may have some superficial appeal, the impracticalities are immense. Madison went to great lengths in Federalist 44 to point out that a constitution, to survive, must be phrased in general terms. His comments were in support of the Necessary and Proper Clause of Article I, Section 8, which had been attacked for its vague grant of power to Congress. He said that the framers might have copied the Articles of Confederation, which prohibited the exercise of any power not *expressly* delegated by the states, or they might have attempted to enumerate congressional powers. The first alternative risked leaving the national government with insufficient power, whereas the second option meant "a complete digest of laws on every subject to which the Constitution relates; accommodated not only to

---

[84]Hugo LaFayette Black, A Constitutional Faith 50 (1968). See his concurring opinion in Smith v. California, 361 U.S. 147, 157 (1959).

[85]Boddie v. Connecticut, 401 U.S. 371, 393 (1971).

[86]Gibson v. Florida Legislative Comm., 372 U.S. 539, 558–59 (1963).

[87]Everson v. Board of Education, 330 U.S. 1, 13 (1947).

[88]Bartkus v. Illinois, 359 U.S. 121, 150 (1959) (dissenting opinion).

the existing state of things, but to all the possible changes which futurity may produce. . . ."

The Articles of Confederation protected state sovereignty by allowing states to retain all powers except those "expressly delegated" to the national government. When that phrase was proposed for the Tenth Amendment, Madison objected to the use of "expressly" because the functions and responsibilities of the Federal Government could not be delineated with such precision. It was impossible to confine a government to the exercise of express powers, for there "must necessarily be admitted powers by implication, unless the Constitution descended to recount every minutiae."[89] On the strength of his argument the word "expressly" was eliminated. Chief Justice Marshall relied on this legislative history when he upheld the power of Congress to establish a national bank, even though such power is not expressly provided for in the Constitution.[90] The Supreme Court has held that "it is undoubtedly true that that which is implied is as much a part of the Constitution as that which is expressed."[91]

Attorney General Meese has criticized *Dred Scott* v. *Sandford*, in which Chief Justice Taney denied that blacks were entitled to the protections accorded to "citizens." Meese cites the decision as evidence that some see the Constitution "as an empty vessel into which each generation may pour its passion and prejudice."[92] But Taney adhered to original intent by limiting the meaning of "citizens" to what it mean in 1787: "No one, we presume, supposes that any change in public opinion or feeling, in relation to this unfortunate race [of blacks], in the civilized nations of Europe or in this country, should induce the court to give to the words of the Constitution a more liberal construction in their favor than they were intended to bear when the instrument was framed and adopted. . . . [Constitutional language] must be construed now as it was understood at the time of its adoption. It is not only the same in words, but the same in meaning. . . ."[93]

Justice Holmes rejected this reasoning. To him a word "is not a crystal, transparent and unchanged, it is the skin of a living thought

[89]1 Annals of Congress 761 (August 18, 1789).
[90]McCulloch v. Maryland, 4 Wheat. 315, 406–7 (1819).
[91]South Carolina v. United States, 199 U.S. 437, 451 (1905).
[92]Edwin Meese III, "The Battle for the Constitution," Policy Rev., No. 35, Winter 1986, at 34.
[93]60 U.S. (19 How.) at 426.

and may vary greatly in color and content according to the circumstances and the time in which it is used."[94] Literalism would create intolerable demands on the amending process, subjecting the country to costly delays and uncertainties in response to issues never anticipated by the framers.

Moreover, a literalist is at sea when two commands of the Constitution, such as free press and fair trial, collide. How is one constitutional value to be "balanced" against another? What guides the Court in deciding between civil rights and state rights? When does government regulation give way to the needs of individual privacy? What "weight" should be given to the press' interest of freedom from searches and seizures by law enforcement officers? When does the right of a free press override the interest of an individual not to be libeled? Where in the Constitution do we find answers to conflicts between workers and employers? Do certain rights, such as those enumerated in the First Amendment, have a "preferred" status?[95] Even if they do, are those rights subordinated to the needs of the government during time of national emergency?[96] Literalism cannot function in this environment: "There is no objectivity in constitutional law because there are no absolutes. Every constitutional question involves a weighing of competing values."[97]

Strict constructionism holds out the promise of understanding the Constitution by examining the text as amplified by the drafters' intent. This method of interpretation did not appeal to the great Chief Justice, John Marshall. In *Gibbons* v. *Ogden*, he penned one of the most elegant refutations of "strict constructionism," in responding to those who believed that the powers in the Constitution should be strictly construed:

> But why ought they to be so construed? Is there one sentence in the constitution which gives countenance to this rule? In the last of the enumerated powers, that which grants, expressly, the means for carrying all others into execution, congress is authorized "to make all laws which shall be necessary and proper"

[94]Towne v. Eisner, 245 U.S. 418, 425 (1918).

[95]Palko v. Connecticut, 302 U.S. 319, 326–27 (1937); Marsh v. Alabama, 326 U.S. 501, 509 (1946); Kovacs v. Cooper, 336 U.S. 77, 106 (1949) (Rutledge, J., dissenting).

[96]Barenblatt v. United States, 360 U.S. 109, 134 (1958).

[97]George D. Braden, "The Search for Objectivity in Constitutional Law," 57 Yale L. J. 571, 594 (1948).

for this purpose. But this limitation on the means which may be used, is not extended to the powers which are conferred; nor is there one sentence in the constitution which has been pointed out by the gentlemen of the bar, or which we have been able to discern, that prescribes this rule. We do not, therefore, think ourselves justified in adopting it.[98]

Marshall inquired into the meaning of strict constructionism. If it meant only the kind of construction that would not "extend words beyond their natural and obvious import, we might question the application of the term, but should not controvert the principle." But he opposed a more strict application:

If they contend for that narrow construction which, in support of some theory not to be found in the constitution, would deny to the government those powers which the words of the grant, as usually understood, import, and which are consistent with the general views and objects of the instrument—for that narrow construction, which would cripple the government, and render it unequal to the objects for which it is declared to be instituted, and to which the powers given, as fairly understood, render it competent—then we cannot perceive the propriety of this strict construction, nor adopt it as the rule by which the constitution is to be expounded.[99]

Marshall returned to the subject with full force:

Powerful and ingenious minds, taking, as postulates, that the powers expressly granted to the government of the union, are to be contracted, by construction, into the narrowest possible compass, and that the original powers of the states are retained, if any possible construction will retain them, may, by a course of well-digested, but refined and metaphysical reasoning, founded on these premises, explain away the constitution of our country, and leave it, a magnificent structure, indeed, to look at, but totally unfit for use.[100]

In the effort to discover another component of strict constructionism—the intentions of the framers—Justice Jackson said despairingly

[98]Gibbons v. Ogden, 22 U.S. (9 Wheat.) 1, 185 (1824).
[99]Id. at 186.
[100]Id. at 220.

at one point: "Just what our forefathers did envision, or would have envisioned had they foreseen modern conditions, must be divined from materials almost as enigmatic as the dreams Joseph was called upon to interpret for Pharaoh."[101] The search for the intent of the framers is complicated by incomplete and unreliable records. For example, the notes of Robert Yates at the Philadelphia Convention were tampered with by Citizen Genet, who hoped to use the doctored notes for partisan objectives.[102]

Which framers do we select, and during what periods of their lives? Do we reconstruct intentions partly from private letters, memoranda, and diaries? Do we focus on the debates at the Philadelphia Convention or also at the state ratifying conventions? How much British, American colonial, and early national history is applicable?[103] The University of Chicago Press published a five-volume work in 1987 entitled *The Founders' Constitution*, which includes public debates, private letters, newspaper broadsides, philosophic essays, and penny pamphlets, all dating from the English colonies in the 1600s to the longest-lived American founders in the 1830s.[104]

Attempts by the Supreme Court to introduce historical evidence have been dismissed by some historians as mere law-office efforts— special pleading for a particular point of view.[105]A recent example of this deficiency is the Court's analysis of the Gramm-Rudman law. In a very strict reading of the separation of powers doctrine, the Court referred to "the famous warning of Montesquieu," quoted by James Madison in Federalist 47, that "There can be no liberty where the legislative and executive powers are united in the same person, or body of magistrates. . . ."[106] The Court totally ignored Madison's crucial qualification. Immediately following the quotation from Montesquieu, Madison said that Montesquieu "did not mean that these departments ought to have no *partial agency* in, or no *control* over, the acts of each other. His meaning, as his own words import, and still more conclusively as illustrated by the example in his eye, can

---

[101]Youngstown Co. v. Sawyer, 343 U.S. 579, 634 (1952) (concurring opinion).

[102]James H. Hutson, "The Creation of the Constitution: The Integrity of the Documentary Record," 65 Tex. L. Rev. 1, 9–12, 14–19 (1986).

[103]William Anderson, "The Intention of the Framers: A Note on Constitutional Interpretation," 49 Am. Pol. Sci. Rev. 340 (1955).

[104]Philip B. Kurland and Ralph Lerner, eds., The Founders' Constitution (1987).

[105]Alfred H. Kelly, "Clio and the Court: An Illicit Love Affair," 1965 Sup. Ct. Rev. 119.

[106]Bowsher v. Synar, 106 S.Ct. 3181, 3186 (1986).

amount to no more than this, that where the *whole* power of one department is exercised by the same hands which possess the *whole* power of another department, the fundamental principles of a free constitution are subverted."[107] It should be obvious from a reading of the statute that the Comptroller General's responsibility in the sequestration process was not an attempt by Congress to place the *entire* executive power in the legislative branch.

The difficulties of literalism are further revealed by examining the Sixth and Eighth Amendments. The Sixth Amendment provides that in all criminal prosecutions the accused shall "be confronted with the witnesses against him." Under certain circumstances, however, the literal language of the Confrontation Clause is ignored. A disruptive defendant may be removed from the courtroom without violating his constitutional right to be present and to confront the witnesses against him.[108] A trial court's ruling in violation of the Confrontation Clause may even be tolerated if the Supreme Court finds the error "harmless."[109] Other exceptions to the Confrontation Clause include the use of hearsay evidence in conspiracy trials.[110]

With regard to the Eighth Amendment, the vagueness of its language prompted several complaints by members of the First Congress. William Smith of South Carolina objected to the Cruel and Unusual Punishments Clause as "being too indefinite."[111] Samuel Livermore of New Hampshire regarded the Clause as unnecessary because it had "no meaning in it."[112] Livermore also criticized the remainder of the amendment: "What is meant by the terms excessive bail? Who are to be the judges? What is understood by excessive fines? It lies with the court to determine."[113] In fact, the question of "excessive fines" is rarely litigated. The issue is more likely to be attacked under the Equal Protection and Due Process Clauses.[114]

Natural Law. In their search for guidance, judges sometimes reach outside the Constitution to discover fundamental or uni-

---

[107]The Federalist (B. Wright ed.) 338 (1961).

[108]Illinois v. Allen, 397 U.S. 337 (1970).

[109]Delaware v. Van Arsdall, 106 S.Ct 1431 (1986).

[110]United States v. Inadi, 106 S.Ct. 1121 (1986); Dutton v. Evans, 400 U.S. 74 (1970).

[111]1 Annals of Congress 782.

[112]Id.

[113]Id.

[114]Williams v. Illinois, 399 U.S. 235 (1970). See also Ex parte Watkins, 32 U.S. (7 Pet.) 568 (1833).

versal principles. This natural law approach, however, remains a continuing source of dispute. Writing in *Calder* v. *Bull* (1798), Justice Iredell urged his colleagues to base their decisions on substantial constitutional grounds rather than mere declarations of opinions regarding the laws of nature. Courts should not declare a statute unconstitutional "merely because it is, in their judgment, contrary to the principles of natural justice. The ideas of natural justice are regulated by no fixed standard: the ablest and the purest men have differed upon the subject."[115]

Justices react defensively to the charge that they merely read their own predilections into the Constitution, especially when interpreting such vague phrases as "due process," "equal protection," "unreasonable searches and seizures," and "cruel and unusual punishments." Nevertheless, Justices who oppose the death penalty argue that it violates the "human dignity" protected by the Constitution[116] and is "no longer morally tolerable in our civilized society."[117] The law of defamation has been drawn not just from the First Amendment but from "our basic concept of the essential dignity and worth of every human being—a concept at the root of any decent system of ordered liberty."[118]

Justice Frankfurter, remembered as the champion of judicial restraint, objected to those who called the interpretation of "due process" a mere matter of judicial caprice. Notwithstanding his general doctrine, Frankfurter struck down actions that "shock the conscience" and "offend the community's sense of fair play and decency."[119] Justice Black, a perennial critic of these opinions, charged that Frankfurter derived his standards basically from natural law, not constitutional law, and that such methods allowed judges to propound their own personal philosophies. Black feared that the appeal to standards outside the Constitution could be used to permit courts to strike down economic regulation, which is what happened during the period of substantive due process.[120] These cases, Black said,

[115]3 U.S. (3 Dall.) at 399

[116]Furman v. Georgia, 408 U.S. 238, 270 (1972) (Brennan, J., dissenting).

[117]Gregg v. Georgia, 428 U.S. 153, 229 (1976) (Brennan, J., dissenting). Footnote omitted.

[118]Rosenblatt v. Baer, 383 U.S. 75, 92 (1966) (Stewart, J., concurring).

[119]Rochin v. California, 342 U.S. 165, 172–73 (1952).

[120]Id. at 176.

show the extent to which the evanescent standards of the majority's philosophy have been used to nullify state legislative programs passed to suppress evil economic practices. What paralyzing role this same philosophy will play in the future economic affairs of this country is impossible to predict. Of even graver concern, however, is the use of the philosophy to nullify the Bill of Rights. I long ago concluded that the accordian-like qualities of this philosophy must inevitably imperil all the individual liberty safeguards specifically enumerated in the Bill of Rights.[121]

Black's concerns are well founded, but the Constitution does have a "higher law" heritage.[122] In *Fletcher* v. *Peck*, Chief Justice Marshall said "there are certain great principles of justice, whose authority is universally acknowledged, that ought not to be entirely disregarded."[123] Justice Johnson in that case was more explicit: "I do not hesitate to declare, that a state does not possess the power of revoking its own grants. But I do it, on a general principle, on the reason and nature of things; a principle that will impose laws even on the Deity."[124]

One need not ascend to celestial jurisprudence to understand the influence of natural law and natural rights on the Constitution. Although it would be untenable to say that the Constitution incorporates all of the Declaration of Independence, it is equally short-sighted to ignore the motivating principles that founded this nation. The incompatibility between the principles embodied in the Declaration of Independence and the institution of slavery sanctioned by the Constitution exploded into the civil war. The concept of a Constitution embodying a set of aspirations, rather than a catalog of rights fixed at the time of the framers, explains why it has been necessary to eliminate discrimination against blacks and women through constitutional amendments, judicial decisions, and statutory actions.

Historical Development. To shed further light on constitutional meaning, judges turn to historical trends that create pressures

[121]Id. at 177 (footnote omitted).

[122]Edward S. Corwin, The "Higher Law" Background of American Constitutional Law (1928); J.A.C. Grant, "The Natural Law Background of Due Process," 31 Colum. L. Rev. 56 (1931).

[123]Fletcher v. Peck, 10 U.S. at 132.

[124]Id. at 143.

and opportunities for legal change. Justice O'Connor has said that when the intent of the framers is unclear, "I believe we must employ both history and reason in our analysis."[125] Willard Hurst regarded the general political, economic, and social history of the United States as "legally competent and relevant evidence for the interpretation of the Constitution."[126] The meaning of "interstate commerce" could not be restricted to the methods of commerce available at the time the Constitution was adopted. The phrase had to keep pace with the progress of the country, extending from stagecoaches to steamboats, from railroads to the telegraph.[127] Chief Justice Burger recognized this role of historical evolution with respect to federalism: "Our conceptions of the limits imposed by federalism are bound to evolve, just as our understanding of Congress' power under the Commerce Clause has evolved."[128]

Economics play a vital role in legal history. Fundamental changes in economic structures over the past century gradually washed away many traditional boundaries between intrastate and interstate commerce. To follow the framers' intent or expectations about commerce in this area would be of little avail. In 1886 the Supreme Court struck down an Illinois railroad statute because it affected, even for the part of the journey within the state, commerce among the states.[129] This decision made national regulation imperative and Congress responded a year later by creating the Interstate Commerce Commission. In 1905 and again in 1922 the Court adopted the "current of commerce" test to permit congressional regulation of stockyards that served as temporary resting places for cattle moving interstate.[130]

During the New Deal the Court at first resisted, but eventually capitulated, to a wholesale expansion of congressional power over commerce. Initially the Court prohibited Congress from regulating commercial activities that were regarded as production and manufacture, or that were "local" or intrastate, or that affected commerce

[125]Wallace v. Jaffree, 472 U.S. 38, 81 (1985) (concurring opinion).

[126]Willard Hurst, "The Role of History," in Edmond Cahn, ed., Supreme Court and Supreme Law 56 (1954).

[127]Pensacola Telegraph Co. v. Western Union Telegraph Co., 96 U.S. 1, 9 (1877).

[128]City of Lafayette v. Louisiana Power & Light Co., 435 U.S. 389, 421 n.2 (1978).

[129]Wabash, &c., Railway Co. v. Illinois, 118 U.S. 557 (1886).

[130]Swift & Co. v. United States, 196 U.S. 375, 399 (1905); Stafford v. Wallace, 258 U.S. 495, 516 (1922).

only "indirectly." By 1937 the court began to embrace what it had accepted intermittently in the past: intrastate commerce having a substantial relation to interstate commerce could be regulated by Congress.[131] Manufacturing was no longer outside congressional control.[132]

Rapid changes in economic conditions have caused the Court to make an about-face in responding to social legislation. Earlier in this century the Court struck down statutes on the ground that the activity to be regulated was not "affected with a public interest."[133] Justices then began to recognize that changes in economic conditions justified increased legislative intervention. What used to be left to free bargaining between worker and employer now required regulation by the government.[134] Laissez-faire notions that might have made sense in a simpler economy were no longer appropriate.[135] Decisions about economic philosophy became matters for legislatures, not courts.[136]

Changes in cultural beliefs explain the various stages of the Eighth Amendment's injunction against "cruel and unusual punishments." A congressional statute, enacted in 1790, required the death penalty for forgery.[137] Such a penalty today would be considered disproportionate to the crime. In 1879, the Supreme Court decided that public shooting was not cruel and unusual.[138] States do not sanction public executions today. The extent to which "cruel and unusual" reflects cultural beliefs and contemporary notions can be seen in interpretations of the Eighth Amendment that rely on the "evolving standards of decency that mark the progress of a maturing society."[139]

---

[131]NLRB v. Jones & Laughlin, 301 U.S. 1 (1937)

[132]United States v. Darby, 312 U.S. 100, 119 (1941). See also Wickard v. Filburn, 317 U.S. 111 (1942).

[133]New State Ice Co. v. Liebmann, 285 U.S. 262 (1932); Williams v. Standard Oil Co., 278 U.S. 235 (1929); Ribnik v. McBride, 277 U.S. 350 (1928); Tyson & Brother v. Banton, 273 U.S. 418 (1927); Wolff Co. v. Industrial Court, 262 U.S. 522 (1923).

[134]Morehead v. N.Y. ex rel. Tipaldo, 298 U.S. 587, 635 (1936) (Stone, J., dissenting).

[135]Olsen v. Nebraska, 313 U.S. 236 (1941), overturning Ribnik v. McBride, 277 U.S. 350 (1928).

[136]Ferguson v. Skrupa, 372 U.S. 726 (1963); Williamson v. Lee Optical Co., 348 U.S. 483, 488 (1955); Day-Brite Lighting, Inc. v. Missouri, 342 U.S. 421 (1952).

[137]1 Stat. 115, § 14 (1790).

[138]Wilkerson v. Utah, 99 U.S. 130 (1879).

[139]Trop v. Dulles, 356 U.S. 86, 101 (1958).

"Contemporary human knowledge" is another criterion that guides judicial interpretations of the Cruel and Unusual Punishments Clause.[140]

In 1972, the Supreme Court declared that death-penalty statutes in Georgia and Texas violated the Cruel and Unusual Punishments Clause.[141] Following this decision, thirty-five states immediately reinstituted the death penalty for certain crimes.[142] After this public endorsement of capital punishment placed strong pressure on the Court to uphold the death penalty, the Court, in 1976, identified the various factors that had to be satisfied before a constitutional execution could occur.[143]

A year later the Court found the death penalty to be disproportionate punishment for the raping of an adult woman.[144] The gradual abandonment of that punishment by most states weighed heavily with the Court as significant evidence of current public judgment.[145] In some cases, judicial references to community opinions and societal consensus may be "merely a convenient verbal counterpane" under which a judge hides personal preference.[146]

The effort over the past decade to give fresh meaning to the Tenth Amendment is also instructive. Historical shifts in notions of federalism are commonplace. In *National League of Cities* v. *Usery* (1976) the Court held that Congress could not regulate "traditional governmental functions" carried out by the states.[147] This doctrine never took root as a workable theory of federalism and was ignored in subsequent decisions.[148] Federal courts found it difficult to distinguish between "traditional" and "nontraditional" state functions. The 1976 doctrine was eventually overturned in 1985. The dissenting opinion by Justice O'Connor illustrates the complexity of relying on the framers' intent: "[T]he Framers were not single-minded. The

[140]Robinson v. California, 370 U.S. 660, 666 (1962).

[141]Furman v. Georgia, 408 U.S. 238 (1972).

[142]Gregg v. Georgia, 428 U.S. 153, 179–80 n.23 (1976).

[143]Id. at 168–76.

[144]Coker v. Georgia, 433 U.S. 584 (1977).

[145]Id. at 593–96.

[146]Arthur S. Miller and Jeffrey H. Bowman, "Slow Dancing on the Killing Ground: The *Willie Francis* Case Revisited," 32 DePaul L. Rev. 1, 26 (1983).

[147]426 U.S. 833 (1976).

[148]Hodel v. Virginia Surface Mining & Recl. Assn., 452 U.S. 264 (1981); FERC v. Mississippi, 456 U.S. 742 (1982); United Transportation Union v. Long Island R. Co., 455 U.S. 678 (1982); EEOC v. Wyoming, 460 U.S. 226 (1983).

Constitution is animated by an array of intentions. . . . Just as surely as the Framers envisioned a National Government capable of solving national problems, they also envisioned a republic whose vitality was assured by the diffusion of power not only among the branches of the Federal Government, but also between the Federal Government and the States."[149]

Justice O'Connor concluded that the proper resolution "lies in weighing state autonomy as a factor in the balance when interpreting the means by which Congress can exercise its authority on the States as States."[150] Can the proper weights be discovered by turning to the framers? Determining the balance between the national government and the states depends to a large extent on the conditions existing at the time of a lawsuit. Originally the national government was vulnerable to state encroachments, and therefore the Court created the doctrines of dual federalism and intergovernmental tax immunity. In *McCulloch* v. *Maryland* (1819), Chief Justice Marshall struck down a state tax on the U.S. Bank by arguing that the power to tax is the power to destroy.[151] After the national government had established its power, the Court began to revisit these doctrines. In 1928 four Justices dissented against a rigid application of reciprocal tax immunity. In one of the dissents, Justice Holmes remarked: "The power to tax is not the power to destroy while this Court sits."[152] Subsequently the Court began to retreat from the notion of strict reciprocity or immunity.[153]

Historical shifts in the meaning of federalism are illustrated more recently by a Supreme Court decision. Although the Court in 1861, "facing the looming shadow of a Civil War," lacked the political power to compel states to comply with federal law, a decision made then was overturned in 1987. The Court now recognized the contemporary power of federal courts to enjoin unconstitutional action by state officials.[154] The decision of the 1861 Court was "the product of an-

[149]Garcia v. San Antonio Metro. Transit Auth., 469 U.S. 528, 581 (1985).
[150]Id. at 588.
[151]4 Wheat. at 427, 431, 432.
[152]Panhandle Oil Co. v. Knox, 277 U.S. 218, 223 (1928).
[153]Graves v. N.Y. ex rel. O'Keefe, 306 U.S. 466, 486 (1939), overturning Collector v. Day, 78 U.S. (11 Wall.) 113, 128–29 (1871).
[154]Puerto Rico v. Branstad, 107 S.Ct. 2802, 2808 (1987), overturning Kentucky v. Dennison, 65 U.S. (24 How.) 66 (1861).

other time,"[155] resting upon "a foundation with which time and the currents of constitutional change have dealt much less favorably."[156]

The impact of historical development is seen in other areas. More than a century of practice became a justification for supporting the exercise of presidential power despite the absence of any express or statutory authority: "long continued practice, known to and acquiesced in by Congress, would raise a presumption . . . of a recognized administrative power of the Executive in the management of the public lands."[157] Justice Holmes, writing in 1920, insisted that a case before the Court has to be considered "in the light of our whole experience and not merely in that of what was said a hundred years ago."[158]

Justices refer to professional journals and studies as a way of keeping law current with changes in American society. The judiciary has been profoundly influenced by the views of social scientists, both conservative and liberal. It has been customary for the Court to go outside the legal record and take "judicial notice" of writings by experts. The opinions of Justice Brandeis introduced a new meaning to the word "authority." He believed "that the law derives its authority from the real conditions of society, and that scholarly writings and other sources of expert opinion often provide the best knowledge of those conditions."[159]

There is good reason to question the competence of judges to evaluate the findings of social scientists and analyze their methodology. The philosophy of Social Darwinism in the late nineteenth and twentieth centuries supplied part of the theoretical justification for a laissez-faire state. This doctrine, reshaped in the hands of judges, helped

[155]107 S.Ct. at 2809.

[156]Id. at 2808.

[157]United States v. Midwest Oil Co., 236 U.S. 459, 472–74 (1915). See also Charles E. Miller, The Supreme Court and the Uses of History (1969); Paul Brest, "The Misconceived Quest for the Original Understanding," 60 B.U. L. Rev. 204 (1980); Frederick Bernays Wiener, Uses and Abuses of Legal History (1962); Sister Marie Carolyn Klinkhamer, "The Use of History in the Supreme Court, 1789–1935," 36 U. Det. L. J. 553 (1959); John Woodford, "The Blinding Light: The Uses of History in Constitutional Interpretation," 31 U. Chi. L. Rev. 502 (1964).

[158]Missouri v. Holland, 252 U.S. 416, 433 (1920). The significance of constitutional provisions "is to be gathered not simply by taking the words and a dictionary, but by considering their origin and the line of their growth." Gompers v. United States, 233 U.S. 604, 610 (1914).

[159]Chester A. Newland, "The Supreme Court and Legal Writing: Learned Journals as Vehicles of an Anti-Trust Lobby?," 48 Geo. L. J. 105, 140 (1959).

support their opposition to social and economic regulation. In time, laissez-faire principles were challenged by the "Brandeis brief," which introduced social and economic facts to justify regulation of factory and working conditions. The use of extralegal data helped undermine the Court's reliance on abstract reasoning about "liberty of contract."[160] Eventually, lawyers on both sides learned how to put together a Brandeis brief to support their case.

The controversy over social science data is evident in the desegregation case of 1954. Segregation, said the Court, generated a feeling of inferiority among black children: "Whatever may have been the extent of psychological knowledge at the time of *Plessy* v. *Ferguson*, this finding [that segregation is detrimental to education] is amply supported by modern authority."[161] Bolstering this sentence was the famous footnote eleven, the wisdom of which has been extensively debated, citing several sociological studies on the effects of discrimination and segregation on children. The risk of citing sociological studies is that a decision, supposedly announcing a fundamental principle of constitutional law, is left exposed to the findings of new studies or the recantations of authorities cited by the Court.[162]

Eclecticism.   If the Constitution is to guide future generations, there must be some flexibility in applying its language. Speaking of a New Deal dispute over the contract clause, the Supreme Court observed:

It is no answer to say that this public need was not apprehended a century ago, or to insist that what the provision of the Constitution meant to the vision of that day it must mean to the vision of our time. If by the statement that what the Constitution meant at the time of its adoption it means to-day, it is intended to say that the great clauses of the Constitution must be confined to the interpretation which the framers, with the con-

[160]Paul L. Rosen, The Supreme Court and Social Science 23–101 (1972).
[161]Brown v. Board of Education, 347 U.S. 483, 494 (1954).
[162]Edmond Cahn, "Jurisprudence," 30 N.Y.U. 1. Rev. 150 (1950); Jack Greenberg, "Social Scientists Take the Stand," 54 Mich. L. Rev. 953 (1956); Herbert Garfinkel, "Social Science Evidence and the School Segregation Case," 21 J. Pol. 37 (1959); "Symposium: Law and Social Science," 5 Vill. L. Rev. 215 (1959–1960); Abraham L. Davis, The United States Supreme Court and the Uses of Social Science Data (1973).

ditions and outlook of their time, would have placed upon them, the statement carries its own refutation.[163]

In interpreting the Constitution, we look partly at the "judicial gloss" added by the courts. It is the responsibility of the judiciary to interpret the law, and under the doctrine of *stare decisis* (stand by the precedents) judges try to honor prior rulings. Nevertheless, sufficient variations and discord among existing precedents allow any number of directions for future decisions. Which elements of an opinion were essential for the result and therefore binding on subsequent courts? Which were peripheral (*obiter dicta*)? At what point do we comb concurring and dissenting opinions?

Judges hold different views about the doctrine of stare decisis. Some are more willing than others to break with prior holdings. The Supreme Court's practice is to apply stare decisis less rigidly to constitutional than to nonconstitutional issues.[164] If the Court "errs" on nonconstitutional matters, legislatures may respond by passing a new statute. Errors of constitutional dimension, however, need attention by the judiciary.[165] Justice Douglas explained that continuity is important for statutory law, for it permits citizens to arrange their business affairs with confidence. Courts should not disturb this sense of security and stability by needlessly disrupting the law.[166] But errors of constitutional doctrine require correction. In the words of Douglas, judges swear to support and defend the Constitution, "not the gloss which his predecessors may have put on it."[167]

Justice Roberts once complained that the Court's change of views "tends to bring adjudications of this tribunal into the same class as a restricted railroad ticket, good for this day and train only."[168] Justice Stewart supported stare decisis by announcing that even if he believed that the Court decided wrongly, and he dissented at the time, subsequent rulings should be governed by what the majority de-

[163]Home Bldg. & Loan Ass'n v. Blaisdell, 290 U.S. 398, 442–43 (1934).

[164]Glidden Co. v. Zdanok, 370 U.S. 530, 543 (1962). See also Edelman v. Jordan, 415 U.S. 651, 671 (1974).

[165]Burnet v. Coronado Oil & Gas Co., 285 U.S. 393, 406–7 (1932) (Brandeis, J., dissenting).

[166]William O. Douglas, "Stare Decisis," 49 Colum. L. Rev. 735, 736 (1949). See also National Bank v. Whitney, 8 Otto (103 U.S.) 99, 102 (1880).

[167]Douglas, "Stare Decisis," 49 Colum. L. Rev. at 736.

[168]Smith v. Allwright, 321 U.S. 649, 669 (1944) (dissenting opinion).

cided.[169] Most judges, however, would consider it irresponsible if they failed to correct a previous decision containing a mistake in constitutional law. The initial discomfort of having the Court reverse itself is more than offset by the enhanced reputation of a Court willing to acknowledge its own errors. Justice Jackson noted: "Of course, it is embarrassing to confess a blunder; it may prove more embarrassing to adhere to it."[170] He declined to bind himself "hand and foot" to prior decisions, even when they were his own. In his own words: "I see no reason why I should be consciously wrong today because I was unconsciously wrong yesterday."[171] Two years later he penned an elegant justification for rejecting prior opinions that have lost their persuasive quality.[172]

Outright reversal of a ruling is rare. More frequent is the practice of ignoring a precedent or "distinguishing" it from the pending case.[173] Prior cases are in effect overruled, but with great delicacy. These silent or tacit overrulings prompted Justice Black to remark of such cases: "Their interment is tactfully accomplished, without ceremony, eulogy, or report of their demise."[174] Judges may argue that the current facts are different or simply reinterpret the precedent. Such techniques avoid the costs of overruling a precedent, but they also produce conflicting case law and uncertainty for those who must obey, interpret, enforce, and practice law.

After reviewing the various approaches to constitutional interpretation, Justice Cardozo described the judge's task as an eclectic exercise that blends in varying proportions the methods of philosophy, history, tradition, logic, and sociology. Rules are replaced by working hypotheses.[175] The pressure of deadlines eliminates many options. Time, political constraints, and other limitations often make it impossible for judges to examine the entire record, pursue promising leads, review all the precedents, and produce original research. The complexity of the task has been summarized by Walter Murphy:

[169]Donovan v. Dewey, 452 U.S. 594, 609 (1981) (dissenting opinion).

[170]United States v. Bryan, 339 U.S. 323 (1950) (concurring opinion).

[171]Massachusetts v. United States, 333 U.S. 611, 639–40 (1948) (dissenting opinion).

[172]McGrath v. Kristensen, 340 U.S. 162, 176–78 (1950) (concurring opinion).

[173]Haig v. Agee, 453 U.S. 280, 310 (1981) (Blackmun, J., concurring). See also Brennan's dissent at 319–20.

[174]Hood & Sons v. Du Mond, 336 U.S. 525, 555 (1949) (dissenting opinion).

[175]Benjamin N. Cardozo, The Nature of the Judicial Process (1921).

To interpret a constitution requires more than ingenious guesses about what its draftsmen were thinking. Constitutional interpretation is an art, an art that must sometimes be both creative and political in the highest sense of that word, for it must apply imperfectly stated general principles to concrete and complex problems of human life and it must produce an authoritative solution. An interpreter who wishes to uphold, defend, maintain, or preserve the American Constitution cannot rationally treat it either as a detailed code or as a compact computer whose machine language is locked in the minds of men long dead.[176]

Philip Bobbitt identified a broad range of techniques used by judges to interpret the Constitution. They go far beyond the concept of original intent. He suggested that if someone took colored pencils to mark through passages of a Supreme Court opinion, using a different color for each technique, the reader would end up with a multicolored picture.[177] This approach to the judicial art of opinion writing describes the work of judges whether they are "activist" or a believer in original intent.

The search of "strict constructionists" by Presidents Nixon, Ford, and Reagan has proved to be illusory, and there is little reason to expect that future appointments will produce Justices who are willing or able to follow a Jurisprudence of Original Intention. Although many conservatives and liberals agree that an activist Court is dangerous to both the country and itself, mechanical formulas of original intent or "neutral principles" are not self-executing because there is no agreement on their meaning.

It is clear from the record of the Philadelphia Convention that the framers reserved the war power to Congress, with the single exception of allowing the President to "repel sudden attacks."[178] Nevertheless, the same Reagan administration that espouses original intent has used military force without any congressional authorization against Libya, Grenada, and Nicaragua. Supporters of presidential war power look beyond original intent to discover a base of legitimacy. In defending the actions of President Lyndon Johnson in Vietnam, the

---

[176] Walter Murphy, "Constitutional Interpretation: The Art of the Historian, Magician, or Statesman?," 87 Yale L. J. 1752, 1771 (1978).

[177] Philip Bobbitt, Constitutional Fate 93–94 (1982).

[178] 2 Farrand 318–19.

legal adviser to the State Department offered this analysis: "In 1787 the world was a far larger place, and the framers probably had in mind attacks upon the United States. In the 20th Century, the world has grown much smaller. An attack on a country far from our shores can impinge directly on the nation's security."[179]

The doctrine of original intent also has important implications for domestic issues. Attorney General Meese supports the Supreme Court's decision in *Brown* v. *Board of Education*, claiming that the Court "was not giving new life to old words, or adapting a 'living,' 'flexible' Constitution to new reality. It was restoring the original principle of the Constitution to constitutional law."[180] Yet there is little basis to believe that the framers of the Fourteenth Amendment intended that it be used to strike down segregated education. The evidence is quite to the contrary.

The difficulty of applying original intent is further suggested by *Wallace* v. *Jaffree* (1985), which struck down Alabama's one minute of silence in public schools for meditation or voluntary prayer.[181] The majority opinion by Justice Stevens mentioned the framers only once, in a footnote reference to James Madison.[182] In her concurrence, Justice O'Connor pointed out that it was impossible to expect the drafters of the First Amendment to have expressed a preference for prayer in public schools because "free public education was virtually nonexistent in the late 18th century."[183]

The position of Justice Rehnquist is even more intriguing because he is often identified as a strict constructionist and an advocate of judicial self-restraint. His dissent in the Alabama prayer case consists of a lengthy review of the framers' intent, concluding from this history that the state statute fit well within the intentions of those who drafted the Bill of Rights.[184] Two years earlier, however, he adopted an entirely different approach in upholding Minnesota's law allowing taxpayers to deduct from their state income-tax returns the expenses they incurred in providing tuition, textbooks, and transportation for children attending elementary or secondary schools, including sectarian institutions. Justice Rehnquist, writing for the 5-to-4 majority,

[179]54 Dep't St. Bull, 474, 484 (1966).
[180]Meese, "Battle for the Constitution," Policy Rev. No. 35, at 34.
[181]472 U.S. 38 (1985).
[182]Id. at 53–54 n.38.
[183]Id. at 80.
[184]Id. at 91–114.

quoted approvingly from Justice Powell's concurrence in *Wolman* v. *Walter*[185] that citizens in the twentieth century

> are quite far removed from the dangers that prompted the Framers to include the Establishment Clause in the Bill of Rights. . . . The risk of significant religious or denominational control over our democratic processes—or even of deep political division along religious lines—is remote, and when viewed against the positive contributions of sectarian schools, any such risk seems entirely tolerable in light of the continuing oversight of this Court.[186]

In other words, the intent of the framers can be dismissed whenever the contemporary Court is confident that it can deal effectively with a resurgence of religious strife.

A more reliable safeguard against judicial activism is the Court's ability to sidestep sensitive issues or decide in such a way as to allow the other branches and state governments to reenter the field and make the necessary adjustments and revisions to court doctrine. Courts are generally sensitive to the restraints of coequal branches and public opinion. When they are not, there are many many methods available to curb the courts and modify their rulings. Judge Kaufman has observed that judges are "mindful that the ultimate justification for their power is public acceptance—acceptance not of every decision, but of the role they play. Without popular support, the power of judicial review would have been eviscerated by political forces long ago."[187]

[185]433 U.S. 229, 263 (1977).

[186]Mueller v. Allen, 463 U.S. 388, 400 (1983), quoting from Justice Powell's concurrence in Wolman v. Walter, 433 U.S. at 263 (1977).

[187]Kaufman, "The Founding Fathers," N.Y. Times Magazine, February 23, 1986, at 69.

3. Threshold Requirements: Husbanding Power and Prestige

The scope of judicial review is circumscribed by rules of self-restraint fashioned by judges. Various court doctrines sketch out the minimum qualities needed to adjudicate a case. These thresholds (or "gatekeeping rules") do more than limit access by litigants. They shield judges from cases that threaten their independence and institutional effectiveness. They ration scarce judicial resources and postpone or avoid decisions on politically sensitive issues. Their abandonment may signal new paths to be followed by an activist court.

Chief Justice Marshall suggested that the boundaries for judicial action were quite fixed: "It is most true that this Court will not take jurisdiction if it should not: but it is equally true, that it must take jurisdiction if it should."[1] The record of the judiciary, however, runs in a different direction. Even when courts have jurisdiction, they may decide not to accept a case for reasons of equity and prudence.[2] What the Court should or should not accept is largely a matter of judicial discretion. Reflecting on his work at the Supreme Court, Justice Brandeis confided: "The most important thing we do is not doing."[3] The deliberate withholding of judicial power often reflects the fact that courts lack ballot-box legitimacy. Although couched in technical jargon, jurisdictional requirements nonetheless become an elementary question of democratic theory.

Judges invoke access rules to promote the adversary system, preserve public support, avoid conflicts with other branches of government, and provide flexibility of action for the judiciary. The doctrines used to pursue those goals include justiciability, standing, mootness, ripeness, political questions, and prudential limitations, all of which help protect an unelected and unrepresentative judiciary. Although efforts are made to distinguish these doctrines, inevitably

[1]Cohens v. Virginia, 6 Wheat. 264, 404 (1821).
[2]E.g., Schlesinger v. Councilman, 420 U.S. 738 (1975), in which the Court decided not to intervene in a military court process.
[3]Alexander M. Bickel, The Unpublished Opinions of Mr. Justice Brandeis 17 (1957).

they overlap. As noted by the Supreme Court: "The standing question thus bears close affinity to questions of ripeness—whether the harm asserted has matured sufficiently to warrant judicial intervention—and of mootness—whether the occasion for judicial intervention persists."[4]

Cases and Controversies

Article III of the Constitution limits the jurisdiction of federal courts to "cases" and "controversies." Courts must determine that they have jurisdiction to hear the case. Jurisdiction is granted both by the Constitution and by statute. Even after accepting jurisdiction, courts may decide that the subject matter is inappropriate for judicial consideration—what the courts call "nonjusticiable." This latter concept, at times synonymous with "political questions," is used to avoid collisions with Congress and the President.[5] It is also applied more broadly to cover issues outside the separation of powers.[6]

As a way to minimize error, miscalculation, and political conflict, courts adopt guidelines to avoid judgment on a large number of constitutional questions. These guidelines only provide very broad direction for judicial activity. However, the rules supply a convenient list of justifications for refusing to decide a case. In a concurring opinion in 1936, Justice Brandeis summarized the rules used by the courts to avoid deciding constitutional questions:

> The Court developed, for its own governance in the cases confessedly within its jurisdiction, a series of rules under which it has avoided passing upon a large part of all the constitutional questions pressed upon it for decision. They are:
>
> 1. The Court will not pass upon the constitutionality of legislation in a friendly, non-adversary, proceeding, declining because to decide such questions "is legitimate only in the last resort, and as a necessity in the determination of real, earnest and vital controversy between individuals. It never was the thought that, by means of a friendly suit, a party

---

[4]Warth v. Seldin, 422 U.S. 490, 499 n.10 (1975).
[5]Baker v. Carr, 369 U.S. 186, 198, 208–34 (1962).
[6]Flast v. Cohen, 392 U.S. 83, 95 (1968).

beaten in the legislature could transfer to the courts an inquiry as to the constitutionality of the legislative act." . . .

2. The Court will not "anticipate a question of constitutional law in advance of the necessity of deciding it." . . .

3. The Court will not "formulate a rule of constitutional law broader than is required by the precise facts to which it is to be applied." . . .

4. The Court will not pass upon a constitutional question although properly presented by the record, if there is also present some other ground upon which the case may be disposed of. This rule has found most varied application. Thus, if a case can be decided on either of two grounds, one involving a constitutional question, the other a question of statutory construction or general law, the Court will decide only the latter. . . . Appeals from the highest court of a state challenging its decision of a question under the Federal Constitution are frequently dismissed because the judgment can be sustained on an independent state ground. . . .

5. The Court will not pass upon the validity of a statute upon complaint on one who fails to show that he is injured by its operation. . . .

6. The Court will not pass upon the constitutionality of a statute at the instance of one who has availed himself of its benefits.

7. "When the validity of an act of the Congress is drawn in question, and even if a serious doubt of constitutionality is raised, it is a cardinal principle that this Court will first ascertain whether a construction of the statute is fairly possible by which the question may be avoided." . . .[7]

To resolve a legal claim, courts need to know that parties have been adversely affected. Abstract or hypothetical questions, removed from a concrete factual setting, prevent courts from reaching an informed judgment. The words "cases" and "controversies" limit the federal courts "to questions presented in an adversary context and

---

[7]Ashwander v. TVA, 297 U.S. 288, 346–48 (1936) (Brandeis, J., concurring). See also Escambia County v. McMillan, 466 U.S. 48 (1984).

in a form historically viewed as capable of resolution through the judicial process."[8]

Adverseness. The adversary system seeks truth by having judges and juries observe a contest between two sets of professional advocates. It assumes that two antagonistic parties, each with a sufficient stake in the outcome, will marshal the best arguments to defend their interests. This clash between the parties "sharpens the presentation of issues upon which the court so largely depends for illumination of difficult constitutional questions."[9]

In a unanimous decision in 1850, Chief Justice Taney warned that two parties bringing an action with the same interest risked being held in contempt of court. The plaintiff and defendant in this case attempted to obtain a decision that they could then use against parties who were not involved in the case and had no knowledge of it.[10] Taney distinguished this case from an "amicable action" in which two parties had a real dispute but agreed to conduct the case in an expeditious, cooperative manner in order to obtain a prompt decision without unnecessary expense or delay.

When a business merger places two competing litigants under the control of the same parties, the case loses its adversary character.[11] Nor is there adverseness when two attorneys bring a collusive or "friendly suit"[12] or when both parties agree on a constitutional issue and want the same result.[13] In one case, however, the Court allowed a president to sue his own company because the board of directors, backed by the stockholders, voted against him and thus created the necessary adverseness.[14]

Courts occasionally consider a case even when both parties agree on the issue. In *United States* v. *Lovett* (1946), the Justice Department agreed with the plaintiff that a provision in a congressional statute was unconstitutional. To protect its interests, Congress passed legislation to create a special counsel. Functioning officially as amicus cu-

[8]Flast v. Cohen, 392 U.S. at 95.
[9]Baker v. Carr, 369 U.S. at 204.
[10]Lord v. Veazie, 49 U.S. 251, 255 (1850).
[11]South Spring Gold Co. v. Amador Gold Co., 145 U.S. 300 (1892).
[12]United States v. Johnson, 319 U.S. 302 (1943).
[13]Moore v. Board of Education, 402 U.S. 47 (1971); but see INS v. Chadha, 462 U.S. 919 (1983) and Goosby v. Osser, 409 U.S. 512, 516–17 (1972).
[14]Carter v. Carter Coal Co., 298 U.S. 238, 286–87 (1936).

riae, the counsel in effect served as counsel for the United States to assure adverseness.[15] In other cases the courts have appointed a special counsel to satisfy the requirement for a genuinely adversary proceeding.[16]

There appeared to be lack of adverseness in the legislative veto case decided by the Supreme Court in 1983. The plaintiff, Jagdish Rai Chadha, sued the Immigration and Naturalization Service (INS), charging that its statutory procedure for deportation was unconstitutional. The government agreed with him. The Ninth Circuit asked both the House of Representatives and the Senate to file briefs as amici curiae. The House argued that Chadha's claim lacked the necessary adverseness because the Service agreed that the statute was invalid, and further argued that its appearance as amicus did not apply the adverseness needed for a case or controversy. The court rejected this reasoning because it would "implicitly approve the untenable result that all agencies could insulate unconstitutional orders and procedures from appellate review simply by agreeing that what they did was unconstitutional."[17]

In affirming the judgment of the Ninth Circuit, the Supreme Court also refused to regard the case as a "friendly, non-adversary, proceeding" between Chadha and the INS. As the Court noted, it would be "a curious result if, in the administration of justice, a person could be denied access to the courts because the Attorney General of the United States agreed with the legal arguments asserted by the individual." From the time of Congress's formal intervention as amici curiae, adverseness was "beyond doubt," and even prior to intervention there was "adequate Art. III adverseness."[18]

Advisory Opinions. The case or controversy requirement was tested in 1790 when Secretary of the Treasury Alexander Hamilton sought the advice of Chief Justice John Jay. Resolutions adopted by the Virginia House of Representatives had challenged the right of the National Government to assume state debts. Hamilton called this resistance "the first symptom of a spirit which must either be killed or it will kill the Constitution of the United States," and urged that

[15]328 U.S. 303, 304 (1946).
[16]Granville-Smith v. Granville-Smith, 349 U.S. 1, 4 (1955).
[17]Chadha v. INS, 634 F.2d 408, 420 (9th Cir. 1980).
[18]INS v. Chadha, 462 U.S. at 939 (1983).

the "collective weight" of the three branches be employed to repudiate the resolutions. Jay replied that it was inadvisable to take any action.[19] Similar efforts by Secretary of State Jefferson in 1793 to obtain advisory opinions were turned aside by the Court. The Justices considered it improper to make extrajudicial decisions, especially because the Constitution gave the President the express power to obtain opinions from the heads of the executive departments.[20]

This same period, however, yields contrary evidence. Chief Justice Jay and his colleagues on the Court advised President Washington in 1790 that the statutory requirement for them to ride circuit was unconstitutional.[21] And in *Hayburn's Case* (1792), two circuit courts explained to President Washington their constitutional objections to a statute passed by Congress that allowed the Secretary of War to countermand judicial decisions.[22] In both of these examples, however, the interests of the courts were directly involved: having to ride circuit and the performance of nonjudicial duties.

The Supreme Court's formal position on advisory opinions appears in *Muskrat* v. *United States* (1911). Congress had authorized certain Indians to bring suit to determine the constitutionality of a prior statute. They were given expedited treatment to the Court of Claims and a right of appeal to the Supreme Court. Justice Day reviewed earlier instances in which federal judges decided that Congress could not impose nonjudicial duties on the courts. The suit, even though authorized by Congress, did not create a case or controversy between adverse parties. It was an effort to obtain the Court's opinion on the validity of congressional statutes. Day said it was inappropriate for the judiciary "to give opinions in the nature of advice concerning legislative action, a function never conferred upon it by the Constitution and against the exercise of which this court has steadily set its face from the beginning."[23]

[19]1 Charles Warren, Supreme Court in United States History 52–53 (1937).

[20]Manley O. Hudson, "Advisory Opinions of National and International Courts," 37 Harv. L. Rev. 970, 976 (1924).

[21]Robert A. Dahlquist, "Advisory Opinions, Extrajudicial Activity and Judicial Advocacy: A Historical Perspective," 14 Sw. U. L. Rev. 46, 50–54 (1983).

[22]2 U.S. (2 Dall.) at 410–14 nn (1792). The statute was constitutionally objectionable because judicial decisions could be set aside by the Secretary of War, in effect converting a judicial decision into a mere advisory opinion. For similar reasons the Court has opposed procedures that make its decisions dependent on executive and legislative actions before being carried out; Gordon v. United States, 117 U.S. 697 (1864).

[23]219 U.S. 346, 362 (1911).

In 1948 the Supreme Court voiced its constitutional objections to a statute that authorized judicial review of orders of the Civil Aeronautics Board. For orders affecting international routes, the President was given final authority and could override the Board. The Court found itself in a no-man's land: unwilling to pass judgment on presidential decisions in this area of foreign affairs, and unwilling to pass judgment on a Board's order that lacked finality:

> To revise or review an administrative decision which has only the force of a recommendation to the President would be to render an advisory opinion in its most obnoxious form—advice that the President has not asked, tendered at the demand of a private litigant, on a subject concededly within the President's exclusive, ultimate control. This Court early and wisely determined that it would not give advisory opinions even when asked by the Chief Executive. It has also been the firm and unvarying practice of Constitutional Courts to render no judgments not binding and conclusive on the parties and none that are subject to later review or alteration by administrative action.[24]

Nevertheless, judges find ways to offer advice to the political branches. Many of them have met with Presidents, legislators, and agency administrators to discuss matters that were being, or could be, litigated.[25] As a nonjudicial function, the Judicial Conference performs an advisory role by commenting on pending legislation.

In their off-bench activities, federal judges have not hesitated to comment on the constitutionality of legislative proposals. After the Supreme Court in *INS* v. *Chadha* (1983) struck down the legislative veto, D.C. Circuit Judge Abner J. Mikva told a House committee that he did not think "there is any question" that a joint resolution of approval or disapproval, as a substitute for the discredited one-House and two-House vetoes, "would pass constitutional muster."[26]

Even in the course of writing an opinion, judges often resort to dicta to advise executive and legislative officers.[27] During his time as

[24]C. & S. Air Lines v. Waterman Corp., 333 U.S. 103, 113–14 (1948). See also Flast v. Cohen, 392 U.S. at 96.

[25]Walter Murphy, The Elements of Judicial Strategy 132–55 (1964).

[26]"Legislative Veto After Chadha," hearings before the House Committee on Rules, 98th Cong., 2d Sess. 600 (1984).

[27]E. F. Albertsworth, "Advisory Functions in Federal Supreme Court," 23 Geo. L. J. 643 (1935).

a federal appellate judge, Griffin B. Bell defended the "discriminate use of obiter dictum in opinion writing." Policy considerations, he said, may dictate the need for "guidance through dictum" in cases where legal concepts are undergoing change: "This is an advisory opinion, no less, but the role of the courts under our system of separation of powers and federalism may call such a practice into play in some situations."[28]

A recent example appears in *Duke Power Co.* v. *Carolina Environmental Study Group* (1978), which rejected a number of procedural arguments offered to postpone decision on the Price-Anderson Act. The Court concluded that any delay in interpreting the statute would frustrate one of its key purposes: "the elimination of doubts concerning the scope of private liability in the event of major nuclear accident." All parties would be adversely affected, said the Court, by deferring a decision.[29] Justice Stevens admitted that the decision would serve the national interest by removing doubts concerning the constitutionality of the Price-Anderson Act, but he did not include among judicial functions the duty to provide advisory opinions on important subjects:

> We are not statesmen; we are judges. When it is necessary to resolve a constitutional issue in the adjudication of an actual case or controversy, it is our duty to do so. But whenever we are persuaded by reasons of expediency to engage in the business of giving legal advice, we chip away a part of the foundation of our independence and our strength.[30]

A year later, in *Bellotti* v. *Baird*, Justice Stevens and three colleagues criticized the Court for rendering an advisory opinion for the state of Massachusetts. In defense, Justice Powell explained that his decision merely provided "some guidance" to the state legislators. In view of the importance of the issue raised (concerning parental consent before an abortion could be performed on an unmarried woman under the age of eighteen), and the "protracted litigation" that had already occurred, Powell thought it would be irresponsible simply to invalidate the state statute "without setting our views as to the con-

---

[28]Griffin B. Bell, "Style in Judicial Writing," 15 J. Pub. L. 214, 217 (1966).
[29]438 U.S. 59, 82 (1978).
[30]Id. at 103 (concurring opinion).

trolling principles." This exchange took place in two intriguing footnotes.[31]

Declaratory Judgments. Parties undertain of their legal rights want courts to determine those rights before injury is done. Otherwise, they might have to violate a law to bring a test case or forego possible rights because of a fear of litigation. By issuing "declaratory judgments," courts can offer preventive relief. Representative Ralph Gilbert explained the advantages of declaratory judgments: "Under the present law [in 1928] you take a step in the dark and then turn on the light to see if you stepped into a hole. Under the declaratory law you turn on the light and then take a step."[32] Unlike other judgments, declaratory relief decides only legal rights; it does not determine damages or the right to coercive relief. To avoid the ban on advisory opinions, such judgments are limited to actual controversies.

Before 1934, declaratory judgments had been issued by Great Britain, India, Scotland, Canada, Australia, and other nations. More than two dozen American states had adopted the practice.[33] Federal courts had also issued what were in effect declaratory judgments, because they determined rights and duties before a law was violated and even before a law had taken effect.[34] To clear up the legal uncertainty, Congress in 1934 passed the Declaratory Judgments Act. In "cases of actual controversy," it gave federal courts the power to declare "rights and other legal relations to any interested party petitioning for such declaration, whether or not further relief is or could be prayed, and such declaration shall have the force and effect of a final judgment or decree and be reviewable as such." In a unanimous decision in 1937, the Supreme Court upheld the constitutionality of this statute.[35] The Court treats the Declaratory Judgment Act as "an authorization, not a command. It gave the federal courts com-

[31]Bellotti v. Baird, 443 U.S. 622, 651–52, 656 (1979).

[32]69 Cong. Rec. 2030 (1928).

[33]H. Rept. No. 1264, 73d Cong., 2d Sess. 1 (1934).

[34]Pierce v. Society of Sisters, 268 U.S. 510, 525 (1925); Village of Euclid v. Ambler Realty Co., 272 U.S. 365 (1926).

[35]Aetna Life Insurance Co. v. Haworth, 300 U.S. 227 (1937). See 48 Stat. 955 (1934); 28 U.S.C. § 2201 (1982).

petence to make a declaration of rights; it did not impose a duty to do so."[36]

Standing to Sue

To satisfy the requirement of a case or controversy, parties bringing an action must have standing to sue. "Generalizations about standing to sue," Justice Douglas said with customary bluntness, "are largely worthless as such."[37] Judges frequently accuse one another of circular reasoning. After the Supreme Court announced that the requirements of standing are met if a taxpayer has the "requisite personal stake in the outcome" of his suite, Justice Harlan chided the Court: "This does not, of course, resolve the standing problem; it merely restates it."[38] A study in 1984 reviewed the Court's effort to find "injury" in order to determine standing: "the Court has so severely manipulated the injury standard that the foundation of standing law is essentially incomprehensible."[39]

The reader forewarned, here are some generalizations. To demonstrate standing, parties must show injury to a legally protected interest, an injury that is real rather than abstract or hypothetical.[40] Injuries may be economic or noneconomic[41], actual or threatened.[42] Injuries may afflict organizations as well as persons.[43] A "threatened" injury can be close cousin to the hypothetical. Five members of the Supreme Court in 1973 held that *allegations* of injury were sufficient to establish standing. Proof of actual injury was not necessary.[44] On

---

[36]Public Affairs Press v. Rickover, 369 U.S. 111, 112 (1962). See also Steffel v. Thompson, 415 U.S. 452 (1974) and Golden v. Zwickler, 394 U.S. 103 (1969).

[37]Data Processing Service v. Camp, 397 U.S. 150, 151 (1970).

[38]Flast v. Cohen, 392 U.S. at 121 (dissenting opinion).

[39]Gene R. Nichol, Jr., "Rethinking Standing," 72 Cal. L. Rev. 68, 70 (1984).

[40]O'Shea v. Littleton, 414 U.S. 488, 494 (1974).

[41]Data Processing Service v. Camp, 397 U.S. at 154.

[42]Linda R.S. v. Richard D., 410 U.S. 614, 617 (1973); Gladstone, Realtors v. Village of Bellwood, 441 U.S. 91, 99 (1979); Muller Optical Co. v. EEOC, 574 F.Supp. 946, 950 (W.D. Tenn. 1983).

[43]Havens Realty Corp. v. Coleman, 455 U.S. 363, 379 n.19 (1982); Warth v. Seldin, 422 U.S. 490, 511 (1975).

[44]United States v. SCRAP, 412 U.S. 669 (1973). Justice Stewart was satisfied with an "attenuated line of causation" linking litigant to an injury; id. at 688. Justices Blackmun and Brennan accepted allegations of harm as sufficient; id. at 699. Justice Doug-

the other hand, actual injury may be inadequate to establish standing if the Court wishes to defer to the states.[45]

Individuals, functioning in the role of private attorneys general, may have standing as "representatives of the public interest."[46] This principle is sometimes extended to permit one party to assert the rights of third parties (*jus tertii*). Federal courts hesitate to resolve a controversy on the basis of the rights of third persons who are not parties to the litigation. There are two reasons:

> First, the courts should not adjudicate such rights unnecessarily, and it may be that . . . holders of those rights either do not wish to assert them, or will be able to enjoy them regardless of whether the in-court litigant is successful or not. . . . Second, third parties themselves usually will be the best proponents of their own rights. The courts depend on effective advocacy, and therefore should prefer to construe legal rights only when the most effective advocates of those rights are before them.[47]

When genuine obstacles prevent a third party from appearing in court (such as the need to maintain anonymity to avoid the loss of rights), the courts allow exceptions.[48] The judiciary may also find it necessary to relax the third-party restriction in order to protect an earlier holding. For example, in 1948 the Supreme Court held that racially restrictive housing covenants could not be enforced in state court because this denied blacks equal protection of the laws under the Fourteenth Amendment.[49] The question then arose whether it was possible to collect damages from white owners who broke restrictive covenants by selling to blacks. Would court action sustaining a damage suit indirectly encourage racial covenants? Could a white owner sued for damages represent the interests of blacks who were not parties to the suit? The Court answered that it was possible, in

---

las agreed with their position; id. at 703. Justice Marshall agreed with the holding on standing; id. at 724.

[45]City of Los Angeles v. Lyons, 461 U.S. 95 (1983) (plaintiff had been subject to a "chokehold" by Los Angeles police).

[46]Scripps-Howard Radio v. Comm'n, 316 U.S. 4, 14 (1942); Scenic Hudson Preservation Conf. v. FPC, 354 F.2d 608, 615–16 (2d Cir. 1965).

[47]Singleton v. Wulff, 428 U.S. 106, 113–14 (1976).

[48]NAACP v. Alabama, 357 U.S. 449 (1958). See also Singleton v. Wulff, 428 U.S. at 114–16, and Note, "Standing to Assert Constitutional Jus Tertii," 88 Harv. L. Rev. 423 (1974).

[49]Shelley v. Kraemer, 334 U.S. 1 (1948).

this "unique situation," for a white to vindicate the rights of blacks.[50] The "third party" issue was largely a legal fiction. The NAACP conducted and financed the case for the white owner.[51]

Although standing is basically a judge-made rule, courts recognize that Congress can, by statute, confer standing upon an individual or a group, and courts may defer to Congress on such matters.[52] However, such statutory phrases as "any person aggrieved" or "adversely affected" allow the courts broad discretion in interpreting what Congress means by standing. Furthermore, Congress cannot compel the courts to grant standing for a suit that, in the opinion of judges, lacks the necessary ingredients of a case or controversy. Congressional efforts to confer standing are limited by the judiciary's exclusive responsibility to determine Article III requirements.[53]

Courts raise and lower the standing barrier depending on circumstances. In *Frothingham* v. *Mellon* (1923), an individual taxpayer was denied standing to challenge the constitutionality of a federal statute that provided appropriations to the states for maternal and infant care. The taxpayer claimed that Congress had exceeded its Article I powers and had invaded territory reserved to the states by the Tenth Amendment. The Supreme Court decided that a federal taxpayer's interest in financing the program was "comparatively minute and indeterminable," and the effect on future taxation "so remote, fluctuating and uncertain" that there was no possibility of a direct injury to confer standing.[54]

The Court's decision appeared to be driven largely by policy rather than constitutional considerations. Lowering the barrier for standing meant increased casework for the judiciary. Other taxpayers would be allowed to challenge any federal statute involving the outlay of public funds.[55] Lowering the barrier might bring the administrative

[50]Barrows v. Jackson, 346 U.S. 249, 255–59 (1953).

[51]Clement E. Vose, Caucasians Only 240–43 (1959). Also on the standing of third parties, see Secretary of State of Md. v. J. H. Munson Co., 467 U.S. 947, 954–59 (1984).

[52]Sierra Club v. Morton, 405 U.S. 727, 732 n.3 (1972); Trafficante v. Metropolitan Life Ins., 409 U.S. 205, 209 (1972); Linda R.S. v. Richard D., 410 U.S. at 617 n.3; Warth v. Seldin, 422 U.S. at 501.

[53]Data Processing Service v. Camp, 397 U.S. at 154; Simon v. Eastern Kentucky Welfare Rights Org., 426 U.S. 26, 41 n.22 (1976). For a strict reading of statutory authorization to bring suit, see Bread PAC v. FEC, 455 U.S. 577 (1982).

[54]262 U.S. 447, 487 (1923).

[55]Id.

process to a standstill, as each disappointed party turned to the courts for possible relief. The Court insisted that a party must not only show that a statute is invalid but that "he has sustained or is immediately in danger of sustaining some direct injury as the result of its enforcement, and not merely that he suffers in some indefinite way in common with people generally."[56]

The decision was criticized because it was unclear whether the Court had announced a constitutional bar to taxpayer suits (compelled by Article III limitations on federal court jurisdiction) or whether the Court had temporarily imposed a rule of self-restraint to be lifted in the future. In later years the Supreme Court admitted that *Frothingham* could be read either way.[57]

The Justice Department interpreted *Frothingham* as an absolute prohibition on taxpayer suits. The Supreme Court discarded that notion in *Flast* v. *Cohen* (1968), which involved a taxpayer's challenge to the use of public funds for religious education. Such a doctrine would put the Government in the position of conceding that a taxpayer would lack standing "even if Congress engaged in such palpably unconstitutional conduct as providing funds for the construction of churches for particular sects."[58] The Court decided to liberalize the rule on standing but only at the cost of substantial doctrinal confusion. It claimed that standing focuses on the party, not the issue: "when standing is placed in issue in a case, the question is whether the person whose standing is challenged is a proper party to request an adjudication of a particular issue and not whether the issue is justiciable." Under this reasoning a party could gain standing and be told, because of the issue, that the case was being dismissed as a political question.[59]

The party/issue dichotomy lost its crispness when the Court attempted to explain why Mrs. Flast had standing and Mrs. Frothingham did not. The Court looked to the substantive issues to determine whether a logical "nexus" existed between the status asserted and the claim adjudicated. The Court identified two aspects of nexus: the taxpayer must establish a logical link between his status and the legislative statute attacked, and the taxpayer must connect his status

[56]Id. at 488.
[57]Flast v. Cohen, 392 U.S. at 92–93.
[58]Id. at 98 n.17.
[59]Id. at 99–100.

with "the precise nature of the constitutional infringement alleged."[60] The Court concluded that both Frothingham and Flast satisfied the first but only Flast satisfied the second. Justice Harlan dissented, unable to understand on what basis the Court could classify the ArticleI/Tenth Amendment position in *Frothingham* as too general, while accepting the First Amendment/Establishment Clause at issue in *Flast* as sufficiently "precise."

The Court decided that it was time to retreat from the absolute barrier of *Frothingham* but could not adequately explain why. The party/issue distinction was unpersuasive. Even the questions of party and injury had become muddled. Did Mrs. Flast have to be a taxpayer to bring suit? Could she have had standing if she lived on interest from tax-exempt bonds and was therefore unable to show injury or a monetary stake? Such fundamental questions were left unanswered.

By lowering the barrier for standing, the Supreme Court not only encouraged more lawsuits but invited collisions with other branches of government. In a later case, Justice Powell commented on the relationship between a relaxed standing policy and the expansion of judicial power: "It seems to be inescapable that allowing unrestricted taxpayer or citizen standing would significantly alter the allocation of power at the national level, with a shift away from a democratic form of government."[61]

The Burger Court raised the requirements for standing. In 1972 it denied standing to an environmental group that wanted to prevent construction of a ski resort in a national park. The Court was deeply split, four Justices arrayed against three.[62] In that same year it refused to decide whether the Army's surveillance of domestic activities constituted a chilling effect on First Amendment liberties. A majority of five Justices, with four dissenting, held that there was insufficient evidence of a direct injury to present a case for resolution in the courts.[63]

In some cases Justices will admit that standing and the merits are

[60]Id. at 102.

[61]United States v. Richardson, 418 U.S. 166, 188 (1974) (concurring opinion).

[62]Sierra Club v. Morton, 405 U.S. 727 (1972).

[63]Laird v. Tatum, 408 U.S. 1 (1972). Curiously, a year later the Court gave standing to five law students to bring an environmental suit against the Interstate Commerce Commission; United States v. SCRAP, 412 U.S. 669 (1973). Evidently, standing *does* depend on the issue.

"inextricably intertwined."[64] The close link between standing and issue is highlighted by a 1974 decision in which the Supreme Court denied standing to a taxpayer who challenged the constitutionality of covert spending by the Central Intelligence Agency (CIA). The Court specifically looked at the issues raised before dismissing the case on standing, even though the constitutional provision (the Statement and Account Clause) is quite as "precise" as the Establishment Clause at stake in *Flast*. More to the point, the Court noted that relief was available through the regular political process.[65]

What was dismissed on standing appeared to turn basically on questions of separation of power. In concurring in this 5-to-4 opinion, Justice Powell urged the Court to abandon *Flast*'s two-part "nexus" test as hopeless. He also explored the separation-of-power question, pointing to the dangers that might await the Court if it relaxed the standing requirements:

> Relaxation of standing requirements is directly related to the expansion of judicial power. It seems to me inescapable that allowing unrestricted taxpayer or citizen standing would significantly alter the allocation of power at the national level, with a shift away from a democratic form of government. I also believe that repeated and essentially head-on confrontations between the life-tenured branch and the representative branches of government will not, in the long run, be beneficial to either. The public confidence essential to the former and the vitality critical to the latter may well erode if we do not exercise self-restraint in the utilization of our power to negative the actions of the other branches. We should be ever mindful of the contradictions that would arise if a democracy were to permit general oversight of the elected branches of government by a nonrepresentative, and in large measure insulated, judicial branch.[66]

Powell concluded that the power of judicial review could be retained only if exercised prudently: "Were we to utilize this power as

[64]Holtzman v. Schlesinger, 414 U.S. 1316, 1319 (1973) (Douglas, J., in chamber). See also Revere v. Massachusetts General Hospital, 463 U.S. 239, 243 n.5 (1983).

[65]United States v. Richardson, 418 U.S. 166 (1974). See also Schlesinger v. Reservists to Stop the War, 418 U.S. 208 (1974), which denied plaintiffs standing to challenge the constitutionality of members of Congress who served in the military reserves, in apparent conflict with the Ineligibility Clause.

[66]United States v. Richardson, 418 U.S. at 188. Footnote omitted.

indiscriminately as is now being urged, we may witness efforts by the representative branches drastically to curb its use."[67] He urged the Court to reaffirm prudential barriers to the doctrine of standing.[68]

The connection between standing and sensitive political issues was evident again in 1975 when the Court announced that the inquiry into standing "involves both constitutional limitations on federal-court jurisdiction and prudential limitations on it exercise. . . . In both dimensions it is founded in concern about the proper—and properly limited—role of the courts in a democratic society."[69] Prudential rules of standing are not constitutionally required but they "serve to limit the role of the courts in resolving public disputes."[70] In a dissenting opinion joined by Justices White and Marshall, Justice Brennan picked additional holes in the Court's doctrine that standing was unrelated to the issue being litigated:

> While the Court gives lip service to the principle, often re-peated in recent years, that "standing in no way depends on the merits of the plaintiff's contention that particular conduct is illegal," . . . in fact the opinion, which tosses out of court al-most every conceivable kind of plaintiff who could be injured by the activity claimed to be unconstitutional, can be explained only by an indefensible hostility to the claim on the merits.[71]

The *Flast* doctrine was further shaken by *Valley Forge College* v. *Americans United* (1982), which denied plaintiffs standing to challenge the transfer of federal property to a Christian college. Justice Rehn-quist, writing for the Court, first argued that the plaintiffs could not sue as taxpayers because the land was transferred under the Prop-erty Clause, not the Taxing and Spending Clause. He then denied that the Establishment Clause gave citizens a personal constitutional right to bring suit. Four Justices dissented, accusing the majority of using a threshold question to decide substantive issues obliquely and to obfuscate legal rights. They wondered on what basis the consti-tutional rights in the Establishment Clause could be enforced in the

[67]Id. at 191.

[68]Id. at 196–97.

[69]Warth v. Seldin, 422 U.S. at 498.

[70]Id. at 500.

[71]Id. at 520. A year later the Supreme Court reiterated the *Flast* doctrine that stand-ing "focuses on the party seeking to get his complaint before a federal court and not on the issues he wishes to have adjudicated." Simon v. Eastern Kentucky Welfare Rights Org., 426 U.S. at 38.

courts. Brennan's dissent, in which Marshall and Blackmun joined, is especially biting: "Blind to history, the Court attempts to distinguish this case from *Flast* by wrenching snippets of language from our opinions, and by perfunctorily applying that language under color of the first prong of *Flast*'s two-part nexus test. The tortuous distinctions thus produced are specious, at best; at worst, they are pernicious to our constitutional heritage."[72]

There have been cases that could have been disposed of on standing but the courts went ahead and reached the merits anyway. In a 1980 case concerning access to CIA documents, the D.C. Circuit agreed that under a controlling Supreme Court precedent the plaintiff lacked standing to bring the suit. Nonetheless, the court found it advisable to reach the merits on the constitutionality of statutory exemptions for the CIA. The court considered that "judicial economy is best served by our resolving all relevant issues at this stage" and proceeded to reject the plaintiff's constitutional claim on the merits.[73]

Much of the confusion about the standing doctrine has its source in the Court's practice of spinning awkward doctrines that are, at bottom, techniques of deferring to the states and to the legislative and executive branches. These basic issues of federalism and separation of powers "have generally been concealed behind a standing discussion concerning the directness of injury or the generalized nature of the claim."[74] Although the law of standing is derived from the case-or-controversy test in Article III, the application of standing rules requires sensitive judgments about the Court's place in a system of democratic government and separated powers.[75]

Mootness

Mootness raises some of the same issues as standing and advisory opinions. Litigants able to establish standing at the outset of a case may find their personal stake diluted or eliminated by subsequent

---

[72]454 U.S. 464, 510 (1982).

[73]Halperin v. CIA, 629 F.2d 144, 146, 152–54 (D.C. Cir. 1980).

[74]Nichol, "Rethinking Standing," 72 Cal. L. Rev., at 101.

[75]See Justice O'Connor's opinion for the Court in Allen v. Wright, 468 U.S. 737, 752, 759–61 (1984). See also David A. Logan, "Standing to Sue: A Proposed Separation of Powers Analysis," 1984 Wisc. L. Rev. 37 (1984), and Antonin Scalia, "The Doctrine of Standing as an Essential Element of the Separation of Powers," 17 Suffolk U. L. Rev. 881 (1983).

events. Because of a change in law or facts, the case or controversy may disappear and leave insufficient adverseness to guide the courts.[76] When the states failed to ratify the Equal Rights Amendment, pending suits regarding the extension of its deadline from March 22, 1979 to June 30, 1982 were mooted.[77] If the action that triggered the complaint ceases, a court may have no means of granting relief.[78] At that point a decision could become, in effect, an advisory opinion. There have been situations where the original plaintiff no longer has a stake in the outcome, but mootness is avoided because the United States intervenes pursuant to statutory authority.[79]

A case is not mooted simply because one party discontinues a contested action. Judicial review cannot be circumvented merely through a strategy of starts and stops. If the controversy is likely to reappear, judicial scrutiny "ought not to be, as they might be, defeated, by short term orders, capable of repetition, yet evading review. . . ."[80] Complaints about an election process, even after a particular election is over, may remain a continuing controversy that requires decision by the courts,[81] but there must be a "reasonable expectation" or "demonstrated probability" that the same controversy will recur.[82]

If the judiciary is unprepared or unwilling to decide an issue, mootness is one avenue of escape. In 1952 the Supreme Court held that a public school Bible-reading case was moot because the child had graduated by the time the case had progressed through the lower courts and reached the Supreme Court. Although other students would be subjected to the same school policy in the future, the Court declared that "no decision we could render now would protect any rights she may once have had, and this Court does not sit to decide

[76]United States v. Hamburg-American Co., 239 U.S. 466 (1916); United States v. Alaska S.S. Co., 253 U.S. 113 (1920); Brockington v. Rhodes, 396 U.S. 41 (1969); Hall v. Beals, 396 U.S. 45 (1969).

[77]National Organization for Women v. Idaho, 459 U.S. 809 (1982).

[78]California v. San Pablo and Tulare Railroad Co., 149 U.S. 308 (1893); Jones v. Montague, 194 U.S. 147 (1904); Richardson v. McChesney, 218 U.S. 487 (1910). See also Sidney A. Diamond, "Federal Jurisdiction to Decide Moot Cases," 94 U. Pa. L. Rev. 125 (1946).

[79]Pasadena City Bd. of Education v. Spangler, 427 U.S. 424, 430–31 (1976).

[80]Southern Pacific Terminal Co. v. ICC, 219 U.S. 498, 515 (1911). See Globe Newspaper Co. v. Superior Court, 457 U.S. 596, 602–03 (1982); United States v. Phosphate Export Corp., 393 U.S. 199, 203 (1968); United States v. W. T. Grant Co., 345 U.S. 629, 632 (1953).

[81]Moore v. Ogilvie, 394 U.S. 814, 816 (1969).

[82]Murphy v. Hunt, 455 U.S. 478 (1982).

arguments after events have put them to rest."[83] The three dissenters, who regarded the case as neither feigned nor collusive, argued that it should be decided on the merits.

In *DeFunis* v. *Odegaard* (1974), a white student denied admission to a law school claimed that the school's affirmative action policy discriminated against him, allowing minorities with lower test scores to enter. He was admitted after a trial court found in his favor. By the time the case reached the Supreme Court he was in his third and final year. The school asssured the Court that he would be allowed to complete his legal studies, regardless of the disposition of the case. The Court refused to reach the merits of the case, considering it moot. Because DeFunis was scheduled to graduate, the Court could provide no remedy for him. Deciding on the merits would not affect his status.[84] If the law school continued its admission policy, the issue could return to the Court.[85] Four Justices dissented, claiming that the issue was of such breadth that it would inevitably return to the Supreme Court and should have been decided on the merits. In one of the dissents, Justice Brennan pointed out that twenty-six amicus briefs had been filed, indicating the extent to which the interest transcended the individual plaintiff.[86] Within a few years another case challenging a university's affirmative action program found its way to the Supreme Court, in *Regents of the University of California* v. *Bakke* (1978), and this time the Court confronted the merits.[87]

When the judiciary is ready to decide an issue, "mootness" will not stand in its way. For example, after a defendant was convicted and sentenced to nine months in prison for drunk driving, his sentence was suspended upon payment of $100 fine and costs. His appeal in the state courts led to a sentence of two years in prison. Subsequently a federal appellate court held that the more drastic sentence violated due process because it discouraged him from using the state's right of appeal. Although he had served his term in prison and could not gain relief from the harsher sentence, the Supreme Court agreed to hear the question of expunging the conviction from his record.[88]

[83]Doremus v. Board of Education, 342 U.S. 429, 433 (1952).

[84]DeFunis v. Odegaard, 416 U.S. 312, 317 (1974).

[85]Id. at 319.

[86]Id. at 350.

[87]438 U.S. 265 (1978). The Supreme Court used mootness to avoid an affirmative action case in County of Los Angeles v. Davis, 440 U.S. 625 (1979).

[88]North Carolina v. Rice, 404 U.S. 244 (1971).

The fact that someone has already served out a sentence does not make the case moot if the person faces deportation or disqualification of citizenship because of the conviction.[89]

To cite another example, in March 1967 the House of Representatives refused to seat Adam Clayton Powell. He was reelected in 1968 and seated in 1969. Was the case moot? The Supreme Court agreed that one of Powell's claims for relief remained a case or controversy, namely, the salary withheld after his exclusion.[90] The Court proceeded to examine the merits of the case and decided that the House had acted unconstitutionally.

In *Roe* v. *Wade* (1973), plaintiffs argued that the Texas criminal abortion laws were unconstitutionally vague and infringed upon their right of privacy. The laws prohibited abortion except on medical advice to save the mother's life. Texas responded that one of the suits, brought by a pregnant single women, was moot because her pregnancy had terminated. Justice Blackmun, writing for the majority, rejected that position:

> But when, as here, pregnancy is a significant fact in the litigation, the normal 226-day human gestation period is so short that the pregnancy will come to term before the usual appellate process is complete. If that termination makes a case moot, pregnancy litigation seldom will survive much beyond the trial stage, and appellate review will be effectively denied. Our law should not be that rigid. Pregnancy often comes more than once to the same woman, and in the general population, if man is to survive, it will always be with us. Pregnancy provides a classic justification for conclusion of nonmootness. It truly could be "capable of repetition, yet evading review."[91]

In 1984 the Supreme Court had an opportunity to dismiss as moot an affirmative action case involving a court order for the dismissal or demotion of white employees who had more seniority than black employees retained. All white employees laid off as a re-

[89]Fiswick v. United States, 329 U.S. 211 (1946).

[90]Powell v. McCormack, 395 U.S. 486, 496 (1969).

[91]410 U.S. 113, 125 (1973). See also Super Tire Engineering Co. v. McCorkle, 416 U.S. 115, 126–27 (1974).

sult of the order were restored to duty a month later. Those demoted were later offered their old positions. Those facts did not prevent the Supreme Court in *Firefighters* v. *Stotts* from deciding the case and reversing the lower court action.[92] Although some of the Justices accused the Court of issuing an advisory opinion,[93] the Court was evidently ready and willing to circumscribe the reach of affirmative action.

The twists and turns of the mootness doctrine reflect the Court's effort to maintain a proper relationship with the other political branches. Dissenting in a mootness case, Justice White noted that the threshold requirements of Article III are not always "consistent with Judicial economy." The "overriding purpose," he said, "is to define the boundaries separating the branches and to keep this Court from assuming a legislative perspective and function."[94]

An excellent example of White's concern occurred in 1987 in a pocket veto case. As a result of lawsuits by Senator Kennedy in the early 1970s, it was agreed by all three branches that pocket vetoes should not be used within a session of Congress, either the first session or the second.[95] The courts left unclear the availability of a pocket veto *between* sessions, but the Ford and Carter administrations reached an accommodation with Congress: pocket vetoes would be used neither within sessions nor between the first and the second sessions. They could be invoked only at the end of the second session, when Congress adjourned sine die.[96]

President Reagan rejected this accommodation by exercising the pocket veto between sessions. After the plaintiff lost in the district court and prevailed in the appeals court, it appeared that the Supreme Court would resolve once and for all the scope of the pocket veto. Instead, it held that the case was moot because the bill at issue expired by its own terms.[97] Although the issue was "capable of repetition," the Court may have decided to duck the issue for the mo-

[92]467 U.S. 561, 568–72 (1984).
[93]Id. at 590 (Stevens, J., concurring) and 594, 599 (Blackmun, J., dissenting).
[94]Sosna v. Iowa, 419 U.S. 393, 418 (1975) (dissenting opinion).
[95]Kennedy v. Sampson, 364 F.Supp. 1075 (D.D.C. 1973); Kennedy v. Sampson, 511 F.2d 430 (D.C. Cir. 1974).
[96]Louis Fisher, Constitutional Conflicts between Congress and the President 153 (1985).
[97]Burke v. Barnes, 107 S.Ct. 734 (1987).

ment because the plaintiff was a member of Congress, and the appeals Court had divided sharply on the question whether Congressmen have standing to sue.[98]

Ripeness

Just as a case brought too late can be moot, a case brought too early may not yet be ripe. Sometimes this results from a failure to exhaust administrative and state remedies. Plaintiffs must show that they have explored all avenues of relief before they turn to the federal courts. Premature consideration by the courts does more than create unnecessary workload. It can deprive judges of information needed for informed adjudication and force them to deal at an abstract, speculative, and hypothetical level. It also discourages settlement in the administrative arena, which may be the most appropriate forum for resolution.

The issue of ripeness was present in a 1947 case brought by twelve federal employees against the Civil Service Commission. They wanted to prevent the Commission from enforcing a section of the Hatch Act that prohibited them from taking "any active part in political management or in political campaigns." The federal workers complained that the statute deprived them of their First Amendment rights of speech, press, and assembly. The Supreme Court regarded the employees' fears of losing their jobs as too speculative:

> The power of courts, and ultimately of this Court, to pass upon the constitutionality of acts of Congress arises only when the interests of litigants require the use of this judicial authority for their protection against actual interference. A hypothetical threat is not enough. We can only speculate as to the kinds of political activity the appellants desire to engage in or as to the contents of their proposed public statements or the circumstances of their publication. It would not accord with judicial responsibility to adjudge, in a matter involving constitutionality, between the

[98]Barnes v. Kline, 759 F.2d 21 (D.C. Cir 1985). See also Barnes v. Carmen, 582 F.Supp. 163 (D.D.C. 1984).

freedom of the individual and requirements of public order except when definite rights appear upon the one side and definite prejudicial interferences upon the other.[99]

The situation of one of the federal employees, George P. Poole, was not hypothetical. He faced dismissal unless he could refute the charges of the Commission that his political activities had violated the Hatch Act. Accepting his suit as a justiciable case, the Court held that disciplinary action under the Hatch Act would not violate the Constitution.

Justices Black and Douglas dissented, believing that the Court should have heard the cases of all twelve litigants. The threat of discharge, they said, was real rather than fanciful, immediate not remote. Douglas observed: "to require these employees first to suffer the hardship of a discharge is not only to make them incur a penalty; it makes inadequate, if not wholly illusory, any legal remedy which they might have. Men who must sacrifice their means of livelihood in order to test their jobs must either pursue prolonged and expensive litigation as unemployed persons or pull up their roots, change their life careers, and seek employment in other fields."[100]

The issue of preventive relief often splits the courts. Should judges rule on a statute before its sanctions have been set in motion? Although a decision might offer relief to threatened individuals, it also requires the courts to rule in advance of a concrete case or controversy. It forces judgments on hypothetical situations that raise remote and abstract issues. Yet judicial inaction can lead to irreparable harm to individuals once a statute is enforced.[101] Judicial review may be both necessary and appropriate to protect individuals before an agency enforces a regulation.[102]

The extreme point is reached when a suit lingers so long in the courts that it becomes "overripe." Justice Black described a case that

[99]United Public Workers v. Mitchell, 330 U.S. 75, 90 (1947). Footnote omitted.

[100]Id. at 117. Footnote omitted. See also Adler v. Board of Education, 342 U.S. 485 (1952) and Cramp v. Board of Public Instruction, 368 U.S. 278 (1961).

[101]Longshoremen's Union v. Boyd, 347 U.S. 222, 224–26 (1954) (Black, J., dissenting).

[102]Abbott Laboratories v. Gardner, 387 U.S. 136 (1967). See also Toilet Goods Assn. v. Gardner, 387 U.S. 158 (1967) and Gardner v. Toilet Goods Assn., 387 U.S. 167 (1967).

bounced around for ten years before the Supreme Court sent it back to the lower courts "because of the staleness of the record."[103]

As with mootness, disposing of a case on the ground of ripeness may delay but not necessarily avoid decision. In 1943 and 1961, the Supreme Court refused to rule on the constitutionality of Connecticut laws that prohibited married couples from using contraceptives or physicians from giving advice about their use.[104] Because the record suggested that the state was unlikely to prosecute offenders, the Court held that it lacked jurisdiction to decide hypothetical cases. In the 1961 case, the Court ignored the fact that the state had closed several birth-control clinics. In one of the dissents, Justice Douglas asked: "What are these people—doctor and patients—to do? Flout the law and go to prison? Violate the law surreptiously and hope they will not get caught? In today's decision we leave them no other alternatives. It is not the choice they need have under the regime of the declaratory judgment and our constitutional system."[105] Justice Harlan, in his dissent, feared that the Court "has indulged in a bit of sleight of hand to be rid of this case."[106] After that decision, the state arrested physicians who had operated a birth-control clinic in New Haven. They were found guilty and fined $100 each. In 1968 the Supreme Court held that they had standing and declared the Connecticut statute invalid under the "penumbra" of the Bill of Rights.[107]

"Ripeness" may provide the means to sidestep momentarily a socially sensitive issue. Immediately after the Court had decided the desegregation case in 1954, it was faced with the constitutionality of a Virginia miscegenation statute. To strike down a law banning interracial marriages would stimulate the fears of the critics of the desegregation decision, who predicted that integrated schools would lead to "mongrelization" of the white race. Indeed, the Supreme Court of Appeals in Virginia had upheld the statute by arguing that the state had a right to preserve the "racial integrity" of its citizens and to regulate the marriage relation "so that it does not have a mongrel

---

[103]Hugo Black, A Constitutional Faith 17 (1968); American Committee v. SACB, 380 U.S. 503 (1965).

[104]Tileson v. Ullman, 318 U.S. 44 (1943); Poe v. Ullman, 367 U.S. 497 (1961).

[105]Poe v. Ullman, 367 U.S. at 513.

[106]Id. at 533.

[107]Griswold v. Connecticut, 381 U.S. 479 (1965).

breed of citizens."[108] The Court returned the case to the lower courts because of the "inadequacy of the record" and the lack of a "properly-presented federal question."[109] In essence, the Court decided to buy some time. Years later, after the principle of desegregation had been safely established, the Court struck down the Virginia statute.[110]

Judicial doctrine and political practicalities were joined in a 1978 case involving a congressional limitation on liability for accidents by private nuclear plants. A "hypothetical" issue, to be sure, but it was intuitively unappealing to insist that the courts await a nuclear catastrophe before deciding. The Court was satisfied that the test of ripeness had been met by two effects already evident from the operation of nuclear power plants: the emission of small quantities of radiation in the air and water, and an increase in the temperature of two lakes used for recreational purposes.[111] "One does not have to await the consummation of threatened injury to obtain preventive relief. If the injury is certainly impending that is enough."[112]

Ripeness sometimes involves the unwillingness of Congress to challenge presidential actions. President Carter's termination of the Taiwan defense treaty was met initially by a Senate resolution declaring that Senate approval was necessary to terminate a mutual defense treaty. But no final vote was ever taken on the resolution. Justice Powell considered the case insufficiently ripe for judicial review. "Prudential considerations" convinced him that disputes between Congress and the President should not be reviewed by the courts "unless and until each branch has taken action asserting its constitutional authority." He said that only when the political branches reach a "constitutional impasse" should the judiciary decide issues affecting the allocation of power between Congress and the Presi-

---

[108]Naim v. Naim, 87 S.E.2d 749, 756 (Va. 1955).

[109]Naim v. Naim, 350 U.S. 891 (1955); 350 U.S. 985 (1956). See Alexander M. Bickel, The Least Dangerous Branch 174 (1962).

[110]Loving v. Virginia, 388 U.S. 1 (1967).

[111]Duke Power Co. v. Carolina Environment Study Group, 438 U.S. 59, 72–74, 81–82 (1978). Also on the need for courts to avoid premature decisions: Adler v. Board of Education, 342 U.S. 485, 497–508 (1952) (Frankfurter, J., dissenting); Socialist Labor Party v. Gilligan, 406 U.S. 583 (1972).

[112]Regional Rail Reorganization Act Cases, 419 U.S. 102, 143 (1974), quoting from Pennsylvania v. West Virginia, 262 U.S. 553, 593 (1923).

dent: "Otherwise, we would encourage small groups or even individual Members of Congress to seek judicial resolution of issues before the normal political process has the opportunity to resolve the conflict."[113] If Congress chose not to confront the President, Powell said "it is not our task to do so."[114]

Political Questions

The "political question" doctrine survives to some extent on circular reasoning. In *Marbury* v. *Madison*, Chief Justice Marshall claimed that "Questions in their nature political . . . can never be made in this court."[115] Yet every question that reaches a court is, by its very nature, political. Justice Homes, hearing a litigant claim that a question concerning a party primary was nonjusticiable because of its political character, said that such an objection "is little more than a play upon words."[116]

Definitional problems are legion. After refusing to decide a war powers case in 1968, a federal judge declared: "Though it is not always a simple matter to define the meaning of the term 'political question,' it is generally used to encompass all questions outside the sphere of judicial power."[117] That definition recalls this dictionary explanation: "violins are small cellos, and cellos are large violins."[118] The issue is not whether a question is "outside the sphere of judicial power," in the sense that fixed principles of jurisdiction can be applied. The test is essentially a political judgment of what is appropriate for the courts for the times. The term political question "applies to all those matters of which the court, at a given time, will be of the opinion that it is impolitic or inexpedient to take jurisdiction."[119]

Beyond questions of definition, there is some doubt whether a political question doctrine even exists in the sense that courts refuse to

[113]Goldwater v. Carter, 444 U.S. 996, 997 (1979).
[114]Id. at 998.
[115]5 U.S. (1 Cr.) 137, 170 (1803).
[116]Nixon v. Herndon, 273 U.S. 536, 540 (1927).
[117]Velvel v. Johnson, 287 F.Supp. 846, 850 (D. Kans. 1968).
[118]John P. Roche, "Judicial Self-Restraint," 49 Am. Pol. Sci. Rev. 762, 768 (1955).
[119]Maurice Finkelstein, "Judicial Self-Limitation," 37 Harv. L. Rev. 338, 344 (1924).

adjudicate certain issues. After reviewing political question cases, Louis Henkin concluded: "the court does not refuse judicial review; it exercises it. It is not dismissing the case or the issue as nonjusticiable; it adjudicates it. It is not refusing to pass on the power of the political branches; it passes upon it, only to affirm that they had the power which had been challenged and that nothing in the Constitution prohibited the particular exercise of it."[120]

In *Baker* v. *Carr* (1962), the Court identified the areas that are generally classified as political questions. *Baker* supplied six criteria to indicate the kinds of questions not subject to judicial resolution. The first criterion is "a textually demonstrable constitutional commitment of the issue to a coordinate political department."[121] However, the very question of whether an issue has been textually committed to a coordinate branch requires judicial interpretation. Moreover, the fact that an area *is* committed to Congress or the President does not automatically produce a political question. As the Supreme Court noted in 1983, "virtually every challenge to the constitutionality of a statute would be a political question" under that reasoning.[122] The Court further pointed out:

> It is correct that this controversy may, in a sense, be termed "political." But the presence of constitutional issues with significant political overtones does not automatically invoke the political question doctrine. Resolution of litigation challenging the constitutional authority of one of the three branches cannot be evaded by courts because the issues have political implications in the sense urged by Congress. *Marbury* v. *Madison*, 1 Cranch 137 (1803), was also a "political" case, involving as it did claims under a judicial commission alleged to have been duly signed by the President but not delivered.[123]

Consider the language of Article I, Section 5, of the Constitution: "Each House shall be the Judge of the Elections, Returns and Qualifications of its own Members." A study in 1954 concluded: "it is up to Congress to pass upon the qualifications of its own members, the

[120]Louis Henkin, "Is There a 'Political Question' Doctrine?," 85 Yale L. J. 597, 606 (1976).
[121]369 U.S. 186, 217 (1962).
[122]INS v. Chadha, 462 U.S. at 941.
[123]Id. at 942–43.

Constitution says as much, leaving nothing for the judges to do."[124] Nevertheless, the courts play a significant role. After the House of Representatives excluded Adam Clayton Powell in 1967, it was widely assumed that no court would or could second-guess that decision. Yet in 1969 the Supreme Court ruled that the House had a duty to seat Powell because he met the standing qualifications set forth in the Constitution. Although the power of Congress to judge the qualifications of its members was a "textually demonstrable constitutional commitment," it was a power to judge only the qualifications expressly provided in the Constitution. The Court said that Congress could not add to them.

Attorneys for the House of Representatives argued that the case was not justiciable because it was impossible for a court to offer effective relief. They said that federal courts could not issue mandamus or injunctions compelling officers or employees of the House to perform certain acts. But coercive relief was not at issue. Powell sought a declaratory judgment to determine his rights independent of the question of relief.[125]

Three years later the same section of the Constitution was before the Court in the case of a contested election. Senator Vance Hartke, a narrow winner in an Indiana race, claimed that the appointment of a recount commission by a state court was prohibited by Article I, Section 5, which grants Congress the power to judge the elections, returns, and qualifications of its members. But another section of the Constitution was involved: Article I, Section 4, giving states the power to prescribe the times, places, and manner of holding elections for Senators and Representatives, subject to alterations by Congress.

The issue was thus the power of Indiana under Section 4 to call for a recount. The Senate had not challenged the recount procedure. It was waiting for the final tally before carrying out its powers under Section 5. Unless Congress acted, Section 4 empowered Indiana to regulate the conduct of senatorial elections.[126] The Court said that the Senate would not be bound by the recount: "The Senate is free to accept or reject the apparent winner in either count, and, if it chooses, to conduct its own recount."[127]

---

[124]John P. Frank, "Political Questions," in Edmond Cahn, ed., Supreme Court and Supreme Law 39 (1954). Footnote omitted.

[125]Powell v. McCormack, 395 U.S. 486 (1969).

[126]Roudebush v. Hartke, 405 U.S. 15, 24 (1972).

[127]Id. at 25–26. Footnotes omitted.

Another state case during this period concerned the deaths of several students at Kent State University in Ohio after the governor had called out the National Guard. The students sought injunctive relief to prevent the governor from taking such actions in the future and to prevent the Guard from future violations of students' constitutional rights. Basically, the students wanted the courts to supervise the future training and operations of the Guard. The Supreme Court regarded those duties as vested solely in Congress by Article I, Section 8, Clause 16, which empowers Congress to provide "for organizing, arming, and disciplining the Militia, and for governing such Part of them as may be employed in the Service of the United States, reserving to the States respectively, the Appointment of the Officers, and the Authority of training the Militia according to the discipline prescribed by Congress." The Court said that such actions were meant to be exercised by the political branches: "it is difficult to conceive of an area of governmental activity in which the courts have less competence."[128]

The Court agreed that the concept of political questions was not of fixed content, and that what was once nonjusticiable in the area of voting rights cases came to be accepted by the courts. But those cases, it said, "represented the Court's efforts to strengthen the political system by assuring a higher level of fairness and responsiveness to the political processes, not the assumption of a continuing judicial review of substantive political judgments entrusted expressly to the coordinate branches of government."[129] There has been no uncertainty about the exclusive responsibility of Congress to determine whether a state satisfies the language of Article IV, Section 4, which requires that the United States "shall guarantee to every State in this Union a Republican Form of Government."[130]

The second criterion in *Baker* v. *Carr* is "a lack of judicially discoverable and manageable standards for resolving" a dispute. One example comes from *Coleman* v. *Miller* (1939). Thirteen years had elapsed before Kansas ratified the Child Labor Amendment. Was that too long a time for state action? The Court decided that it lacked statutory and constitutional criteria to make a judicial determination. The question of a reasonable time involved "an appraisal of a great vari-

[128]Gilligan v. Morgan, 413 U.S. 1, 10 (1973).
[129]Id. at 11.
[130]Luther v. Borden, 7 How. 1 (1849); Pacific Telephone Co. v. Oregon, 223 U.S. 118 (1912).

ety of relevant conditions, political, social and economic, which can hardly be said to be within the appropriate range of evidence receivable in a court of justice. . . ."[131]

Another example is *C. & S. Airlines* v. *Waterman Corp.* (1948). The courts were asked to review certain orders issued by the Civil Aeronautics Board involving overseas and foreign air transportation. The orders were subject to presidential review, possibly thrusting the courts into an advisory opinion role. But the Supreme Court stated that the President, "both as Commander-in-Chief and as the Nation's organ for foreign affairs, has available intelligence services whose reports are not and ought not to be published to the world. It would be intolerable that courts, without the relevant information, should review and perhaps nullify actions of the Executive taken on information properly held secret."[132]

The Court went on to say that "the very nature of executive decisions as to foreign policy is political, not judicial. Such decisions are wholly confided by our Constitution to the political departments of the government, Executive and Legislature."[133] This statement is far too broad. As the Court later noted in *Baker* v. *Carr*, "it is error to suppose that every case or controversy which touches foreign relations lies beyond judicial cognizance."[134]

Certain matters of foreign policy are too sensitive for the courts to handle. When President Carter terminated the defense treaty with Taiwan, Senator Barry Goldwater asked the courts to declare the termination invalid. The case reached the Supreme Court a few weeks before the scheduled termination. Justice Rehnquist attracted three other colleagues to his position that the issue represented a nonjusticiable political question. The Court was being asked to settle a dispute between the executive and legislative branches, "each of which has resources available to protect and assert its interests, resources not available to private litigants outside the judicial forum."[135]

---

[131]307 U.S. 433, 453 (1939). In a concurrence, Justices Black, Roberts, Frankfurter, and Douglas objected that the Court had indulged in an advisory opinion because Congress possessed exclusive power over the amending process and was not bound by any court order. Id. at 459–60.

[132]333 U.S. 103, 111 (1948).

[133]Id.

[134]369 U.S. at 211.

[135]Goldwater v. Carter, 444 U.S. at 1004.

The third criterion is "the impossibility of deciding without an initial policy determination of a kind clearly for nonjudicial discretion." This criterion is laced with circularity and basically restates the issue. It would cover reapportionment in 1946 but not after 1962.[136] At the present time, it covers the issue whether President Reagan violated the War Powers Resolution by sending military advisers to El Salvador. A district court held that the factfinding necessary to resolve the dispute rendered the case nonjusticiable. The questions were "appropriate for congressional, not judicial, investigation and determination."[137]

The fourth criterion is "the impossibility of a court's undertaking independent resolution without expressing lack of the respect due coordinate branches of government." This factor exists in every case involving separation of powers, but it offers little guidance in resolving particular controversies. Whether in the Nixon tapes case or the exclusion of Adam Clayton Powell by the House of Representatives, the Court's judgment often challenges and overrides decisions made by coordinate branches.

"An unusual need for unquestioning adherence to a political decision already made" constitutes the fifth criterion. Professor Henkin said that he did not know "of any case from which Justice Brennan might have derived such a principle."[138] Some recent possibilities might include President Carter's termination of the Taiwan defense treaty and his handling of Iranian assets.[139]

Finally, the sixth is "the potentiality of embarrassment from multifarious pronouncements by various departments on one question." Despite this guideline, the Supreme Court told the House of Representatives that Adam Clayton Powell should be seated. However, this criterion retains usefulness in matters regarding the recognition of foreign governments,[140] political boundaries,[141] envoys,[142] the dates

---

[136]Colegrove v. Green, 328 U.S. 549 (1946); Baker v. Carr, 369 U.S. 186 (1962).

[137]Crockett v. Reagan, 558 F.Supp. 893, 898 (D.D.C. 1982).

[138]Henkin, "Political Question Doctrine," 85 Yale L. J., at 605–06 n.26.

[139]Goldwater v. Carter, 444 U.S. 996 (1979); Dames & Moore v. Regan, 453 U.S. 654 (1981). See also Idaho v. Freeman, 529 F.Supp. 1107, 1140–41 (D. Idaho 1981), regarding Idaho's rescission of its vote to ratify the Equal Rights Amendment.

[140]Rose v. Himely, 4 Cr. 241 (1808); Gelston v. Hoyt, 3 Wheat. 246 (1818).

[141]Foster v. Neilson, 2 Pet. 253 (1829); Williams v. Suffolk Insurance Co., 13 Pet. 415 (1839).

[142]Ex parte Hitz, 111 U.S. 766 (1884).

for beginning and ending wars,[143] calling out the militia,[144] and an alien's eligibility for federal benefits.[145]

Virtues and Vices

Rules of self-restraint are part of the complex process of drawing limits on judicial power. Some scholars argue that prudence dictates restrictions on judicial activity. Others warn that the contemporary Court has confused the concept of justiciability and abdicated its duty to decide proper cases and controversies. The use of threshold requirements to avoid or delay judicial decision has sparked a number of lively debates.

A particularly stimulating exchange involved Alexander M. Bickel and Gerald Gunther. Writing in 1961, Bickel urged the Court to discover means of sidestepping some issues that might damage its prestige and institutional effectiveness. Such techniques he called the "passive virtues." Bickel rejected the doctrine that Chief Justice Marshall announced in 1821:

> It is most true that this court will not take jurisdiction if it should not; but it is equally true, that it must take jurisdiction if it should. The judiciary cannot, as the legislature may, avoid a measure because it approaches the confines of the constitution. We cannot pass it by because it is doubtful. With whatever doubts, and whatever difficulties, a case may be attended, we must decide it if it is brought before us. We have no more right to decline the exercise of jurisdiction which is given, than to usurp that which is not given. The one or the other would be treason to the constitution.[146]

Bickel denied that Congress, simply by conferring jurisdiction, could compel the Court to adjudicate certain types of cases. Regardless of the disputes that found their way to the Court's doorstep because of

[143]Martin v. Mott, 12 Wheat. 19 (1827); Commercial Trust Co. v. Miller, 262 U.S. 51 (1923).

[144]Martin v. Mott, 12 Wheat. 19 (1827).

[145]Mathews v. Diaz, 426 U.S. 67, 81–84 (1976).

[146]Alexander M. Bickel, "The Supreme Court, 1960 Term—Foreword: The Passive Virtues," 75 Harv. L. Rev. 40, 42–43 (1961), quoting from Cohens v. Virginia, 19 U.S. (6 Wheat.) 264, 404 (1821)

statutory requirements, the Court retained discretion to decline the exercise of jurisdiction, whether by denying certiorari or by dismissing appeals from the states "for the want of a substantial federal question."[147] To Bickel, these methods of avoiding a decision on the merits were essential attributes of an unelected judiciary in a democratic society, particularly "a large and heterogeneous" society like the United States. Such societies would "explode" unless they exercised the "arts of compromise" and discovered ways "to muddle through." Bickel neatly capsulized his position: "No good society can be unprincipled; and no viable society can be principled-ridden."[148]

Although Bickel felt strongly that the Court could not survive solely on principled judgments, and that some degree of expediency was necessary, he recognized that these traits might appear unsavory and morally offensive. He attempted to blunt critiques by claiming that the considerations open to the Court "are for the most part prudential in character, but they should not be predilectional, sentimental, or irrational."[149] To behave in this fashion would diminish the prestige and legitimacy of the Court.

Bickel was answered by Gerald Gunther in an article entitled "The Subtle Vices of the 'Passive Virtues.' " Gunther says that Bickel found himself caught between two unacceptable options: the entreaties of the realists who claimed that constitutional law resembled nihilism more than principled interpretation and those who embraced purely principled action. Gunther writes that Bickel "cannot bear to abandon the requirement of principle in constitutional adjudication; he cannot bear the inexpedient results of unflinching adherence to principle. He is put to an excruciating choice; his response to avoid the choice, to seek escape routes."[150] Bickel's guidelines invited not compromise and accommodation but the "surrender of principle to expediency."[151] Unchanneled discretion would gain the upper hand over the prudence and wisdom that Bickel espoused.[152]

Bickel admitted that the Court could not invalidate legislation without a principled basis. The courts were not justified in declaring

[147]75 Harv. L. Rev. at 46.
[148]Id. at 49.
[149]Id. at 79.
[150]Gerald Gunther, "The Subtle Vices of the 'Passive Virtues'—A Comment on Principle and Expediency in Judicial Review," 64 Colum. L. Rev. 1, 5 (1964).
[151]Id.
[152]Id. at 10.

laws invalid by resorting to "judicial impressionism."[153] His difficulty lay with two other judicial duties: the power to validate legislation and to avoid a decision. Although decisions upholding a legislative or executive action are not meant to endorse the wisdom of the action, the public might interpret it that way. The same problem exists when the Court refuses to decide a case. Judicial avoidance through the use of thresholds may result in public misapprehension that the courts find the challenged action unobjectionable on constitutional grounds.[154] In either event, the Court is implicated in policies and political choices that Bickel wanted the judiciary to stay clear of.

Bickel's dilemma was not different than the Court's. The judiciary cannot accept nihilism and it cannot discover a principled means of discharging its duties. Law professors write eloquently about constitutional principles, but they attract few colleagues to their cause. Moreover, their formulations are often devoid of the considerations that the Court must keep in mind as it operates within a society that disperses power among many institutions.

[153] Id. at 6.
[154] Id. at 7–8.

4. Judicial Organization

It is tempting to dismiss judicial organization as a technical or esoteric matter. Yet organizational issues present questions of power. Changes in institutional boundaries and processes dramatically affect the flow of power at the federal-state level and among the three branches of the national government. The process of appointing judges is heavily lobbied by all sectors, public and private. Judicial tenure, removal, and compensation are perennial sources of conflict. The appropriate role of judicial lobbying remains a subject of great sensitivity.

Federal Court System

Long before the American colonies declared their separation from England, the idea of an independent judiciary had secured a firm foothold. The Act of Settlement, passed by England in 1701, contributed to judicial autonomy by guaranteeing judges tenure during good behavior. The power to constitute courts in the American colonies, however, was vested in the governor and council, creatures of the King. The assemblies were allowed to create courts only for small causes, subject always to the King's veto.[1]

The principle of judicial independence appears in several sections of the Declaration of Independence, which charged that the King had "obstructed the Administration of Justice, by refusing his Assent to Laws for establishing Judiciary Powers." Because of disputes between the British Crown and several of the colonies, laws establishing courts of justice were struck down repeatedly, sometimes eliminating courts for long stretches of time.[2] The Declaration of Independence also criticized the King for making judges "dependent on his Will

[1]Julius Goebel, Jr., 1 History of the Supreme Court of the United States: Antecedents and Beginnings 12–13 (1971).

[2]Edward Dumbauld, The Declaration of Independence and What It Means Today 108–12 (1950).

alone, for the Tenure of their Offices, and the Amount and Payment of their Salaries." Despite the Act of Settlement, the English government insisted that colonial judges serve at the King's pleasure. This policy produced bitter resistance in New York, New Jersey, Pennsylvania, North Carolina, South Carolina, and Massachusetts, where colonial legislatures wanted judges to have tenure during good behavior.[3] Following the break with England, several American colonies included tenure and salary provisions in their constitutions to secure judicial independence.

After the colonies cut ties with England, state governments authorized vessels to prey on British shipping. A judicial system was needed to dispose of "prizes" taken during those raids. State admiralty courts made the initial determination, but appeals beyond that level required the attention of the Continental Congress. From 1776 to 1780, appeals were handled first by temporary committees and then by a standing committee, until Congress, in May 1780, created a "Court of Appeals in Cases of Capture." This tribunal took direction from the Continental Congress and even from the Secretary for Foreign Affairs.[4] The Court of Appeals continued to function until delegates arrived at Philadelphia in May 1787 to draft a new constitution.

The record of the Continental Congress offered convincing evidence that one branch could not efficiently administer all functions of government: legislative, executive, and judicial. The behavior of state legislatures supplied alarming proof that individual liberties were endangered whenever power was concentrated in one branch, even if popularly elected. In various ways the legislatures had tried to usurp executive and judicial powers that state constitutions formally vested in separate branches.[5] Problems of interstate commerce and internal disunity threatened the nation.

The delegates to the Philadelphia Convention recognized the need for executive and judicial independence. They explored the possibility of setting up a Council of Revision, consisting of the executive and "a convenient number of the National Judiciary," to examine all

[3]Id. at 112–15.

[4]Goebel, History of the Supreme Court, at 178–79; Henry J. Bourguignon, The First Federal Court: The Federal Appellate Prize Court of the American Revolution (1977).

[5]Louis Fisher, President and Congress 6–22, 251–70 (1972).

bills from the legislature before they became law. Rejection by the council could be overridden by the legislature.[6] The convention turned down the proposal because the delegates wanted the Supreme Court to interpret the law without any prior participation.[7] The framers decided to vest the veto power exclusively in the President.

Article III of the Constitution created a separate judicial branch. The judges, both of the Supreme and inferior courts, "shall hold their Offices during good Behaviour, and shall, at stated Times, receive for their Services, a Compensation, which shall not be diminished during their continuance in Office." The Constitution vests the judicial power of the United States "in one supreme Court, and in such inferior Courts as the Congress may from time to time ordain and establish." The word "may" implies that the establishment of lower courts is discretionary, and some members of the First Congress proposed to do only the minimum: create a Supreme Court for national issues and rely on existing state courts for most local needs. The Judiciary Bill of 1789, as first drafted by the Senate, opted for federal district courts. Senator Richard Henry Lee's amendment, which would have restricted those courts to cases of admiralty and maritime matters (like the Court of Appeals in Cases of Capture), was rejected.[8]

During debate on the Bill of Rights, there were similar efforts in the House of Representatives to limit inferior courts to questions of admiralty.[9] These, too, were unsuccessful. Action on the Judiciary Bill of 1789 produced new resistance against the creation of federal district courts, but again the House rejected the idea of relying on state courts.[10] Madison warned that the courts in many states "cannot be trusted with the execution of Federal laws." Because of limited tenure and possible salary reductions, some courts were so dependent on state legislatures "that to make the Federal laws dependent on them, would throw us back into all the embarrassments which characterized our former situation."[11] By a vote of 31 to 11, the House

[6] 1 Farrand 21.
[7] Id. at 97–98 (Elbridge Gerry and Rufus King). See also 1 Farrand 104, 108 (James Madison) and 2 Farrand 73–80, 294–95, 298–301.
[8] Charles Warren, "New Light on the History of the Federal Judiciary Act of 1789," 37 Harv. L. Rev. 49, 67 (1923).
[9] 1 Annals of Congress 762 (August 18, 1789) and 777–78 (August 22, 1789),
[10] Id. at 783 (August 24, 1789).
[11] Id. at 812–13 (August 29, 1789).

decisively rejected a motion to establish only State Courts of Admiralty with no district courts.[12]

The Judiciary Act of 1789 provided for a Chief Justice and five Associate Justices for the Supreme Court. It divided the United States into thirteen districts, with a federal judge for each district, and created three circuits to handle appellate cases: the eastern, middle, and southern circuits. The circuit courts met twice a year in each district and consisted of any two Justices of Supreme Court and one district judge from that circuit. District judges could not vote in any case of appeal or error from their decision. Section 25 of the Judiciary Act also solidified federal control over the states by conferring upon the Supreme Court a supervisory role over state courts.

The Justices of the Supreme Court complained bitterly about their circuit court duties. Riding circuit was an arduous and hazardous enterprise. It was important during this period to select a young man "whose bonds would knit if he chanced to be thrown from his carriage as he made progress over rutty highways."[13] Participation in circuit cases had another drawback: a Justice might have to review his own decision when the case reached the Supreme Court. All six Justices appealed to President Washington and to Congress to reduce their labors. They advised Washington that the burdens placed upon them were "so excessive that we cannot forbear representing them in strong and explicit terms." Although willing to make personal sacrifices, "we cannot reconcile ourselves to the idea of existing in exile from our families."[14] The communication to Congress was even more pointed. The Justices set forth the following objections:

> That the task of holding twenty-seven circuit courts a year, in the different States, from New Hampshire to Georgia, besides two sessions of the Supreme Court at Philadelphia, in the two most severe seasons of the year, is a task which, considering the extent of the United States, and the small number of judges, is too burdensome.
>
> That to require of the judges to pass the greater part of their days on the road, and at inns, and at a distance from their

[12]Id. at 834 (August 31, 1789).

[13]Charles Fairman, "The Retirement of Federal Judges," 51 Harv. L. Rev. 397, 404–5 (1938).

[14]1 Am. State Papers 51–52 (1834).

families, is a requisition which, in their opinion, should not be made unless in cases of necessity.

That some of the present judges do not enjoy health and strength of body to enable them to undergo the toilsome journeys through different climates and seasons, which they are called upon to undertake; nor is it probable that any set of judges, however robust, would be able to support, and punctually execute, such severe duties for any length of time.[15]

Congress offered modest relief in 1793 by allowing the attendance of only one Justice for the holding of circuit court.[16] Circuit riding did have one advantage: it allowed Justices to influence public opinion. During their instructions to grand juries, it was not uncommon for members of the Supreme Court to go beyond the formal charge and push ideas of civic virtues and other political values.[17]

With six Justices to cover three circuits, each Justice now had to ride circuit only once a year. Pressure for relief resulted in the ill-fated Judiciary Act of 1801, which divided the country into six circuits and promised to terminate circuit riding by creating sixteen circuit judges. President John Adams elevated six district judges to those positions and also named three Senators and one Representative to the vacant district judgeships.[18]

Although the creation of circuit judges had been proposed for several years, the statute creating them was not signed until the closing days of the Adams administration. After President Adams hastily filled the positions and allotted them to loyal Federalists, the Jeffersonains condemned the "midnight judges bill" as unconscionable. They accused the Federalists of trying to accomplish through judicial appointments what had just been denied them in the national election. The judiciary appeared to be a "hospital for worn-out political parties."[19] The Judiciary Act of 1801 also reduced the number of Supreme Court Justices from six to five, effective with the next vacancy. The reduction might have been justified because the work of the

[15]Id. at 52.

[16]1 Stat. 333 (1793).

[17]Ralph Lerner, "The Supreme Court as Republican Schoolmaster," 1967 Sup. Ct. Rev. 127.

[18]Max Farrand, "The Judiciary Act of 1801," 5 Am. Hist. Rev. 682 (1900); 2 Stat. 89, § 7 (1801).

[19]William A. Sutherland, "Politics and the Supreme Court," 48 Am. L. Rev. 390, 394 (1914).

Justices had been cut back by eliminating circuit duties.[20] Moreover, five Justices would avoid the possibility of tie votes. Jeffersonians interpreted the change less charitably. The reduction decreased Jefferson's opportunity to appoint his own candidate to the High Court. The new Congress promptly repealed the Judiciary Act of 1801.

The size of the Supreme Court fluctuated throughout the nineteenth century. A seventh Justice was added in 1807 to reflect the creation of a new judicial circuit. The size of the Supreme Court rose to nine in 1837, again reflecting the westward expansion, and to ten by 1863 (to accommodate the Pacific circuit). Three years later Congress lowered the permanent size of the Court to seven, although the membership never fell below eight. The reduction is usually interpreted as a slap against President Andrew Johnson, depriving him of an opportunity to fill vacancies. The Radical Republicans feared that his appointees to the Court would oppose Reconstruction policies.[21] His nomination of Henry Stanbery as an Associate Justice had to be withdrawn because Congress had reduced the Court's size. But Johnson signed the bill and its legislative history does not suggest an attack on the Court. In fact, Chief Justice Salmon P. Chase, in pursuit of higher salaries for the Supreme Court, supported a reduction to seven members.[22] As a U.S. Senator, Chase had proposed that no vacancies be filled until the court's membership fell to six. He justified this smaller number because of reduced duties once Justices were relieved of their responsibility for riding circuit.[23]

Legislation in 1869 brought the Court back to its present size of nine members. By 1890 the statutory duty of Supreme Court Justices to attend circuit was "practically a dead letter."[24] A major step in judicial reorganization occurred in 1891 when Congress created a separate system of appellate courts, producing three tiers: district (trial) courts, circuit (appellate) courts, and the Supreme Court. A comprehensive "Judges Bill" in 1925 gave the Supreme Court greater discretion to grant or deny petitions of appeal from the lower courts.

[20]S. Rept. No. 711, 75th Cong., 1st Sess. 12 (1937).

[21]Id. at 13.

[22]Charles Fairman, 6 History of the Supreme Court of the United States: Reconstruction and Reunion 163–71 (1971); Cong. Globe, 39th Cong. 3909 (July 18, 1866); Stanley I. Kutler, Judicial Power and Reconstruction Politics 48–63 (1968).

[23]Cong. Globe, 33d Cong., 2d Sess. 216–17 (1855).

[24]Felix Frankfurter and James M. Landis, The Business of the Supreme Court 87 (1928).

By 1891 there were nine circuit courts of appeals. The Tenth Circuit, split from the Eighth, appeared in 1929. When the workload of the Fifth Circuit grew too large, Congress divided it in 1981, forming the Eleventh Circuit. Together with the D.C. Circuit, that made twelve courts of appeals. In 1982 Congress established the Court of Appeals for the Federal Circuit by merging the Court of Claims with the Court of Customs and Patent Appeals. Unlike the other twelve circuits, which cover a specific geographical area and possess general jurisdiction, this newly established court is nationwide and limited in subject matter jurisdiction.

As a means of expediting action, Congress requires the submission of some disputes to a three-judge court consisting of district and appellate judges. Initially these courts were established to limit the interference of federal courts with state statutes. In *Ex parte Young* (1908), the Supreme Court held that an attempt by a state officer to enforce an unconstitutional statute is an action without authority and therefore unprotected by a state's sovereign capacity. The Court concluded that a state had no power to give such officers immunity from federal jurisdiction.[25] This opinion not only broadened the power of the federal courts but allowed a single federal judge to enjoin a state officer from enforcing a state statute.

Congress at first responded by considering a bill to remove injunctive powers from federal district and circuit judges in cases where the state was a party. Senator Lee Overman said in 1908 that "we have come to a sad day when one subordinate Federal judge can enjoin the officer of a sovereign State from proceeding to enforce the laws of the State passed by the legislature of his own State, and thereby suspending for a time the laws of the State."[26] As finally enacted into law, Congress adopted a more moderate approach by requiring three federal judges, including a Supreme Court Justice or a circuit judge, to hear applications to enjoin the enforcement of state statutes on constitutional grounds. Their determinations would be appealable directly to the Supreme Court.[27] The requirement for a Supreme Court Justice was later removed.[28]

[25] 209 U.S. 123 (1908).
[26] 42 Cong. Rec. 4847 (1908).
[27] 36 Stat. 557, § 17 (1910); 36 Stat. 1150, § 266 (1911); 42 Cong. Rec. 4846–59 (1908); 45 Cong. Rec. 7253–57 (1910).
[28] 38 Stat. 220 (1913).

Three-judge courts placed an administrative burden on the federal judiciary, requiring three judges to do what might be done by one. In 1976, Congress eliminated the requirement that three-judge courts be convened whenever an injunction is requested against a state law on constitutional grounds.[29] These courts continue to be used in cases involving legislative apportionment and cases specifically mandated by Congress.[30] Over the years, the jurisdiction of three-judge courts has been cut substantially.[31]

Congress has established various organizations to help the judiciary. In 1922 it created the Judicial Conference to coordinate the legislative requests and administrative actions of the federal courts. Two years after Roosevelt's abortive court-packing scheme in 1937, Congress created judicial councils in each circuit to improve the efficiency of court administration. At the same time, Congress addressed the anomaly, if not impropriety, of having the Justice Department administer the courts, including their budgeting, auditing, and accounting functions. Clearly it was inappropriate for a chief litigant in the courts (the Justice Department) to handle such matters. To eliminate this separation-of-power problem, Congress created the Administrative Office of the United States Courts to take care of the managerial, research, statistical, and budgetary needs of the national judiciary.[32] In 1967, a Federal Judicial Center was set up to study methods of improving judicial administration.[33]

Legislative and Specialized Courts

In addition to "constitutional courts" established by Congress pursuant to Article III of the Constitution, Congress creates other courts to carry out legislative duties. Drawing on various sections of the Constitution, Congress has set up territorial courts, legislative courts, military courts, and the courts of the District of Columbia. Judges

[29]90 Stat. 1119 (1976).

[30]28 U.S.C. § 2284 (1982).

[31]Robert L. Stern and Eugene Gressman, Supreme Court Practice 70–74, 90–98 (1978).

[32]53 Stat. 1223 (1939); 84 Cong. Rec. 5791–93, 9308–10, 9396–97, 9559, 9695–96, 10316, 10386–87 (1939).

[33]81 Stat. 664 (1967).

sitting on those courts are not automatically entitled to the rights of life tenure and irreducible compensation guaranteed to Article III federal judges.

Territorial Courts.   Section 3 of Article IV gives Congress the power "to dispose of and make all needful Rules and Regulations respecting the territory or other Property belonging to the United States." After Spain ceded Florida to the United States in 1819, Congress established a territorial government in Florida and its legislature created a court system that gave judges a term of four years. This system was challenged as a violation of the requirement in Article III that judges serve "during good Behavior." The Supreme Court ruled that the territorial courts of Florida were not constitutional courts. They were legislative courts, created under Section 3 of Article IV.[34]

Under its authority to govern territories, Congress established district courts in the Commonwealth of Puerto Rico and in the Territories of Guam, the Virgin Islands, the former Canal Zone, and the Northern Mariana Islands. The district court of Puerto Rico is classified as an Article III federal district court. Its judges hold office during good behavior; territorial judges serve eight-year terms. Similar to territorial courts are the consular courts established by Congress. The Supreme Court has called these legislative courts, created to carry out the constitutional powers regarding treaties and commerce with foreign nations.[35]

Legislative Courts.   Congress has established a number of Article I, legislative courts. It created the Court of Claims in 1855 to help members of Congress handle the large number of claims presented by citizens against the United States. The responsibility for determining these claims "belongs primarily to Congress as an incident of its power to pay the debts of the United States."[36] At the beginning, the Court of Claims served an advisory role. Members of

---

[34]American Ins. Co. v. Canter, 26 U.S. (1 Pet.) 511, 545 (1828). Also on territorial courts see Benner v. Porter, 9 How. 235 (1850); Hornbuckle v. Toombs, 18 Wall. 648 (1874); Reynolds v. United States, 98 U.S. 145 (1878); The "City of Panama," 101 U.S. 453 (1880); and Romeu v. Todd, 206 U.S. 358 (1907).

[35]Ex parte Bakelite Corp., 279 U.S. 438, 451 (1929), footnote omitted. See In re Ross, 140 U.S. 453 (1891).

[36]Ex parte Bakelite, 279 U.S. at 452.

Congress had to evaluate its recommendations and sift through reams of supporting documents. Subsequent statutes made some of the judgments binding, gradually transforming the Court of Claims from an investigative body to an adjudicatory agency. The ability to issue advisory rulings is one of the tests used by the Supreme Court to distinguish between legislative and constitutional courts: "A duty to give decisions which are advisory only, and so without force as judicial judgments, may be laid on a legislative court, but not on a constitutional court established under Article III."[37] As long as the Court of Claims rendered advisory opinions on legislative questions referred to it by Congress, the Supreme Court treated it as an Article I court. Its judges lacked the constitutional protections of tenure and salary.[38] In 1953, Congress made the Court of Claims an Article III court.[39]

The United States Customs Court also illustrates the congressional need to delegate some of its constitutional responsibilities to other bodies. In 1890, Congress established within the Department of Treasury a Board of General Appraisers to review the decisions of appraisers and collectors at U.S. ports. In 1926 the Board was replaced by the United States Customs Court. There was no change in powers, duties, or even personnel.[40] In 1956 Congress made the Customs Court an Article III court and in 1980 changed its name to the Court of International Trade.[41]

Congress created a Court of Customs Appeal in 1909 to review final decisions of the Board of General Appraisers. The Court was established pursuant to the power of Congress to lay and collect duties on imports.[42] The statute had been silent about judicial tenure. In response to the argument that Congress intended the court to be

[37]Id. at 454, footnote omitted. Because of its advisory nature, the Court of Claims was categorized as a legislative court in Gordon v. United States, 117 U.S. 697 (1864) and in In re Sanborn, 148 U.S. 222 (1893). Some early decisions treated the Court of Claims as an Article III court—e.g., United States v. Union Pacific Co., 98 U.S. 569, 603 (1878)—but the Supreme Court later regarded such remarks as obiter dicta (see Ex parte Bakelite, 279 U.S. at 455).

[38]Williams v. United States, 289 U.S. 553, 569 (1933). See Jeffrey M. Glosser, "Congressional Reference Cases in the United States Court of Claims: An Historical and Current Perspective," 25 Am. U. L. Rev. 595 (1976).

[39]67 Stat. 226 (1953).

[40]Ex parte Bakelite, 279 U.S. at 457.

[41]70 Stat. 532 (1956); 94 Stat. 1727 (1980).

[42]Ex parte Bakelite, 279 U.S. at 458–59.

a constitutional one with judges holding office during good behavior, the Supreme Court rejected that position as "fallacious [for it] mistakenly assumes that whether a court is of one class or the other depends on the intention of Congress, whereas the true test lies in the power under which the court was created and in the jurisdiction conferred."[43] Congress granted the judges life tenure in 1930, a year after the Court's opinion.[44]

Congress had authorized temporary assignments of circuit and district judges to the Court of Customs Appeals when vacancies occurred or when any of its members were disqualified or otherwise unable to act. In 1929 the Supreme Court held this provision invalid, for Congress was not empowered to make the Court of Customs Appeals a constitutional court.[45] In 1958 Congress changed the court (by now called the Court of Customs and Patent Appeals) to an Article III court. Legislation in 1982 folded this court into the Court of Appeals for the Federal Circuit.[46]

The authority of the Supreme Court to exercise appellate jurisdiction over legislative courts depends on the finality of their judgments. If a legislative court merely renders an advisory opinion there is no appeal (and nothing to appeal); constitutional courts should not perform nonjudicial functions.[47] But if a legislative court exercises judicial duties, the Supreme Court may review its decisions.[48] The Court has also held that legislative courts may handle only disputes between government and private citizens in noncriminal matters (except for military crimes). Issues between individuals are matters of private rights to be adjudicated solely by Article III Courts.[49]

From this record it is clear that Congress may choose to resolve questions within its own chambers; delegate them to executive agencies; or vest them in adjudicatory bodies, either Article I or Article III. Functions therefore float from one branch to another as Congress searches for the most effective means of discharging its duties.

[43]Id. at 459.
[44]46 Stat. 590, 762 (1930).
[45]Ex parte Bakelite, 279 U.S. at 460.
[46]72 Stat. 848 (1958); 96 Stat. 25 (1982).
[47]Postum Cereal Co. v. Calif. Fig Nut Co., 272 U.S. 693 (1927); Federal Radio Comm'n v. Gen'l Elec. Co., 281 U.S. 464, 469 (1930).
[48]Pope v. United States, 323 U.S. 1, 13–14 (1944).
[49]Northern Pipeline Const. v. Marathon Pipe Line Co., 458 U.S. 50 (1982). See nn. 24 and 25 in this decision.

What is "legislative" at one stage becomes "administrative" at another and "judicial" still later. The increased authority of the judiciary is due in large measure to these congressional delegations. Despite conventional brickbats hurled at "Government by Judiciary" and the "Imperial Judiciary," the issue is not a simple one of usurpation. A large proportion of the decisions made by courts result from statutory assignments.

The United States Tax Court is one of the few legislative courts to retain its Article I status. Created in 1924 as the Board of Tax Appeals, it was placed within the Treasury Department as "an independent agency in the executive branch of the Government."[50] In 1929 the Supreme Court regarded the Board of Tax Appeals not as a court but as an executive or administrative board.[51] Studies treated it "for all practical purposes" as a legislative court.[52] Legislation in 1942 and 1969 changed the name of the Board to the "Tax Court of the United States" and gave it Article I status.[53] All decisions of the Tax Court, other than small tax cases, are subject to review by the United States Court of Appeals and by the Supreme Court.

Military Courts. A third class of specialized courts derives from the power of Congress under Article I, Section 8, to "make Rules for the Government and Regulation of the land and naval Forces." Congress had provided that criminal behavior in the military shall be tried by court-martial proceedings, not by courts established under Article III. The United States Court of Military Appeals, composed of three judges with fifteen-year terms, is an Article I court. Military courts need not satisfy all of the specific procedural protections offered by Article III courts.[54]

In 1969 the Supreme Court attempted to subject certain military questions to the jurisdiction of civilian courts. It held that to be under military jurisdiction, a crime must be "service connected." Otherwise, members of the military are entitled to a civilian trial, includ-

[50]43 Stat. 338 (1924).

[51]Old Colony Trust Co. v. Commissioner of Internal Revenue, 279 U.S. 716, 725 (1929).

[52]Robert E. Cushman, "The Constitutional Status of the Independent Regulatory Commissions," 24 Corn. L. Q. 13, 44 (1938).

[53]56 Stat. 957 (1942); 83 Stat. 30 (1969).

[54]Palmore v. United States, 411 U.S. 389, 404 (1973).

130

ing the benefits of an indictment by grand jury and trial by jury.[55] In his dissent, Justice Harlan (joined by Stewart and White) said that the Court "has grasped for itself the making of a determination which the Constitution has placed in the hands of the Congress, and that in so doing the Court has thrown the law in this realm into a demoralizing state of uncertainty."[56]

Harlan's arrow was well aimed. So confusing was the service-connected doctrine that the Court abandoned it in 1987. Jurisdiction of a court-martial now depends solely on the accused's status as a member of the armed forces.[57] The Court announced that Congress "has primary responsibility for the delicate task of balancing the rights of servicemen against the needs of the military."[58] The three dissenters—Justices Marshall, Brennan, and Blackmun—recognized that it was up to Congress "to avoid the consequences of this case."[59] In other recent decisions involving the rights of members of the military, the Court stated that remedies lie with Congress, not with the courts.[60]

District of Columbia Courts. Under Article I, Section 8, Congress exercises "exclusive Legislation in all Cases whatsoever, over such District." The Supreme Court has recognized that congressional power over the District of Columbia "encompasses the *full* authority of government, and thus, necessarily, the Executive and Judicial powers as well as the Legislative."[61] Initially the Court regarded the D.C. courts as legislative, not constitutional.[62] As late as 1930 the Supreme Court stated that D.C. courts "are not created under the judiciary article of the Constitution but are legislative courts. . . ."[63] Yet three years later the Court reasoned that because the district was formed

---

[55]O'Callahan v. Parker, 395 U.S. 258 (1969).

[56]Id. at 275.

[57]Solorio v. United States, 107 S.Ct. 2924 (1987).

[58]Id. at 2931.

[59]Id. at 2941.

[60]United States v. Johnson, 107 S.Ct. 2063 (1987); United States v. Stanley, 107 S.Ct. 3054 (1987).

[61]Northern Pipeline Const. v. Marathon Pipe Line Co., 458 U.S. at 76. Emphasis in original.

[62]Keller v. Potomac Electric Power Co., 261 U.S. 428, 441–43 (1923); Postum Cereal Co. v. Calif. Fig Nut Co., 272 U.S. 693, 700 (1927); Ex parte Bakelite Corp., 279 U.S. 438, 450 (1929).

[63]Federal Radio Comm'n v. Gen'l Elec. Co., 281 U.S. 464, 468 (1930).

from territory belonging to Maryland and Virginia, District inhabitants should continue to enjoy their former constitutional rights and protections. Therefore, D.C. courts were considered constitutional courts established under Article III.[64]

In 1973 the Supreme Court narrowed its decision by distinguishing between two classes of D.C. courts: federal courts with Article III judges (the U.S. District Court for the District of Columbia and the U.S. Court of Appeals for the D.C. Circuit) and strictly local courts created pursuant to Article I (the Superior Court and the D.C. Court of Appeals). Defendants charged with a felony under the D.C. Code may be tried by a judge who lacks Article III protections of tenure and salary. The Court compared a District resident to that of a citizen in any other state charged with violating a state criminal law. Citizens in the D.C. courts are "no more disadvantaged and no more entitled to an Art. III judge than any other citizen of any of the 50 States who is tried for a strictly local crime."[65]

Bankruptcy Courts.   The demarcation between Article I and III courts remains a source of disagreement among Justices of the Supreme Court. In 1982 the Court struck down as unconstitutional a court system created by Congress in 1978 to handle thousands of bankruptcy cases. Previously, federal district courts relied on referees (called "judges") to conduct bankruptcy proceedings. The referee's final order could be appealed to a district court. The 1978 legislation eliminated the referee system and established a bankruptcy court in each federal district. The judges of those courts were appointed by the President (subject to Senate advice and consent) for fourteen-year terms and could be removed by the judicial council of the circuit. Their salaries could be decreased by Congress. Technically, the bankruptcy courts were not considered a legislative court but an "adjunct" to the district court.

In 1982 the Supreme Court denied that Congress could establish specialized courts to carry out every one of its Article I powers. Although Congress has constitutional authority under Article I, Section 8, to establish "uniform Laws on the subject of Bankruptcies throughout the United States," this authority did not permit Con-

[64]O'Donoghue v. United States, 289 U.S. 516 (1933).
[65]Palmore v. United States, 411 U.S. at 410.

gress to rely on a non-Article III court. Such reasoning, said the Court, "threatens to supplant completely our system of adjudication in independent Art. III tribunals and replace it with a system of 'specialized' legislative courts."[66] Laws respecting bankruptcy, unlike the limited geographical area of the District of Columbia, "are clearly laws of national applicability and affairs of national concern."[67] Nor were the bankruptcy courts comparable with the federal magistrates established by Congress and upheld by the Court in 1980.[68] The responsibilities of magistrates were far more narrow, and they were appointed and subject to removal by the district court.[69] The Court concluded that the Bankruptcy Act of 1978 had removed essential attributes of judicial power from the Article III district court and vested them in a non-Article III body.[70]

If the statute was defective, the judiciary shared the blame. After the House of Representatives had given bankruptcy judges life tenure within an Article III system, federal judges lobbied to defeat that proposal in the Senate. They did not want bankruptcy judges elevated to their status.[71] The Court delayed the effectiveness of its decision for three months to give Congress time to pass remedial legislation. After Congress failed to pass legislation within the time allotted by the Court (again because federal judges opposed the conversion of bankruptcy judges to Article III status), the bankruptcy courts operated under interim rules issued by the Judicial Conference. Ironically, the result of the Court's separation-of-powers decision was a concentration of power in the courts. The bankruptcy courts operated on an emergency rule written by the judiciary; the courts sustained that rule after it was challenged in lawsuits; and the rule was administered by the courts.

Two years after the Supreme Court's decision, Congress finally

[66]Northern Pipeline Const. v. Marathon Pipe Line Co., 458 U.S. at 73.

[67]Id. at 2874.

[68]United States v. Raddatz, 447 U.S. 667 (1980). In 1983 the Ninth Circuit held that the 1979 amendments to the Magistrates Act, allowing magistrates to enter final judgments without de novo review by the district courts, violated Article III of the Constitution; Pacemaker Diagnostic Clinic of America v. Instromedix, 712 F.2d 1305 (9th Cir. 1983). On rehearing, however, the en banc court decided that consent of the parties cured any constitutional defects; 725 F.2d 537 (9th Cir. 1984).

[69]Northern Pipeline Const. v. Marathon Pipe Line Co., 458 U.S. at 82–83.

[70]Id. at 87.

[71]Jonathan C. Rose, "Shortsightedness Plagues Bankruptcy Courts' History," Legal Times, February 27, 1984, at 16.

passed legislation to reinstate the bankruptcy courts. When President Reagan signed the bill, he questioned several of its provisions. The Justice Department had advised him that the provision seeking to continue in office all existing bankruptcy judges was inconsistent with the appointments clause of the Constitution.[72] The authority of all sitting bankruptcy judges had expired several weeks before the bill was signed into law. The administration therefore argued that Congress had "appointed" about two hundred judges by reinstating the courts.[73] Although Congress passed amendments to the bankruptcy statute, it did not satisfy Reagan's objections.[74]

The strict reading of the Supreme Court on bankruptcy judges should not obscure the extent of adjudication that takes place outside Article III courts. In 1985, the Court in a unanimous decision upheld the arbitration provision of the Federal Insecticide, Fungicide, and Rodenticide Act. The Court decided that agency adjudication posed only a minimum threat to Article III judicial powers: "practical attention to substance rather than doctrinaire reliance on formal categories should inform application of Article III."[75]

A year later the Court upheld another case of agency adjudication. In 1976, as a means of promoting the congressional goal of resolving disputes in an efficient manner, the Commodity Futures Trading Commission issued a regulation allowing it to adjudicate counterclaims. A typical dispute would involve a customer bringing a claim against a broker, charging that a debit in the customer's account resulted from the broker's violation of the Commodity Exchange Act. The broker would then file a counterclaim, explaining that the debit reflected the customer's lack of success in the market. The Supreme Court, by a 7-to-2 vote, refused to adopt "formalistic and unbending rules" to decide the separation of power issue.[76] Such rules might "unduly constrict Congress' ability to take needed and innovative action pursuant to its Article I powers."[77] The Court avoided a doctrinaire insistence that every adjudicatory function be discharged by an Article III court. A number of factors were weighed "with an eye to

[72] 20 Wkly Comp. Pres. Doc. 1011 (July 10, 1984).

[73] C.Q. Wkly Rept., July 7, 1984, p. 1665.

[74] 98 Stat. 2704 (1984). See 20 Wkly Comp. Pres. Doc. 1580 (October 19, 1984).

[75] Thomas v. Union Carbide Agric. Products, 473 U.S. 568, 587 (1985).

[76] Commodity Futures Trading Commission v. Schor, 106 U.S. 3245, 3258 (1986).

[77] Id.

the practical effect that the congressional action will have on the constitutionally assigned role of the federal judiciary."[78]

The Appointment Process

The delegates at the Constitutional Convention rejected the British system of executive appointment, associating it with official corruption and debasement of the judiciary. Initially they decided to place the power to select judges with Congress. Next they considered vesting that responsibility solely in the Senate. Only late in the Convention did they settle on joint action by the President and the Senate.[79] The President, under Article II of the Constitution, shall nominate "and by and with the Advice and Consent of the Senate, shall appoint . . . Judges of the Supreme Court." The Constitution also permits Congress to vest the appointment of "inferior officers" in the President alone, in the courts, or in the head of the executive departments.

Subjecting federal judges to presidential nomination and Senate confirmation creates an intensely political process. Appointments to the Supreme Court "are highly political appointments by the nation's chief political figure to a highly political body."[80] From an early date, Senators wielded considerable power in choosing nominees for federal judgeships. Members of the Supreme Court (especially Chief Justice Taft) have lobbied vigorously for their candidates. Other sectors of government are active. An unusually candid judge remarked: "A judge is a lawyer who knew a governor."[81] Private organizations participate. The American Bar Association (ABA), organized in 1878, plays a key role. Its influence increased during the Truman administration when it established a special committee to judge the professional qualifications of candidates. Acting on names submitted by the

[78]Id.

[79]1 Farrand 21, 63, 119–28, 232–33; 1 Farrand 41–44, 80–83, 121. See John Ferling, "The Senate and Federal Judges," 2 Capitol Studies 57 (1974).

[80]Michael A. Kahn, "The Politics of the Appointment Process: An Analysis of Why Learned Hand Was Never Appointed to the Supreme Court," 25 Stan. L. Rev. 251, 283 (1973).

[81]Fred Rodell, Woe Unto You, Lawyers! 36 (1939).

Attorney General, the committee informs the chairman of the Senate Judiciary Committee whether a nominee to the Supreme Court fits the category of "well qualified," "not opposed," or "not qualified." The ABA categories for the lower courts are "exceptionally well qualified," "well qualified," "qualified," or "not qualified."[82]

President Carter altered the selection process for appellate judges by establishing nominating panels. They were directed to recommend five candidates for each vacancy, allowing the President to select the nominee. As part of an accommodation, Senators continued to control nominations for district judges, although some opted for a panel system. Through this procedure, Carter was able to place on the federal courts an unprecedented number of blacks, women, and Hispanics, far exceeding the record of previous Presidents.[83] When President Reagan took office, he abolished the judicial nominating commissions for appellate judges. The effect was to increase the Senate's influence. He also placed far less emphasis on recruiting women and minorities.[84]

The power to nominate Supreme Court Justices can produce sudden shifts in judicial policy. Slight changes in the composition of the Supreme Court have reversed previous ruling. In 1870 the Court reviewed a congressional statute that treated paper money as legal tender for discharging prior debts. Voting 4 to 3, the Court declared the statute unconstitutional. The partisanship that raged throughout the post–Civil War period did not bypass the courts. The four Justices in the majority were Democrats; the three dissenters were Republicans. In the lower federal courts, almost every Democratic judge pronounced the statute unconstitutional, whereas nearly every Republican judge sustained it.[85]

---

[82]See Joel B. Grossman, Lawyers and Judges: The ABA and the Politics of Judicial Selection (1965); Harold W. Chase, Federal Judges: The Appointing Process (1972); American Bar Association, Standing Committee on Federal Judiciary 4–5, 8 (1983).

[83]Sheldon Goldman, "Carter's Judicial Appointments: A Lasting Legacy," 64 Judicature 344 (1981).

[84]David F. Pike, "A New Way of Selecting U.S. Judges," National Law Journal, September 14, 1981, at 3, 17, 21; David F. Pike, "The Court-Packing Plans," National Law Journal, August 29, 1983, at 1, 26, 27, 31; W. Gary Fowler, "Judicial Selection Under Reagan and Carter: A Comparison of Their Initial Recommendation Procedures," 67 Judicature 265 (1984).

[85]Hepburn v. Griswold, 8 Wall. (75 U.S.) 603 (1870); Charles Fairman, "Mr. Justice Bradley's Appointment to the Supreme Court and the Legal Tender Cases," 54 Harv. L. Rev. 1128, 1131 (1941).

The retirement of Justice Grier and the authorization by Congress the previous year of a new Justice allowed President Grant to appoint two members. His first two appointments were ill-starred. The Senate rejected his Attorney General, Ebenezer Hoar, while his second nominee, Edwin Stanton, died four days after being confirmed.[86] Those nominations were made before the Court's decision. He had reason to believe that his next two appointments, submitted after the decision, would support the statute. William Strong, as a member of the Supreme Court of Pennsylvania, had already sustained the Legal Tender Act. Joseph P. Bradley appeared to be no less sympathetic. Fifteen months after the Legal Tender Act had been declared unconstitutional, the reconstituted Court upheld the Act by a 5 to 4 margin. Strong and Bradley joined the original three dissenters to form the majority; the four Justices who decided the case in 1870 now found themselves in the minority.[87]

The transition from the Warren Court to the Burger Court also produced reversals of prior decisions (or efforts by the Court to "distinguish" prior holdings for current judicial policy). In 1971, a 5 to 4 majority—including two newcomers, Chief Justice Burger and Justice Blackmun—upheld a statutory procedure that stripped an individual of his citizenship. The Court thus narrowed earlier holdings that citizenship could not be taken away unless voluntarily renounced.[88] Justice Black protested that Fourteenth Amendment protections for American citizenship "should not be blown around by every passing political wind that changes the composition of this Court."[89]

No doubt Black was frustrated by policy shifts from the Warren Court to the Burger Court, but he himself had been part of the Roosevelt nominations that helped chart a new course in constitutional interpretation. In 1974, when Nixon appointments to the Supreme Court helped reverse a decision announced two years earlier, Justice Stewart remarked: "A basic change in the law upon a ground no firmer than a change in our membership invites the popular mis-

---

[86]S. Rept. No. 711, 75th Cong., 1st Sess. 13 (1937).
[87]Legal Tender Cases, 12 Wall. (79 U.S.) 457 (1871). See Sidney Ratner, "Was the Supreme Court Packed by President Grant?," 50 Pol. Sci. Q. 343 (1935).
[88]Schneider v. Rusk, 377 U.S. 163 (1964); Afroyim v. Rusk, 387 U.S. 253 (1967).
[89]Rogers v. Bellei, 401 U.S. 815, 837 (1971) (dissenting opinion).

conception that this institution is little different from the two political branches of the government."[90]

Although it may be disconcerting that decisions sometimes turn on the most recent appointments, changes in the Court's composition enable it to incorporate contemporary ideas and attitudes. Justice Jackson denied that this fact did any violence to the notion of an independent, nonpolitical judiciary:

> . . . let us not deceive ourselves; long-sustained public opinion does influence the process of constitutional interpretation. Each new member of the ever-changing personnel of our courts brings to his task the assumptions and accustomed thought of a later period. The practical play of the forces of politics is such that judicial power has often delayed but never permanently defeated the persistent will of a substantial majority.[91]

The Senate has refused to confirm almost one out of every five presidential nominations to the Supreme Court. Twenty-five nominees have either been rejected, had their names submitted without Senate action, or been forced to withdraw. Most of those actions (eighteen) occurred before 1900. After the Senate rejected John J. Parker in 1930, confirmation of Supreme Court nominees seemed an automatic step. That pattern ended in 1968 when the Senate refused to advance Associate Justice Abe Fortas to the position of Chief Justice. Fortas, subjected to embarrassing questions about his acceptance of fees from private parties, eventually asked President Johnson to withdraw his nomination. Homer Thornberry, picked by Johnson to fill Fortas's seat as Associate Justice, then withdrew his name. A year later, with impeachment proceedings gearing up against him because of financial and personal improprieties, Fortas resigned from the Court.[92]

The Supreme Court remained embroiled in political controversy

[90]Mitchell v. W. T. Grant Co., 416 U.S. 600, 636 (1974), reversing Fuentes v. Shevin, 407 U.S. 67 (1972).

[91]Robert H. Jackson, "Maintaining Our Freedoms: The Role of the Judiciary," delivered to the American Bar Association, Boston, Massachusetts, August 24, 1953; reprinted in *Vital Speeches*, No. 24, Vol. xix, p. 761 (October 1, 1953).

[92]William F. Swindler, "The Politics of 'Advice and Consent,'" 56 A.B.A.J. 533 (1970) and Robert Shogun, A Question of Judgment: The Fortas Case and the Struggle for the Supreme Court (1972).

in 1969 when the Senate rejected Nixon's nomination of Clement F. Haynsworth, Jr., to the Supreme Court. The ethical test applied by Republicans against Fortas was now turned against Haynsworth by Democrats. A year later the Senate rejected Nixon's next nominee, G. Harrold Carswell, who lacked the qualifications for Associate Justice. In 1971, after the resignations of Hugo Black and John Harlan, Nixon made matters still worse by considering a list of candidates who were clearly unqualified for the High Bench.[93] Nixon finally nominated Lewis Powell, Jr., and William Rehnquist, both of whom the Senate confirmed.

The emphasis given by Nixon to the sociopolitical views of judicial candidates merely underscores the entanglement of law and politics. Senators, too, in expressing their advice and consent, feel at liberty to evaluate a nominee's political and constitutional philosophy in order to maintain a balance of views on the Court.[94] As shown by the hearings in 1981 on the nomination of Sandra Day O'Connor to the Court, her personal and judicial philosophy on the exceedingly sensitive issue of abortion was a matter of recurrent interest to Senators and one on which she was willing to state her views. Although she told the Senate Judiciary Committee that the personal views and philosophies of a judge "should be set aside insofar as it is possible to do that in resolving matters that come before the Court," and that issues should be decided on the facts of a particular case and the law applicable to those facts, she said that "my own view in the area of abortion is that I am opposed to it as a matter of birth control or otherwise."[95]

The Senate's rejection of two nominees by Nixon to the Supreme Court was duplicated in 1987. President Reagan nominated Judge Robert H. Bork, a conservative member of the D.C. Circuit, to replace the more moderate Justice Powell. All observers recognized this as a critical nomination, especially after Reagan's selection of Sandra Day O'Connor in 1981, Antonin Scalia in 1986, and the elevation of William Rehnquist as Chief Justice in 1986. Powell, a cen-

[93]James F. Simon, In His Own Image: The Supreme Court in Richard Nixon's America 215–51 (1973).

[94]Senate Committee on the Judiciary, "Advice and Consent on Supreme Court Nominations," 94th Cong., 2d Sess. (Committee Print 1976). See L. A. Powe, Jr., "The Senate and the Court: Questioning a Nominee," 54 Tex. L. Rev 891 (1976).

[95]"Nomination of Sandra Day O'Connor," hearings before the Senate Committee on the Judiciary, 97th Cong., 1st Sess. 60–61 (1981).

trist, had supplied a swing vote on the Burger Court. The addition of Bork might allow conservatives on the Court to reverse a number of important decisions, including the abortion case of 1973.

In his writings and speeches, Bork had used blunt, pungent, and provocative language to challenge previous Court rulings in the areas of civil rights, women's rights, the First Amendment, abortion, privacy, reapportionment, and criminal law. The NAACP announced its opposition to Bork, as did women's groups and other organizations, including the influential People for the American Way. The ACLU decided to set aside its fifty-one-year policy of not taking stands on Supreme Court nominees and promptly voted unanimously to oppose Bork.

Bork's fortunes slipped from week to week. The ABA committee supplied a split vote, ten supporting him as "well qualified," four finding him "not qualified," and one voting "not opposed" (which means minimally qualified and not among the best available). The White House made a tactical blunder by trying to paint Bork as a moderate. Because of this label, conservative groups were unable to mobilize their support. Opponents of Bork charged that he had made a "confirmation conversion," raising questions of integrity and consistency. That issue was reinforced when Bork described his earlier ventures into socialism and libertarianism.

Senate Democrats had gained control of the Senate in 1986, allowing them to decide the witness list and map out a hearings strategy. In that election, a number of conservative Republican Senators from the south were replaced by moderate Democrats. The Democrats voted against Bork for several reasons. Because Reagan campaigned against them, they owed him nothing. The black vote was an important factor in the victories of southern Democrats. Also for his part, Bork failed to convince the wavering southern Senators that he had a consistent judicial philosophy. On numerous occasions he gave the appearance of backtracking ("recanting") on key issues. How Bork's theory of "original intent" would be applied was left in doubt. The Senate Judiciary Committee voted 9 to 5 to reject him; the vote in the full Senate for rejection was 58 to 42.

After this defeat, Reagan announced on October 29, 1987, the nomination of Judge Douglas H. Ginsburg of the D.C. Circuit. Reagan's announcement was truculent, combative, and spiteful. When the Senate began to examine Ginsburg's credentials, his qualifications were of modest dimensions: age 41, less than a year on the bench, and little contribution to constitutional law beyond antitrust and government regulation. For his nomination to the D.C. Circuit he claimed that he had appeared in court 34 times to try a case to judgment. In fact, his total courtroom experience amounted to an hour-long appellate court argument. It was also disclosed that he owned $140,000 in cable television stock while handling cable television matters in the Justice Department, raising serious questions of conflict of interest. When he admitted smoking marijuana into his thirties, as a professor of law, the support in the conservative community completely evaporated. This disclosure was particularly damaging because of Reagan's strong campaign against drugs and the administration's heavy emphasis on law and order. Within nine days of the nomination, Reagan received Ginsburg's request to withdraw his name.

The Senate is denied a role in the confirmation process when the President makes recess appointments to the Supreme Court. Under Article II, Section 2, the President "shall have Power to fill up all Vacancies that may happen during the Recess of the Senate, by granting Commissions which may expire at the End of their next Session." During the 1950s, President Eisenhower placed three men on the Supreme Court while the Senate recessed: Earl Warren, William J. Brennan, Jr., and Potter Stewart. All three joined the Court and participated in decisions before the Senate had an opportunity to review their qualifications and vote to confirm. In each case the Senate gave its advice and consent, but the experience convinced most Senators that the procedure was unhealthy both for the Senate and the Court.

A report by the House Judiciary Committee in 1959 pointed out that more than fifty federal judges serving at that time went on the bench under recess appointments by Presidents Coolidge through Eisenhower. The report concluded that recess appointments of federal judges violated the principle of lifetime tenure. How could federal judges serving under a recess appointment maintain total independence of mind? If a judge is to be questioned by a Senate committee during confirmation hearings, that might influence the direction and content of his or her decision. A nominee who declined a recess appointment to the federal judiciary volunteered this com-

141

ment: "I do not think a judge should have to look over his shoulder to see whom he may be offending by his decision."[96]

In 1960 Senator Philip Hart introduced a resolution to discourage recess appointments to the courts. Opponents of the resolution argued that the President had to make recess appointments because of the heavy judicial workload. The Senate passed the resolution, 48 to 37, voting essentially along party lines. The resolution stated the sense of the Senate that the making of recess appointments to the Supreme Court "may not be wholly consistent with the best interests of the Supreme Court, the nominee who may be involved, the litigants before the Court, nor indeed the people of the United States, and that such appointments, therefore, should not be made except under unusual circumstances and for the purpose of preventing or ending a demonstrable breakdown in the administration of the Court's business."[97] Although the resolution is not legally binding, no President after Eisenhower has made recess appointments to the Supreme Court.

The President's constitutional authority to make recess appointments to the federal courts was upheld by the Second Circuit in 1962.[98] However, in 1983 a panel of the Ninth Circuit (building on the Supreme Court's bankruptcy court decision of the previous year) held that the President's constitutional power under Article II to make recess appointments could not supplant the lifetime tenure granted judges under Article III. Federal judges serving under a recess appointment lacked the independence required by the Constitution to exercise judicial power.[99] The panel was reversed in 1985 by an en banc ruling of the Ninth Circuit. The full court found no reason to favor one Article of the Constitution over another. The President's recess appointment power was of general character. There was no basis "to carve out an exception from the recess power for federal judges."[100] Moreover, recess appointments of federal judges had been practiced for almost two hundred years. The court claimed that the

---

[96]House Committee on the Judiciary, "Recess Appointments of Federal Judges" (Committee Print January 1959), at iii. See Note, "Recess Appointments to the Supreme Court—Constitutional But Unwise?," 10 Stan. L. Rev. 124 (1957).

[97]106 Cong. Rec. 18130–45 (1960).

[98]United States v. Allocco, 305 F.2d 704 (2d Cir. 1962), cert. denied, 371 U.S. 964 (1963).

[99]United States v. Woodley, 726 F.2d 1328 (9th Cir. 1983).

[100]United States v. Woodley, 751 F.2d 1008, 1010 (9th Cir. 1985), cert. denied, 106 S.Ct. 1269 (1986).

historical record demonstrated "an unbroken acceptance of the President's use of the recess power to appoint federal judges by the three branches of government."[101] The court took no notice of the Senate's action in 1960. Although there have been approximately three hundred judicial recess appointments since 1789,[102] the dissenters noted that there had been only one such appointment since 1964.[103]

There is no agreement on the qualifications appropriate for judicial appointments. Two giants on the Supreme Court, Oliver Wendell Holmes and Benjamin Cardozo, had years of experience as state judges. The "greatness" of the Supreme Court Justice, however, does not seem to depend on prior judicial experience. Some of the most prominent members of the Court, including John Marshall, Joseph Story, Samuel Miller, Charles Evans Hughes, Louis D. Brandeis, Harlan F. Stone, Hugo Black, William O. Douglas, Robert H. Jackson, Felix Frankfurter, and Earl Warren, had no previous experience either as a state or federal judge. Justice Frankfurter believed that it could be said "without qualification that the correlation between prior judicial experience and fitness for the Supreme Court is zero."[104] Competence turns less on technical mastery than on experience in public affairs and broad political understanding.

Tenure and Removal

Under Article III of the Constitution, judges "both of the supreme and inferior Courts, shall hold their Offices during good Behaviour." Article I gives the House of Representatives the sole power of impeachment and the Senate has the sole power to try all impeachments. A two-thirds majority of the Senate is required for conviction. Judges may be removed from office "on Impeachment for, and Conviction of, Treason, Bribery, or other high Crimes and Misdemeanors."

The impeachment process is cumbersome and suitable only for

[101]Id. at 1011.
[102]Id.
[103]Id. at 1024.
[104]Felix Frankfurter, "The Supreme Court in the Mirror of Justices," 105 U. Pa. L. Rev. 781, 795 (1957). See Loren P. Beth, "Judge into Justice: Should Supreme Court Appointees Have Judicial Experience?," 58 So. Atl. Q. 521 (1959).

grave offenses. The need to remove judges for lesser offenses has long been recognized. In Federalist 79, Alexander Hamilton said that "insanity, without any formal or express provision, may be safely pronounced to be a virtual disqualification" for federal judges. However, he did not explain how judges would be removed for that cause. If insanity is a basis for removal, what of senility, incompetence, disability, alcoholism, laziness, and other deficiences that may fall short of an impeachable offense?[105]

A rare example of a federal judge impeached and removed from office occurred in 1803 in the case of John Pickering. He was charged with misconduct in a trial and for being on the bench while intoxicated.[106] Supreme Court Justice Samuel Chase was impeached in 1804 but acquitted. Actions were brought against a number of other federal judges, many of whom preferred to resign from office rather than defend themselves against the charges.[107] Still other federal judges withdrew quietly from the bench before prosecutors could launch a full-scale investigation.[108]

To encourage aged and infirm judges to leave the bench, Congress passed legislation in 1869 to authorize the payment of full salary to any federal judge who resigned at or after age 70 after completing at least ten years service on the bench.[109] For Justices with less than the required ten years, Congress has passed special statutes to provide full retirement benefits. One example is Justice Ward Hunt, whose poor health prevented him from discharging his labors on the Court. After Congress passed a special bill for him in 1882, he resigned.[110]

Article I judges, such as territorial judges, have been removed by Presidents because they were not entitled to life tenure.[111] Article III

[105]See Robert Kramer and Jerome A. Barrow, "The Constitutionality of Removal and Mandatory Retirement Procedures for the Federal Judiciary: The Meaning of 'During Good Behavior,'" 35 G.W. L. Rev. 455 (1970).

[106]3 A. Hinds, Precedents of the House of Representatives §§ 2319–41 (1907).

[107]Carl L. Shipley, "Legislative Control of Judicial Behavior," 35 Law & Contemp. Prob. 178, 190–91 (1970).

[108]Joseph Borkin, The Corrupt Judge 27–28, 120, 181, 200, 200–201, 225, 226, 229, 230, 231, 233, 235, 245, 256, 257 (1962). See also p. 204.

[109]16 Stat. 44, § 5 (1869).

[110]22 Stat. 2 (1882); Charles Fairman, "The Retirement of Federal Justices," 51 Harv. L. Rev. 397 (1938).

[111]United States v. Guthrie, 58 U.S. (17 How). 284, 288–89 (1854); 5 Op. Att'y Gen. 288, 291 (1851); and McAllister v. United States, 141 U.S. 174 (1891).

judges are immune from removal, other than by impeachment. Nevertheless, they are subject to prosecution by the Justice Department for criminal offenses. The First Congress passed legislation requiring that judges convicted of accepting a bribe "shall forever be disqualified to hold any office of honour, trust or profit under the United States."[112] Moreover, any federal judge who engages in the practice of law "is guilty of a high misdemeanor."[113]

Criminal prosecutions have been used to drive corrupt judges from the bench. Senior Judge Martin T. Manton of the Second Circuit resigned in 1939 after Thomas E. Dewey, then a young district attorney, uncovered actions that amounted to the sale of a judicial office. Manton was convicted for taking bribes, borrowing money from litigants, and engaging in other practices to shore up his intricate and shaky financial empire. In his appeal to the Supreme Court, Manton offered an imaginative argument against his prosecution: "From a broad viewpoint, it serves no public policy for a high judicial officer to be convicted of a judicial crime. It tends to destroy the confidence of the people in the courts."[114] And so it does.

In 1973, Judge Otto Kerner, Jr., of the Seventh Circuit was found guilty of bribery, perjury, tax evasion, and other crimes, most of which occurred during his previous service as governor of Illinois. On appeal, Kerner argued that the Constitution provided only one way to remove a judge—impeachment. The Seventh Circuit decided that judicial immunity did not exempt judges from the operation of criminal laws and affirmed Kerner's conviction.[115]

Kerner's prosecution primarily concerned his actions before joining the bench. A different issue arose in the early 1980s when the Justice Department charged U.S. District Judge Alcee L. Hastings with criminal activities while sitting as a judge. The Eleventh Circuit decided in 1982 that Hastings could be prosecuted.[116] After a jury acquitted him in 1983, a judicial inquiry panel conducted its own investigation into charges of misconduct. Hastings challenged the constitutionality of this inquiry, claiming that it undermined his independence as a federal judge. Nevertheless, this investigation and

[112]1 Stat. 117, § 21 (1790).
[113]62 Stat. 908, § 454 (1948); 28 U.S.C. § 454 (1982).
[114]Borkin, Corrupt Judge, at 23.
[115]United States v. Isaacs, 493 F.2d 1124 (7th Cir. 1974).
[116]United States v. Hastings, 681 F.2d 706 (11th Cir. 1982), cert. denied, 459 U.S. 1203 (1983).

disciplinary procedure was upheld by the courts.[117] Hastings has encountered continuing difficulties, to be discussed later. In 1984, U.S. District Judge Harry Claiborne was found guilty of income tax evasion.[118] Two years later he was impeached and removed by Congress. In 1986, U.S. District Judge Walter L. Nixon, Jr., of Mississippi was convicted of lying to a federal grand jury.[119]

Once nominated and appointed to the bench, a few judges have been vulnerable to the charge that they violated the "ineligibility clause" of the Constitution. Article I, Section 6, Clause 2, provides that no Senator or Representative "shall, during the Time for which he was elected, be appointed to any Civil Office under the Authority of the United States, which shall have been created, or the Emoluments whereof shall have been encreased during such time." Hugo Black's nomination to the Supreme Court in 1937 was challenged because a retirement system for the judiciary had been enacted that year while Black served as U.S. Senator. The Supreme Court avoided the issue by holding that the plaintiff in this case, an attorney who practiced before the Court, lacked standing to bring suit.[120]

A more recent challenge concerned Abner Mikva, a member of Congress nominated by President Carter to the D.C. Circuit. Because of Mikva's longtime advocacy of gun control, the National Rifle Association (NRA) spent an estimated $700,000 to block his nomination. Failing that, the NRA went to court and raised the issue of ineligibility. Working through Senator James McClure, who served as plaintiff, the NRA argued that the salaries of federal judges had been increased during Mikva's term in Congress.[121] A three-judge court ruled that McClure lacked standing to challenge the validity of an appointment of a federal judge. The court said that McClure and his colleagues had had their opportunity to vote against Mikva's confirmation. Senators on the losing side could not then ask the judiciary to reverse the Senate's action.[122]

---

[117]Hastings v. Judicial Conference of United States, 593 F.Supp. 1371 (D.D.C. 1984); In the Matter of Certain Complaints Under Investigation, 783 F.2d 1488 (11th Cir. 1986).

[118]United States v. Claiborne, 727 F.2d 842 (9th Cir. 1984).

[119]Washington Post, February 10, 1986, at A7.

[120]81 Cong. Rec. 9075–76, 9094–96 (1937); Ex parte Levitt, 302 U.S. 633 (1937).

[121]Mark K. Benenson, "A Well-Armed NRA Draws a Bead on High-Caliber Judge," The National Law Journal, October 13, 1980, at 15, 40.

[122]McClure v. Carter, 513 F.Supp. 265 (D. Idaho 1981), aff'd sub. nom. McClure v. Reagan, 454 U.S. 1025 (1981).

Statutory procedures are available for judges to retire on grounds of disability. Any federal judge appointed to hold office during good behavior "who becomes permanently disabled from performing his duties" may retire and be replaced by a presidential appointee, by and with the advice and consent of the Senate. A federal judge retiring under this procedure must certify to the President his disability in writing. If a judge fails to act, a majority of the members of the judicial council of his circuit may sign a certificate of disability and submit it to the President. Once the President finds that the judge is "unable to discharge efficiently all the duties of his office by reason of permanent mental or physical disability," and that an additional judge is needed, the President may make the appointment with the advice and consent of the Senate.[123]

Another provision of the U.S. Code authorizes each judicial council to make all necessary orders for the effective administration of court business. Judges "shall promptly carry into effect all orders of the judicial council."[124] The judicial council for the Tenth Circuit relied on this provision in the 1960s to order Judge Stephen S. Chandler of the Western District of Oklahoma to "take no action whatsoever in any case or proceeding now or hereafter pending in his court." The council had found that Chandler, noted for his eccentric behavior, was unable or unwilling to discharge his judicial duties. The order did not remove Chandler from office; it removed the office from him.

In 1966 the Supreme Court denied an application to stay the council's order. Justices Black and Douglas, in their dissent, argued that Congress did not (and could not) authorize judicial councils to discipline judges and remove their powers. The only constitutional method, they said, was impeachment.[125] The judicial council later modified its order, allowing Chandler to retain his cases but withholding any new assignments. When the Supreme Court denied a motion by Chandler to nullify the modified order, Black and Douglas again dissented.[126]

By 1979, all judicial councils had implemented rules for the processing of complaints against federal judges, but the rules lacked uni-

[123]28 U.S.C. § 372(b) (1982).
[124]Id. at § 332(d).
[125]Chandler v. Judicial Council, 382 U.S. 1003 (1966).
[126]Chandler v. Judicial Council, 398 U.S. 74 (1970). For background on Judge Chandler, see Joseph C. Goulden, The Benchwarmers 206–49 (1974).

147

formity and were silent on key issues. Building on this system, Congress passed legislation in 1980 that assigns to the councils the responsibility for investigating charges against judges. This statutory process is intended to complement the existing impeachment procedure, which Congress considered too cumbersome and unwieldy to deal with most cases of judicial misconduct. Some members argued that impeachment was the only constitutionally permissible means of disciplining federal judges, but Congress passed the bill after careful consideration of the constitutional issues.[127]

The statute contemplates charges of inefficiency or ineffectiveness resulting from mental or physical disability (conditions that may not be impeachable). The legislation does not encompass complaints against the merits of a decision on the conduct of judges unconnected with their judicial duties. The 1980 statute was upheld by a district court in 1984 and by the Eleventh Circuit in 1986.[128] The Eleventh Circuit explained that the statute, far from intruding upon the independence of the judiciary, serves to strengthen the ability of courts to maintain an independent power. Without some form of judicial complaint procedure, short of impeachment, "courts would be virtually alone among public and professional occupations in lacking a means to clean house."[129] The Eleventh Circuit went on to say:

> If judges cannot or will not keep their own house in order, pressures from the public and legislature might result in withdrawal of needed financial support or in the creation of investigatory mechanisms outside the judicial branch which, to a greater degree than the Act, would threaten judicial independence. Considerations of this sort were at the heart of the present legislation.[130]

The 1980 statute also allows a judicial council, after determining that a judge has engaged in conduct constituting one or more grounds

[127]94 Stat. 2035 (1980). See S. Rept. No. 362, 96th Cong., 1st Sess. (1979) and H. Rept. No. 1313, 96th Cong., 2d Sess. (1980).

[128]Hastings v. Judicial Conference of the United States, 593 F.Supp. 1371 (D.D.C. 1984). This decision was vacated in part and remanded in Hastings v. Judicial Conference of the United States, 770 F.2d 1093 (D.C. Cir. 1985). The appellate court ruled that the question of constitutionality on the 1980 statute was premature.

[129]In the Matter of Certain Complaints Under Investigation, 783 F.2d 1488, 1507 (11th Cir. 1986).

[130]Id.

for impeachment, to certify this determination for the Judicial Conference, which may then present a report to the House of Representatives for possible impeachment proceedings. The Eleventh Circuit concluded that the Constitution's grant to the House of Representatives of the exclusive power of impeachment does not prevent Congress from authorizing the judiciary, through its administrative bodies, to conduct an investigation of an Article III judge and present its findings to the House.[131] This statutory procedure was upheld by the D.C. Circuit in 1987.[132] Also in 1987, the Judicial Conference invoked the 1980 statute to vote unanimously for a recommendation to the House of Representatives that it consider impeaching U.S. District Court Judge Alcee L. Hastings.

Compensation

Judicial independence would be short-lived if the salaries of judges could be cut by legislators. Federal judges appointed to Article III courts are entitled to a compensation "which shall not be diminished during their Continuance in Office." In Federalist 79, Hamilton said that next to permanency in office "nothing can contribute more to the independence of the judges than a fixed provision for their support. . . . In the general course of human nature, a power over a man's subsistence amounts to a power over his will." That principle had been embodied in the Declaration of Independence, which attacked the British King for making colonial judges "dependent on his Will alone, for the Tenure of their Offices, and the Amount and Payment of their Salaries."

The no-diminution clause of the Constitution was challenged in 1802 when Congress repealed the judiciary act of the previous year. The effect was to abolish sixteen circuit judges and their salaries. Supporters of the repeal argued that it was irrational to expect a judge to hold office during good behavior and to continue receiving payment if the office no longer existed. A salary could not exist without an office.[133] A case challenging the right of Congress to abolish

---

[131]Id. at 1510–12.

[132]Hastings v. Judicial Conference of U.S., 829 F.2d 91 (D.C. Cir. 1987).

[133]William S. Carpenter, "Repeal of the Judiciary Act of 1801," 9 Am. Pol. Sci. Rev. 519, 524–25 (1951); Richard E. Ellis, The Jeffersonian Crisis: Courts and Politics in the Young Republic 36–38 (1971).

the circuit courts reached the Supreme Court in 1803, but the Court declined to overturn the statute.[134]

The compensation issue was not raised again until 1862, when Congress passed legislation to subject federal salaries to a tax of three percent. Chief Justice Taney wrote to the Secretary of the Treasury, objecting that the measure was unconstitutional and void as applied to federal judges. Although the taxes were collected, in 1869 Attorney General Hoar agreed with Taney's position. The Government discontinued the tax on judges' salaries and distributed refunds. Subsequent tax bills included an exemption for federal judges.[135]

The issue was revived by the Sixteenth Amendment, giving Congress the power to lay and collect taxes on incomes "from whatever source derived." In 1920 the Supreme Court held unconstitutional a federal income tax that had been levied against Article III judges. Justice Holmes, in a dissent that would later become the majority position, denied that the no-diminution clause exonerated federal judges "from the ordinary duties of a citizen." To require someone from the judicial branch to pay taxes like other people "cannot possibly be made an instrument to attack his independence as a judge."[136] Nineteen years later the Supreme Court held that a federal tax could be applied to Article III judges without violating the Constitution. Writing for the majority, Justice Frankfurter said that the objection to including judges in the class of citizens subject to taxation "is to trivialize the great historic experience on which the framers based the safeguards of Article III, § 1."[137]

Retrenchment efforts during the Great Depression triggered new litigation on the no-diminution clause. The Economy Act of 1932 applied percentage reductions to the salaries of all federal employees, including judges except those "whose compensation may not, under the Constitution, be diminished during their continuance in office." The Comptroller General ruled that the salaries of judges of the D.C. Court of Appeals and the D.C. Superior Court could be reduced because they were members of legislative, not constitutional,

---

[134]Stuart v. Laird, 5 U.S. (1 Cr.) 299 (1803). See George L. Haskins, "Law Versus Politics in the Early Years of the Marshall Court," 130 U. Pa. L. Rev. 1, 12 (1981).

[135]13 Op. Att'y Gen. 161 (1869). See Evans v. Gore, 253 U.S. 245, 257–59 (1920).

[136]Evans v. Gore, 253 U.S. at 265.

[137]O'Malley v. Woodrough, 307 U.S. 277, 282 (1939). Footnote omitted.

courts. His decision followed Supreme Court doctrines handed down as recently as 1930.[138] But in 1933 the Supreme Court broke new ground by treating the D.C. judiciary as constitutional courts.[139]

The Supreme Court also held that the Economy Act of 1932 permitted Congress to reduce the compensation of judges of the Court of Claims, considered at that time a legislative court.[140] A year later the Court ruled that Congress could not reduce the *retirement* pay of an Article III judge. The Court noted that retired judges continue to perform judicial duties and are entitled to the protection of the no-diminution clause.[141]

Congress used its power of the purse in 1937 to encourage some of the older, conservative Justices to leave the Supreme Court and make way for replacements by President Franklin D. Roosevelt. Legislation enacted on March 1, 1937, provided for retirement benefits that amounted to full pay at regular salaries, with the stipulation that retired Justices could be called upon by the Chief Justice to perform judicial duties.[142] With this financial incentive, Justice Van Devanter retired in June 1937 and Justice Sutherland in January 1938. Chief Justice Hughes later remarked: "I have reason to believe that they would have retired earlier, had it not been for the failure of Congress to make good its promise to continue to pay in full the salaries of Justices who resigned."[143]

Nothing in the Constitution or caselaw prevents Congress from giving judges a smaller pay raise than other federal employees or no increase at all. In 1964, members of Congress raised their pay by $7,500 while limiting the members of the Supreme Court to an increase of $4,500. The legislative record suggests that some members of Congress may have wanted to use the power of the purse to penalize the Court for its recent decisions. However, the smaller raise for the judiciary could be justified on other grounds: the more generous retirement system for the courts, the need for Congressmen

[138]Federal Radio Comm'n v. Gen'l Elec. Co., 281 U.S. at 468.
[139]O'Donoghue v. United States, 289 U.S. 516 (1933), as modified by Palmore v. United States, 411 U.S. 389 (1973).
[140]Williams v. United States, 289 U.S. 553 (1933).
[141]Booth v. United States, 291 U.S. 339 (1934).
[142]50 Stat. 24 (1937).
[143]David J. Danelski and Joseph S. Tulchin, eds., The Autobiographical Notes of Charles Evans Hughes 302 (1973).

to maintain two residences, and the extra costs they bear in traveling home to see constituents.[144]

As a way to protest their salary levels, 140 federal judges brought an action in the 1970s to claim that their salaries had been diminished unconstitutionally because pay had not kept pace with inflation. The courts found no merit to this argument,[145] but the case did call attention to the problem of adjusting federal salaries. In 1967 Congress decided to forego its periodic efforts to adjust federal salaries and delegated that politically sensitive task to a Quadrennial Commission and the President. Subsequent delegations allowed annual cost-of-living raises to take effect without congressional action. In four consecutive years (1976–1979) Congress passed statutes to stop or reduce authorized cost-of-living increases for all federal employees, including judges. A number of federal judges filed suit, claiming that these actions violated the no-diminution clause of the Constitution. In 1980 the Supreme Court held that Congress, under the provisions of the salary statutes, could disapprove scheduled pay increases for the judiciary provided it acted before October 1 of a new fiscal year (when they automatically took effect). The Court allowed two of the statutory actions taken prior to October 1 and struck down two others that came too late.[146]

As a result of this decision, judicial salaries moved well ahead of executive and legislative pay schedules. Congress retaliated in 1981 by passing legislation to require specific congressional authorization before any future pay raise for federal judges could take effect. The language effectively eliminated future automatic increases for the judiciary.[147] Recent legislation allows judicial salaries to be increased unless Congress, within a thirty-day period, passes a joint resolution of disapproval.[148]

[144]110 Cong. Rec. 17912, 18032–33 (1964). For further details see John R. Schmidhauser and Larry L. Berg, The Supreme Court and Congress 8–12 (1972).

[145]Atkins v. United States, 556 F.2d 1028 (Ct. Cl. 1977), cert. denied, 434 U.S. 1009 (1978).

[146]United States v. Will, 449 U.S. 200 (1980).

[147]95 Stat. 1200, § 140 (1981).

[148]99 Stat. 1322, § 135 (1985).

Judicial Lobbying

To preserve their reputation for impartiality, objectivity, and independence, judges traditionally abstain from political activities that are the daily fare of executives and legislators. Judicial activities, both on and off the bench, are expected to be free from impropriety and the *appearance* of impropriety.

Before coming to the bench, however, most judges have been active in legislatures, government agencies, and other aspects of political life. They are unlikely, upon confirmation, to adopt the manner and habits of a cloistered judge; nor should they. Legislation often has a direct bearing on the courts, justifying the active participation of judges at the bill-drafting and congressional hearing stages. Canon 4 of the American Bar Association's code of Judicial Conduct permits a judge to "appear at a public hearing before an executive or legislative body or official on matters concerning the law, the legal system, and the administration of justice, and he may otherwise consult with an executive or legislative body or official, but only on matters concerning the administration of justice" and never by casting doubt on his capacity to decide impartially any issue that may come before him.[149]

With the 1982 publication of *The Brandeis/Frankfurter Connection* by Bruce Allen Murphy, the public was surprised to learn that Justice Brandeis, over a period of years, had secretly paid more than $50,000 to Felix Frankfurter to advance Brandeis's political views.[150] The financial arrangement ended when Brandeis left the Court in 1939. Frankfurter joined the Court that year and remained deeply enmeshed in politics. He drafted legislative proposals for the Roosevelt administration, helped staff the upper echelons of the War Department, and lent his assistance to Roosevelt's reelection campaign in 1940.

---

[149]See 2 O.L.C. 30 (1978).

[150]Bruce Allen Murphy, The Brandeis/Frankfurter Connection 40–45, 83–89 (1982). Their financial arrangement had been noted previously by Murphy in "Elements of Extrajudicial Strategy: A Look at the Political Roles of Justices Brandeis and Frankfurter," 69 Geo. L. J. 101, 111–14 (1980) and by H. N. Hirsch, The Enigma of Felix Frankfurter 44, 85, 225 (1981).

The details of Frankfurter's activities are particularly noteworthy. As a member of the Court he described himself as a "political eunuch," claiming that the Court "has no excuse for being unless it's a monastery."[151] In 1943 he entered in his diary: "I did not come on to the Court to play politics," and yet he was unremitting in trying to cultivate the support of his brethren.[152] A year later he confided to a friend: "I have an austere and even sacerdotal view of the position of a judge on this Court, and that means I have nothing to say on matters that come within a thousand miles of what may fairly be called politics."[153] In his published opinions, Frankfurter declared that the authority of the Supreme Court depended on its "complete detachment, in fact and in appearance, from political entanglements . . . ."[154]

Although Frankfurter distinguished himself for hypocrisy, other Justices were also drawn to off-the-bench activities. The contacts between Brandeis and President Franklin D. Roosevelt had already been noted in the literature.[155] Taft, Frankfurter, Byrnes, and Fortas, while on the Court, met frequently with Presidents and discussed public issues.[156]

Much earlier examples illustrate the difficulty that some members of the Supreme Court have had in drawing a line between law and politics. During the Court's first two decades, individual Justices campaigned for political candidates, ran for political office, and accepted political duties that came their way. Chief Justice John Jay was sent as special envoy to negotiate a treaty with England. Chief Justice Oliver Ellsworth followed that precedent by negotiating a treaty with France.[157]

After Chief Justice Marshall issued his decision in *McCulloch* v. *Maryland* (1819), arguing in favor of broad implied powers for the

[151]Murphy, Brandeis/Frankfurter Connection, at 9.

[152]Joseph P. Lash, ed., From the Diaries of Felix Frankfurter 175 (1975).

[153]Murphy, Brandeis/Frankfurter Connection, at 259–60.

[154]Baker v. Carr, 369 U.S. 186, 267 (1962) (dissenting opinion).

[155]Philippa Strum, "Justice Brandeis and President Roosevelt," reprinted in Walter F. Murphy and C. Herman Pritchett, eds., Courts, Judges, and Politics 187–90 (1979).

[156]See Max Freedman, ed., Roosevelt and Frankfurter: Their Correspondence (1967); John P. MacKenzie, The Appearance of Justice 1–33 (1974); and "Nonjudicial Activities of Supreme Court Justices and Other Federal Judges," hearings before the Senate Committee on the Judiciary, 91st Cong., 1st Sess. (1969).

[157]For a recapitulation of extrajudicial activities of Supreme Court Justices, see Murphy, The Brandeis/Frankfurter Connection, at 345–63.

federal government, a series of anonymous articles appeared in a Richmond newspaper attacking the decision and championing states' rights. The first few critiques were probably written by William Brockenbrough, a state judge from Virginia. Marshall could not bear to let the charges go unanswered. Working through his colleague Justice Bushrod Washington, Marshall penned a number of anonymous rebuttals (signed A Friend of the Union) and published them in a Philadelphia newspaper. Four more critiques appeared in the Richmond newspaper, this time by Judge Spencer Roane of the Virginia Court of Appeals (who used the pseudonym Hampden). Marshall answered them as well, signing his name A Friend of the Constitution.[158] Justice Story, while serving for over twenty years as president of a Massachusetts branch of the United States Bank, tried to influence Treasury Department officials to secure large deposits in his bank and helped Daniel Webster draft a reply to President Jackson's veto of the Bank's charter in 1832.[159]

Many avenues are available to Justices who want to affect the course of political events. Public addresses, law review articles, and contacts with reporters, scholars, and magazine writers are methods of extending judicial influence beyond official actions.[160] These communications are not supposed to prejudge an issue that might be litigated, but judges are often outspoken about sensitive matters that are likely to take the form of a lawsuit. In a magazine article published in 1955, Chief Justice Warren included the following remarks in a section on needed reforms: "Unequal justice is a contradiction in terms. Yet access to justice is unequal in parts of our country. Suspects are sometimes arrested, tried and convicted without being adequately informed of their right to counsel. Even when he knows of this right, many a citizen cannot afford to exercise it."[161] These precise issues were later adjudicated in such cases as *Gideon*, *Escobedo*, and *Miranda*.[162]

[158]Gerald Gunther, ed., John Marshall's Defense of *McCulloch* v. *Maryland* (1969).

[159]G. Edward White, The American Political Tradition 41 (1976); Gerald T. Dunne, Justice Joseph Story and the Rise of the Supreme Court 301–2, 328–31 (1970).

[160]Walter Murphy, Elements of Judicial Strategy 123–97 (1964).

[161]Chief Justice Earl Warren, "The Law and the Future," Fortune (November 1955), reprinted in Henry M. Christman, ed., The Public Papers of Chief Justice Earl Warren 230 (1959).

[162]Gideon v. Wainwright, 372 U.S. 335 (1963); Escobedo v. Illinois, 378 U.S. 478 (1964); Miranda v. Arizona, 384 U.S. 436 (1966).

The Chief Justice prepares an annual "year-ender," summing up the problems, needs, and accomplishments of federal courts. He also delivers an annual report on the state of the judiciary, sometimes using these forums to criticize Congress for its actions and inactions. Proposals have been introduced for an annual "State of the Judiciary" address, to be delivered by the Chief Justice to a joint session of Congress. This proposal passed the Senate in 1980, but the House took no action.[163]

The Judicial Conference is the principal institutional body for preparing a legislative agenda. The organization dates back to 1922, when Congress directed the Chief Justice to call an annual conference of the senior circuit judges. The objective was to make a comprehensive survey of cases pending before the federal courts: their number and character, cases disposed of, and backlog. The potential for judicial lobbying did not go unnoticed. Representative Clarence F. Lea predicted that the conference "will become the propaganda organization for legislation for the benefit of the Federal judiciary."[164]

As the law now reads, the Chief Justice submits to Congress "an annual report of the proceedings of the Judicial Conference and its recommendations for legislation."[165] These reports are submitted twice a year, covering the spring and fall meetings of the Conference. Because the meetings are largely devoted to administrative and legislative matters rather than judicial duties, there has been pressure to open them to the public. Opponents of this reform proposal concede that the Conference is a creature of Congress and subject to further statutory change, but so are federal district and appellate courts. They argue that the principle of judicial independence should cover the proceedings of the Judicial Conference. The following exchange in 1980 between Senator Dennis DeConcini and U.S. District Judge Elmo B. Hunter explores the proper scope of judicial lobbying:

> *Senator DeConcini.* Let me go to one other area. Do you agree that the Judicial Conference is involved in what might be termed to be lobbying, or at least bringing to the Congress

[163]126 Cong. Rec. 23397 (1980).

[164]62 Cong. Rec. 203 (1921). For the origin and development of the Judicial Conference, see Peter Graham Fish, The Politics of Federal Judicial Administration (1973).

[165]28 U.S.C. § 331 (1982).

certain information in order to persuade them that certain laws should be changed as they relate to the court?

Judge Hunter. Senator, I give a qualified yes to that. We do not ask you or tell you or advise you how to pass on bills unless you invite our comments. We are very careful.

My committee simply will not respond concerning legislation unless the invitation originates with one or the other of the bodies of the Congress. . . .

Senator DeConcini. You see, when we had the matter of the judicial conduct and disability [bill] we didn't ask but every member of the committee received a lengthy letter in the Senate explaining the opposition to it. We did not ask you to do that.

I do not object to your doing it. My point is only that I do not think that it is quite correct when you say that the Judicial Conference responds only to requests.

At this point Judge Hunter referred to the annual seminars held in Williamsburg, Virginia, sponsored by the Brookings Institution:

Judge Hunter. I wish to respond fully. If there was any violation of our policy that we respond only at the request of Congress, you can lay that blame on me. The policy is firm and intact. Perhaps I misjudged the application of it.

I attended the seminar which was held in Virginia in which Members of the House and Senate were invited and attended, together with members of the judiciary, together with the Attorney General, and it was a very helpful seminar. Out of that seminar I thought that I heard an invitation to advise the Congress at any time of any pressing need or problem of the judiciary. Perhaps I misunderstood that message.[166]

Federal judges also influence public policy by serving on executive or legislative commissions that report their findings. This type of activity, such as Justice Roberts's service on the committee that investigated the Pearl Harbor disaster and the role of Chief Justice Warren as chairman of the commission that investigated the assassination of President John F. Kennedy, has been criticized as an im-

[166]"Judicial Conference and Councils in the Sunshine Act, S. 2045," hearings before the Senate Committee on the Judiciary, 96th Cong., 2d Sess. 19–21 (1980).

proper involvement in nonjudicial duties. There are substantial risks that this activity will compromise the independence of the judiciary and that judges might have to disqualify themselves on a case involving the extrajudicial assignment. In 1967 a three-judge court upheld a statute that authorized U.S. district judges to appoint members of the D.C. Board of Education. Both the majority and the dissent by Judge Skelly Wright agreed that this participation might require disqualification.[167]

These types of problems persist. In 1983 President Reagan established a commission on organized crime. To chair the commission, he named Judge Irving R. Kaufman from the Second Circuit. The commission was directed to conduct a study and make judicial and legislative recommendations by March 1, 1986.[168] A lawsuit challenged Kaufman's participation on the commission on the ground that it violated the separation-of-power doctrine. In 1985 the Eleventh Circuit agreed that impartiality is threatened when federal judges serve on an executive commission: "A judge who is charged with assisting and improving enforcement efforts against organized crime must adopt a pro-government perspective which is ill-suited to his obligation to be neutral in the courtroom."[169] Even if a judge could satisfy himself that he could separate his participation on the commission from his judicial duties, "it is not clear that litigants could sustain equal faith in his impartiality."[170] The selection of Judge Kaufman raised particularly serious issues because he is a judge from a jurisdiction with "a well-publicized problem with organized crime."[171]

The Third Circuit reached a different result in 1986. It held that the presence of an active federal judge like Kaufman on a presidential commission does not violate the separation-of-power doctrine. The court pointed out that service on the commission is voluntary, nor coerced, and that judges possess special expertise in the field of judicial administration.[172] The first point does not address the problem of bias, and the second point could be satisfied simply by having

[167]Hobson v. Hansen, 265 F.Supp. 902 (D.D.C. 1967) (three-judge court).

[168]Public Papers of the Presidents, 1983, Book II, at 1092–96.

[169]Application of President's Commission on Organized Crime, 763 F.2d 1191, 1197 (11th Cir. 1985).

[170]Id.

[171]Id. at 1198.

[172]Matter of President's Commission on Organized Crime, 783 F.2d 370 (3d Cir. 1986).

158

judges testify before the commission or submit statements for the record.

Federal judges were also selected to serve on the U.S. Sentencing Commission, which Congress established in 1984 as "an independent commission in the judicial branch."[173] The President appointed the members of the commission, and they were confirmed by the Senate. The statute required that at least three members be federal judges. The purpose of the commission is to set guidelines for judges to follow in sentencing, with the objective of reducing the disparities that exist in penalties with similar crimes. William W. Wilkins, Jr., a federal district judge from South Carolina, was named chairman. The other two judges included George E. MacKinnon of the D.C. Circuit and Stephen G. Breyer of the First Circuit.

A controversy developed in 1987 when the Justice Department urged the commission to write new rules to permit the death penalty for federal crimes. The commission's vice chairman, Judge Breyer, questioned whether it was appropriate for "a technically oriented commission in the judicial branch to get into the business of deciding whether or not capital punishment is sound policy." Assistant Attorney General Charles J. Cooper, head of the Office of Legal Counsel in the Justice Department, claimed that the commission should be regarded as an executive agency.[174]

There are also substantial constitutional questions about the organization, duties, and powers of the Sentencing Commission. It is unusual in several respects. Unlike the crime commission, the recommendations of the Sentencing Commission would become law unless Congress passed a joint resolution of disapproval within a specific period of time. The recommendations became effective on November 1, 1987. Moreover, this lawmaking body is composed partly of federal judges and partly of nonjudges, all subject to removal from the commission by the President.[175] A lawsuit has been filed challenging the commission on separation-of-powers grounds. The suit claims that Congress improperly delegated its legislative duties to a judicial body.

[173]98 Stat. 2017 (1984).

[174]Howard Kurtz, "Toward a Federal Death Penalty," Washington Post, January 13, 1987, at A21.

[175]Alan B. Morrison, "A Fatal Flaw," The National Law Journal, January 26, 1987, at 15, 28–29.

The lobbying activities of Chief Justice Burger attracted press attention in 1978. On the eve of a Senate vote on the bankruptcy bill, he called Senator DeConcini and several other members of the Senate Judiciary Committee. DeConcini told reporters that Burger accused him of being "irresponsible" for supporting the legislation and said that the bill "was a political sale and he was going to the President and have him veto it." Calling the charge "a slap in the face of the entire Senate," DeConcini described Burger as being "very, very irate and rude." He "just screamed at me" and "not only lobbied, but pressured and attempted to be intimidating."[176] Representative Don Edwards, head of the House subcommittee responsible for the bankruptcy bill, said that he welcomed the views of judges but only when presented in "a scholarly, judicious way, in writing or in hearings, not in telephone calls once a bill has gone to the floor."[177]

As is customary for most members of the judiciary, Chief Justice Burger did not respond directly to DeConcini's charges. Within a month, however, while accepting an award in New York City, Burger defended his participation in the legislative process. He pointed out that the separation-of-power doctrine is sufficiently flexible and practical to permit an overlapping of functions, such as the appearance of the Solicitor General and members of Congress in court proceedings. Similarly, "participation in legislative and executive decisions which affect the judicial system is an absolute obligation of judges, as it is of lawyers. . . . It is entirely appropriate for judges to comment upon issues which affect the courts."[178]

Burger resisted some judicial activities he viewed as inappropriate. In 1981, a number of federal judges wanted to form an association to lobby Congress for higher salaries and fringe benefits. Interested judges would contribute $200 and list the members of Congress they felt comfortable contacting about judicial salaries. Burger advised the judges that the position of the federal judiciary should be expressed through the Judicial Conference.[179] Nevertheless, the group was

[176]"Senator Slams Burger on Move to Thwart Bill," National Law Journal, October 16, 1978; "Burger Wants Judges to Speak Up to Congress," Washington Post, October 26, 1978, at A13.

[177]"Lobbying By Burger Provokes Criticism," New York Times, November 19, 1978, at 39.

[178]Speech of October 25, 1978, accepting the Fordham-Stein Award in New York City.

[179]"U.S. Judges Want Lobby; Burger Against Proposal," National Law Journal, June 29, 1981, at 2, 10.

formed and consists of about three hundred judges in an organization called the Federal Judges Association. Several Senators in 1984 complained about this kind of judicial lobbying and requested the Comptroller General to investigate possible violations of the Lobbying with Appropriated Moneys Act.[180]

[180]For criticism of this group, see the floor statement by Jeremiah Denton, 130 Cong. Rec. S2267–70 (daily ed. March 2, 1984).

5. Decisionmaking: Process and Strategy

Publication of *The Brethren* in 1979 promised a rare glimpse into the inner sanctum of the Supreme Court. The authors claimed that for nearly two centuries the Supreme Court had made its decisions "in absolute secrecy."[1] In fact, the deliberative process of the Court has been studied and scrutinized for years. Scholars have had access to internal memoranda, conference notes, diaries, draft opinions, and correspondence by the Justices. Members of the Court and their law clerks publish widely. Drawing on those materials, we have a fairly detailed picture of the process that Justices use to make decisions.[2]

The Supreme Court begins its term on the first Monday in October and ends in late June or early July of the following year. A term is designated by the October date (the 1987 term began October 5, 1987). During these approximately nine months, the court selects cases, hears oral argument, writes opinions, and announces decisions. After recessing for the summer, the Justices continue to review petitions in preparation for the new term and are called upon to decide emergency petitions brought to their attention. Although decisions by the Supreme Court require a quorum of six, in certain cases individual Justices may stay the execution and enforcement of lower court orders and give aggrieved parties time to petition the full Court for review. Each Justice performs other duties when assigned to one of the judicial circuits.

On rare occasions the Court convenes in the summer in special session to deal with urgent matters. For example, the Court met on June 18, 1953, to consider Justice Douglas's stay in the execution of

---

[1]Bob Woodward and Scott Armstrong, The Brethren: Inside the Supreme Court 1 (1979).

[2]Of many commendable studies, special note should be made of J. Woodford Howard, Jr., Mr. Justice Murphy 231–496 (1968); Walter F. Murphy, Elements of Judicial Strategy (1964); and Alpheus Thomas Mason, Harlan Fiske Stone: Pillar of the Law (1956). In the years since *The Brethren*, a number of superb studies have appeared on decisionmaking within the Supreme Court, including Bernard Schwartz, Super Chief (1983) and David M. O'Brien, Storm Center (1986).

Ethel and Julius Rosenberg, convicted of delivering atomic bomb information to the Soviet Union. On June 19 the Court vacated the stay and the Rosenbergs were executed that day. Another special session occurred on August 28, 1958, when the Court convened to consider a lower court order enforcing a desegregation plan for Little Rock High School. The Court unanimously upheld the lower court on September 12, three days before the school's scheduled opening.

Jurisdiction: Original and Appellate

The Constitution assigns to the Supreme Court judicial power in "all Cases, in Law and Equity, arising under this Constitution, the Laws of the United States, and Treaties made, or which shall be made under their Authority." The types of cases identified in the Constitution are those affecting ambassadors, other public ministers, and consuls; admiralty and maritime cases; controversies in which the United States is a party; and controversies between two or more states, between a state and a citizen of another state, between citizens of different states, between citizens of the same state claiming lands under grants of different states, and between a state (or its citizens) and foreign states, citizens, or subjects.

This jurisdiction divides between original and appellate. In all cases affecting ambassadors, other public ministers, and consuls, and those in which a state shall be a party, the Supreme Court has original jurisdiction. These cases may be taken directly to the Court without action by lower courts. Only rarely does a case of original jurisdiction concern ambassadors, diplomats, and consuls. Most of the cases involve litigation between states, such as disputes over boundaries and water rights.[3]

"Original" appears to imply exclusively, suggesting that what is granted by the Constitution cannot be abridged or altered by Congress. Nevertheless, Congress has passed legislation that divides original jurisdiction into two categories: original and exclusive jurisdiction, and original but not exclusive jurisdiction.[4] For the latter, lower federal courts share concurrent jurisdiction.

[3] Note, "The Original Jurisdiction of the United States Supreme Court," 11 Stan. L. Rev. 665 (1959).
[4] 28 U.S.C. § 1251 (1982).

Congress has restricted the jurisdiction of federal courts by establishing criteria for "federal questions." Until 1980, certain federal court cases required at least $10,000 in dispute. The purpose was to reduce case congestion in the federal courts. That amount was eliminated in 1980.[5] Congress wanted to resolve the anomaly faced by persons whose rights had been violated but were barred from the courts because they had not suffered a sufficient economic injury.[6] Dollar thresholds remain for "diversity" jurisdiction (where federal courts consider cases involving state law if the parties are from different states).[7]

Court jurisdiction may seem like a technical matter of interest only to specialists and practitioners of the law. But jurisdiction means political power. A question of jurisdiction provoked the first constitutional amendment adopted after the Bill of Rights. In *Chisholm* v. *Georgia* (1793), the Court held that states could be sued in federal courts by citizens of another state.[8] The public outcry was so deep and swift that the Eleventh Amendment, overriding *Chisholm,* passed both Houses of Congress in 1794 and was ratified by the states in 1798.

Dockets. Each year the Supreme Court receives between four thousand and five thousand petitions for review. A few cases concern original jurisdiction and are placed on the Original Docket. This class is not obligatory on the Court. To fall within the category of original jurisdiction, the case must constitute a proper "controversy."[9] Original jurisdiction is used sparingly to protect the Court's increased workload with its appellate docket.[10] The Court is especially reluctant to become a court of first instance and assume the factfinding function of a trial court, a task for which the Court considers itself "ill-equipped."[11] To assist in the handling of its original jurisdiction

[5]94 Stat. 2369 (1980). See 31 U.S.C. § 1331 (1982).
[6]H. Rept. No. 1461, 91st Cong., 2d Sess. (1980).
[7]31 U.S.C. § 1332 (1982).
[8]2 Dall. (2 U.S.) 419 (1793).
[9]Maryland v. Louisiana, 451 U.S. 725, 735–36 (1981).
[10]Illinois v. City of Milwaukee, 406 U.S. 91, 93–94 (1972).
[11]Ohio v. Wyandotte, 401 U.S. 493, 498 (1971). See Julie Vick Stevenson, "Exclusive Original Jurisdiction of the United States Supreme Court: Does It Still Exist?," 1982 B.Y.U. L. Rev. 727 (1982).

docket, the Court appoints Special Masters to study an issue and present recommendations.[12]

Most of the petitions concern appeals. Over the past century the basic thrust of court reforms has been to alleviate the Supreme Court's burden of appellate cases, first by creating circuit courts of appeals in 1891. Later, Congress limited appeals to the Supreme Court and substituted the discretionary writ of certiorari in 1925.

Cases reach the Supreme Court by one of four routes. First, some parties come to the Court as a matter of statutory right. Congress has passed a number of statutes to provide for direct appeal, preferred treatment, and expedited action. In recent years, however, Congress has begun converting some of these statutes to discretionary review.[13] All nine Justices of the Supreme Court have communicated to Congress their request that mandatory jurisdiction be eliminated.[14]

Although this jurisdiction is supposedly mandatory or obligatory on the Court, in practice the Court exercises considerable discretion.[15] To handle the volume of these appeals, the Court often disposes of cases without written opinion. It has been estimated that more than eighty percent of the appeals have been disposed of summarily in recent years without oral argument or further briefing.[16] There is substantial disagreement as to how lower courts should accept the precedential value of summary dismissals and affirmances. In *Hicks* v. *Miranda* (1975), the Court instructed lower courts that these summary decisions are on the merits and should be treated with the same substantive respect as other holdings.[17] But in subsequent decisions the Court has pointed out that summary actions do not have the same authority as decisions reached after plenary consideration.[18] The issue remains a source of great confusion.[19]

Writs of certiorari are a second route to the Supreme Court. By

---

[12]E.g., United States v. California, 447 U.S. 1 (1980).

[13]H. Rept. No. 824 (Part 1), 97th Cong., 2d Sess. 6 (1982).

[14]See letter from all nine Justices to Congressman Kastenmeier, June 17, 1982, reprinted at H. Rept. No. 986, 98th Cong., 2d Sess. 27–28 (1984).

[15]Erwin N. Griswold, "Rationing Justice—The Supreme Court's Caseload and What the Court Does Not Do," 60 Corn. L. Rev. 335, 344–46 (1975).

[16]Robert L. Stern and Eugene Gressman, Supreme Court Practice 503 (1978).

[17]422 U.S. 332, 343–45 (1975).

[18]Metromedia, Inc. v. San Diego, 453 U.S. 490, 500 (1981).

[19]See dissent by Justice Brennan in Colorado Springs Amusements, Ltd. v. Rizzo, 428 U.S. 913 (1976).

"granting cert" the Court calls up the records of a lower court, a decision that is wholly discretionary. Third, petitions for review are submitted by indigents, including prison inmates, sometimes in the form of handwritten notes. These requests, called *in forma pauperis* (in the manner of a pauper), numbered a few dozen in 1930 and now range about two thousand a term. Fourth, an appellate court may submit a writ of certification to seek instruction on a question of law.[20] This procedure is seldom used, for it forces the Court to decide questions of law without the important guidance of findings and conclusions by the lower courts.

Before 1970, petitions for certiorari and appeals covered by a docketing fee were placed on an Appellate Docket. All petitions and appeals filed in forma pauperis, together with applications for extraordinary writs (e.g., habeas corpus), were placed on a Miscellaneous Docket. Since 1970, all cases other than those within original jurisdiction are placed on a single Docket.[21] A numbering system allows for the traditional distinction between Appellate and Miscellaneous, and statistics supplied each year in the *Harvard Law Review* rely on those classifications.[22]

The Writ of Certiorari. The Supreme Court controls its workload largely by exercising discretionary authority over cases coming to it for review. The discretionary writ of certiorari was initiated by the Evarts Act of 1891 and the Judicial Code of 1911,[23] but the primary source of discretion awaited the "Judges Bill" of 1925. That statute eliminated direct review by the Supreme Court of decisions in the district courts and greatly expanded the use of the writ of certiorari.[24]

Most of the decisions of the Supreme Court involve cert denials. Under Rule 17 of the Supreme Court, a review on writ of certiorari "is not a matter of right, but of judicial discretion, and will be granted only when there are special and important reasons therefor." Among the reasons listed in Rule 17 are conflicts between federal courts of appeals, between a federal court of appeals and a state court of last

---

[20]28 U.S.C. § 1254 (1982).

[21]Stern and Gressman, Supreme Court Practice, at 33–34.

[22]See 96 Harv. L. Rev. 308 (1982).

[23]26 Stat. 826, 828 (1891); 36 Stat. 1087, 1157 (1911). See also 38 Stat. 790 (1914).

[24]43 Stat. 936 (1925).

resort, and over federal questions decided by different state courts of last resort.[25] The fact that a question is important and lower courts are in clear conflict, however, is insufficient in itself to grant cert.[26]

Justices look for cases that present broad issues on the administration of the law, substantive constitutional questions, the construction of important federal statutes, and serious questions of public law.[27] The Court is likely to take a case in which an act of Congress or a state statute has been declared unconstitutional.[28] In a 1949 address, Chief Justice Vinson advised lawyers who prepare petitions for certiorari to spend "a little less time discussing the merits of their cases and a little more time demonstrating why it is important that the Court should hear them. . . . If [a petition for certiorari] only succeeds in demonstrating that the decision below may be erroneous, it has not fulfilled its purpose."[29]

Other factors explain why the Court accepts a writ of certiorari. The literature on "cue theory" points to a key ingredient—the federal government's decision to seek review. The Court relies heavily on the seasoned judgment of the Solicitor General to bring only those cases that merit appeal. When that factor combines with other elements (the presence of a civil liberty issue, conflict between circuits, a lower court decision in which judges are divided), granting a petition is even more likely.[30] Justice Powell noted in 1979 that the Court feels "a special responsibility to protect the liberties guaranteed by the Bill of Rights. Thus, a fairly high percentage of the cases that we

[25]U.S. Code Annotated, Title 28: Rules (1984); see S. Sidney Ulmer, "The Supreme Court's Certiorari Decisions: Conflict as a Predictive Variable," 78 Am. Pol. Sci. Rev. 901 (1984).

[26]Greco v. Orange Memorial Hospital Corp., 423 U.S. 1000 (1975).

[27]Tom C. Clark, "Some Thoughts on Supreme Court Practice," address of April 13, 1959, reprinted in Alan F. Westin, ed., An Autobiography of the Supreme Court 296–97 (1963).

[28]Byron R. White, "The Work of the Supreme Court: A Nuts and Bolts Description," 54 N.Y. State Bar J. 346, 349 (1982).

[29]69 S.Ct. vi (1949). For advice from someone who clerked for three Supreme Court Justices, see E. Barrett Prettyman, Jr., "Petitioning the United States Supreme Court—A Primer for Hopeful Neophytes," 51 Va. L. Rev. 582 (1965).

[30]Joseph Tanenhaus et al., "The Supreme Court's Certiorari Jurisdiction: Cue Theory," in Glendon Schubert, ed., Judicial Decision-Making 111–32 (1963). For a critique of the Tanenhaus study, see Doris Marie Provine, Case Selection in the United States Supreme Court 77–83 (1980). A detailed study of the factors that motivated the Court to grant cert appears in Stern and Gressman, Supreme Court Practice, at 254–317.

take for review involve claims by citizens—often quite humble citizens—that government has infringed upon their rights under the Constitution."[31]

At various times in its history the Court has accepted an issue from a lower court because it appeared that the executive and legislative branches were unwilling to act. An appellate judge said that "waiting for the legislature is not productive. The legislature doesn't legislate. Courts have had to do a good deal of stuff that would be better for the legislature to have done. But it's better for courts to do them than no one."[32] Presumably the same attitude prevailed on the Supreme Court, but only recently have its members publicly admitted this function. Justice Powell has said that judicial independence gives the Court "a freedom to make decisions that perhaps are necessary for our society, decisions that the legislative branch may be reluctant to make."[33] Justice Blackman elaborated on that same point in 1982. Asked whether desegregation was an example where the courts had to do more because other branches did less, he replied:

Well, one can come up with a lot of possible examples. That is one. One man, one vote is another one. And many of the sex discrimination cases perhaps are others. If one goes back twenty-five years, certainly things are different because of judicial intervention. I can remember when I was a law clerk a case came up concerning the possibility of a federal judge intervening in the administration of a prison and it was unheard of in those days. That was a problem for the prison administrative authorities. And now, of course, in recent years—and by what I mean twenty years anyway—there have been many instances where the courts, in effect, have taken constitutional rights inside the prison doors, not all of them. Because once a man is incarcerated he loses to a great degree rights that he would otherwise have as one who is not in prison. But there are certain things still there to which he has access and should be protected.[34]

[31]"Constitutional Interpretation: An Interview with Justice Lewis Powell," Kenyon College Alumni Bulletin, Summer 1979, at 17.

[32]J. Woodford Howard, Jr., Courts of Appeals in the Federal Judicial System 163 n. (1981).

[33]Powell, "Constitutional Interpretation," at 15.

[34]"A Justice Speaks Out: A Conversation with Harry A. Blackmun," Cable News Network, Inc., December 4, 1982, at 10–11.

Of the four thousand to five thousand cases received each year, less than two hundred are accepted for oral argument and full opinions. In evaluating the petitions, Justices dismiss many as frivolous and "dead-list" them (deny them cert) without further deliberation. In recent years the Court has replaced the "dead list" with a "discuss list," which includes the cases deemed worthy of discussion.[35] Examples of frivolous petitions include: "Are Negroes in fact Indians and therefore entitled to Indians' exemptions from federal income taxes?"; "Are the federal income tax laws unconstitutional insofar as they do not provide a deduction for depletion of the human body?"; and "Does a ban on drivers turning right on a red light constitute an unreasonable burden on interstate commerce?"[36] When an appeal or petition for writ of certiorari is frivolous, Rule 49.2 of the Supreme Court authorizes the award of appropriate damages to the party sued. In a rare invocation of this rule in 1983, the Court ordered an individual to pay $500 in legal expenses incurred by University of Nebraska regents in responding to his suit. The action appeared to reflect a growing concern among members of the Court that its caseload was becoming unmanageable.[37] Fines have been levied against attorneys for bringing frivolous cases.[38] In 1985 the Court declined to adopt Chief Justice Burger's recommendation to fine the attorney.[39]

Justices try to avoid cases where the legal issue is overpowered by emotional ingredients. When the Court reviewed cert petitions in 1975 to clarify the rights available to criminal defendants, it deliberately passed over the petition of someone who had been convicted for strangling, raping, and beheading a woman, followed by an attempt to skin her.[40] It would have been impossible for the Court to

[35]John Paul Stevens, "The Life Span of a Judge-Made Rule," 58 N.Y.U. L. Rev. 1, 13 (1983).

[36]William J. Brennan, Jr., "The National Court of Appeals: Another Dissent," 40 U. Chi. L. Rev. 473, 478 (1973).

[37]Tatum v. Regents of the University of Nebraska-Lincoln, 462 U.S. 1117 (1983). See Washington Post, June 15, 1983, at A16, and Note, "Penalties for Frivolous Appeals," 43 Harv. L. Rev. 113 (1929).

[38]"Chief Justice Complains of Rising Case Backlog," Washington Post, December 30, 1985, at A3. See James J. Kilpatrick, "Nonsense in the Court," Washington Post, December 26, 1985, at A19, and interview with Warren E. Burger, "Unclogging the Courts—Chief Justice Speaks Out," U.S. News & World Report, February 22, 1982, at 39–40.

[39]Talamini v. Allstate Insurance Co., 470 U.S. 1067 (1985); Crumpacker v. Indiana Supreme Court Disciplinary Commission, 470 U.S. 1074 (1985).

[40]Liva Baker, Miranda: Crime, Law and Politics 105 (1983).

announce new legal principles in the midst of such ghastly circumstances.

In theory, Justices make a personal judgment on each of the thousands of petitions received annually. However, they depend on their law clerks to prepare memoranda that summarize the facts of a case and recommend acceptance or rejection.[41] Some of the Justices, including Rehnquist, White, Blackmun, O'Connor, and Scalia, participate in a "cert pool" to divvy up the work. In 1982, Justice Stevens said that he found it necessary to delegate "a great deal of responsibility in the review of certiorari petitions to my law clerks." He estimated that he looked at the papers in less than twenty percent of the cases filed.[42]

Justices meet at a Friday conference to discuss and vote on the petitions that survive their initial review. A single Justice may set a case for decision at conference. As a symbol of unity, Justices shake hands upon entering the conference room. These gestures preserve an atmosphere of civility in an institution compelled to deal with some of the most fractious issues in society. Maintaining a measure of collegiality among nine strong personalities is no small feat. Members of the Court work together over long periods and under intense pressures. Someone who alienates colleagues one week may need their votes to control a close question the following week.

To preserve confidentiality in the conference room, only the Justices are present. The junior Justice sits closest to the door, receiving and delivering messages that flow in and out of the room. Some political scientists reported that the rectangular table in the conference room had been chopped into three pieces by Chief Justice Burger and converted into an inverted U-shaped table, supposedly to prevent the liberal Douglas from sitting opposite him in direct confrontation. Justice Powell reassured his readers in 1975 that the conference table "retains its pristine shape; there has been no hacking or sawing; the justices occupy their seats in the traditional order of seniority."[43] Visitors to the room find the table intact.

---

[41]William H. Rehnquist, "Who Writes Decisions of the Supreme Court?," U.S. News & World Report, December 13, 1957, at 74–75. Rehnquist claimed that law clerks exerted a liberal influence on the Court, a charge disputed by Alexander M. Bickel, "The Court: An Indictment Analyzed," New York Times Magazine, April 27, 1958, at 16ff.

[42]John Paul Stevens, "Some Thoughts on Judicial Restraint," 66 Judicature 177, 179 (1982).

[43]Lewis F. Powell, Jr., "Myths and Misconceptions about the Supreme Court," 61

The Chief Justice begins the discussion of each case. He summarizes the facts, analyzes the law, and announces his proposed vote. He is followed by the other Justices in order of seniority, from the senior Associate Justice down to the newest Justice. Before the Warren Court, voting was done in the opposite manner: the junior Justice voted first and the Chief Justice last.[44] Toward the end of his service, Warren persuaded the Justices to vote in the same order as they had spoken.[45]

Four votes are needed to grant certiorari. There are exceptions to this rule. On some occasions less than four votes have been sufficient.[46] On the other hand, cert can be denied even though four Justice dissent.[47]

Justice Frankfurter sparked a dispute by claiming that a vote to grant cert did not obligate a Justice to vote later on the merits. He insisted that he would be free to dismiss the writ as "improvidently granted." Had other Justices adopted his policy, the Court might have lacked a sufficient number of members to decide a case after accepting it for review. Justice Douglas said that the "integrity of the four-vote rule on certiorari would . . . be impaired" if the Court granted cert, heard argument, and then dismissed the writ as improvidently granted.[48] In rebuttal, Frankfurter noted that dismissal at this stage was warranted when cases appeared to be nothing more than "legal sports" that did not merit a decision by the Court.[49] Frankfurter regularly dissented in cases in which cert was granted to evaluate evidence concerning the liability of employers for worker injuries (Federal Employees' Liability Act and Jones Act cases). He

---

A.B.A.J. 1344 (1975). See Glendon Schubert, Judicial Policy Making 134 (1977), and Howard Ball, Courts and Politics 254 (1980). For a discussion of some of the practices in conference, see William H. Rehnquist, "Sunshine in the Third Branch," 16 Washburn L. J. 559 (1977).

[44]In a 1963 article, Justice Brennan stated that voting began with the junior Justice; William J. Brennan, Jr., "Inside View of the High Court," New York Times Magazine, October 6, 1963, at 100. Justice Clark, in 1956, also said that the junior Justice voted first, 19 F.R.D. 303, 307, as did Justice Frankfurter in 1953, "Chief Justices I Have Known," 39 Va. L. Rev. 883, 903.

[45]Walter F. Murphy and C. Herman Pritchett, eds., Courts, Judges, and Politics 657 (1979). This account is supported by a 1982 interview with Justice Blackmun, "A Justice Speaks Out," at 21.

[46]David M. O'Brien, Storm Center 191–92 (1986).

[47]Drake v. Zant, 449 U.S. 999 (1980). On a cert denial, Justices Brennan, Marshall, Stewart, and White dissented.

[48]United States v. Shannon, 342 U.S. 288, 298 (1952).

[49]Id. at 294–95.

regarded granting cert in these cases to be an abuse of judicial discretion and a misuse of judicial power.[50] The record shows that there are instances where the Court grants cert and later, on the basis of changed circumstances, dismisses the writ of certiorari as improvidently granted.[51]

Justices must address a wide range of complex cases at each conference. Docket sheets are provided to record each step of the process from deciding to hear a case to postconference voting. Conference notes are a summary record of the arguments of each Justice on the merits of the case. Whoever is selected to draft the opinion can review the conference notes and craft an argument that will attract the maximum number of votes. At any point, however, votes may be changed before the opinion of the Court reaches its final stage.

Each year the Court grants cert in about six or seven percent of the petitions reviewed. Most of those are selected from the Appellate Docket. Relatively few come from the Miscellaneous Docket. One of the most significant "pauper's cases" was initiated by Clarence Earl Gideon. His petition to the Court in 1962 resulted in a major decision granting the right to counsel for indigents.[52]

In denying cert, the Court seldom offers an explanation. When it does, the reason is usually brief if not cryptic. More light is shed when Justices write a dissenting opinion on cert denials. This practice, which has grown significantly in recent decades, calls into question the Court's traditional position that cert denial means a refusal to take a case and nothing more.[53] If dissenting Justices strongly voice their reasons and argue the merits, it may appear that the majority denying cert considered and rejected those arguments.[54] Justices often differ on the significance to be attached to dissents on cert denial.[55] Speculation as to intent is hazardous. Even when Justices

---

[50]McBride v. Toledo Terminal R. Co., 354 U.S. 517, 517–20 (1957); Ferguson v. Moore-McCormack Lines, 352 U.S. 521, 524–58 (1957).

[51]Conway v. California Adult Authority, 396 U.S. 107 (1969). See Joan Maisel Leiman, "The Rule of Four," 57 Colum. L. Rev. 975 (1957); John Paul Stevens, "The Life Span of a Judge-Made Rule," 58 N.Y.U. L. Rev. 1 (1983).

[52]Gideon v. Wainwright, 372 U.S. 335 (1963). See Anthony Lewis, Gideon's Trumpet (1964), for an instructive account of *in forma pauperis* petitions.

[53]Darr v. Burford, 339 U.S. 200, 226 (1950) (Frankfurter, J., dissenting).

[54]Peter Linzer, "The Meaning of Certiorari Denials," 79 Colum. L. Rev. 1127 (1979).

[55]See differing views of Justices Blackmun and Marshall in United States v. Kras,

think that a lower court is wrong, they may vote to deny an application simply because they regard the federal question as insubstantial or poorly timed for review.[56] Cases that appear to fall within the guidelines of Rule 17 are rejected because Justices must watch their bulging caseload.[57] A petition raising an important legal issue may be denied if it appears that procedural grounds will prevent a decision on the question.[58] And some Justices resist granting cert because of a belief in judicial restraint.[59]

From Oral Argument to Decision

After a case receives four votes from Justices meeting in conference, it is transferred to the oral argument list. If Justices conclude that a question is clearly controlled by one of the Court's earlier decisions, they may summarily dispose of a lower court decision without oral argument. Of the approximately 275 cases the Court accepts each year, about 100 are decided summarily. In *Snepp* v. *United States* (1980), for example, the Court decided a case involving press and speech restrictions on former government employees without hearing oral argument.[60] Summary disposition carries the risk of depriving the Court of crucial information. It can also suggest a "rush to judgment."

The Pentagon Papers Case of 1971 marked another occasion when the Court moved with extraordinary speed. Beginning with the *New York Times*'s publication of a secret Pentagon study on the origins and

---

409 U.S. 434, 443, 460–61 (1973). Justices Stevens, Brennan, and Stewart objected when the Court gave a brief reason for denying cert ("for failure to file petition within time provided"); County of Sonoma v. Isbell, 439 U.S. 996 (1978).

[56]William J. Brennan, Jr., "State Court Decisions and the Supreme Court," in Westin, Autobiography of the Supreme Court, at 301–2.

[57]See the lengthy statement by Justice White, dissenting from a denial of cert in Brown Transport Corp. v. Atcon, 439 U.S. 1014–15 (1978). Chief Justice Burger agreed with White's analysis of workload problems; id. at 1025–32.

[58]"Chief Justice Vinson and His Law Clerks," 49 Nw U. L. Rev. 26, 29 (1954).

[59]Provine, Case Selection, at 104–30. In Singleton v. Commissioner of Internal Revenue, 439 U.S. 940, 942–46 (1978), Justice Stevens explained his objections to the practice of writing separate opinions of dissent on cert denials.

[60]444 U.S. 507. See also Recznik v. City of Lorain, 393 U.S. 166 (1968), in which the Court simultaneously granted cert, reversed, and remanded, all without oral argument.

conduct of the Vietnam War, only seventeen days were consumed for action by two district courts, two appellate courts, and the Supreme Court. The *New York Times*'s petitions and motions were filed with the Supreme Court on June 24 at eleven A.M. The government filed its motion later that evening. Oral argument took place on June 26. The record in the *Times* case did not arrive until seven or eight o'clock the previous evening. The briefs of the parties were received less than two hours before oral argument. Four days later the Court announced its decision, upholding the right of the press to publish material from the Pentagon study. Despite protests from several Justices, the Court moved quickly to protect the First Amendment right of the press to publish without prior restraint.[61]

The number of full opinions each year ranges between 140 and 150. In preparing for oral argument, counsel for each side submits briefs and records, which are distributed to each Justice. The Court hears oral argument in public session from Monday through Thursday, listening to cases from ten A.M. to noon and from one to three P.M. Usually one hour is set aside for each case. Although briefs are important, members of the judiciary have noted that there are some judges "who listen better than they read and who are more receptive to the spoken than the written word."[62] The impressions they receive during oral argument often carry with them into the conference room a few days later. Moreover, oral argument gives an opportunity for judges to explore with counsel key issues left undeveloped in the briefs.

During oral argument, the Chief Justice sits in the center of a raised bench with the senior Associate Justice to his right and the next ranking Justice to his left. Other Justices are arranged by seniority alternately to his right and left, leaving the most junior Justice positioned farthest to his left. Some justices rely on a "bench memorandum" to digest the facts and arguments of both sides and provide guidance during the questioning of counsel. Judicial styles differ at oral argument. Justice Douglas asked few questions and regarded many of them from colleagues as attempts to lobby Justices for votes rather than to illuminate issues.[63]

---

[61]New York Times v. United States, 403 U.S. 713 (1971). See Martin Shapiro, The Pentagon Papers and the Courts 125 (1972).

[62]John M. Harlan, "What Part Does the Oral Argument Play in the Conduct of an Appeal?," 41 Corn. L. Q. 6 (1955).

[63]William O. Douglas, The Court Years 181 (1981).

To divide the time between hearing cases and writing opinions, the Court alternates between several weeks or oral argument and several weeks of recess to write opinions and study appeals and cert petitions. If the Chief Justice has voted with the majority in conference, he assigns the majority opinions either to himself or to another Justice. When the Chief Justice is in the minority, the senior Justice voting with the majority assigns the case. The dissenters decide who shall write the dissenting opinion. Each Justice may write a separate opinion, concurrence, or dissent.

The assignment of opinions recognizes the need to distribute workload fairly, the different speeds with which Justices complete their research and writing, and the availability of expertise within the Court. Chief Justice Vinson, a former member of the House Ways and Means Committee and Secretary of the Treasury, preferred to handle tax cases.[64]

Although Justices are appointed for life and are immune from periodic campaigning for electoral office, they know that the ability to write acceptable opinions depends on sensitivity to the public. This consideration affects the assignment of opinions. In 1944, Chief Justice Stone initially assigned the Texas "White Primary" case to Justice Frankfurter. Justice Jackson expressed his misgivings to both Frankfurter and Stone, suggesting that because of "Southern sensibilities" it was unwise to have a Vienna-born Jew, raised in New England (the seat of the abolition movement), write the majority opinion striking down the Texas statute. With Frankfurter's knowledge and consent, Stone transferred the assignment to Stanley Reed, a native-born, Protestant, and old-time Kentuckian. Reed was also a Democrat of long standing, whereas Frankfurter's past ties to the Democratic party were suspect.[65]

Recusal. Under English common law, judges could be disqualified for direct interest in a case but never for bias. Such an admission would have conceded the capacity for partiality or favoritism in a judge.[66] Many of the early Justices on the Supreme Court failed to recuse (remove) themselves from cases that, under today's

---

[64]Chief Justice Vinson, 499 Nw. U. L. Rev., at 31–32.

[65]Alpheus T. Mason, Harlan Fiske Stone: Pillar of the Law 614–15 (1968).

[66]John P. Frank, "Disqualification of Judges," 56 Yale L. J. 605, 609–10 (1947), and Lois G. Forer, "Psychiatric Evidence in the Recusation of Judges," 73 Harv. L. Rev. 1325, 1327 (1960).

standards, would call for disqualification. Justice Story decided cases involving the United States Bank while serving as president of a Massachusetts branch of the National Bank. Chief Justice Marshall wrote *Marbury* v. *Madison* after serving as the Secretary of State who refused to deliver the commission of office. In that same year, however, Marshall withdrew from *Stuart* v. *Laird* because he had tried the case earlier in the circuit court.[67]

Based on statutory guidelines, court decisions, judicial codes, and personal standards, judges withdraw from certain cases.[68] Judges disqualify themselves to maintain the appearance of impartiality and due process. Chief Justice Stone and Justice Jackson did not take part in a 1942 decision because as former Attorneys General they had helped prosecute the case.[69] Justice Frankfurter, believing that judges "on the whole" are able to lay aside private views in discharging their judicial function, felt that under some circumstances "reason cannot control the subconscious influence of feelings of which it is unaware," and under those conditions recusal was an appropriate step.[70] Judge Haynsworth's failure to recuse himself in several cases in the Fourth Circuit became a key reason for the Senate's rejection of him to the Supreme Court in 1969.

Justice Jackson shocked the country in June 1946 by issuing a blistering attack on Justice Black. This extraordinary public revelation of a bitter feud between two members of the Supreme Court had its origins in a 1945 decision in which Black was part of a 5 to 4 majority upholding the right of coal miners.[71] Jackson wrote a dissent that quoted from a Senate debate in 1937 to show that Black, as a Senator, provided legislative history contrary to the majority's decision. It was also known that the chief counsel for the miners in the 1945 case was Black's former law partner.

The coal company petitioned for a rehearing, asking whether Black could render impartial justice given his connection with the legislation and the chief counsel. All members of the Court agreed that the motion for a rehearing should be denied, because the decision to

[67]1 Cr. 299, 308 (1803).

[68]See 28 U.S.C. §§ 144, 455 (1982), and David C. Hjelmfelt, "Statutory Disqualification of Federal Judges," 30 Kans. L. Rev. 255 (1982).

[69]United States v. Bethlehem Steel Corp., 315 U.S. 289, 309 (1942).

[70]Public Utilities Comm'n v. Pollak, 343 U.S. 451, 466–67 (1952). See also discussion at United States v. Grinnell Corp., 384 U.S. 563, 580–83 (1966).

[71]Jewell Ridge Corp. v. Local No. 6167, 325 U.S. 161 (1945).

disqualify oneself is purely a personal judgment to be exercised by each Justice. However, Jackson did not want to imply, by silence, that everyone on the Court supported Black's decision. When the Court denied the motion, Jackson wrote a concurring opinion, explaining that disqualification was not a decision for the full Court. Each Justice had to make that determination for himself. Frankfurter joined Jackson's concurrence.[72] Black's supporters were outraged by the concurrence because it drew attention to the issue of disqualification.

A newspaper article in May 1946 reported that Black regarded Jackson's concurrence as a gratuitous insult and a slur on Black's honor. The dispute was intensified by the pending selection of a Chief Justice by President Truman. Jackson hoped to be named. Black was dead-set against it. According to the newspaper story, Black threatened to resign if Truman selected Jackson as Chief Justice.[73] Black refused to comment on these newspaper accounts.

While Jackson was in Nuremberg serving as Special Prosecutor for the Nazi trials, Truman nominated Fred Vinson to be Chief Justice. Jackson was convinced that Black had a hand in denying him the promotion. From Nuremberg, Jackson cabled the Judiciary Committee to set forth his views on the 1945 dispute. He said that after he announced his decision to write a concurrence on the petition for a rehearing, Black became "very angry" and warned that any opinion that discussed the subject at all would mean "a declaration of war." Jackson told Black that he would "not stand for any more of his bullying and that, whatever I would otherwise do, I would now have to write my opinion to keep self-respect in the face of his threats." Alluding to reports that had been published critical of his role, Jackson remarked: "If war is declared on me I propose to wage it with the weapons of the open warrior, not those of the stealthy assassin." Jackson warned that if Black failed to disqualify himself in comparable cases in the future, "I will make my Jewell Ridge opinion look like a letter of recommendation by comparison."[74]

Justice Rehnquist was asked to recuse himself from *Laird* v. *Tatum* because he had earlier testified on the subject while serving as an official in the Justice Department. In a highly unusual memoran-

[72]Jewell Ridge Coal Corp. v. Local No. 6167, 325 U.S. 897 (1945).
[73]Doris Fleeson, "Supreme Court Feud," [Washington] Evening Star, May 16, 1946, at A-15.
[74]New York Times, June 11, 1946, at 2:6.

dum, Rehnquist agreed that disqualification would have been required had he signed a pleading or brief in the case or actively participated in it. In two earlier cases he withdrew for those reasons.[75] But he disagreed that testimony or the expression of one's views were adequate grounds for recusal. He also pointed out that disqualification of a Supreme Court Justice presents problems that do not exist in a lower court where one judge may substitute for another.[76] Rehnquist's participation in *Laird* v. *Tatum* resurfaced as an issue in 1986 during his nomination hearings to be Chief Justice.[77]

Drafting Opinions. The process of writing opinions begins with the briefs prepared by opposing counsel, research by law clerks and library staff, and the knowledge that Justices acquire from decades of experience in public and private life. These drafts are printed within the Court building and circulated among the Justices. Comments are written on the drafts; memoranda are exchanged. Often a forceful dissent may persuade members of the majority to change their position, creating a new majority from the old dissenting position. Chief Justice Vinson once remarked that an opinion circulated as a dissent "sometimes has so much in logic, reason, and authority to support it that it becomes the opinion of the Court."[78] Draft opinions may be so influential in modifying the Court's final decision that they are never published.[79] The threat of a dissent can force changes in the majority opinion.[80]

The role of law clerks is sometimes described in sensational terms, as though they displace the functions of judges. Because of the growing importance of law clerks, Senator John Stennis suggested in 1958 that it might be appropriate to subject them to confirmation by the Senate.[81] Publication of *The Brethren* in 1979 catapulted clerks to a

[75]409 U.S. 824, 828–29 (1972).

[76]Id. at 837–38. See also Rehnquist's "Sense and Nonsense About Judicial Ethics," 28 Record Ass'n Bar of the City of N.Y. 694 (1973). Failure of judges to recuse themselves can lead to a decision being vacated; Aetna Life Insurance Co. v. Lavoie, 106 S.Ct. 1580 (1986).

[77]"Nomination of Justice William Hubbs Rehnquist," hearings before the Senate Committee on the Judiciary, 99th Cong., 2d Sess. 182–86, 198, 230–61 (1986).

[78]69 S.Ct. x (1949).

[79]Alexander M. Bickel, The Unpublished Opinions of Mr. Justice Brandeis (1967).

[80]Murphy, Judicial Strategy, at 57–60.

[81]104 Cong. Rec. 8107–08 (1958).

seemingly pivotal role in making judicial policy, but this study depended heavily on interviews with clerks who no doubt found it tempting to embroider a bit on their contributions to public law.

Judges in the prime of life are unlikely to defer to the opinions of clerks fresh out of law school, however much the clerks may stimulate new ideas and approaches. Clerks come and go, but the persistence of a Justice's writing style is compelling evidence that they do their own work. Yet clerks do more than check footnotes, review cert petitions, and perform minor editing tasks. Depending on the judge they work for, they might be asked to prepare a "prototype or aspirant opinion" to guide the thinking of the court.[82] Because of heavy court workload, judges are often inclined to let clerks do the preliminary draft of an opinion.[83]

The legal profession no longer suggests that the sole duty of a judge is to place a constitutional provision beside a challenged statute to see if the latter squares with the former.[84] Still, the belief that judges, in the act of deciding, are able to put aside their personal value systems retains a following. Justice Frankfurter made an eloquent plea for this concept of judicial deliberation:

> It is asked with sophomoric brightness, does a man cease to be himself when he becomes a Justice? Does he change his character by putting on a gown? No, he does not change his character. He brings his whole experience, his training, his outlook, his social, intellectual and moral environment with him when he takes a seat on the Supreme Bench. But a judge worth his salt is in the grip of his function. The intellectual habits of self-discipline which govern his mind are as much a part of him as the influence of the interest he may have represented at the bar, often much more so.[85]

It would be superficial to suggest that judges use their office simply to disseminate personal views, but decisions of individual judges flow at least in part from their own values and attitudes. Justice Miller,

[82]Frank M. Coffin, The Ways of a Judge: Reflections from the Federal Appellate Bench 69 (1980).

[83]J. Woodford Howard, Jr., Courts of Appeals in the Federal Judicial System 200 (1981). See also Coffin, Ways of a Judge, at 69–71, 145–66.

[84]See Justice Roberts's opinion in United States v. Butler, 297 U.S. 1, 62 (1936).

[85]Felix Frankfurter, "Some Observations on the Nature of the Judicial Process of Supreme Court Litigation," 98 Proceedings Am. Phil. Soc. 233, 238 (1954).

who served on the Supreme Court from 1862 to 1890, despaired of the fixed views and predispositions of those on the bench: "It is vain to contend with judges who have been at the bar the advocates for forty years of rail road companies, and all the forms of associated capital, when they are called upon to decide cases where such interests are in contest. All their training, all their feelings are from the start in favor of those who need no such influence."[86]

Although the votes of judges cannot be predicted with mathematical accuracy, attorneys are sophisticated enough to engage in "forum shopping" to find the court that augurs best for their client. Judicial independence and objectivity remain important values in the administration of justice, but by now it is routine to recognize definite alignments and alliances among judges.[87] Even members of the judiciary acknowledge the existence of blocs. When Justice Blackmun joined the Supreme Court he calculated there were two Justices on the right, two on the left, and "five of us in the center."[88] Justice O'Connor's appearance in 1981 added another conservative voice to that of Chief Justice Burger and Justice Rehnquist. Blackmun, meanwhile, now found himself voting more frequently with the liberal bloc of Justices Brennan and Marshall. Blocs are not necessarily stable. They change over time and vary with the issue. A well-known shift occurred in 1937 when Hughes and Roberts altered their interpretation of the commerce power of Congress. During the Burger Court, Justices Blackmun, Powell, Stevens, and White formed part of a "floating center," casting the votes necessary to build a majority by joining either with the liberal votes of Brennan and Marshall or the conservative wing of Burger, O'Connor, and Rehnquist.

Members of the judiciary sometimes complain that their decisions are distorted by the press. Mistakes and misconceptions by reporters are likely, given the time pressures between the announcement of a decision and the deadlines imposed by newspapers, magazines, and broadcast services. These pressures have been partly relieved by several changes over the past few decades. In 1965 the Supreme Court, instead of handing down all opinions on "Decision Monday," began

[86]Charles Fairman, Mr. Justice Miller and the Supreme Court 374 (1939). For a dissection of various claims of impersonal judgments by judges, see George D. Braden, "The Search for Objectivity in Constitutional Law," 57 Yale L. J. 571 (1948).

[87]A pioneering study is by C. Herman Pritchett, The Roosevelt Court: A Study in Judicial Politics and Values, 1937–1947 (1948).

[88]Blackmun, "A Justice Speaks Out," at 22.

delivering some of its decisions on other days of the week. The Court also started meeting at ten A.M. rather than noon; these extra hours eased deadlines for reporters. To assure more accurate and sophisticated coverage, major newspapers and wire services began selecting reporters with law degrees or special training in the law.[89]

Some of the "distortions" in the press come from Justices who use careless language in concurring and dissenting opinions, or from those who fail, in the statement for the Court, to correct misconceptions that appear in separate opinions. When the Supreme Court announced the school prayer decision in 1962, Justice Douglas's concurrence suggested that the decision would cover ceremonial observances of a religious nature, such as the Court's traditional invocation when it convenes and the offering of a daily prayer by a chaplain in Congress.[90] Such speculations, well beyond the issue before the Court, helped fuel public confusion and outrage. When opinions contain sharp crossfire between Justices, "news reporters and the public at large are likely to lose sight of the law in what appears (to the uninitiated at least) to be a battle of men and not of law."[91] The prayer case was also grossly misrepresented by the president of the American Bar Association, who weighed in with the warning that the decision would require elimination of the motto "In God We Trust" from all coins.[92] The public impression never recovered from these irresponsible readings.

The judiciary's ability to communicate accurately to the public requires a writing style that is precise and economical. Judges advise opinion writers to use familiar words and short sentences. They prefer simplicity, clarity, brevity, and a direct and vigorous style.[93] Justice Jackson gloried in the "short Saxon word that pierces the mind like a spear and the simple figure that lights the understanding."[94] Nevertheless, judges have personal idiosyncrasies that produce affec-

---

[89]John P. MacKenzie, "The Warren Court and the Press," 67 Mich. L. Rev. 303, 314–15 (1968). See also David L. Grey, The Supreme Court and the News Media (1968).

[90]Engel v. Vitale, 370 U.S. 421, 439–42 (1962).

[91]Chester A. Newland, "Press Coverage of the United States Supreme Court," 17 West. Pol. Q. 15, 24–25 (1964).

[92]Id. at 28.

[93]Griffin B. Bell, "Style in Judicial Writing," 15 J. Pub. L. 214 (1966).

[94]Robert H. Jackson, "Advocacy Before the Supreme Court: Suggestions for Effective Case Presentations," 37 A.B.A.J. 801, 863–64 (1951).

tation, ornate prose, and verbosity. Ambiguity is also likely when several strong-minded individuals must agree on a single statement: "The Court must function as an institution, which means that at least five Justices must commonly agree on a given statement. This may require use of terms that mean one thing to one Justice and something else to another, thus getting rid of the case at hand and postponing the problem of precision to a future day that may never come."[95]

Jerome Frank, in a law review article signed Anon Y. Mous, decried the temptation of some judges to ape the English style of writing. He singled out Cardozo for special criticism for imitating eighteenth-century English and allowing archaisms and circumlocutions to obscure his opinions. Sentences that are baroque and rococo, although perhaps satisfying to the author's ego, are confusing to the reader. Elaborate metaphors, inverted phrases, and negative constructions rob an opinion not only of clarity but of persuasive force. Instead of adopting the style of the English upper class, Frank urges judges to use the direct and powerful American speech of Justices Holmes, Jackson, Black, and Douglas. He quotes Cardozo that "Justice is not there unless there is also understanding."[96]

In deciding a particular case, judges often stray from the central issue and add extraneous matter in the form of obiter dicta. Because these remarks are not necessary to the basic decision, they are not binding as legal precedent. But they can serve as the functional equivalent of an advisory opinion, supplying guidance to the future direction of legal thinking. In striking down a statute, a court might suggest to legislators how the law could be rewritten.[97] As Griffin Bell noted during his service as a federal appellate judge, "the role of courts under our system of separation of powers and federalism may call such a practice into play in some situations."[98]

Coherence and "principled decisionmaking" are difficult virtues to achieve for a multimember Court that necessarily operates as a committee, attempting to stitch together a decision that can attract a majority. Compromises are needed. The difficulty is compounded by

[95]John P. Frank, Marble Palace 134–35 (1958).

[96]Anon Y. Mous, "The Speech of Judges: A Dissenting Opinion," 29 Va. L. Rev. 625, 638 (1943). For a discussion of judicial writing styles, see Benjamin N. Cardozo, "Law and Literature," 14 Yale Rev. 699 (1925).

[97]E. F. Albertsworth, "Advisory Functions in Federal Supreme Court," 23 Geo. L. J. 643, 650–63 (1935).

[98]Bell, "Style," 15 J. Pub. L., at 217.

the practice of moving a step at a time, responding to the concrete case at hand. As noted by one scholar, the Court "is in the unenviable posture of a committee attempting to draft a horse by placing very short lines on a very large drawing-board at irregular intervals during which the membership of the committee constantly changes."[99]

Unanimity and Dissent

The Supreme Court initially followed the British practice of allowing each Justice to write opinions seriatim. Rather than announce a single opinion representing the collective position of the majority, the Justices delivered independent statements.[100] Before John Marshall's appointment as Chief Justice, the Court had begun to deliver an opinion for the entire Court rather than a string of seriatim opinions.[101] Marshall reinforced that direction, believing that a single decision strengthened the Court's power and dignity. He selected one Justice (usually himself) to write the majority opinion. Dissents were rare. Jefferson delivered a stinging rebuke to the Chief Justice for departing from seriatim decisions: "An opinion is huddled up in conclave, perhaps by a majority of one, delivered as if unanimous, and with the silent acquiescence of lazy or timid associates, by a crafty chief judge, who sophisticates the law to his own mind, by the turn of his own reasoning."[102]

Jefferson's critique was written in 1820, about two decades after Marshall had joined the Court, and appeared to be triggered by Marshall's broad nationalist ruling in *McCulloch* v. *Maryland* (1819). Seriatim opinions had offered a definite benefit: each Justice was accountable for articulating the rationale behind a decision. But Marshall wanted the Court to develop an institutional view, moving away from personal positions to a more generalized principle for the majority.

The harmony within the early Marshall Court depended partly on

[99] Anthony G. Amsterdam, "Perspectives on the Fourth Amendment," 58 Minn. L. Rev. 349, 350 (1974).
[100] Karl M. ZoBell, "Division of Opinion in the Supreme Court: A History of Judicial Disintegration," 44 Corn. L. Q. 186, 192–93 (1959).
[101] 4 Dall. 1–11 (1799). But see seriatim opinions at 18–20 and 39–46, both cases delivered in 1800.
[102] 15 The Writings of Thomas Jefferson 298 (Memorial ed. 1904). Letter of December 25, 1820 to Thomas Richie.

residential arrangements. The Justices lived together in the same lodginghouse on Capitol Hill, taking their meals at a common table. Justice Story described the members of the Marshall Court as "united as one. . . . We moot every question as we proceed, and . . . conferences at our lodgings often come to a very quick, and, I trust, a very accurate opinion, in a few hours."[103]

This cohesiveness did not last long on the Marshall Court. Dissents became more frequent in later years and under future Chief Justices. At various times throughout history, however, members of the Court have placed a premium on unanimity. In 1922, Justice McReynolds wrote a majority opinion that provoked dissents from Brandeis, Clarke, and Pitney. Chief Justice Taft scheduled a reargument and by the time he wrote the new majority opinion, Clarke and Pitney had retired. Taft sought Brandeis's views and eventually produced a unanimous opinion, with which McReynolds concurred.[104]

At the urging of colleagues who fear that dissents will damage the corporate reputation of the Supreme Court, Justices have been willing to convert a dissent into a concurring opinion. Labeling it a concurrence, however, is often an inadequate mask to cover the dissenting view.[105] It is not unusual for Justices to concur in the judgment or result while shredding the logic, reasoning, and precedents contained in the opinion of the Court.[106] Justices may decide to write a concurrence rather than join the Court's opinion because they are "not sure what it means."[107]

Justices also withhold dissents when the case is less significant to them. Such accommodations create a reservoir of good will, promote

[103]James Sterling Young. The Washington Community 77 (1966).

[104]Alpheus Thomas Mason, "William Howard Taft," in Leon Friedman and Fred L. Israel, eds., The Justices of the United States Supreme Court (1969), iii, 2114, and Bickel, Mr. Justice Brandeis, at 111–13. The Case was Sonneborn Bros. v. Cureton, 262 U.S. 506 (1923).

[105]CIA v. Sims, 471 U.S. 159, 181–94 (1985) (Marshall and Brennan, JJ., concurring). Justice Murphy, under the urgings of colleagues, changed his dissent in *Hirabayashi* v. *United States* to a concurrence. See Murphy, Judicial Strategy, at 46–47, and Howard, Mr. Justice Murphy, at 302–9.

[106]Murphy v. Waterfront Comm'n, 378 U.S. 52, 80–92 (1964) (Harlan, J., concurring); Warden v. Hayden, 387 U.S. 294, 310–12 (1967) (Fortas, J. and Warren, C.J., concurring); Argersinger v. Hamlin, 407 U.S. 25, 41–44 (1972). (Burger, C.J., concurring) and 44–46 (Powell, J., concurring, joined by Rehnquist, J.).

[107]Edwards v. Arizona, 451 U.S. 477, 488 (1981) (Powell and Rehnquist, JJ., concurring).

institutional harmony, and allow the acquiescent Justice to call upon a colleague at some future time for reciprocal favors—perhaps a fourth vote to grant certiorari.[108] Justices may also promise to withdraw a separate concurring opinion if its substance is incorporated in the Court's opinion.[109] Justice Blackmun remarked in a 1986 concurrence: "Our experience should tell us that the concessions extracted as the price of joining an opinion may influence its shape as decisively as the sentiments of its nominal author."[110]

During preparation for the desegregation case of 1954, members of the Court felt strongly that unanimity was crucial in building public acceptance of its decision. Discreet pressure was applied to Justices to ward off concurring and dissenting opinions. Chief Justice Warren realized that once a Justice had announced his position it would be more difficult for him to change his thinking, "so we decided that we could dispense with our usual custom of formally expressing our individual views at the first conference and would confine ourselves for a time to informal discussion of the briefs, the arguments made at the hearing, and our own independent research for each conference day, reserving our final opinions until the discussions were concluded." By following this process, the Court agreed unanimously that the "separate but equal" doctrine had no place in public education.[111]

In earlier rulings, the Court relied on *per curiam* opinions (unsigned opinions "for the court") to reduce friction. This technique permitted the Justices to present a united front and avoid details or legal interpretations that might have fractured the Court and communicated more information to the public than the Court thought prudent. In one of the early racial discrimination cases before the desegregation case, Justice Frankfurter explained in a letter to Chief Justice Vinson that the per curiam "should set forth as briefly and as unargumentatively as possible" the Court's position. "In short," Frankfurter wrote, "our *per cur.* should avoid every possibility of serving as a target for contention. . . ."[112]

[108]Murphy, Judicial Strategy, at 52–53.
[109]H. N. Hirsch, The Enigma of Felix Frankfurter 190 (1981).
[110]Aetna Life Insurance Co. v. Lavoie, 106 S.Ct. at 1591.
[111]Earl Warren, "Inside the Supreme Court," 239 Atlantic Monthly 35–36 (April 1977).
[112]Dennis J. Hutchinson, "Unanimity and Desegregation: Decisionmaking in the

When Governor Orval Faubus and the Arkansas legislature fought to retain the state's system of segregated schools, the Supreme Court reaffirmed the principle it had enunciated in 1954. To underscore its unanimity, the names of all nine Justices were listed, including the three who joined the Court since 1954. Frankfurter frustrated this strategy by insisting on a separate concurrence, agreeing to file it a week after the Court released its opinion. Warren, Black, and Brennan were furious. Frankfurter's only justification for the extra statement was that he had a special responsibility to lecture Southern lawyers and law professors who had been his students at Harvard Law School.[113]

In 1974, with President Nixon threatening to defy any judicial effort to make him surrender the Watergate tapes, the Supreme Court once again produced a unanimous ruling.[114] By forcing a united front and rejecting Nixon's broad claim of executive privilege, the Court played a crucial role in bringing about his resignation. But the very process of generating a unanimous opinion invited generalization at so high a plane that the result obfuscated the law of executive privilege.[115] This is an ever-present risk. Attracting a few additional votes may dilute legal principles to such an extent that some Justices in the original majority may decide to write concurring or even dissenting opinions.

Unanimity in these cases helped prepare the public for important rulings. In other situations, however, a multiplicity of opinions may be enlightening. In the Steel Seizure Case of 1952, for example, every member of the six-man majority wrote a separate opinion discussing the limits of presidential power. The country was therefore privy to nuances and complexities that would have been obscured by a broad ruling satisfactory to the majority. Multiplicity gave room for sophisticated explorations of the source and scope of executive powers.

Supreme Court, 1948–1958," 68 Geo. L. J. 1, 9 (1979). For objections to per curiams that fail to cite authorities and the reasons for a decision, see "Supreme Court Per Curiam Practice: A Critique," 69 Harv. L. Rev. 707 (1956).

[113]Bernard Schwartz, Super Chief 302–3 (1983); Cooper v. Aaron, 358 U.S. 1 (1958).
[114]United States v. Nixon, 418 U.S. 683 (1974).
[115]Louis Henkin, "Executive Privilege: Mr. Nixon Loses But the Presidency Largely Prevails," 22 UCLA L. Rev. 40 (1974); William Van Alstyne, "A Political and Constitutional Review of *United States* v. *Nixon*," 22 UCLA L. Rev. 116 (1974).

Concurring opinions may be the means of foreshadowing future developments in the direction of law.

With the growth in the number of cases that raise constitutional issues, separate concurring and dissenting opinions have increased dramatically. Justice Rehnquist suggested that it "may well be that the nature of constitutional adjudication invites, at least, if it does not require, more separate opinions than does adjudication of issues of law in other areas."[116] Of special concern is the inability of the Court to prepare a decision that attracts a majority of the Justices. Instead, the Court delivers a plurality opinion that creates confusion in the lower courts and other branches of government. The number of plurality opinions by the Burger Court exceeds the number of all previous Courts.[117]

Dissents. Shortly before returning to the Supreme Court, this time as Chief Justice, Charles Evans Hughes wrote eloquently on the deliberative process of the judiciary. He recognized that a dissenting opinion can damage the appearance of justice that the public needs in a court of last resort. However, he felt it far more injurious to obtain unanimity by concealing genuine differences, for "what must ultimately sustain the court in public confidence is the character and independence of the judges." While not encouraging dissents born of a captious spirit or an inability to cooperate with others, he believed that a dissenting opinion based on deep thought and feeling could be "an appeal to the brooding spirit of the law, to the intelligence of a future day, when a later decision may possibly correct the error into which the dissenting judge believes the court to have been betrayed."[118]

Following this tradition, Justice Douglas explained why dissents are necessary in a democratic society. The lawyer's search for certainty is illusory because law "is not what has been or is—law in the lawyer's sense is the prediction of things to come, the prediction of

[116]Justice William H. Rehnquist, "The Supreme Court: Past and Present," 59 A.B.A.J. 361, 363 (1973).
[117]Note, "Plurality Decisions and Judicial Decisionmaking," 94 Harv. L. Rev. 1127 (1981); John F. Davis and William L. Reynolds, "Judicial Cripples: Plurality Opinions in the Supreme Court," 1974 Duke L. J. 59.
[118]Charles Evans Hughes, The Supreme Court of the United States 68 (1928).

what decree will be written by designated judges on specified facts."[119] He acknowledged that legal certainty and unanimity are possible both under the fascist and communist systems: "They are not only possible; they are indispensable; for complete subservience to the political regime is a *sine qua non* to judicial survival under either system."[120]

Dissents may force the majority to clarify and tighten its opinion. They can also serve as a precursor for a future majority holding. Justice Harlan's dissents in the *Civil Rights Cases* (1883), in *Plessy* v. *Ferguson* (1895), and other race cases offered a broad interpretation of the Fourteenth Amendment in protecting the rights of blacks. This doctrine gained strength in some of the lower courts more than a half century later and foreshadowed the eventual overruling of *Plessy*.[121] The dissents of Justice Holmes, especially in economic regulation cases, later carried the day for the Court. Justice Stone was a lone dissenter in the first flag-salute case in 1940, involving the religious freedoms of Jehovah's Witnesses.[122] Two years later, three Justices from the majority publicly announced that the decision "was wrongly decided."[123] The following year the Court reversed its 1940 ruling, vindicating Stone's position.[124] In 1942 the Court split 6 to 3, deciding that indigent defendants did not have a right to counsel in state court for all felonies. By 1963 the position of the three dissenters had been elevated to the majority viewpoint.[125]

For a judicial body, dissent carries substantial costs. Justice Edward D. White, himself dissenting in an 1895 opinion, said that the "only purpose which an elaborate dissent can accomplish, if any, is to weaken the effect of the opinion of the majority, and thus engender want of confidence in the conclusions of courts of last resort."[126] Dissents

[119]William O. Douglas, "The Dissent: A Safeguard of Democracy," 32 J. Am. Jud. Soc. 104, 104 (1948).

[120]Id. at 105.

[121]Loren P. Beth, "Justice Harlan and the Uses of Dissent," 49 Am. Pol. Sci. Rev. 1085, 1086–92 (1955).

[122]Minersville School District v. Gobitis, 310 U.S. 586, 601 (1940).

[123]Jones v. Opelika, 316 U.S. 584, 624 (1942). The Justices were Black, Douglas, and Murphy.

[124]West Virginia Board of Education v. Barnette, 319 U.S. 624 (1943).

[125]Betts v. Brady, 316 U.S. 455, 474 (1942); Gideon v. Wainwright, 372 U.S. 335 (1963).

[126]Pollock v. Farmers' Loan & Trust Co., 157 U.S. 429, 608 (1895) (White, J., dissenting).

detract from institutional unity and may exacerbate tensions within a court, which is by nature a collegial body. Those tensions are heightened by sarcastic dissents that question the integrity or intellectual ability of a fellow judge. Dissents can be especially irresponsible when they confuse or distort the holding of the Court.[127]

Some members of the judiciary feel a special obligation to express their dissent when constitutional questions are at stake. Said Justice Moody in a 1908 dissent:

> Under ordinary circumstances, where the judgment rests exclusively, as it does here, upon a mere interpretation of the words of a law, which may be readily changed by the lawmaking branches of the Government, if they be so minded, a difference of opinion may well be left without expression. But where the judgment is a judicial condemnation of an act of a coordinate branch of our Government it is so grave a step that no member of the court can escape his own responsibility, or be justified in suppressing his own views, if unhappily they have not found expression in those of his associates.[128]

The choice between writing a dissent and joining the majority remains an individual matter, often reflecting a Justice's value toward continuity and institutional cohesiveness. Although Justice Harlan dissented in *Miranda* v. *Arizona* (1966), the principle of stare decisis prompted him to acquiesce in subsequent applications of *Miranda*.[129] Justices White and Stewart, who also dissented in *Miranda*, felt free to express their continuing disagreement with that decision.[130]

Caseload Burdens

The number of cases before the Supreme Court has increased dramatically over the years, especially in recent decades. In this era of "rights consciousness," a larger number of individuals and organi-

[127]Robert H. Jackson, The Supreme Court in the American System of Government 16–19 (1955).

[128]The Employers' Liability Cases, 207 U.S. 463, 504–05 (1908). For a similar view, see Justice Story's dissent in Briscoe v. Bank of Kentucky, 11 Pet. 256, 328 (1837).

[129]Orozco v. Texas, 394 U.S. 324, 328 (1969).

[130]Id. at 328–31.

zations go to court either to secure rights or to enforce rights already established by statute. The victories of blacks in the desegregation cases encouraged other "disfranchised" groups to enter the courts. Consumers, environmentalists, Native Americans, senior citizens, the disabled, women, Mexican Americans, and a variety of public interest law firms filed suit to pursue their goals.[131] The result is an engine that stimulates litigation. The creation of additional district and appellate judgeships allows more plaintiffs and attorneys to enter the courts. Further aggravating the workload are dozens of statutes passed by Congress creating new causes of action, providing expedited methods of appeal, imposing duties on the judiciary, and awarding fees for attorneys.

In 1971, Chief Justice Burger appointed a group to study the growing caseload of the Supreme Court. Called the Freund Committee, the group recommended that Congress establish a seven-member National Court of Appeals to screen petitions filed with the Supreme Court and to certify four hundred or so cases considered the most worthy. The Supreme Court would select from that list, but no appeal would lie from the cases rejected by the National Court of Appeals. The Committee's recommendation paralleled those announced earlier by Burger.[132] The previous Chief Justice, Earl Warren, criticized the Committee's screening idea as a naive proposal from people unfamiliar with the Court's decisional process. He also objected to giving the National Court limited power to resolve conflicting decisions among the circuits.[133]

A second study, prepared by the Hruska Commission, was released in 1975. It too proposed a National Court of Appeals, but not to screen cases for the Supreme Court. A new court would be established to handle cases referred to it by the Supreme Court or appellate courts. In 1983, Chief Justice Burger offered his own version of a National Court of Appeals. He suggested a temporary court, drawn from appellate judges in each circuit, to resolve conflicts between appellate courts. A major restructuring of the judicial system, he

[131]Susan M. Olson, "The Political Evolution of Interest Group Litigation," in Richard A. L. Giambitta, et al., eds., Governing Through Courts 225–58 (1981).

[132]"Interview with Chief Justice Warren E. Burger," U.S. News & World Report, December 14, 1970, at 43.

[133]Earl Warren, "The Proposed New 'National Court of Appeals'," 28 Record Ass'n Bar of the City of N.Y. 627, 637, 642 (1973).

warned, was necessary to "avoid a breakdown of the system—or of some of the justices."[134]

Other members of the Supreme Court have voiced alarm about the size of its casework. Justice Stevens, in a highly unusual revelation of the Court's decisionmaking process and the role of law clerks, said in 1982 that per curiam opinions were generally written "by an anonymous member" of the staff.[135] Justices White, Marshall, Powell, and Rehnquist have all called attention to the growing caseload and the delegation of judicial tasks to staff members.[136]

Although a majority of the present Court share a common concern about heavy caseloads, specific solutions are not so obvious. The Justices are unanimous in wanting to replace the Court's obligatory jurisdiction with discretionary review on certiorari, and in 1982 and 1984 the House of Representatives passed such legislation.[137] For more fundamental changes, however, there is no agreement.

Most cases decided by the Supreme Court are discretionary in character, and to that extent the Court's workload is self-imposed. Justices frequently complain that the Court accepts cases of an insignificant character. Dissenting in a 1982 per curiam ruling, Justice Stevens objected that the case was not "of sufficient importance to warrant full briefing and argument," was not "worthy of an opinion signed by a Member of this Court," and reflected "the ever-increasing impersonalization and bureaucratization of the federal judicial system."[138] The workload increases when the Court reaches out to decide matters that might have been left to state courts or to slow percolation in the federal courts. In 1985, Justice Stevens (joined by Justices Brennan and Marshall) noted in dissent:

> Much of the Court's "burdensome" workload is a product of its own aggressiveness in this area [of Fourth Amendment cases]. By promoting the Supreme Court of the United States as the High Magistrate for every warrantless search and seizure, this

[134]Washington Post, February 7, 1983, at A1.
[135]Stevens, "Judicial Restraint," 66 Judicature, at 178. For qualifications, see n.3 in his article.
[136]Washington Post, September 24, 1982, at A3.
[137]128 Cong. Rec. H7269–75 (daily ed. September 20, 1982); 130 Cong. Rec. H9287–88 (daily ed. September 11, 1984).
[138]Board of Education of Rogers, Ark. v. McCluskey, 458 U.S. 966, 972 (1982).

practice has burdened the argument docket with cases presenting fact-bound errors of minimal significance. It has also encouraged state legal officers to file petitions for certiorari in even the most frivolous search and seizure cases.[139]

Justice Stevens has warned that a National Court of Appeals (along the lines of the Hruska Commission) would aggravate the Supreme Court's workload. Justices would have to manage not only their own docket but that of an intermediate court as well.[140] However, Stevens supports the Freund Committee's idea of a court to screen petitions before they reach the Supreme Court. He would also allow that court to *decide* (not merely recommend) the granting of cert. Through such a change he hopes to augment the power of the intermediate court and overcome the resistance of appellate judges who fear they will be saddled with a routine screening function.[141] Justice White has objected to the creation of a special court that would sift through petitions and decide which cases the Supreme Court would hear.[142]

Justice Brennan has been a persistent critic of proposals to allow a special court to screen cases for the Supreme Court. He called the screening function "second to none in importance."[143] From his perspective, the dissenting opinions in denying cert represent an important foundation for the development of legal doctrine and the formation of future majority positions. He would not delegate to a separate court the responsibility for screening, a process he calls "inherently subjective" in nature and one that helps educate Justices on contemporary issues.[144]

Some of the workload problems could be relieved by withdrawing nonjudicial duties from the Court. At present, the Chief Justice is a member of the Board of Regents of the Smithsonian Institution.[145] He is also a Trustee of the National Gallery of Art[146] and of the

[139]California v. Carney, 471 U.S. 386, 396 (1985). Footnotes omitted.

[140]Stevens, "Judicial Restraint," 66 Judicature, at 179.

[141]Id. at 181–82.

[142]Byron R. White, "Challenges for the U.S. Supreme Court and the Bar: Contemporary Reflections," 51 Antitrust L. J. 275, 281–82 (1982).

[143]William J. Brennan, Jr., "The National Court of Appeals: Another dissent," 40 U. Chi. L. Rev. 473, 477 (1973).

[144]Id. at 480–81. See also William J. Brennan, Jr., "Some Thoughts on the Supreme Court's Workload," 66 Judicature 233 (1983); Ruth Bader Ginsburg and Peter W. Huber, "The Intercircuit Committee," 100 Harv. L. Rev. 1417 (1987).

[145]20 U.S.C. § 42 (1982).

[146]Id. at § 72.

Joseph H. Hirshhorn Museum and Sculpture Garden.[147] He is responsible for appointing someone from the judicial branch to the National Historical Publications and Records Commission.[148] Carrying out these extraneous duties seems to belie the claim that the Court is pressed to the limit with its caseload.

The Lower Courts

The federal judicial system consists of three tiers: district courts for trying a case (trial courts), circuit courts of appeals (appellate courts), and the Supreme Court. In addition, a myriad of specialized courts carry out adjudicatory duties.

Very few of the appellate decisions are taken to the Supreme Court. Of those that do reach the Court, an even smaller number are accepted and decided—somewhere in the range of one or two percent of the total.[149] This statistic reflects the principle that our federal judicial system entitles a litigant to only one appeal. As Chief Justice Taft noted, the rights of litigants are "sufficiently protected by a hearing or trial in the courts of first instance, and by one review in an immediate appellate Federal court."[150] Taft's position has been buttressed over the years by congressional actions that have extended the Court's discretionary authority.

Because the Supreme Court reviews only a small fraction of the cases decided at the lower level, appellate judges exercise "critical and usually final authority" over state and federal lawsuits.[151] The opportunity for error is limited by structuring appellate courts on a collegial basis. Decisions are usually made by a panel of three judges who rotate from panel to panel and form different combinations. The policy of rotation "decreases the ability of litigants to anticipate the court's exact composition and, by diversifying personnel, inhibits the formation of polarizing blocs or cliques."[152]

[147]Id. at § 76cc.
[148]44 U.S.C. § 1501 (1982).
[149]J. Woodford Howard, Jr., Courts of Appeals in the Federal Judicial System 57–58 (1981).
[150]William Howard Taft, "The Jurisdiction of the Supreme Court Under the Act of February 13, 1925," 35 Yale L. J. 1, 2 (1925).
[151]Frank M. Coffin, The Ways of a Judge 4 (1980).
[152]Howard, Court of Appeals, at 190.

Three-judge panels allow circuits to hear and decide more cases, but the panel system can produce contradictory rulings within the same circuit. To resolve these conflicts and address particularly important issues, the entire appellate court may sit en banc. By bringing all judges in the circuit together to sit on a case, however, the court may invite polarization and dissenting opinions.[153] En banc decisions can also produce panels of unwieldy size. When the Fifth Circuit grew in size to twenty-six judges, Chief Judge Godbold said that its en banc sessions "performed somewhat like a legislative body. It divided up into groups, with judges seeking accommodation on some ground that, while maybe not ideal for everybody, was at least agreeable to a majority. Its function became almost legislative, and, therefore, antithetical to the way that appellate courts normally operate."[154]

Judges acting in a collegial setting are able to challenge each other's mistakes and work cooperatively toward a consensus. Some appellate judges, by dint of their intellectual ability, have set the tone for the entire nation. As said of Learned Hand, for many decades a distinguished judge for the Second Circuit: "although he obeys the Supreme Court's decisions, many of those decisions have been based on rules of his own making. When he whistles a Supreme-Court tune, frequently it is really his own."[155]

Compared with appellate judges, district judges work in isolation. As the first and only court that most litigants in the federal system see, the district court occupies a crucial position. District judges not only receive the great mass of federal cases but settle in final form most of the disputes submitted to them. Unlike appellate courts, there are no colleagues to review their work formally and no need for conferences to hammer out differences and produce a compromise acceptable to several members of a court. Whereas appellate judges have jurisdiction over a territory comprising a number of states, district judges have strong ties to their local community. They are selected in part because they were born and educated in their district,

[153]Judah I. Labovitz, "En Banc Procedure in the Federal Courts of Appeals," 111 U. Pa. L. Rev. 220 (1962); A. Lamar Alexander, Jr., "En Banc Hearings in the Federal Courts of Appeals: Accommodating Institutional Responsibilities" (2 Parts), 40 N.Y.U. L. Rev. 563, 726 (1965).

[154]15 The Third Branch 2 (July 1983).

[155]Jerome N. Frank, "Some Reflections on Judge Learned Hand," 24 U. Chi. L. Rev. 666, 681 (1957).

practiced law there, and participated in local politics. These local allegiances affect their decisions in such areas as civil rights, environmental law, and labor relations.[156] As public opinion turned against the Vietnam War, federal district judges responded by handing down lighter sentences against draft resisters.[157] Appellate judges, more likely to reflect national than local concerns, sometimes characterize their work as having "to pull a lot of chestnuts out of the fire for district judges who must face lots of parochial pressures."[158] One appellate judge explained: "Circuit judges are not more courageous or more enlightened than district judges. They are just not on the firing line, not as exposed to built-in pressures and allegiances, not as tied by birth, education, residence, professional experience and other ties to one state and to one section of a state. And rarely do they have to condemn and enjoin their golfing, fishing, or gin rummy companions."[159]

Several factors supply uniformity to district court decisions and offset the centrifugal forces of localism. The exposure to standard textbooks in law school contributes a common framework. Review by appellate courts and the Supreme Court adds general guidance, either explicitly through decisions and remands or implicitly through the threat of review. Federal rules for civil and criminal procedure provide another source for uniformity among district judges. Finally, district judges see a broader context when they circulate outside their local environment and participate in the Judicial Conference of the United States, the Judicial Conference of the circuit, and Judicial Councils.[160]

State courts, by basing their rulings not on the U.S. Constitution but on rights guaranteed in their state constitutions, can insulate

[156]J. W. Peltason, Fifty-Eight Lonely Men: Southern Federal Judges and School Desegregation (1961); Kenneth Vines, "Federal District Judges and Race Relations Cases in the South," 26 J. Pol. 337 (1964). See also Herbert M. Kritzen, "Political Correlates of the Behavior of Federal District Judges: A 'Best Case' Analysis," 40 J. Pol. 25 (1978).

[157]Beverly B. Cook, "Public Opinion and Federal Judicial Policy," 21 Am. J. Pol. Sci. 567 (1977).

[158]Howard, Court of Appeals, at 145–56 (note). See Robert A. Carp and C. K. Rowland, Policymaking and Politics in the Federal District Courts (1983).

[159]John Minor Wisdom [Judge of the Fifth Circuit], "The Frictionmaking, Exacerbating Political Role of the Federal Courts," 21 Sw. L. J. 411, 420 (1967).

[160]Richard J. Richardson and Kenneth N. Vines, The Politics of Federal Courts: Lower Courts in the United States 108–12 (1970).

themselves from review by the federal judiciary. Although state courts have had the reputation as constitutional backwaters, especially in civil rights, civil liberties, and criminal procedures, throughout their history they have often pressed for policies that were several steps ahead of the national government. Justice Brandeis encouraged the idea of states operating as "laboratories" for the nation, experimenting with social and economic legislation that might later be applied by the federal government.

It is not unusual to see the Supreme Court, in announcing a new right or doctrine in constitutional law, point to several dozen states who had already led the way. In *Mapp* v. *Ohio* (1961), for example, the Court noted that almost two-thirds of the States were opposed to the use of the exclusionary rule before 1949, but more than half of those "since passing upon it, by their own legislative or judicial decision, have wholly or partly adopted or adhered to" the rule of excluding evidence illegally obtained.[161] State sentiments on the death penalty were an obvious influence behind the Court's repositioning between 1972 and 1976, first opposing the death penalty and then supporting it with qualifications.[162]

The independence of state courts is expressed in the school financing cases. In 1973, the Supreme Court rejected the argument that property-based financing systems violate the Equal Protection Clause by favoring students from affluent districts.[163] The Court's decision did not prevent state courts from reaching the opposite conclusion in interpreting the equal protection clauses of their own constitutions.[164] State courts may interpret individual liberties more expansively than the U.S. Supreme Court. For example, on the question of handing out leaflets in shopping centers, state courts can give greater weight to First Amendment interests than to the rights of property owners.[165]

In 1980, the Supreme Court concluded that Congress could deny funds to indigent women seeking an abortion.[166] When the issue of

[161]367 U.S. 643, 651 (1961).
[162]Furman v. Georgia, 408 U.S. 238 (1972); Gregg v. Georgia, 428 U.S. 153, 179–81 (1976).
[163]San Antonio School District v. Rodriguez, 411 U.S. 1 (1973).
[164]Serrano v. Priest, 557 P.2d 929 (Cal. 1977); Robinson v. Cahill, 303 A.2d 273 (N.J. 1973).
[165]PruneYard Shopping Center v. Robins, 447 U.S. 74, 81 (1980).
[166]Harris v. McRae, 448 U.S. 297 (1980).

public funding is framed entirely as a state matter to be decided under the state constitution, the results may differ from the Court's ruling. The California legislature restricted the circumstances under which public funds would be authorized to pay abortions for Medi-Cal recipients. The California courts struck down these statutes as unconstitutional. They reasoned that the state has no constitutional obligation to provide medical care to the poor, but once it does it bears the heavy burden of justifying a provision that withholds benefits from otherwise qualified individuals solely because they choose to exercise their constitutional rights to have an abortion.[167] A similar decision was issued by the New Jersey judiciary, overturning a state law that prohibited Medicaid funding for abortions except where medically necessary to preserve the mother's life.[168]

By the 1980s, states were once again being touted as innovative forces for social change and individual rights.[169] Speaking in 1984, Justice Brennan accused his own court of "both isolated and systematic violations of civil liberties" and said that more and more citizens were turning to state courts for relief.[170] When the Supreme Court in 1984 announced a broadening of the good-faith defense regarding the exclusionary rule, thus giving an advantage to law enforcement officers over the rights of citizens subject to search and seizure, states were free to offer increased protection for Fourth Amendment rights.[171] In a New York case, the exclusionary rule for illegally obtained evidence under the state constitution was held not subject to the good-faith defense.[172]

When the federal courts began to take on a conservative cast after appointments by President Reagan, some litigants depended on state courts to protect individual rights. The legal director of the Texas Civil Liberties Union remarked: "The state judges like it. Finally they get to act like federal judges and declare something unconstitutional.

---

[167]Committee to Defend Reprod. Rights v. Myers, 625 P.2d 779 (Cal. 1981).

[168]Right to Choose v. Byrne, 450 A.2d 925 (N.J. 1982).

[169]Fred Barbash, "State Courts Expanding Individual Rights," Washington Post, April 2, 1984, at A1; Lanny Proffer, "State Courts and Civil Liberties," 13 State Legislatures 28 (September 1987).

[170]"Brennan Says Rulings Violated Civil Liberties," Washington Post, October 25, 1984, at A3.

[171]United States v. Leon, 468 U.S. 897 (1984); Massachusetts v. Sheppard, 468 U.S. 981 (1984).

[172]People v. Bigelow, 488 N.E.2d 451 (N.Y. 1985).

They are proud that they can protect rights better than the federal courts can."[173]

To cultivate comity and mutual respect between the national and state levels, federal courts abstain in some areas. It would be impossible and self-destructive for federal courts to intervene in every state matter. This abstention doctrine, as an exercise of discretionary authority, is invoked by the Supreme Court to avoid "needless friction" with the administration of state affairs.[174] The general policy is to wait until the highest state court has disposed of a constitutional issue.

The policy of abstention has been waived when state statutes are vulnerable on their face for abridging free expression or discouraging protecting activities. Federal courts intervene in these cases to prevent state officials from invoking a statute in bad faith, without any hope of success, for the sole purpose of harassing minorities or their organizations. This exception to the abstention doctrine is aimed at statutes that are so vague or overbroad that they threaten First Amendment freedoms.[175]

In the case of a pending state criminal proceeding, federal courts intervene only under extraordinary circumstances: where the danger of irreparable loss is both great and immediate, and where the threat to federally protected rights cannot be eliminated during the course of the trial.[176] Noninterference by the Supreme Court often provokes biting dissents that regard federalism and the abstention doctrine as a cloak used to cover constitutional violations by state officials. Justice Brennan in one case remarked: "Under the banner of vague, undefined notions of equity, comity, and federalism, the Court has embarked upon the dangerous course of condoning both isolated . . . and systematic . . . violations of civil liberties."[177]

---

[173]Carl H. Loewenson, Jr., "ACLU turns to state courts and constitutions to protect rights," Civil Liberties, Winter 1985, at 7. See Ronald K. L. Collins, et al., "State High Courts, State Constitutions, and Individual Rights Litigation Since 1980: A Judicial Survey," 13 Hast. Const. L. Q. 599 (1986).

[174]Railroad Commission v. Pullman, 312 U.S. 496, 500–501 (1941).

[175]Dombrowski v. Pfister, 380 U.S. 479 (1965); Zwickler v. Koota, 389 U.S. 241 (1967).

[176]Younger v. Harris, 401 U.S. 37 (1971); Samuels v. Mackell, 401 U.S. 66 (1971). The policy of noninterference also applies to certain state civil proceedings; Huffman v. Pursue, Ltd., 420 U.S. 592 (1975).

[177]Juidice v. Vail, 430 U.S. 327, 346 (1977). See also the dissents in Paul v. Davis, 424 U.S. 693 (1976) and Rizzo v. Goode, 423 U.S. 362 (1976).

Paradoxically, Brennan has been a strong champion of the state courts as guardians of individual liberties.[178] If federal remedies are unavailable from the Supreme Court because of the abstention doctrine and other policies of noninterference, he urges the state courts "to step into the breach" and increase their protection of individual rights.[179] Federal judges have expressed dismay about the extent to which significant constitutional issues are now being decided by state courts rather than the federal judiciary.[180]

[178]William J. Brennan, Jr., "Guardians of Our Liberties—State Courts No Less Than Federal," 15 Judges' Journal 82 (1976).

[179]William J. Brennan, Jr., "State Constitutions and the Protection of Individual Rights," 90 Harv. L. Rev. 489, 503 (1977).

[180]Ruggero J. Aldisert, "State Courts and Federalism in the 1980's: Comment," 22 Wm. & Mary L. Rev. 821 (1981).

6. Efforts to Curb the Court

Justice Stone once lectured his brethren: "the only check upon our own exercise of power is our own sense of self-restraint."[1] While that is an important check, it is by no means the only one. Judges act within an environment that constantly tests the reasonableness and acceptability of their rulings. Courts hand down the "last word" only for an instant, for after the release of an opinion the process of interaction begins: with Congress, the President, executive agencies, states, professional associations, law journals, and the public at large.

Earlier chapters identified some of the constraints that operate on the judiciary: the President's power to appoint; the Senate's power to confirm; congressional power over the purse, impeachment, and court jurisdiction; and the force of public opinion, the press, and scholarly studies. Other restraints, covered in this chapter, include constitutional amendments, statutory reversals, changing the number of Justices (court packing), withdrawing jurisdiction, and noncompliance with court rulings. The concept of "coordinate construction"—assigning the task of constitutional interpretation to all three branches—is explored in the final chapter.

Court-curbing periods often emerge when the judiciary acts by nullifying statutes, particularly those passed by Congress. But the judiciary can also create enemies by *upholding* legislation, such as the broad nationalist rulings issued by Chief Justice John Marshall. To restrain the courts, members of Congress can introduce a variety of legislative bills and constitutional amendments. Hearings are held to explore ways of curbing the judiciary. State legislatures prepare petitions of protest; state judges pass resolutions of "concern" if not condemnation. To reduce the tension, the federal judiciary may decide to conduct a partial and possibly graceful retreat.

Some of the most intense judicial-congressional confrontations occurred between 1858 and 1869 (reflecting the *Dred Scott* case and

[1]United States v. Butler, 297 U.S. 1, 79 (1936).

200

congressional efforts to protect Reconstruction legislation), 1935 and 1937 (reacting to the Court's nullification of New Deal legislation), and 1955 and 1959 (triggered by decisions involving desegregation, congressional investigation, and national security).[2] A new round of court-curbing efforts began in the late 1970s to challenge judicial rulings on school prayers, school busing, and abortion.

The judiciary is most likely to be out of step with Congress or the President during periods of electoral and partisan realignment, when the country is undergoing sharp shifts in political directions while the courts retain the orientation of an age gone by.[3] During earlier periods, attacks on the judiciary were a common pastime of liberal groups: Jeffersonians, Jacksonians, Radical Republicans, La Follette Republicans, and New Deal Democrats. However, conservatives dominated the confrontation between 1955 and 1959 and have inspired most of the court-curbing efforts since then.

Constitutional Amendments

Whenever two-thirds of both Houses of Congress deem it necessary, they may propose amendments to the Constitution. Ratification requires three-fourths of the states. Alternatively, two-thirds of the states may call a convention for constitutional amendment, but thus far all successful amendments have been initiated by Congress. The process of amending the Constitution is extraordinarily difficult and time consuming.[4] On only four occasions has Congress successfully used constitutional amendments to reverse Supreme Court decisions.

The Eleventh Amendment responded to *Chisholm* v. *Georgia* (1793), which decided that a state could be sued in federal court by a plaintiff from another state.[5] The lower house of the Georgia legislature adopted the modest proposal that any federal marshal attempting to

---

[2]See Stuart S. Nagel, "Court-Curbing Periods in American History," 18 Vand. L. Rev. 925 (1965). For a review of proposals to remedy judicial activism, see Charles Grove Haines, The American Doctrine of Judicial Supremacy 467–99 (1932).

[3]Richard Funston, "The Supreme Court and Critical Elections," 69 Am. Pol. Sci. Rev. 795 (1975); David Adamany, "Legitimacy, Realigning Elections, and the Supreme Court," 1973 Wisc. L. Rev. 790.

[4]Robert G. Dixon, Jr., "Article V: The Comatose Article of Our Living Constitution?," 66 Mich. L. Rev. 931 (1968).

[5]2 U.S. (2 Dall.) 419 (1973).

enforce that ruling would be guilty of a felony and hanged until death "without the benefit of the clergy."[6] To protect states from a flood of costly citizen suits, Congress quickly passed a constitutional amendment. Although a sufficient number of states ratified it by 1795, it was not until 1798 that President John Adams notified Congress that the amendment was effective.[7] The Eleventh Amendment reads: "The Judicial power of the United States shall not be construed to extend to any suit in law or equity, commenced or prosecuted against one of the United States by Citizens of another State, or by Citizens or Subjects of any Foreign States."

The Eleventh Amendment has not provided the states with the blanket immunity from suits that might have been anticipated. Extensive litigation has shaped the meaning of this constitutional amendment. Although it does not expressly bar suits against a state by its own citizens, the Supreme Court has consistently held that a state is subject to such suits only if it consents.[8] The Eleventh Amendment does not even give states total immunity from suits filed by citizens from other states. The doctrine that a state may not be sued in its own courts, without its consent, does not yield absolute immunity from suit in the court of another state.[9]

Furthermore, the meaning of the Eleventh Amendment has been substantially affected by the Fourteenth Amendment. The Eleventh Amendment only prohibits suits directed against the *states*. Suits are allowed against state *officers* who are charged with denying due process or equal protection under the Fourteenth Amendment. The theory is that an officer acting illegally is functioning as an individual rather than a state official.[10] This theory does not support a suit against a state official who is used simply as a conduit to recover

[6]Clyde E. Jacobs, The Eleventh Amendment and Sovereign Immunity 57 (1972).
[7]Id. at 67.
[8]Employees v. Missouri Public Health Dept., 411 U.S. 279, 280 (1973); Parden v. Terminal R. Co., 377 U.S. 184, 186 (1964); Great Northern Life Ins. Co. v. Read, 322 U.S. 47, 51 (1944); Duhne v. New Jersey, 251 U.S. 311 (1920); Hans v. Louisiana, 134 U.S. 1 (1890).
[9]Nevada v. Hall, 440 U.S. 410 (1979).
[10]Ex parte Young, 209 U.S. 123 (1908); Smyth v. Ames, 169 U.S. 466, 518–19 (1898). See also Truax v. Raich, 239 U.S. 33 (1915); William A. Fletcher, "A Historical Interpretation of the Eleventh Amendment: A Narrow Construction of an Affirmative Grant of Jurisdiction Rather Than a Prohibition Against Jurisdiction," 35 Stan. L. Rev. 1033 (1983); Doyle Mathis, "The Eleventh Amendment: Adoption and Interpretation," 2 Ga. L. Rev. 207 (1968).

money from the state. Even if not named in such a case, the state is the real party and is entitled to sovereign immunity.[11]

Constitutional amendments were used to nullify the Supreme Court's 1857 decision in *Dred Scott* v. *Sandford,* which held that blacks as a class were not citizens protected by the Constitution.[12] After the nation had divided militarily on the issue, North against South, the decision of the slave states to secede from the Union allowed the abolitionist forces in Congress to pass a constitutional amendment to prohibit slavery. Senator Charles Sumner argued that the issue of slavery could not be decided merely by reading the Constitution or what the courts had said about it: "In dealing with this subject, it has not been the Constitution, so much as human nature itself, which has been at fault. Let the people change, and the Constitution will change also; for the Constitution is but the shadow, while the people are the substance."[13] The courts, he said, "will not perform the duty of the hour" to abolish slavery, and had in fact interpreted the Constitution to favor it.[14] A constitutional amendment would bring the Constitution "into avowed harmony" with the principle in the Declaration of Independence that all men are created equal.[15]

Ratified in 1865, the Thirteenth Amendment provides: "Neither slavery nor involuntary servitude, except as a punishment for crime whereof the party shall have been duly convicted, shall exist within the United States, or any place subject to their jurisdiction." Specific rights for emancipated blacks were secured by the Fourteenth Amendment, which was ratified in 1868. Section One provides: "All persons born or naturalized in the United States and subject to the jurisdiction thereof, are citizens of the United states and of the State wherein they reside." The Fifteenth Amendment ratified in 1870, gave blacks the right to vote.

The Sixteenth Amendment overruled *Pollock* v. *Farmers' Loan and Trust Co.* (1895), which struck down a federal income tax.[16] The need to finance national expansion and new international responsibilities, combined with a desire to reduce the dependence on high tariffs as

[11]Alabama v. Pugh, 438 U.S. 781 (1978); Ford Motor Co. v. Department of Treasury, 323 U.S. 459 (1945).
[12]60 U.S. (19 How.) 393 (1857).
[13]Cong. Globe, 38th Cong., 1st Sess. 1480 (1864).
[14]Id. at 1482.
[15]Id.
[16]157 U.S. 429 (1895).

the main source of revenue, set in motion the drive for a constitutional amendment.[17] Ratified in 1913, the Sixteenth Amendment gave Congress the power "to lay and collect taxes on incomes, from whatever source derived, without apportionment among the several States, and without regard to any census or enumeration."

The Twenty-sixth Amendment was ratified in 1971 to overturn *Oregon* v. *Mitchell,* a Supreme Court decision of the previous year that had voided a congressional effort to lower the minimum voting age in state elections to eighteen.[18] As a way to encourage youths to participate constructively in the political process and to avoid the cost of a dual registration system of eighteen years for national elections and twenty-one years for state and local elections, Congress sent a constitutional amendment to the states. In record time, three months later, a sufficient number of states had ratified this language: "The right of citizens of the United States, who are eighteen years of age or older, to vote shall not be denied or abridged by the United States or any State on account of age."

Other constitutional amendments, driven by seemingly irresistible political forces, have fallen by the wayside. A successful amendment process requires an extraordinary combination of social, economic, and political forces. If any one of these factors is absent, an amendment may fail. For example, Congress made a concerted effort in 1964 to amend the Constitution to overturn the Supreme Court's decisions in the reapportionment and school prayer cases. Because of delays by House committees and filibusters on the Senate side, these efforts proved fruitless.[19]

Even when Congress reacts against a court decision by clearing an amendment for ratification by the states, the hurdles are immense. After the Supreme Court in 1918 and 1922 denied Congress the right to regulate child labor conditions, opponents of the court rulings tried unsuccessfully to reverse them by constitutional amendment.[20] In 1924 both houses of Congress passed a constitutional amendment to give Congress the power to "limit, regulate and prohibit the labor of persons under 18 years of age." By 1937, only

[17]Alan P. Grimes, Democracy and the Amendments to the Constitution 66–74 (1978).
[18]400 U.S. 112 (1970).
[19]Harry P. Stumpf, "Congressional Response to Supreme Court Rulings: The Interaction of Law and Politics," 14 J. Pub. L. 377, 378–81 (1965).
[20]Hammer v. Dagenhart, 247 U.S. 251 (1918); Bailey v. Drexel Furniture Co., 259 U.S. 20 (1922).

twenty-eight of the necessary thirty-six states had ratified the amendment. The issue became moot after Congress passed the Fair Labor Standards Act of 1938 to regulate child labor and the Supreme Court upheld the statute three years later.[21]

Once the Constitution is successfully amended to overturn a Court decision, there is no guarantee that the judiciary will interpret the amendment consistent with the intent of the framers and ratifiers. Although the Thirteenth, Fourteenth, and Fifteenth Amendments were meant to overturn *Dred Scott* and protect the rights of blacks, such decisions as *The Civil Rights Cases* (1883) and *Plessy* v. *Ferguson* (1896) were more in line with racial attitudes that flourished before the Civil War.[22]

In addition to constitutional amendments aimed at particular decisions, there have been other proposals aimed at curbing the courts' strength by imposing certain procedural requirements. These amendments have in every instance been unsuccessful. Of recurring interest are the following: requiring more than a majority of Justices to strike down a statute[23]; subjecting the Court's decisions to another tribunal, such as the Senate or a judicial body consisting of a judge from each state[24]; submitting the Court's decisions to popular referenda[25]; allowing Congress by two-thirds vote to override a Court decision just as it does a presidential veto[26]; and making laws held unconstitutional by the Court valid if reenacted by Congress.[27]

Other amendments have been directed at the Court's tenure and qualifications: allowing the removal of Supreme Court Justices and other federal judges by majority vote of each house of Congress[28]; restricting the term of a Justice to a set number of years[29]; having

---

[21]United States v. Darby, 312 U.S. 100 (1941).

[22]Civil Rights Cases, 109 U.S. 3 (1883); Plessy v. Ferguson, 163 U.S. 537 (1896).

[23]Maurice S. Culp, "A Survey of the Proposals to Limit or Deny the Power of Judicial Review by the Supreme Court of the United States," 4 Ind. L. J. 386, 392–98 (1929); H.J. Res. 293, 92d Cong., 1st Sess. (1971). Cong. Olin Earl Teague (D-Tex.)

[24]Culp, "A Survey," 4 Ind. L. J., at 387–90; Charles S. Hyneman, The Supreme Court on Trial 51 (1963); Philip B. Kurland, "The Court of the Union or *Julius Caesar* Revised," 39 Notre Dame Lawyer 636 (1964).

[25]Hyneman, Supreme Court on Trial, at 52.

[26]H.J. Res. 574, 92d Cong., 1st Sess. (1971). Cong. George W. Andrews (D-Ala.).

[27]Shelden D. Elliott, "Court-Curbing Proposals in Congress," 33 Notre Dame Lawyer 597, 606 (1958).

[28]Culp, "A Survey," 4 Ind. L. J., at 475–76.

[29]Elliott, "Court-Curbing Proposals," 33 Notre Dame Lawyer, at 602–03.

Justices retire at the age of seventy-five years[30]; requiring direct election from the judicial districts[31]; itemizing the qualifications for Justices, such as requiring prior judicial service in the highest court of a state or excluding anyone who has, within the preceding five years, served in the executive or legislative branches[32]; and vesting the appointment of Justices in judges from the highest state courts.[33] Although unsuccessful in every case, these amendments serve the purpose of venting popular and professional resentment toward court decisions and may even temper future rulings.

State legislatures have requested constitutional conventions to reverse certain rulings of the Supreme Court. In response to the reapportionment decisions, Senator Everett Dirksen urged that a convention be held to amend the Constitution to permit one house of a state legislature to be apportioned on a basis other than population. His campaign fell two short of the necessary two-thirds of the states.[34] Following the Supreme Court's abortion decision in *Roe* v. *Wade* (1973), nineteen states have submitted applications to convene a convention to provide fetuses with the right to life.[35]

Statutory Reversals

When decisions turn on the interpretation of federal statutes, Congress may overturn a ruling simply by passing a new statute to clarify legislative intent. The private sector often uses Congress as an "appellate court" to reverse judicial interpretations of a statute. Such actions were rare before 1944 but became almost routine after that.[36] At a congressional hearing in 1959, Congressman Wilbur Mills leaned across the witness table and told a company president: "It seems that it is becoming more and more almost a full-time job of the Congress to correct the Supreme Court's desire to legislate." The company

[30]Owen J. Roberts, "Now Is the Time: Fortifying the Supreme Court's Independence," 35 A.B.A.J. 1, 1–2 (1949).

[31]Elliott, "Court-Curbing Proposals," 33 Notre Dame Lawyer, at 603.

[32]Id. at 604.

[33]Id.

[34]S. Rept. No. 135, 99th Cong., 1st Sess. 12–13 (1985).

[35]Id. at 13.

[36]John R. Schmidhauser and Larry L. Berg, The Supreme Court and Congress 141 (1972), citing the work of Alan Westin.

president, seeking to have a major Supreme Court decision modified to his advantage, nodded his approval.[37] Members of Congress have little doubt about their authority to overturn the Court in such cases. Senator Alexander Wiley told a witness in 1946:

> What is being worked out here today is part of the mechanics of our constitutional system of checks and balances. . . . I need hardly point out to my colleagues that the founding fathers contemplated three strong and independent branches of government—legislative, judicial and executive—each of which was, insofar as possible, to tend to its own knitting. That means that the legislative branch, which is Congress, should do the legislating. When this delicate system of checks and balances is thrown out of balance, as I believe it is [by the decision here] the very foundation of our Republic is endangered . . . and Congress must reverse the Court.[38]

Judicial-legislative conversations have helped shape the meaning of the Freedom of Information Act. In one case, thirty-three members of the House of Representatives went to court to obtain documents prepared for President Nixon concerning an underground nuclear test. In 1973, the Supreme Court decided that it had no authority to examine the documents *in camera* to sift out "nonsecret components" for their release.[39] Congress passed legislation a year later to override the decision, clearly authorizing federal courts to examine sensitive records in judges' chambers.[40]

A combination of court decisions and congressional statutes have defined the difficult area of job rights for pregnant women. In 1976, the Supreme Court upheld a company's disability plan that gave benefits for nonoccupational sickness and accidents but not for disabilities arising from pregnancy. The Court decided that the plan did not violate Title VII of the Civil Rights Act of 1964.[41] Congress passed legislation in 1978 to reverse this decision. The statute amended Title VII to prohibit employment discrimination on the basis of preg-

---

[37]Emmette S. Redford, et al., Politics and Government in the United States 518 (1965).

[38]Schmidhauser and Berg, Supreme Court, at 141–42.

[39]EPA v. Mink, 410 U.S. 73, 81 (1973).

[40]88 Stat. 1562, § 4(B) (1974). See CIA v. Sims, 471 U.S. 159, 189–90 (1985).

[41]General Electric Co. v. Gilbert, 429 U.S. 125 (1976).

nancy and to require fringe benefit and insurance plans to cover pregnant workers.[42]

A recent example of statutory reversal involved *Smith* v. *Robinson* (1984), in which the Supreme Court held that parents who brought legal action to obtain schooling for their handicapped child were not entitled to attorney's fees if they prevailed in the litigation. Congress had passed legislation to provide special education to handicapped children, but the Court decided from the statutory arrangement that Congress had not intended that attorney's fees be awarded.[43] Justice Brennan, writing a dissent joined by Justices Marshall and Stevens, said that "with today's decision . . . Congress will now have to take the time to revisit the matter" of attorney's fees.[44] Legislation was introduced to amend the Education of the Handicapped Act to authorize the award of attorney's fees to prevailing parties. The statute reversing the Court's decision was enacted in 1986.[45]

Another successful congressional effort concerned the case of *Grove City College* v. *Bell* (1984). Title IX of the Education Amendments of 1972 prohibited sex discrimination in any education program or activity that received federal financial assistance. After the Reagan administration had issued statements indicating that its interpretation of Title IX was not as broad as previous administrations, the House of Representatives on November 16, 1983, passed a resolution by a vote of 414 to 8 opposing the administration's position. The resolution stated the sense of the House that Title IX and regulations issued pursuant to the title "should not be amended or altered in any manner which will lessen the comprehensive coverage of such statute in eliminating gender discrimination throughout the American educational system."[46] The resolution, of course, was not legally binding, but it was passed because the Supreme Court was about to hear oral argument on the *Grove City* case. As Congressman Paul Simon noted: "Passing this resolution the House can send the Court a signal

[42]92 Stat. 2076 (1978). See California Federal S. & L. v. Guerra, 107 S.Ct. 683 (1987).
[43]Smith v. Robinson, 468 U.S. 992 (1984).
[44]Id. at 1030–31.
[45]100 Stat. 796 (1986). For legislative history, see S. Rept. No. 112, 99th Cong., 1st Sess. (1985); 131 Cong. Rec. S10396–401 (daily ed. July 30, 1985), H9964–73 (daily ed. November 12, 1985); 132 Cong. Rec. S9277–79 (daily ed. July 17, 1986), H4841–45 (daily ed. July 24, 1986).
[46]129 Cong. Rec. H10085 (daily ed. November 16, 1983).

that we believe that no institution should be allowed to discriminate on the basis of sex if it receives Federal funds."[47]

The issue before the Court was whether Title IX meant that federal funds would be terminated only for specific programs in which discrimination occurs or for the entire educational institution. The Supreme Court adopted the narrower interpretation.[48] Justices Brennan and Marshall dissented in part, stating that the Court was ignoring congressional intent for institutionwide coverage. They also noted the change in position by the Reagan administration: "The interpretation of statutes as important as Title IX should not be subjected so easily to shifts in policy by the executive branch."[49]

Within four months the House of Representatives, by a vote of 375 to 32, passed legislation to amend not only Title IX but also three other statutes to adopt broad coverage of the antidiscrimination provisions.[50] The Senate resisted action that year, however.[51] When Congress returned to the battle in 1985 and 1986, the issue was now complicated by questions of church-state and abortion.[52] Finally, in 1988, Congress was able to forge a compromise. President Reagan vetoed the measure, but both houses overrode the veto to enact the broader coverage for civil rights that had been rejected in *Grove City*.

Court Packing

Congress has altered the number of Justices on the Supreme Court throughout its history. Congress authorized six Justices in 1789, lowered that to five in the ill-fated Judiciary Act of 1801, returned it to six a year later, and increased the number in subsequent years to keep pace with the creation of new circuits. Since 1869 the number of Justices has remained fixed at nine. Appointments to the Court have often produced marked changes in judicial policy, as witnessed by the abrupt shift in the Legal Tender Cases (discussed in Chapter

[47]Id. at H10087.
[48]465 U.S. 555 (1984).
[49]Id. at 603.
[50]130 Cong. Rec. H7018–57 (daily ed. June 26, 1984).
[51]" 'Grove City' Rights Bill Shelved by Senate," Cong. Q. Wkly Rept., October 6, 1984, at 2430–33.
[52]1985 CQ Almanac, at 230–32; Cong. Q. Wkly Rept., October 25, 1986, at 2665.

Four), but in none of these earlier instances was the change in court size linked so blatantly to changing judicial policy as in FDR's court-packing plan.

In his Inaugural Address in 1933, Franklin D. Roosevelt struck a confident note for presidential-judicial relations. He said that the Constitution "is so simple and practical that it is possible always to meet extraordinary needs by changes in emphasis and arrangement without loss of essential form." Privately, he tempered his bright hopes with the knowledge that members on the Supreme Court were essentially conservative and business oriented.

Presidential optimism was routed on "Black Monday," May 27, 1935, when the Supreme Court unanimously struck down the National Industrial Recovery Act (NIRA).[53] On that same day it ruled that Presidents could remove members of independent regulatory commissions only by following the statutory reasons for removal[54], and it held unconstitutional a statute for the relief of farm mortgagors.[55] The fact that all nine Justices had declared the NIRA unconstitutional suggested the futility of trying to "pack" the Court. Feeling betrayed by the liberal members on the Court, Roosevelt asked plaintively: "Well, where was Ben Cardozo? And what about old Isaiah [Brandeis]?"[56] Direct attacks on the Court were shelved after the public reacted unfavorably to Roosevelt's sneering accusation at a press conference that the Justices had adopted a "horse-and-buggy definition of interstate commerce."[57] At a cabinet meeting in December 1935, Roosevelt reviewed several methods of restraining the Court. Packing the Court, Interior Secretary Harold Ickes recorded in his diary, "was a distasteful idea."[58]

Roosevelt's indignation at the judiciary was further aroused on January 6, 1936, when the Court struck down the processing tax in the Agricultural Adjustment Act. The ruling divided the Court, 6 to 3, with Justice Stone penning a stinging dissent. He reminded his colleagues on the Court that they were not the only branch of gov-

---

[53]Schechter Corp. v. United States, 295 U.S. 495 (1935).

[54]Humphrey's Executor v. United States, 295 U.S. 602 (1935).

[55]Louisville Bank v. Radford, 295 U.S. 555 (1935).

[56]William E. Leuchtenburg, "The Origins of Franklin D. Roosevelt's 'Court-Packing' Plan," 1966 Sup. Ct. Rev. 347, 357.

[57]Id. at 357–59; 4 Public Papers and Addresses of Franklin D. Roosevelt 221 (1941).

[58]1 The Secret Diary of Harold L. Ickes 495 (1953).

ernment assumed to have the capacity to govern.[59] This time there appeared to be a groundswell of support in the country for adding to the Court younger Justices more attuned to the temper of the times.[60] Yet Roosevelt bided his time, not wanting to give his opponents in an election year the opportunity to rally behind the Constitution and the Court. Other decisions in 1936, striking down federal and state laws, provided extra incentives to curb the Court. Some of those decisions attracted three to four dissents.[61] The climate for curbing the Court was further encouraged by the national popularity of *The Nine Old Men* (1936), a caustic portrait of the Justices written by Drew Pearson and Robert Allen. Peppered by such chapters as "The Lord High Executioners," the book charged that "justice has no relation whatsoever to popular will. Adminstrations may come and go, the temper of the people may reverse itself, economic conditions may be revolutionalized, the Nine Old Men sit on."[62]

Roosevelt's landslide victory in 1936, capturing all but two states, paved the way for a direct assault on the Court. Constitutional amendments seemed to him wholly impracticable. They were difficult to frame and nearly impossible to pass. Statutory remedies, such as requiring a unanimous or 8-to-1 decision in the Supreme Court to invalidate a law, were of doubtful constitutionality and could be easily overturned by the Court.[63] After rejecting a number of alternatives, he considered court packing the only feasible solution.

Working closely with his Attorney General and Solicitor General, but without the advice of congressional leaders, Roosevelt ordered the preparation of a draft bill. The President would be authorized to nominate Justices to the Supreme Court whenever an incumbent over the age of seventy declined to resign or retire. He proposed the same procedure for the lower courts, limiting the number of additional appointments to fifty and setting the maximum size of the Supreme Court at fifteen. Under this scenario, Roosevelt could name

[59]United States v. Butler, 297 U.S. at 87.

[60]Leuchtenburg, "Court-Packing Plan," 1966 Sup. Ct. Rev. at 366–68.

[61]Jones v. SEC, 298 U.S. 1 (1936) (Cardozo, Brandeis, and Stone dissenting); St. Joseph Stock Yards Co. v. United States, 298 U.S. 38 (1936) (Cardozo, Brandeis, and Stone dissenting in part); Carter v. Carter Coal Co., 298 U.S. 238 (1936); Morehead v. New York ex rel. Tipaldo, 298 U.S. 587 (1936) (Hughes, Brandeis, Stone, and Cardozo dissenting).

[62]Drew Pearson and Robert S. Allen, The Nine Old Men 322–23 (1936).

[63]6 Public Papers and Addresses of Franklin D. Roosevelt 76–77 (1941).

as many as six new Justices to the Supreme Court. When he submitted his proposal to Congress on February 5, 1937, he attempted to disguise it primarily as an economy and efficiency measure. The addition of more Justices would help relieve the delay and congestion he claimed resulted from aged or infirm judges.[64] His "indirection" (a euphemism for his deception and deviousness) offended some potential supporters. Robert H. Jackson, who served as Solicitor General and Attorney General under Roosevelt before being appointed to the Supreme Court in 1941, admitted that the plan "lacked the simplicity and clarity which was the President's genius and, to men not learned in the procedures of the Court, much of it seemed technical and confusing."[65]

Roosevelt soon revealed his real purpose: to pack the Supreme Court with liberal Justices. In a "fireside chat" on March 9, 1937, he told the country that he wanted a Supreme Court that "will enforce the Constitution as written." But a mechanical application of that document by six additional Justices would not alleviate the problem Roosevelt faced. Later in that address he called for judges "who will bring to the Courts a present-day sense of the Constitution." He wanted "younger men who have had personal experience and contact with modern facts and circumstances." More concretely, he promised to appoint Justices "who will not undertake to override the judgment of the Congress on legislative policy." The result of this reform, he said, would be a "reinvigorated, liberal-minded Judiciary."[66]

The Senate Judiciary Committee reported Roosevelt's bill adversely. The term "adverse" is actually too tepid, for the report methodically and mercilessly shreds the bill's premises, structure, content, and motivation. This searing indictment constituted an extraordinary determination on the part of the committee to pulverize Roosevelt's creation and bury it forever. The first of six reasons for rejecting the plan bluntly noted: "the bill does not accomplish any one of the objectives for which it was originally offered."[67] Among other points in this scathing attack, the committee said that the courts "with the oldest judges have the best records in the disposition of business." The bill called for retirement only for judges who had

---

[64]Id. at 35–50, 51–66.

[65]Robert H. Jackson, The Struggle for Judicial Supremacy 189 (1941).

[66]6 Public Papers and Addresses of Franklin D. Roosevelt 122–33 (1941).

[67]S. Rept. No. 711, 75th Cong., 1st Sess. 3 (1937).

served for ten years (penalizing not age itself but age combined with experience). Nothing in the bill prevented Roosevelt from nominating someone sixty-nine years and eleven months of age without prior judicial service. The result could be a Court of fifteen members, all of them over seventy, and with no means of altering its composition. To the committee, the bill had one purpose and one purpose only: to apply force to the judiciary.[68] The report's harsh language was designed to repudiate the bill so emphatically that no President would ever float the idea again:

> This is the first time in the history of our country that a proposal to alter the decisions of the court by enlarging its personnel has been so boldly made. Let us meet it. Let us now set a salutary precedent that will never be violated. Let us, of the Seventy-fifth Congress, in words that will never be disregarded by any succeeding Congress, declare that we would rather have an independent Court, a fearless Court, a Court that will dare to announce its honest opinions in what it believes to be the defense of the liberties of the people, than a Court that, out of fear or sense of obligation to the appointing power, or factional passion, approves any measure we may enact. We are not the judges of the judges. We are not above the Constitution.[69]

In its summary, the committee recommended the rejection of the bill "as a needless, futile, and utterly dangerous abandonment of constitutional principle. It was presented to the Congress in a most intricate form and for reasons that obscured its real purpose." The President's bill "should be so emphatically rejected that its parallel will never again be presented to the free representatives of the free people of America."[70]

The Committee's position was reinforced by a letter from Chief Justice Hughes stating that the Court was "fully abreast of its work" and there was "no congestion of cases upon our calendar." With respect to the suggestion that with more Justices on the Court it could hear cases in divisions or as panels, he called attention to the requirement in Article III that the judicial power shall be vested in one Supreme Court: "The Constitution does not appear to authorize two

[68]Id. at 8.
[69]Id. at 14
[70]Id. at 23.

or more Supreme Courts or two or more parts of a supreme court functioning in effect as separate courts." He explained that because of the shortness of time he had been unable to consult with all members of the Court, "but I am confident that it is in accord with the views of the Justices." He had been able to consult with Justices Van Devanter and Brandeis "and I am at liberty to say that the statement is approved by them."[71] Felix Frankfurter, who would join the Court within a few years as a Roosevelt appointee, regarded Hughes's letter as "indefensible on several scores: it was disingenuous in saying there wasn't time to consult other colleagues, and it grossly violated the settled practice of the Court against giving advisory opinions in so far as it expressed views regarding Article 3 (I talked pretty plainly to Brandeis about this)."[72]

A number of unexpected developments sealed the fate of the court-packing bill. Senate Majority Leader Joe Robinson, who Roosevelt hoped would steer the bill through the Senate, died on July 14 after a week of debate in the sweltering capital.[73] By that time the Court had already begun to modify some of its earlier rulings. On March 29, 1937, it upheld a state law establishing a minimum-wage law for women, basically reversing a decision handed down ten months earlier.[74] This reversal occurred because of a change in position by Justice Roberts, or what has been called the "switch in time that saved nine." But before FDR submitted his court-packing plan, Roberts had already broken with his doctrinaire laissez-faire colleagues. In 1934 he wrote an opinion upholding a New York law that set prices.[75] He was also in the process of altering his views on minimum-wage legislation. With Roberts's support, the Court was prepared to sustain such legislation in the fall of 1936 but had delayed its ruling

[71]Id. at 38–40. Letter of March 21, 1937 from Chief Justice Hughes to Senator Burton K. Wheeler.

[72]Max Freedman, anno., Roosevelt and Frankfurter: Their Correspondence, 1928–1945, at 402 (1967). Letter to C. C. Burlingham, June 9, 1937.

[73]William E. Leuchtenburg, "Franklin D. Roosevelt's Supreme Court 'Packing Plan,' " in Harold M. Hollingsworth and William F. Holmes, eds., Essays on the New Deal 102–05 (1969). See also Joseph Alsop and Turner Catledge, The 168 Days (1938), and Leonard Baker, Back to Back: The Duel Between FDR and the Supreme Court (1967).

[74]West Coast Hotel Co. v. Parrish, 300 U.S. 379 (1937), overturning Adkins v. Children's Hospital, 261 U.S. 525 (1923) and "distinguishing" (in fact reversing) Morehead v. New York ex rel. Tipaldo, 298 U.S. 587 (1936).

[75]Nebbia v. New York, 291 U.S. 502 (1934).

because of Justice Stone's illness.[76] Late in 1936, Roberts had voted with the liberals to affirm a state unemployment insurance law.[77]

Other decisions in 1937 confirmed that the Court had become more accepting of New Deal programs.[78] Roosevelt remarked with obvious relish: "The old minority of 1935 and 1936 had become the majority of 1937—without a single new appointment of a justice!"[79] Because Congress finally passed legislation early in 1937 providing for full judicial pay during retirement, Justice Van Devanter stepped down on June 2, 1937, giving Roosevelt his first chance in more than four years to nominate a Justice to the Supreme Court. Other retirements were imminent. Within a matter of months, the need for the court-packing plan had evaporated. President Roosevelt would be able to "reorganize" the Court without action on his bill.[80]

Withdrawing Jurisdiction

During the past decade Congress has been under strong pressure to withdraw the Supreme Court's jurisdiciton to hear appeals in cases of abortion, school busing, school prayer, and other issues on the conservatives' "social agenda." This strategy is based on language in Article III of the Constitution: "The Supreme Court shall have appellate jurisdiction, both as to law and fact, with such exceptions, and under such regulations, as the Congress shall make." The Exceptions

[76]Felix Frankfurter, "Mr. Justice Roberts," 104 U. Pa. L. Rev. 311 (1955); 2 Merlo J. Pusey, Charles Evans Hughes 757 (1963); David J. Danelski and Joseph S. Tulchin, eds., The Autobiographical Notes of Charles Evans Hughes 312 (1973). For a challenge to Roberts's recollection of key events in 1936, see Clement E. Vose, Constitutional Change: Amendment Politics and Supreme Court Litigation Since 1900 228–34 (1972).

[77]W.H.H. Chamberlin, Inc. v. Andrews, 299 U.S. 515, decided November 23, 1936. The Court was equally divided. For Roberts's vote, see John W. Chambers, "The Big Switch: Justice Roberts and the Minimum-Wage Cases," 10 Labor Hist. 44, 57 (1969).

[78]Virginian Ry. v. Federation, 300 U.S. 515 (1937); Wright v. Vinton Branch, 300 U.S. 440 (1937); NLRB v. Jones & Laughlin, 301 U.S. 1 (1937); NLRB v. Fruehauf Co., 301 U.S. 49 (1937); NLRB v. Clothing Co., 301 U.S. 58 (1937); Steward Machine Co. v. Davis, 301 U.S. 548 (1937); Helvering v. Davis, 301 U.S. 619 (1937).

[79]6 Public Papers and Addresses of Franklin D. Roosevelt lxviii (1941).

[80]For the fluctuation of public opinion during congressional consideration of the Court-packing plan, see Frank V. Cantell, "Public Opinion and the Legislative Process," 40 Am. Pol. Sci. Rev. 924 (1946).

Clause, it is argued, gives Congress plenary power to determine the Court's appellate jurisdiction.[81]

Although this approach appears to be grounded on constitutional language, the Exceptions Clause must be read in concert with other provisions in the Constitution. An aggressive use of the Exceptions Clause by Congress would make an exception the rule and deny citizens access to the Supreme Court to vindicate constitutional rights. Stripping the Supreme Court of jurisdiction to hear certain issues would vest ultimate judicial authority in the lower federal and state courts, producing contradictory and conflicting legal doctrines.

A more radical proposal would prevent even the lower federal courts from ruling on specific social issues. Under Article III, the judicial power is vested in a Supreme Court "and in such inferior Courts as the Congress may from time to time ordain and establish." Because Congress creates the lower courts, it may by statute confer, define, and withdraw jurisdiction.[82] Although Congress has withdrawn jurisdiction to adjudicate certain issues, the exercise of that power "is subject to compliance with at least the requirements of the Fifth Amendment. That is to say, while Congress has the undoubted power to give, withhold, and restrict the jurisdiction of courts other than the Supreme Court, it must not so exercise that power as to deprive any person of life, liberty, or property without due process of law or to take private property without just compensation."[83] To deny the lower federal courts jurisdiction to hear claims arising under the Constitution would upset the system of checks and balances, alter the balance of power between the national government and the states, and strengthen the force of majority rule over individual rights.[84]

---

[81]John P. East, "The Case for Withdrawal of Jurisdiction," in Patrick B. McGuigan and Randall R. Rader, eds., A Blueprint for Judicial Reform 29–36 (1981). See also other essays in this book for conservative strategy to restrict the judiciary. For an interesting challenge by a prominent conservative, see the views of Senator Barry Goldwater, who warned that court-curbing bills run afoul of the separation-of-powers doctrine and the principle of judicial independence. 128 Cong. Rec. S1040 (daily ed. February 24, 1982).

[82]Sheldon v. Sill, 49 U.S. (8 How.) 441, 449 (1850).

[83]Battaglia v. General Motors Corp., 169 F.2d 254, 257 (2d Cir. 1948), footnote omitted, cert. denied, 335 U.S. 887 (1948). See Richard E. Morgan, "The Portal-to-Portal Pay Case," in C. Herman Pritchett and Alan F. Westin, eds., The Third Branch of Government 50–82 (1963).

[84]Association of the Bar of the City of New York, "Jurisdiction-Stripping Proposals in Congress: The Threat to Constitutional Review," December 1981.

Congress has denied judicial review for certain agency actions, such as decisions by the Administrator of the Veterans' Administration. Nevertheless, the Court has held that constitutional issues resulting from those actions may still be appealed to the federal courts.[85] The immunity from judicial review applies only to administrative decisions that raise no constitutional questions.

Withdrawing appellate jurisdiction from the Supreme Court and withdrawing jurisdiction from the lower federal courts would undercut the Supremacy Clause in Article VI, which states that the Constitution and federal laws "made in Pursuance thereof . . . shall be the supreme Law of the Land; and the Judges in every State shall be bound thereby, any Thing in the Constitution or Laws of any State to the contrary notwithstanding." In 1982 the chief justices of the highest state courts issued a unanimous resolution expressing "serious concerns" about bills introduced in Congress to give the states sole authority to decide certain social issues. Among other objections, the chief justices pointed out that the result of such legislation would be contrary to what conservatives professed to be their goal. Instead of overturning Supreme Court decisions, they would be "cast in stone" when state judges continued to honor their oaths to obey the federal constitution and to give full force (pursuant to the Supremacy Clause) to Supreme Court precedents. The practical effect, therefore, would be to place a body of legal doctrine outside the reach of federal courts or state courts either to alter or overrule.[86]

Members of Congress have also attempted to use their power to enforce the Fourteenth Amendment as a lever to alter the jurisdiction of the federal courts. Section 5 of the Fourteenth Amendment gives Congress the power "to enforce, by appropriate legislation," the provisions of that amendment. In 1981 the Senate Judiciary Committee held hearings on a bill that looked to Section 5 as the vehicle for overturning the Supreme Court's 1973 abortion decision. The hearings covered the scope of Section 5, the issue of whether it would be exercising judgments over "facts" or "law," and a possible shift of balance of power between the national government and the states.[87]

---

[85]Johnson v. Robison, 415 U.S. 361 (1974); Hernandez v. Veterans' Administration, 415 U.S. 391 (1974).

[86]128 Cong. Rec. 689–90 (1982).

[87]"The Human Life Bill," hearings before the Senate Committee on the Judiciary, 97th Cong., 1st Sess. (1981).

217

In a number of early decisions, the Supreme Court recognized the power of Congress to make exceptions and to regulate the Court's appellate jurisdiction.[88] For example, in 1847 the Court stated that it possessed "no appellate power in any case, unless conferred upon it by act of Congress; nor can it, when conferred be exercised in any other form, or by any other mode of proceeding than that which the law prescribes."[89] These early decisions stated the congressional power too broadly, as will be shown.

The leading case for empowering Congress to withdraw appellate jurisdiction from the Supreme Court is *Ex parte McCardle* (1869). In 1868, Congress withdrew the Court's jurisdiction to review circuit court judgments on habeas corpus actions. The clear purpose was to prevent the Court from deciding a case on the constitutionality of the Reconstruction military government in the South, even though the Court had already heard oral argument in the case of William McCardle. He had been held in custody awaiting trial by military commission, charged with publishing articles that incited "insurrection, disorder, and violence." Under an act of February 5, 1867, he petitioned a federal circuit court for the writ of habeas corpus. The writ was issued, directing the military commander to deliver McCardle to a federal marshal. After the commander complied with the writ (denying that the restraint was unlawful), the circuit court rejected McCardle's petition.

At that point McCardle appealed to the Supreme Court. On February 17, 1868, the Court dismissed the government's argument that the Court lacked jurisdiction to hear the case.[90] The case was argued March 2, 3, 4, and 9. Before the Court could meet in conference to decide the case, Congress passed legislation to nullify McCardle's relief under the act of February 5, 1867. The new legislation provided that the portion of the 1867 statute that authorized an appeal from the judgment of the circuit court to the Supreme Court, "or the exercise of any such jurisdiction by said Supreme Court on appeals which have been or may hereafter be taken, be, and the same is, hereby repealed."[91] Congress wanted to sweep McCardle's case from

---

[88]Wiscart v. Dauchy, 3 Dall. 321 (1796); Durousseau v. United States, 10 U.S. (6 Cr.) 306 (1810); Daniels v. Railroad Co., 70 U.S. (3 Wall.) 250, 254 (1866).

[89]Barry v. Mercein, 5 How. 103, 119 (1847).

[90]Ex parte McCardle, 73 U.S. (6 Wall.) 318 (1868).

[91]15 Stat. 44, § 2 (1868). Congress had to override President Johnson's veto.

the docket, fearing that the Court might use it to invalidate the Reconstruction laws.[92]

In a unanimous opinion upholding the repeal statute, Chief Justice Chase stated that the Court was "not at liberty to inquire into the motives of the legislature. We can only examine into its power under the Constitution; and the power to make exceptions to the appellate jurisdiction of this court is given by express words."[93] The Court dismissed the case for want of jurisdiction. The Court might have used Section 14 of the Judiciary Act of 1789 to review habeas corpus actions.[94] But to do this in the face of the repealer act, with the prospect of overturning Reconstruction legislation, invited a high-risk collision with Congress. The House of Representatives had already passed legislation to require a two-thirds majority of the Court to invalidate a federal statute, and some of the more rambunctious Radicals wanted to abolish the Supreme Court.[95]

There is some question whether Congress acted under the Exceptions Clause, even though it forms the basis for the Court's decision. Congress may have merely repealed a special statutory right of access that it had previously granted. As the Court noted later in *Ex parte Yerger,* Congress did not repeal alternative rights of access, such as under the Judiciary Act of 1789 and later statutes that expanded the writ of habeas corpus.[96]

McCardle remains in a shadowy realm, surrounded on both sides by conflicting cases that both limit and legitimate congressional power under the Exceptions Clause. Shortly after *McCardle*, the Supreme Court decided *United States* v. *Klein* (1872), which involved a congressional attempt to use the appropriations power to nullify the President's power to pardon. The Court said that Congress had overstepped its authority, first by trying to limit a presidential power granted by the Constitution, and second by preventing a presidential pardon or amnesty from being admitted as evidence in court. The

---

[92]William W. Van Alstyne, "A Critical Guide to Ex Parte McCardle," 15 Ariz. L. Rev. 229, 239–41 (1979).

[93]Ex parte McCardle, 74 U.S. (7 Wall.) 506, 514 (1869).

[94]"All the before-mentioned courts of the United States [including the Supreme Court], shall have power to issue writs of . . . *habeas corpus.*" 1 Stat. 81–82, § 14; Van Alstyne, "Critical Guide," 15 Ariz. L. Rev., at 246.

[95]Walter Murphy, Elements of Judicial Strategy 194 (1964).

[96]75 U.S. (8 Wall.) 85, 101–2 (1869). See Van Alstyne, "Critical Guide," 15 Ariz. L. Rev. at 250–51.

statute was meant to strip the Supreme Court of its jurisdiction over such cases. The Court agreed that the Exceptions Clause gave Congress the power to deny the right of appeal in a particular class of cases, but it could not withhold appellate jurisdiction "as a means to an end" if the end was forbidden under the Constitution. In this case, the effect of withholding appellate jurisdiction was to prescribe rules of decision for the judiciary in a pending case.[97]

The *Klein* case suggests one limit on the power of Congress under the Exceptions Clause. Other restrictions exist. For example, Congress could not extend certain rights and then attempt, through the Exceptions Clause, to exclude a particular race or religious group. Such actions would violate the Due Process Clause and the First Amendment. Other prohibited actions would include a congressional effort to deny access to federal courts "to all but white Anglo-Saxon Protestants, or to all who voted in the latest election for a losing candidate."[98]

Although the Supreme Court has announced since *McCardle* and *Klein* that its appellate jurisdiction "is confined within such limits as Congress sees fit to prescribe,"[99] the establishment of exceptions and regulations must give "due regard to all the provisions of the Constitution."[100] For district and appellate courts, Congress "may give, withhold or restrict such jurisdiction at its discretion, provided it be not extended beyond the boundaries fixed by the Constitution."[101] The Court has allowed Congress to limit the availability of certain judicial remedies, such as prohibiting district courts from issuing injunctions to control labor disputes[102] or the enforcement of price regulations.[103]

These precedents cannot be read to justify the exclusion of whole areas of constitutional law from the Supreme Court.[104] The mere

[97]80 U.S. (13 Wall.) 128, 146 (1872).

[98]Statement by Prof. Laurence H. Tribe, 127 Cong. Rec. 13360 (1981).

[99]The "Francis Wright," 105 U.S. 381, 385 (1881). A similar statement appears in Railroad Co. v. Grant, 98 U.S. 396 (1878).

[100]United States v. Bitty, 208 U.S. 393, 399–400 (1908).

[101]Kline v. Burke Const. Co., 260 U.S. 226, 234 (1922).

[102]Lauf v. E.G. Shinner & Co., 303 U.S. 323 (1938).

[103]Lockerty v. Phillips, 319 U.S. 182 (1943). See also Yakus v. United States, 321 U.S. 414, 427–31 (1944).

[104]For studies cautioning unbounded use of the Exceptions Clause, see Lawrence Gene Sager, "The Supreme Court, 1980 Term—Foreword: Constitutional Limitations on Congress' Authority to Regulate the Jurisdiction of the Federal Courts," 95 Harv.

existence of a power does not mean that it may be used without limit. Such a construction runs counter to the basic principles of constitutionalism, separation of powers, and checks and balances. Congress has the "power" to determine the size of the Supreme Court, but the availability of that power did not support Roosevelt's effort to pack the Court. Indeed, the Senate Judiciary Committee rejected the proposal with such force that it hoped no President would ever dare repeat the suggestion. The President has the "power" to withhold documents and appropriations, but we live under a system that recognizes limits on executive privilege and impoundment. The Court has the "power" to declare presidential and congressional acts unconstitutional, but it can exercise that power effectively only by acknowledging its place within the political system. The use of the Exceptions Clause must take due regard for an independent judiciary, the Supremacy Clause, and the constitutional rights available to citizens.

Noncompliance

In a masterful phrase, rendered almost hypnotic by its elegance, Justice Jackson said "We are not final because we are infallible, but we are infallible only because we are final."[105] The historical record demonstrates convincingly that the Supreme Court is neither infallible nor final. The lack of finality is evident in the fluid quality of its decisions, reshaped over the years by all three branches. Furthermore, the Court often experiences substantial difficulty in obtaining full compliance with decisions when they are handed down. Noncompliance is a direct threat to the Court's dignity, authority, legitimacy, and reputation. Justice Holmes warned the Court to avoid great social changes, for there was "no use talking about a law that will not be willingly obeyed by at least 90 percent of the population."[106]

L. Rev. 17 (1981); Leonard G. Ratner, "Congressional Power over the Appellate Jurisdiction of the Supreme Court," 109 U. Pa. L. Rev. 157 (1960); and Henry M. Hart, Jr., "The Power of Congress to Limit the Jurisdiction of Federal Courts: An Exercise in Dialectic," 66 Harv. L. Rev. 1362 (1953).

[105]Brown v. Allen, 344 U.S. 443, 540 (1953).

[106]Recollection by Thomas G. Corcoran, who clerked for Holmes; R. Gordon Hoxie, ed., The White House: Organization and Operations 94 (1971).

In theory, judicial opinions are binding on the public and the other branches of government. In practice, judicial opinions are implemented with varying degrees of fidelity by local and federal officials.[107] Noncompliance sometimes results from deliberate evasion, as in the South's "massive resistance" to the desegregation cases. Unintentional violations may also occur but can be relieved by adequate education and clear judicial rulings. In between these two positions are various shades of avoidance and evasion.

One source of noncompliance is poor communication of judicial opinions. Scholars have found that most people do not know or understand decisions rendered by the courts. Instead, they receive abbreviated interpretations, often erroneous, from the media and local officials. For various reasons, the media has difficulty providing adequate coverage of the courts.[108]

The sheer force of inertia can limit compliance. Court decisions must pass through the perceptual screens of citizens who believe that current practices can persist with only slight modifications. Twenty years after *Engel* v. *Vitale* (1962), which struck down state-sponsored prayers in public schools, school authorities continue to set aside time during the day for students to say prayers.[109] Local officials may prefer to reinterpret judicial decisions on church-state separation to minimize the level of conflict and dissension within their communities.[110]

Finally, decisions of the Supreme Court and appellate courts are filtered by district courts and state courts. Lower courts, legislatures, and administrators have a number of ways to avoid full compliance. Lower courts can reinterpret rulings. Parties can relitigate to delay implementation or appeal to legislators to reverse a ruling that turns on statutory interpretation. When the Supreme Court reverses a lower court decision, it may remand the case for disposition "not inconsis-

---

[107]For an excellent synthesis of this literature, see Charles A. Johnson and Bradley C. Canon, Judicial Policies: Implementation and Impact (1984).

[108]Stephen L. Wasby, The Impact of the United States Supreme Court 83–99 (1970).

[109]David E. Rosenbaum, "Prayer in Many Schoolrooms Continues Despite '62 Ruling," New York Times, March 11, 1984, Section 1, at 1, 3.

[110]Kenneth M. Dolbeare and Phillip E. Hammond, The School Prayer Decisions: From Court Policy to Local Practice (1971); Frank J. Sorauf, "*Zorach* v. *Clauson*: The Impact of a Supreme Court Decision," 53 Am. Pol. Sci. Rev. 777 (1959); Gordon Patric, "The Impact of a Court Decision: Aftermath of the McCollum Case," 6 J. Pub. L. 455 (1957).

tent with this opinion." In this new round, the litigant who prevailed in the Supreme Court may lose in the lower courts.[111]

If the Court's opinion is a quilt stitched together from disparate strands of conflicting views in the majority, the leeway for lower courts will be substantial. Ambiguities can result from "inadvertence, or because of a deliberate fudging or vagueness built into the opinion to secure the support of a wavering colleague."[112] When the Supreme Court is unable to muster a majority of Justices behind a decision, and instead merely releases a plurality opinion, a confused message is sent to lower courts (state and federal) and to the legislative and executive branches.[113]

Even for opinions that are more coherent and principled, judges in the lower courts have considerable latitude in applying Supreme Court doctrine. Justice Thurgood Marshall, after dissenting in a decision that reversed the Second Circuit, later met with the judges and urged them to read the Court's decision narrowly.[114] In 1985, Justice Brennan said that the Court's rulings on *Miranda*-type cases "have led nearly every lower court to reject its simplistic reasoning."[115] The Court's reasoning "is sufficiently obscure and qualified as to leave state and federal courts with continued authority to combat obvious flouting by the authorities of the privileges against self-incrimination."[116]

After the Supreme Court handed down its desegregation decision in 1954, lower court judges followed different paths in implementing the ruling. Some were faithful; others were either defiant or evasive. Many federal judges were torn between the edict of the High Court and the sentiments and customs of their local communities.[117] It has been said that the Constitution is what the Supreme Court says it is,

[111]Note, "Evasion of Supreme Court Mandates in Cases Remanded to State Courts Since 1941," 67 Harv. L. Rev. 1251 (1954).

[112]John F. Davis and William L. Reynolds, "Judicial Cripples: Plurality Opinions in the Supreme Court," 1974 Duke L. J. 59, 71.

[113]Note, "Plurality Decisions and Judicial Decisionmaking," 94 Harv. L. Rev. 1127 (1981).

[114]Sotirios A. Barber, On What the Constitution Means 3 (1984).

[115]Oregon v. Elstad, 470 U.S. 298, 320 (1985) (dissenting opinion).

[116]Id. at 346.

[117]J. W. Peltason, Fifty-Eight Lonely Men: Southern Federal Judges and School Desegregation (1961); Walter F. Murphy, "Lower Court Checks on Supreme Court Power," 53 Am. Pol. Sci. Rev. 1017 (1959).

but Supreme Court decisions often mean what district courts say they mean.[118]

The problems of compliance can be appreciated by studying the response to the Supreme Court's decision in *INS* v. *Chadha* (1983), which invalidated the "legislative veto." Although the Court had announced one of the most important separation-of-powers cases of all time, the practical effect was not nearly as sweeping as the Court's decision.

The Court announced that future congressional efforts to alter "the legal rights, duties and relations of persons" outside the legislative branch must follow the full lawmaking process: passage of a bill or joint resolution by both of houses of Congress and presentment of that measure to the President for his signature or veto.[119] The Court lectured Congress that it could no longer rely on the legislative veto as "a convenient shortcut" to control executive agencies.[120] Instead, "legislation by the national Congress [must] be a step-by-step, deliberate and deliberative process."[121] According to the Court, the framers insisted that "the legislative power of the Federal Government be exercised in accord with a single, finely wrought and exhaustively considered, procedure."[122]

This meant that Congress could not use methods short of a public law to control executive actions. Under the legislative veto accommodation, dating back to 1932, Congress had delegated authority to the executive branch on the condition that certain administrative actions be delayed for a specified number of days. During that period, Congress had an opportunity to approve or disapprove without further presidential involvement. Congress acted by a one-house veto (simple resolution of either house), a two-house veto (concurrent resolution of both houses), and committee veto. The very essence of the legislative veto was that it could be invoked without risk of a presidential veto. Congressional approvals or disapprovals were not submitted to the President.

The legislative-veto procedure represented a classic quid pro quo. It attempted to reconcile the interests of both branches: the desire

---

[118]Jack W. Peltason, Federal Courts in the Political Process 14 (1955).
[119]462 U.S. 919, 952 (1983).
[120]Id. at 958.
[121]Id. at 959.
[122]Id. at 951.

of agencies for greater discretionary authority and the need of Congress to maintain control short of passing another public law. The procedure offered benefits for both sides. Congress gained a "shortcut" because its approval or disapproval was not sent to the President, but the executive branch also enjoyed shortcuts. At the close of the legislative review period, administration proposals became law just as if they had been enacted by Congress.

Even with *Chadha,* the need for a quid pro quo continues. The decision stimulated the executive and legislative branches to find ingenious and novel methods of achieving basically the same goals: broad delegations of legislative power by Congress to the agencies, checked by congressional controls that do not need enactment of another law. Some of the new legislative vetoes are informal and nonstatutory. A few rely on convoluted uses of the rulemaking powers available to the House and the Senate. Others are indistinguishable from the legislative veto supposedly struck down by the Court. The persistence of these executive-legislative compacts demonstrates the distance between the Court's theory and the operations of government. Both executive officials and legislators seek ways to avoid the theory of lawmaking espoused in *Chadha.*

It came as a surprise to some observers that Congress continued to place legislative vetoes in bills after the Court's decision and President Reagan continued to sign the bills into law. From the time of the Court's decision on June 23, 1983 to the end of the 99th Congress (October 18, 1986), 102 new legislative vetoes, generally the committee-veto variety, were enacted into law in twenty-four different statutes.

A flagrant case of noncompliance? A sign of disrespect for the courts? An alarming challenge to the time-honored belief that the Supreme Court has the last word on constitutional questions? Perhaps, but the Court painted with too broad a brush and offered a simplistic solution that is unacceptable to Congress and the agencies. The decision has been eroded by open defiance and subtle evasion. Neither consequence is attractive, but much of the responsibility for this situation belongs on the doorstep of the Court.

Some of the legislative vetoes enacted since *Chadha* are easy to spot. Most of them vest control in the Appropriations Committees.[123] Other

---

[123]For specific examples, see Louis Fisher, "Judicial Misjudgments About the Law-

legislative vetoes are more subtle. A continuing resolution provided that foreign assistance funds allocated to each country "shall not exceed those provided in fiscal year 1983 or those provided in the budget estimates for each country, whichever are lower, unless submitted through the regular reprogramming procedures of the Committees on Appropriations."[124] Those procedures provide for prior approval by committee. The District of Columbia Appropriation Act for fiscal 1984 prohibited funds from being obligated or spent by reprogramming "except pursuant to advance approval of the reprogramming granted according to the procedure set forth" in two House reports, both of which required prior approval by the Appropriations Committees.[125]

One year after *Chadha*, President Reagan received an appropriations bill that contained a number of committees vetoes. He signed the bill into law but asked Congress to stop adding provisions the Court had held unconstitutional. Moreover, he said he would implement the law in a manner consistent with *Chadha*, clearly announcing his intent that the administration did not feel legally bound by the committee vetoes.[126] The House Appropriations Committee responded by reviewing an agreement it had entered into four years previously with the National Aeronautics and Space Administration (NASA). Dollar caps were set on various NASA programs, usually at the level requested in the President's budget. The agreement allowed NASA to exceed the caps with the approval of the Appropriations Committees. Because of Reagan's threat to ignore committee controls, the House Appropriations Committee said it was necessary to repeal the accommodation. It would eliminate the committee veto *and* NASA's discretionary authority. Both sides stood to lose. The Appropriations Committees would not be able to veto NASA proposals; NASA would not be able to exceed ceilings without obtaining authority from Congress in a separate public law.[127]

Neither NASA nor the Appropriations Committees wanted to enact a law just to exceed a cap. To avoid this kind of administrative

---

making Process: The Legislative Veto Case," 45 Pub. Adm. Rev. 705, 706–7 (Special Issue, November 1985).

[124]97 Stat. 736 (1983).

[125]Id. at 827.

[126]20 Wkly Comp. Pres. Doc. 1040 (July 18, 1984).

[127]H. Rept. No. 916, 98th Cong., 2d Sess. 48 (1984).

rigidity, NASA Administrator James M. Beggs wrote to both committees and proposed that his agency and the committees agree informally that NASA would not exceed the caps without committee approval. Under the agreement, the statutory funding ceilings and the committee-approval mechanisms would be removed from future appropriations bills. Instead, the ceilings would be identified in the conference report accompanying NASA appropriations and confirmed by NASA in its submission of an annual operating plan.[128]

In short, the agency would continue to honor legislative vetoes but they would be informal rather than statutory. By converting the legislative veto to nonstatutory status, NASA is not legally bound by the agreement. Violation of the agreement, however, could provoke the Appropriations Committees to place caps in the appropriations bill and force the agency to lift them only through the enactment of another public law. Beggs's letter reveals the pragmatic sense of give-and-take that is customary between executive agencies and congressional committees. It also underscores the impracticality and unreality of the doctrines enunciated in *Chadha*.

The NASA agreement describes a world of informal agency-committee accommodations that were solidly in place before *Chadha*. No doubt these agreements will continue (and probably increase), notwithstanding the Court's strictures on the proper steps for lawmaking. Reprogramming procedures have been followed for at least three to four decades. As an informal accommodation between the branches, they allow agencies to shift funds within an appropriations account provided they obtain committee approval for major changes. This arrangement benefits both branches. Congress can appropriate in lump sums and monitor major deviations through the reprogramming procedure. Without this system, Congress would have to appropriate with far greater itemization and agencies would lose flexibility to adjust to changing requirements as the fiscal year unfolds.[129]

Statutes after *Chadha* may rely more heavily on notification to designated committees before an agency acts. Notification does not raise a constitutional issue, because it falls within the report-and-wait cat-

[128]The letter is reprinted in Fisher, "Judicial Misjudgments," 45 Pub. Adm. Rev., at 707.
[129]For more detail on the reprogramming process, see Louis Fisher, Presidential Spending Power 75–98 (1975).

egory already sanctioned by prior Court rulings.[130] In a practical sense, notification requirements in a statute can become a code word to indicate the need for a committee's prior approval. Only in highly unusual circumstances will an agency defy a committee or subcommittee. Nonstatutory legislative vetoes are not legal in effect. They are, however, in effect legal. Agencies are aware of the penalties that can be invoked by Congress if they decide to violate understandings and working relationships with their review committees.

What is now prohibitied directly by *Chadha* can be accomplished indirectly through House and Senate rules. In the 1950s, President Eisenhower objected to statutory provisions that required agencies to "come into agreement" with committees before implementing an administrative action. Such provisions, the Justice Department claimed, violated the constitutional principle of separated powers.[131] Congress retaliated by changing its internal procedure so that funds could be appropriated for a project only after the authorizing committees had passed a resolution of approval. The form had changed; the substance of committee veto remained unscathed. Nevertheless, the Justice Department accepted the committee resolution as a valid form of action because it was directed at Congress (the Appropriations Committees) rather than at the executive branch. By relying on the authorization-appropriation distinction, Congress retained its committee veto.[132]

These examples suggest some of the methods available to Congress and the executive branch to maintain the functional equivalent of a legislataive veto. Neither branch wants the static model of separated powers offered by the Court. The inevitable result is a record of noncompliance, subtle evasion, and a system of lawmaking that is now more convoluted, cumbersome, and covert than before. In many cases the Court's decision simply drove underground a set of legislative and committee vetoes that used to operate in plain sight. No one should be misled if the number of legislative vetoes placed in statutes gradually declines over the years. Fading from view will not mean disappearance. In one form or another, legislative vetoes will

[130]Sibbach v. Wilson, 312 U.S. 1, 14–15 (1941) and INS v. Chadha, 462 U.S. at 935 n.9.

[131]41 Op. Att'y Gen. 230 (1955); 41 Op. Att'y Gen. 300 (1957).

[132]See Public Papers of the Presidents, 1972, at 627.

remain an important method for reconciling legislative and executive interests.

"Judicial sacrosanctity" can be a useful rallying cry to protect the independence of the courts from external attacks. The concept is a powerful talisman for warding off major court-curbing efforts, such as court packing or the withdrawal of appellate jurisdiction. However, it is much less effective in preventing Congress from passing laws to reverse statutory interpretations by the courts.[133] Because these reversals are well within the realm of political legitimacy, they are buttressed by the intervention of interest groups.[134]

No one doubts the right of Congress to pass legislation that overturns what it considers to be judicial misinterpretations of statutes. But even when the courts render a constitutional interpretation, it is usually only a matter of time before Congress prevails if it wants to. Through changes in the composition of courts or adjustments in the attitudes of judges who continue to sit, a determined majority in Congress is likely to have its way.[135] At some point a similar statute, struck down in the past as unconstitutional, will find acceptance in the courts. If Congress fails to act, judicial policy (as with child labor and the definition of federal commerce) can dictate national policy for decades.[136]

It could be said that congressional challenges to the Court threaten to usurp judicial responsibilities. If the Constitution could be interpreted in mechanical fashion, left unchanged over the years and with few dissenting or even concurring opinions, and if the record were barren of instances in which the judiciary had reversed itself, this argument might have merit. But if the function of the Supreme Court is to apply the general language of the Constitution to changing needs,

[133]Stumpf, "Congressional Response," 14 J. Pub. L. at 383–91.

[134]Id. at 391–92; Note, "Congressional Reversal of Supreme Court Decisions; 1945–1957," 71 Harv. L. Rev. 1324, 1336 (1958). For confirmation of Stumpf's views, see Schmidhauser and Berg, Supreme Court, at 171–76.

[135]Robert A. Dahl, "Decision-Making in a Democracy: The Supreme Court as a National Policy-Maker," 6 J. Pub. L. 279 (1957). For a partial challenge to Dahl's thesis, see Jonathan D. Casper, "The Supreme Court and National Policy Making," 70 Am. Pol. Sci. Rev. 50 (1976).

[136]Johnson and Canon, Judicial Policies, at 230–36.

and if the Constitution is developmental rather than static in meaning, "there can hardly be any doubt remaining of the propriety of legislation which calls upon the court to reconsider its decisions, to adapt its opinions anew."[137]

Through what Alexander Bickel once called the Court's "continuing colloquy" with the political branches and society at large, the judiciary's search for constitutional principles can be reconciled with democratic values.[138] The extent of this colloquy is the subject of the final chapter.

[137]Harold W. Bowman, "Congress and the Supreme Court," 25 Pol. Sci. Q. 20, 33 (1910).

[138]Alexander M. Bickel, The Least Dangerous Branch 240 (1962). For this thesis, see also John Agresto. The Supreme Court and Constitutional Democracy (1984).

7. Coordinate Construction

The study of constitutional law is devoted almost entirely to the workings of the judiciary. Even those who explore the politics of constitutional law do so on the assumption that the ultimate act of constitutional interpretation is the prerogative of the courts. The writings of legal realists and, more recently, the Critical Legal Studies school abound with insights concerning the interactions between courts and the world around them. The legal realists recognized that judges make law, despite protestations to the contrary in court decisions, and the critical legal studies group routinely accepts decisions as political pronouncements that affect class relationships. But these studies still place the judiciary at the center of the constitutional universe, discharging its role as authoritative expounder of a text.

There are some exceptions to this general trend. A few legal textbooks, by including sections on congressional and presidential participation, challenge the notion that constitutional law is a monopoly of the judiciary.[1] On the whole, however, the record justifies the conclusion by Professor W. Michael Reisman that because the Constitution is believed to be a document interpreted solely by judges, rather than a much broader process in which nonjudicial actors also participate, "there is no comprehensive course on constitutional law in any meaningful sense in American law schools."[2]

In our political system the executive and legislative branches necessarily share with the judiciary a major role in interpreting the Constitution. Under the doctrine of "coordinate construction," the President and members of Congress have both the authority and the competence to engage in constitutional interpretation, not only before the courts decide but afterwards as well. All three branches per-

[1]Laurence H. Tribe. American Constitutional Law iv, 33 (1978); Paul Brest, Processes of Constitutional Law 21–29 (1975); Paul Brest and Sanford Levinson, Processes of Constitutional Law 903–1015; Gerald Gunther, Constitutional Law 21–29 (1985).

[2]W. Michael Reisman, "International Incidents: Introduction to a New Genre in the Study of International Law," 10 Yale J. Int'l L. 1, 8 n.13 (1984).

form a valuable, broad, and ongoing function in helping to shape the meaning of the Constitution.

The history of constitutional law amply supports these generalizations, but evidently there is something profoundly upsetting about a challenge to judicial monopoly. In 1986, as I was about to leave for the Far East to give talks on constitutional law, I was advised to contact a state judge who had just returned from that area. I asked whether he had encountered any misconceptions about American law. He said he had: people in the Far East had the same mistaken view in America that constitutional law is made only by the U.S. Supreme Court. He insisted that state courts make significant contributions to constitutional law, and I agreed. Then I asked if he thought the legislative and executive branches also had a role in shaping constitutional law. He replied with a note of sadness: "No, I am sorry to say it is all done by judges." An interesting and revealing comment! Open the door slightly to allow state judges to enter the inner sanctum but seal it promptly to prevent any legislative or executive intruders.

The feelings on this issue are acute. In 1986, Attorney General Edwin Meese III gave an address at Tulane University in which he distinguished between the Constitution and constitutional law. He referred to the first as fundamental law, capable of change only by constitutional amendment, whereas the second represents only the body of law developed by the Supreme Court. He quoted from constitutional historian Charles Warren that "however the Court may interpret the provisions of the Constitution, it is still the Constitution which is the law, not the decisions of the Court." He cited Justice Frankfurter to the same effect: "The ultimate touchstone of constitutionality is the Constitution itself and not what we have said about it."

Meese was careful to explain that Warren and Frankfurter did not mean that Supreme Court decisions lack the character of law. The decisions bind the parties to the case and require the executive branch to enforce the decisions. But the decisions do not," Meese said, "establish a 'supreme Law of the Land' that is binding on all persons and parts of government, henceforth and forevermore."[3] Obviously

---

[3]"The Law of the Constitution," a Bicentennial Lecture by the Honorable Edwin Meese III, Attorney General of the United States, The Tulane University, October 21, 1986, New Orleans, La.

that is so, for otherwise the Court could never reverse itself, which it does with some regularity.

Nevertheless, the address by Meese sent shock waves across the country. He touched a raw nerve in the legal community and the press. Some columnists called the speech a "stink bomb" that showed disrespect for the Court.[4] One newspaper column claimed that the speech invited anarchy.[5] Other commentators predicted "enormous chaos" if Meese's view ever prevailed.[6]

One suspects that if the speech had been given by someone else, shorn of the unfortunate references to Judge Manion and the Little Rock Case, it would have passed largely unnoticed. It does little more than review the commonplace about constitutional history. Although the Supreme Court claims that it alone delivers the "final word" on the meaning of the Constitution, congressional and executive practices over a number of years etch deep marks on constitutional law. Many of their determinations never reach the courts or, when they do, are avoided through the use of threshold tests erected by the judiciary. On some constitutional issues, the Court not only lacks the final word but has no word at all. As noted in Chapter Three, when the judiciary refuses to decide a case because it falls within the category of "political question," members of Congress and executive officials must dispose of the issue. Generally the Court decides to ratify the customs and accommodations entered into by the other two branches. On those rare occasions where the Court strikes down their actions, it may be only a matter of time before the political branches prevail. No decision by the Court is ever final if the nation remains unsettled and seriously divided over a constitutional issue.

Three-Branch Interpretation

All public officers—executive, legislative, and judicial—are constitutionally required by Article VI, Clause 3, "to support this Constitu-

---

[4]Michael Kinsley, "Meese's Stink Bomb," Washington Post, October 29, 1986, at A19.

[5]Anthony Lewis, "Law or Power?," N.Y. Times, October 27, 1986, at A23.

[6]Howard Kurtz, "Meese's View on Court Rulings Assailed, Defended," Washington Post, October 24, 1986, at A12.

tion." As elaborated by statute, executive and legislative officials "solemnly swear (or affirm) . . . [to] support and defend the Constitution of the United States against all enemies, foreign and domestic; . . . bear true faith and allegiance to the same; . . . take this obligation freely, without any mental reservation or purpose of evasion; and . . . well and faithfully discharge the duties [of their office]."[7] Members of Congress determine constitutional questions at the time a bill is under consideration. Executive officials carry out the same responsibility when they draft bills for congressional consideration or when they review bills presented to the President for his signature or veto.

Some provisions of the Constitution are addressed explicitly to members of Congress and should not be evaded because of the availability of judicial review. Under Article I, Section 9, "No Bill of Attainder or ex post facto law *shall be passed*" (emphasis added). Members have a responsibility to determine constitutional questions before, not after, a bill passes. The First Amendment commands that Congress *"shall make no law. . . ."* (emphasis added). Members are expected to legislate with a sensitivity to constitutional values and issues. It is irresponsible to legislate blindly, expecting the judiciary to identify and correct constitutional defects.[8]

Coordinate construction is more than a theory. Given the nature of our political system, it is a necessity. Long before the courts offered their interpretations, Congress and the executive branch gave close attention to such issues as judicial review, the Bank of the United States, Congress's investigative power, slavery, internal improvements, federalism, the warmaking power, treaties and foreign relations, interstate commerce, the President's removal power, and the legislative veto.[9] Congressional debate was intense, informed, and

[7]5 U.S.C. § 3331 (1982).

[8]Paul Brest, "The Conscientious Legislator's Guide to Constitutional Interpretation," 27 Stan. L. Rev. 585, 587 (1975).

[9]William G. Andrews, Coordinate Magistrates: Constitutional Law by Congress and the President 1–20 (judicial review), 21–43 (Bank), 44–64 (slavery), 65–95 (interstate commerce), 109–30 (removal power), 131–44 (war powers) (1969). For early debate on internal improvements, see William Letwin, ed., A Documentary History of American Economic Policy Since 1789 53–84 (1961). See also James Hart, The American Presidency in Action 78–111 (treaties and foreign relations), 152–248 (removal power) (1948); Charles Miller, The Supreme Court and the Uses of History 52–70, 205–10 (removal power) (1969); Donald G. Morgan, Congress and the Constitution 49–57 (removal power), 101–18 (investigative power), 140–59 (interstate commerce), 184–

diligent. In the early decades it had to be, given the paucity of direction at that time from the Supreme Court and the lower courts.

Coordinate construction is strongly present in "The Decision of 1789." The debate by the First Congress on the President's removal power occupies several hundred pages of the *Annals of Congress* and constitutes an extraordinarily able analysis of implied powers. Some members concluded that because the Senate forms part of the appointing power, it must also be included in the process of removing executive officials. Others believed that executive officials could be removed solely through the constitutional process of impeachment. A third camp argued that the power of Congress to create an office includes the power to attach any condition Congress deems appropriate for tenure and removal. A fourth school insisted that the removal power belonged exclusively to the President as an incident of his executive power.[10]

Could this issue be resolved in Congress, pursuant to the statutory process, or submitted to the courts? Nine days before the House debated the removal power, Madison took the floor to explain a list of constitutional amendments known collectively as the Bill of Rights. He predicted that "independent tribunals of justice will consider themselves in a peculiar manner the guardians of those rights; they will be an impenetrable bulwark against every assumption of power in the Legislative or Executive."[11]

Some members of Congress took this literally to mean that all constitutional issues had to be decided by the courts. When the House took up the removal power, Madison saw no need to defer to the judiciary. He found no merit to the notion that "it would be officious in this branch of the Legislature to expound the Constitution, so far as it relates to the division of power between the President and the Senate."[12] To Madison it was "incontrovertibly of as much importance to this branch of the Government as to any other, that the Constitution should be preserved entire. It is our duty, so far as it depends upon us, to take care that the powers of the Constitution be

---

203 (legislative veto) (1966); Abraham D. Sofaer, War, Foreign Affairs and Constitutional Power (1976) (discussing deliberations by Congress from 1789 to 1829).

[10]Louis Fisher, Constitutional Conflicts between Congress and the President 60–66 (1985).

[11]1 Annals of Congress 439 (June 8, 1789).

[12]Id. at 500.

preserved entire to every department of Government. . . ."[13] He continued:

> But the great objection drawn from the source to which the last arguments would lead us is, that the Legislature itself has no right to expound the Constitution; that wherever its meaning is doubtful, you must leave it to take its course, until the Judiciary is called upon to declare its meaning. I acknowledge, in the ordinary course of Government, that the exposition of the laws and Constitution devolves upon the Judiciary. But I beg to know, upon what principles it can be contended, that any one department draws from the Constitution greater powers than another, in marking out the limits of the powers of the several departments? The Constitution is the charter of the people to the Government; it specifies certain great powers as absolutely granted, and marks out the departments to exercise them. If the Constitutional boundary of either be brought into question, I do not see that any one of these independent departments has more right than another to declare their sentiments on that point.[14]

The scope of the President's removal power was addressed fully in *Myers* v. *United States* (1926). To determine the dimensions of this power, Chief Justice Taft turned to the debate of 1789 for guidance. After studying the discussion in the House of Representatives, day by day and vote by vote, he concluded that there was not the "slightest doubt" that the vote "was, and was intended to be, a legislative declaration that the power to remove officers appointed by the President and the Senate vested in the President alone. . . ."[15] The debate in 1789 held special significance. As Taft noted, Madison was "a leader in the House, as he had been in the Convention." Madison's arguments in support of the President's implied power of removal "were masterly, and he carried the House."[16]

Taft relied on the legislative debate in the First Congress not because a congressional determination on a constitutional issue

[13]Id.
[14]Id.
[15]272 U.S. 52, 114 (1926).
[16]Id. at 115.

is conclusive, but, first, because of our agreement with the reasons upon which it is avowedly based; second, because this was the decision of the First Congress, on a question of primary importance in the organization of the Government, made within two years of the Constitutional Convention and within a much shorter time after its ratification; and, third, because that Congress numbered among its leaders those who had been members of the Convention.[17]

Taft concluded that the power of removal "must remain where the Constitution places it, with the President, as part of the executive power, in accordance with the legislative decision of 1789 which we have been considering."[18]

While Taft based his decision on the congressional debates of 1789, the dissenters in *Myers* looked to that same record and other congressional actions to reach the opposite conclusion. Justice McReynolds, reviewing an 1835 Senate debate, described the danger of placing unrestrained power in the Executive to remove officials.[19] He pointed to the adoption of civil service reforms as a method of protecting officeholders from arbitrary removal. He identified the many statutes enacted by Congress to restrict the President's removal power.[20] His interpretation of the debates in 1789 did not produce the same impression of unrestrained executive power that Taft had discovered.[21]

Practices since 1789 helped to reinforce "the right of Congress to impose restrictions" on the President's removal power.[22] Justice Brandeis's dissent in *Myers* included a long list of statutes that had curbed the removal power. That record convinced him that a "persistent legislative practice which involves a delimitation of the respective powers of Congress and the President, and which has been so established and maintained, should be deemed tantamount to judi-

---

[17]Id. at 136.
[18]Id. at 161. For Justice Sutherland's reliance on a statement by Congressman John Marshall in 1800 and a Senate report in 1816 to define the President's foreign affairs powers, see United States v. Curtiss-Wright, 299 U.S. 304, 319 (1936).
[19]Id. at 179–81.
[20]Id. at 181.
[21]Id. at 193–99.
[22]Id. at 202 (McReynolds, J., dissenting).

cial construction, in the absence of any decision by any court to the contrary."[23]

Taft's doctrinaire decision cannot be reconciled with the statutes, enacted on numerous occasions, that limited the President's power to remove executive officers who exercised quasi-legislative and quasi-judicial powers. Indeed, the Supreme Court recognized the legitimacy of these congressional efforts to limit the President's removal power.[24] Judicial interpretations were constantly challenged and altered by congressional determinations.

Thomas Jefferson, Andrew Jackson, and Abraham Lincoln developed various formulations of the doctrine of coordinate construction. Jefferson believed that each branch of government would act as an independent guardian of the Constitution. Regarding the Alien and Sedition Acts as patently unconstitutional, he and his followers were appalled when the federal courts failed to strike them down.[25] Once in office as President, Jefferson "discharged every person under punishment or prosecution under the sedition law."[26] He believed "that law to be a nullity, as absolute and as palpable as if Congress had ordered us to fall down and worship a golden image; and that it was as much my duty to arrest its execution in every stage, as it would have been to have rescued from the fiery furnace those who should have been cast into it for refusing to worship the image."[27]

Under Jefferson's theory, the three branches must be "co-ordinate and independent of each another."[28] Decisions by one branch, including judicial interpretations of constitutional questions, were to be given "no control to another branch."[29] Each branch "has an equal right to decide for itself what is the meaning of the Constitution in

---

[23]Id. at 283 (citing United States v. Midwest Oil Co., 236 U.S. 459, 469 [1915]).

[24]See Wiener v. United States, 357 U.S. 349 (1958) (President lacked authority to remove a member of an adjudicatory commission); Humphrey's Executor v. United States, 295 U.S. 602 (1935) (Congress may restrict President's power to remove officers performing quasi-judicial and quasi-legislative duties).

[25]1 Charles Warren, The Supreme Court in United States History 215 (1937).

[26]11 Writings of Thomas Jefferson 43 (Bergh. ed 1904) (letter to Mrs. John Adams, July 22, 1804).

[27]Id. at 43–44.

[28]Id. at 213 (letter to George Hay, June 2, 1807).

[29]Id. at 213–14. For further insight into Jefferson's position on the nullity of the Alien and Sedition Act, see 12 Writings of Thomas Jefferson 288–90 (letter to Wilson C. Nicholas, June 13, 1809); 14 Writings of Thomas Jefferson 116 (letter to Gideon Granger, March 9, 1814).

the cases submitted to its action; and especially, where it is to act ultimately and without appeal."[30] This latter qualification suggests that each branch is supreme on certain constitutional questions. The difficulty with Jefferson's doctrine is that he neglects to identify those questions. Without specifying the areas of supremacy, the country might face a multitude of conflicting and shifting interpretations, none with any greater significance or "finality" than another. All would have equal weight. The risk of Jefferson's theory is substantial. What would have happened in 1974 had President Nixon, in the confrontation over the Watergate tapes, insisted that his interpretation of executive privilege had comparable merit and authority to that of the Supreme Court?[31]

It should be said of the Sedition Act of 1798 that not only did Jefferson regard it as a nullity, so did much of the country. Although the statute was never tested in the courts, it expired by its terms in 1801 and was rejected, as the Supreme Court noted in 1964, in the "court of history."[32] Congress determined that the Sedition Act was "unconstitutional, null, and void," and appropriated funds to reimburse those who had been fined under the statute.[33]

Jackson inherited the Jeffersonian distrust of the judiciary, but looked to the federal courts as a potential ally to combat the nullification doctrine. To keep the nation intact, it might be necessary for the presidency and the judiciary to join forces.[34] He announced his own theory of coordinate construction in a message vetoing the bill in 1832 to recharter the Bank of the United States. The Supreme Court had upheld the constitutionality of the Bank,[35] and advocates of the Bank maintained that "its constitutionality in all its features

[30]15 Writings of Thomas Jefferson 214 (letter to Judge Spencer Roane, September 6, 1819).

[31]John Agresto, The America and Constitutional Democracy 83 (1984). In United States v. Nixon, 418 U.S. 683 (1974), the Supreme Court held that the separation of powers doctrine cannot justify an absolute, unqualified presidential privilege of immunity from judicial process in all circumstances.

[32]New York Times Co. v. Sullivan, 376 U.S. 254, 276 (1964).

[33]H. Rept. No. 86, 26th Cong., 1st Sess. 2 (1840); 6 Stat. 802, chap. 45 (1840).

[34]Richard P. Longaker, "Andrew Jackson and the Judiciary," 71 Pol. Sci. Q. 341 (1956). Despite Jackson's well-known animosity for some members of the judiciary, particularly Chief Justice John Marshall, and political conflict between Jackson and the courts, Jackson was a firm believer in the importance of a vigorous and powerful court system and the principle of judicial review. Id. at 364.

[35]McCulloch v. Maryland, 17 U.S. (4 Wheat.) 315 (1819).

ought to be considered as settled by precedent and by the decision of the Supreme Court."[36] Jackson disagreed, saying that "mere precedent" should not be decisive in questions of constitutional power "except where the acquiescence of the people and the States can be considered as well settled."[37] The history of the Bank, he pointed out, shouted with contradictions. After supporting the Bank in 1791, Congress voted against it in 1811 and again in 1815. A year later Congress favored the Bank. Sentiment from the states was generally hostile to the Bank.[38] His message hammers home the theory of coordinate construction:

> If the opinion of the Supreme Court covered the whole ground of this act, it ought not to control the coordinate authorities of this Government. The Congress, the Executive, and the Court must each for itself be guided by its own opinion of the Constitution. Each public officer who takes an oath to support the Constitution swears that he will support it as he understands it, and not as it is understood by others. It is as much the duty of the House of Representatives, of the Senate, and of the President to decide upon the constitutionality of any bill or resolution which may be presented to them for passage or approval as it is of the supreme judges when it may be brought before them for judicial decision. The opinion of the judges has no more authority over Congress than the opinion of Congress has over the judges, and on that point the President is independent of both. The authority of the Supreme Court must not, therefore, be permitted to control the Congress or the Executive when acting in their legislative capacities, but to have only such influence as the force of their reasoning may deserve.[39]

Jackson's theory of coordinate construction embodies a number of constraints not found in Jefferson's model. Judicial precedents could govern other branches if they acquiesced. The Court's authority did not extend to Congress or the Executive "when acting in their legislative capacities" unless the reasoning of the Court prevailed. Jackson insisted that each public officer should support the Constitution "as

[36] 3 Messages and Papers of the Presidents 1144 (1897).
[37] Id. at 1145.
[38] Id.
[39] Id.

he understands it, and not as it is understood by others." He did not embrace, however, the Jeffersonians' unyielding hostility toward the courts.

Also compatible with democratic principles and the rule of law is Lincoln's speech at Springfield, Illinois, on July 17, 1858. Stephen Douglas, his opponent in the 1858 Senate race, supported the Supreme Court's decision the previous year in *Dred Scott v. Sandford.* Lincoln limited his support of that decision by saying that "in so far as it decided in favor of Dred Scott's master and against Dred Scott and his family, I do not propose to disturb or resist the decision."[40] However, Lincoln rejected Douglas's wholehearted endorsement, which Lincoln characterized as having "the citizen conform his vote to that decision; the Member of Congress, his; the President, his use of the veto power. [Douglas] would make it a rule of political action for the people and all the departments of the government."[41] By resisting the decision "as a political rule," Lincoln said he would "disturb no right of property, create no disorder, excite no mobs."[42]

What Lincoln challenged was the inference in *Dred Scott* that the nation should remain divided between freemen and slaves. He opposed the spread of slavery to the new territories and rejected the Court's decision as a basis for nationalizing Negro slavery. His philosophy of government was drawn not from Chief Justice Taney's opinion in *Dred Scott* but the principles incorporated in the Declaration of Independence. He asked Douglas and his adherents if they wanted to amend the Declaration to read that "all men are created equal except negroes."[43]

> My declarations upon this subject of negro slavery may be misrepresented, but can not be misunderstood. I have said that I do not understand the Declaration to mean that all men were created equal in all respects. They are not our equal in color; but I suppose that it does mean to declare that all men are equal in some respects; they are equal in their right to "life, liberty, and the pursuit of happiness." Certainly the negro is not our equal in color—perhaps not in many other respects; still, in the right to put into his mouth the bread that his own

[40] 2 Collected Works of Abraham Lincoln 516 (R. Basler ed. 1953).
[41] Id.
[42] Id.
[43] Id. at 520.

241

hands have earned, he is the equal of every other man, white or black. In pointing out that more has been given you, you can not be justified in taking away the little which has been given him. All I ask for the negro is that if you do like him, let him alone. If God gave him but little, that little let him enjoy.[44]

Lincoln refused to defer to *Dred Scott* and allow it to set the moral tone and political direction of the United States. At stake was not an abstract or technical question of law but rather the future of the country. Every citizen had a duty to express opinions and help shape the contours of constitutional structures and rights. Harold Hyman has said that mid-nineteenth-century Americans "were not inclined to leave to private lawyers any more than to public men the conception, execution, and interpretation of public law. The conviction was general that no aristocracy existed with respect to the Constitution. Like politics, with which it was inextricably joined, the Constitution was everybody's business."[45]

Lincoln regarded the Supreme Court as a coequal, not superior, branch of government. The Court existed as one branch of a political system, subject to a combination of checks and balances, including the force of public opinion. Thus, in his inaugural address in 1861, he denied that constitutional questions could be settled solely by the Supreme Court. If government policy on "vital questions affecting the whole people is to be irrevocably fixed" by the Supreme Court, "the people will have ceased to be their own rulers."[46] Congress and the President were free to reach their own constitutional judgments, even if at odds with past Court rulings, and then let the Court decide again.

The Last-Word Dogma. Beginning with Chief Justice Marshall's declaration in *Marbury* v. *Madison* that it is "emphatically the province and duty of the judicial department to say what the law is,"[47] the Supreme Court regularly insists that it alone delivers the "final word" on the meaning of the Constitution. According to a 1958

[44]Id.
[45]Harold M. Hyman, A More Perfect Union: The Impact of the Civil War and Reconstruction of the Constitution 6 (1975).
[46]7 Messages and Papers of the Presidents 3210.
[47]5 U.S. (1 Cr.) 137, 177 (1803).

decision, *Marbury* "declared the basic principle that the federal judiciary is supreme in the exposition of the law of the Constitution."[48] The Court reasserted this principle in 1962: "Deciding whether a matter has in any measure been committed by the Constitution to another branch of government, or whether action of that branch exceeds whatever authority has been committed, is itself a delicate exercise in constitutional interpretation, and is a responsibility of this Court as ultimate interpreter of the Constitution."[49]

"Ultimate interpreter" does not mean exclusive interpreter. The courts expect other branches of government to interpret the Constitution in their initial deliberations. "In the performance of assigned constitutional duties each branch of the Government must initially interpret the Constitution, and the interpretation of its powers by any branch is due great respect from the others."[50] Congressional interpretations are given substantial weight in some circumstances, even to the point of becoming the controlling factor.[51]

Congressional and executive practices over a number of years have been instrumental in fixing the meaning of the Constitution.[52] The Supreme Court, upholding the President's removal power in 1903, based its ruling largely on the "universal practice of the government for over a century."[53] Presidential action in which Congress acquiesced can become a justification for the exercise of power.[54] The

[48]Cooper v. Aaron, 358 U.S. 1, 18 (1958).

[49]Baker v. Carr, 369 U.S. 186, 211 (1962). The notion that the Supreme Court is the "ultimate interpreter" was repeated in Powell v. McCormack, 395 U.S. 486, 549 (1969).

[50]United States v. Nixon, 418 U.S. 683, 703 (1974).

[51]See Rostker v. Goldberg, 453 U.S. 57, 64 (1981). (In the context of a challenge to male-only registration for military service, the Court noted: "The customary deference accorded the judgments of Congress is certainly appropriate when, as here, Congress specifically considered the Act's constitutionality.")

[52]See Stuart v. Laird, 5 U.S. (1 Cr.) 299, 309 (1803). (Dismissing a challenge that the Judiciary Act of 1789 was unconstitutional, the Court stated that "practice, and acquiescence under it, for a period of several years, commencing with the organization of the judicial system, affords an irresistible answer, and has indeed fixed the construction. It is a contemporary interpretation of the most forcible nature.")

[53]Shurtleff v. United States, 189 U.S. 311, 316 (1903).

[54]See United States v. Midwest Oil Co., 236 U.S. 459, 474 (1915). (Presidential decisions over a period of years "clearly indicate that the long-continued practice, known to and acquiesced in by Congress, would raise a presumption that the withdrawals had been made in pursuance of its consent or of a recognized administrative power of the Executive in the management of the public lands.")

cumulative force of these customs has helped to transform the Constitution over time.[55]

Justice Jackson claimed that decisions by the Supreme Court "are not final because we are infallible, but we are infallible only because we are final."[56] As the historical record proves overwhelmingly, the Court is neither final nor infallible. Judicial decisions rest undisturbed only to the extent that Congress, the President, and the general public find the decisions convincing, reasonable, and acceptable. Otherwise, the debate on constitutional principles will continue.

Being "ultimate interpreter" does not grant the judiciary superiority in the sense that final judgments are unreviewable. Eight years before writing *Dred Scott,* Chief Justice Taney wrote a dissenting opinion in which he noted that the Court's opinion "upon the construction of the Constitution is always open to discussion when it is supposed to have been founded in error, and that its judicial authority should hereafter depend altogether on the force of the reasoning by which it is supported."[57] Referring to Taney's dissent, Justice Frankfurter spoke about the need for "judicial exegesis" in interpreting broadly phrased charters like the Constitution. To Frankfurter, "the ultimate touchstone of constitutionality is the Constitution itself and not what we have said about it."[58] Before joining the Court, Frankfurter put this point more bluntly to President Franklin D. Roosevelt: "People have been taught to believe that when the Supreme Court speaks it is not they who speak but the Constitution, whereas, of course, in so many vital cases, it is *they* who speak and not the Constitution."[59]

Edward S. Corwin supplied his own twist to this message: "The *juristic* conception of judicial review invokes a miracle. It supposes a kind of transubstantiation whereby the Court's opinion of its Constitution . . . becomes the very body and blood of the Constitution."[60]

---

[55]For an effective critique of court doctrines on custom and acquiescence, see Michael J. Glennon, "The Use of Custom in Resolving Separation of Powers Disputes," 64 B.U.L. Rev. 109 (1984).

[56]Brown v. Allen, 344 U.S. 443, 540 (1953) (Jackson, J., concurring).

[57]The Passenger Cases, 48 U.S. (7 How.) 283, 470 (1849) (Taney, C.J., dissenting).

[58]Graves v. New York ex rel. O'Keefe, 306 U.S. 466, 491–92 (1939).

[59]Max Freedman, anno., Roosevelt and Frankfurter: Their Correspondence 383 (1967).

[60]Edward S. Corwin, Court Over the Constitution: A Study of Judicial Review as an Instrument of Popular Government 68 (1938).

Corwin did not exaggerate. Writing in 1930, Professor Felix Frankfurter made this claim: "In good truth, the Supreme Court *is* the Constitution."[61] Two experts in constitutional law began their book with a chapter entitled "The Court is the Constitution."[62]

The Constitution's bicentennial stimulated additional hyperbole for judicial supremacy. In 1987, at the American Bar Association meeting, Chief Justice Rehnquist stated that the Supreme Court, "sitting at the apex of that judiciary, was made the final arbiter of questions of constitutional law."[63] A reporter summarized these results of a national survey: "Six in 10 of those responding said correctly that the Supreme Court is the final authority on constitutional change."[64] The six, of course, were incorrect. Constitutional change can occur without any judicial involvement, as with the amendment process.

What is "final" at one stage of our political development may be reopened at some later date, leading to fresh interpretation and overrulings of past judicial doctrines. Courts are the ultimate interpreter of a particular case, not the larger issue of which that case is a part. Justice White remarked in a dissenting opinion in 1970: "this Court is not alone in being obliged to construe the Constitution in the course of its work; nor does it even approach having a monopoly on the wisdom and insight appropriate to the task."[65] Disagreement with a decision may lead to new litigation that tests the same issue. At times the Supreme Court signals its willingness to review previous decisions and perhaps overturn them.

The most famous utterance concerning judicial supremacy is usually taken from context to produce a misleading impression. Speaking before the Elmira Chamber of Commerce in 1907, Charles Evans Hughes, at that time governor of New York, said: "We are under a Constitution, but the Constitution is what the judges say it is. . . ."[66] First, these were impromptu remarks. He abandoned his prepared speech to respond to critics who opposed giving power to a commis-

---

[61]Felix Frankfurter, "The United States Supreme Court Molding the Constitution," 32 Current Hist. 235, 240 (1930). Emphasis in original.

[62]Alpheas Thomas Mason and William M. Beaney, The Supreme Court in a Free Society (1968).

[63]Washington Post, February 16, 1987, at A3.

[64]Washington Post, February 15, 1987, at A13.

[65]Welsh v. United States, 398 U.S. 333, 370 (1970).

[66]Addresses and Papers of Charles Evans Hughes 139 (1908).

sion to investigate abuses by railroads.[67] Hughes feared that without such powers in the hands of a commission, these divisive matters would be the subject of lawsuits damaging to the courts. Far from regarding the courts as a supreme body, he thought their duties had to be carefully circumscribed. Here is the full context:

> I have the highest regard for the courts. My whole life has been spent in work conditioned upon respect for the courts. I reckon him one of the worst enemies of the community who will talk lightly of the dignity of the bench. We are under a Constitution, but the Constitution is what the judges say it is, and the judiciary is the safeguard of our liberty and of our property under the Constitution. I do not want to see any direct assault upon the courts, nor do I want to see any indirect assault upon the courts. And I tell you, ladies and gentlemen, no more insidious assault could be made upon the independence and esteem of the judiciary than to burden it with these questions of administration,—questions which lie close to the public impatience, and in regard to which the people are going to insist on having administration by officers directly accountable to them.[68]

Hughes warned that any effort to place these issues with the judiciary "would swamp your courts with administrative burdens and expose them to the fire of public criticism in connection with matters of this description, from which I hope they will be safeguarded." Were the courts to decide these matters, "free from that direct accounting to which administrative officers are subject, you will soon find a propaganda advocating a short-term judiciary, and you will turn upon our courts—the final safeguard of our liberties—that hostile and perhaps violent criticism from which they should be shielded and will be shielded if left with the jurisdictions which it was intended they should exercise."[69]

In various ways the process of constitutional interpretation has become a shared enterprise, calling upon the best efforts of the Su-

[67]Id. at 133.

[68]Id. at 139–40

[69]Id. at 141–42. See also Hughes's later reflection on his Elmira address; David J. Danelski and Joseph S. Tulchin, eds., The Autobiographical Notes of Charles Evans Hughes 143–44 (1973).

preme Court, Congress, the President, executive agencies, the states, and the public at large.

Judicial Invitations

During the 1930s and 1940s, after Congress and the Court had gone back and forth on a tax issue, the Court invited Congress to pass legislation and challenge previous rulings: "There is no reason to doubt that this Court may fall into error as may other branches of the Government. Nothing in the history or attitude of this Court should give rise to legislative embarrassment if in the performance of its duty a legislative body feels impelled to enact laws which may require the Court to reexamine its previous judgment or doctrine."[70] The Court explained that it is less able than other branches "to extricate itself from error," because it can reconsider a matter "only when it is again properly brought before it as a case or controversy."[71] Statutory action is often necessary to permit the Court to review and possibly to overturn its previous holdings. Congress may feel that it is not only its right but its duty to present a question once more to the Court, hoping to elicit a more favorable ruling.[72] By overruling itself, the Court admits its ability on an earlier occasion to commit error. "Congress and the courts," said Justice Stone, "both unhappily may falter or be mistaken in the performance of their constitutional duty."[73]

A type of implicit invitation appeared in *Leisy* v. *Hardin* (1890). Building on the "original package" doctrine of *Brown* v. *Maryland* (1827),[74] the Court ruled that a state's prohibition of intoxicating liquors could not be applied to original packages or kegs. Only after the original package was broken into smaller packages could the state exercise control. The power of Congress over commerce, even if not expressly stated in a statute, appeared to override state police powers

[70]Helvering v. Griffiths, 318 U.S. 371, 400–401 (1943).
[71]Id. at 401.
[72]Compare Ashton v. Cameron County Dist., 298 U.S. 513 (1936), striking down sections of the Bankruptcy Act of 1934, and United States v. Bekins, 304 U.S. 27, 33 (1938), sustaining Chapter X of the Bankruptcy Act of 1937.
[73]United States v. Butler, 297 U.S. 1, 87 (1936) (Stone, J., dissenting).
[74]25 U.S. (12 Wheat.) 419, 441 (1827).

247

and local options. The Court qualified its opinion by saying that the states could not exclude incoming articles "without congressional permission."[75]

As a result of the Court's decision, imaginative entrepreneurs opened up "original-package saloons" making it impossible for the states to exercise any control. Brewers and distillers from outside the state could package their goods "even in the shape of a vial containing a single drink."[76] Within a matter of months Congress considered legislation to overturn the decision. The irreverent attitude in Congress is reflected in remarks by Senator George Edmunds of Vermont. The opinions of the Supreme Court regarding Congress "are of no more value to us than ours are to it. We are just as independent of the Supreme Court of the United States as it is of us, and every judge will admit it." If members of Congress concluded that the Court had made an error "are we to stop and say that is the end of the law and the mission of civilization in the United States for that reason? I take it not." Further consideration by the Court might produce a different result: "as they have often done, it may be their mission next year to change their opinion and say that the rule ought to be the other way."[77]

Congress quickly overturned the decision by passing legislation that made intoxicating liquors, upon their arrival in a state or territory, subject to the police powers "to the same extent and in the same manner as though such liquids or liquors had been produced in such State or Territory, and shall not be exempt therefrom by reason of being introduced therein in original packages or otherwise."[78] The Supreme Court upheld the constitutionality of this statute.[79]

The give-and-take between Congress and the judiciary is illustrated by the insurance cases. In 1869 the Supreme Court held that states could regulate insurance because it was not a "transaction of commerce."[80] That holding, along with 150 years of precedents, was overturned in 1944 when the Court interpreted the transaction of insurance business across state lines as interstate commerce subject

[75]Leisy v. Hardin, 135 U.S. 100, 125 (1890).
[76]21 Cong. Rec. 4954 (1890).
[77]Id. at 4964.
[78]26 Stat. 313 (1890).
[79]In re Rahrer, 140 U.S. 545 (1891).
[80]Paul v. Virginia, 8 Wall. 168 (1869).

to congressional regulation. The Court said that Congress had not intended to exempt the insurance business from the Sherman Anti-trust Act.[81]

The Court sent a mixed message. On the one hand, it said that the "real answer before us is to be found in the Commerce Clause itself and in some of the great cases which interpret it,"[82] which suggests that the matter was solely for the courts. At the same time, its ruling was conditioned on "the absence of Congressional action" and was placed in the context of "the continued absence of conflicting Congressional action."[83] Evidently, the "real answer" depended on what Congress decided to do: "Our basic responsibility in interpreting the Commerce Clause is to make certain that the power to govern intercourse among the states remains where the Constitution placed it. That power, as held by this Court from the beginning, is vested in the Congress, available to be exercised for the national welfare as Congress shall deem necessary."[84] If exceptions were to be written into the Sherman Act, "they must come from the Congress, not this Court."[85]

Congress quickly passed the McCarran Act, authorizing states to regulate insurance.[86] Acting under cover of this statute, states were once again allowed to regulate and tax the business of insurance. In unanimously upholding the McCarran Act, the Court confessed that the "history of judicial limitation of congressional power over commerce, when exercised affirmatively, has been more largely one of retreat than of ultimate victory."[87]

During the Reagan administration, all three branches wrestled with the constitutionality of the "fairness doctrine," with the judiciary eventually inviting the other two branches to resolve the matter. The Federal Communications Commission (FCC) had developed the doctrine to require broadcasters to present public issues and give each side of an issue fair coverage. In 1969, the Supreme Court held that this agency regulation was consistent with congressional policy and

[81]United States v. South-Eastern Underwriters Assn., 322 U.S. 533 (1944).
[82]Id. at 549.
[83]Id. at 548, 549.
[84]Id. at 552–53.
[85]Id. at 561.
[86]59 Stat. 33 (1945).
[87]Prudential Ins. Co. v. Benjamin, 328 U.S. 408, 415 (1946).

did not violate the First Amendment.[88] Congress had supported the fairness doctrine in 1959, but in oblique fashion.[89]

The fairness doctrine depended largely on the limited number of access points available to licensees for radio and television. If outlets increased because of technology, the doctrine's rationale would be undermined. In a footnote to a 1984 decision, the Supreme Court recognized that the emergence of cable and satellite television created new channels for the public. However, "without some signal from Congress or the FCC" that technological development required revision of broadcasting regulation, the Court was not prepared to challenge the fairness doctrine.[90]

The FCC chairman had criticized the doctrine as unconstitutional and threatened to abolish it. In 1985 the Commission released a report that concluded that the doctrine violates the First Amendment and no longer serves the public interest. However, it declined to institute a rulemaking to eliminate or modify the doctrine. On the basis of that report, a party brought suit and asked the D.C. Circuit to consider the constitutionality of the doctrine. The D.C. Circuit refused on the ground that the report did not constitute "agency action" subject to its review.[91] On the same day, the D.C. Circuit returned a case to the FCC because it had failed to give adequate consideration to a station owner's constitutional arguments regarding the fairness doctrine. The Commission regarded Congress and the courts as more appropriate arenas for deciding the constitutional question. The D.C. Circuit, however, decided it might benefit from the FCC's analysis, even if the Commission felt political pressure from Congress to avoid a final conclusion.[92] It noted that federal officials are not only bound by the Constitution but they take an oath to support and defend it: "To enforce a Commission-generated policy that the Commission itself believes is unconstitutional may well constitute a violation of that oath. . . ."[93]

Congress passed legislation in 1987 to codify the fairness doctrine, but President Reagan vetoed the bill. He stated that the doctrine was

[88]Red Lion Broadcasting Co. v. FCC, 395 U.S. 367 (1969).
[89]73 Stat. 557 (1959).
[90]FCC v. League of Women Voters of California, 468 U.S. 364, 377–78 n.11 (1984). See also n.12 at 378–79.
[91]Radio-Television News Directors Ass'n v. FCC. 809 F.2d 860 (D.C. Cir. 1987).
[92]Meredith Corp. v. FCC, 809 F.2d 863, 872 (D.C. Cir. 1987).
[93]Id. at 874.

antagonistic to the First Amendment and was no longer justified because of new media outlets such as cable television.[94] On June 23, the Senate voted to refer the vetoed bill to committee. On August 4, the FCC unanimously abolished the fairness doctrine, claiming that it represented an unconstitutional restriction on free speech.[95]

Uninvited Collisions

After courts hand down a decision, a disappointed Congress may decide to test the firmness of the Court's conclusion by passing new legislation and provoking further litigation. The history of child labor legislation offers a striking example. The first child labor law passed by Congress in 1916 was based on the commerce power. The Supreme Court invalidated that statute in 1918.[96] Congress bounced back a year later with another statute on child labor, this time based on the taxing power. The Court struck it down in 1922.[97] Undaunted, Congress passed a constitutional amendment in 1924 to give it the power to regulate child labor.[98] By 1937, however, only twenty-eight of the necessary thirty-six states had ratified the amendment. On its final effort, Congress returned to the commerce power by including a child labor provision in the Fair Labor Standards Act of 1938.[99] This time a unanimous Court upheld the statute.[100]

In 1956 the Supreme Court invalidated a state sedition law because the Smith Act, passed by Congress, regulated the same subject. The Court concluded that it had been the intent of Congress to occupy the whole field of sedition.[101] The author of the Smith Act, Congressman Howard W. Smith, immediately denied that he had ever intended the result reached by the Court. In fact, even before the Court decided the question, he criticized the holding of the Supreme Court of Pennsylvania that the Smith Act preempted state

[94]23 Wkly Comp. Pres. Doc. 715 (June 19, 1987).
[95]"FCC Kills 'Fairness Doctrine," But Congress Will Renew Fight," Cong. Q. Wkly Rept., August 8, 1987, at 1796.
[96]Hammer v. Dagenhart, 247 U.S. 251 (1918).
[97]Bailey v. Drexel Furniture Co., 259 U.S. 20 (1922).
[98]65 Cong. Rec. 7295, 10142 (1924).
[99]52 Stat. 1060, 1067 (1938).
[100]United States v. Darby, 312 U.S. 100 (1941).
[101]Pennsylvania v. Nelson, 350 U.S. 497, 504 (1956).

efforts to regulate sedition.[102] He introduced a bill to prohibit the courts from construing a congressional statute "as indicating an intent on the part of Congress to occupy the field in which such act operates, to the exclusion of all State laws on the same subject matter, unless such act contains an express provision to that effect."[103]

Congressional committees reported legislation to permit concurrent jurisdiction by the Federal Government and the states in the area of sedition and subversion. The legislation would also have prohibited courts from using intent or implication to decide questions of federal preemption over state activities. These bills were never enacted.[104] However, Smith's bill was debated at length on the House floor in 1958.[105] He explained that the purpose of his bill was to say to the Supreme Court: "Do not undertake to read the minds of the Congress; we, in the Congress, think ourselves more capable of knowing our minds than the Supreme Court. . . . We are telling you that when we get ready to repeal a State law or preempt a field, we will say so and we will not leave it to the Supreme Court to guess whether we are or not."[106] His bill passed the House of Representatives by the vote of 241 to 155.[107] The measure was never taken up on the Senate floor.

In 1959, these bills were again under consideration.[108] Shortly before the legislation was debated by the House, the Court "distinguished" its 1956 decision and held that a state could investigate subversive activities against itself. To this extent state and federal sedition laws could coexist.[109] The modifiction in 1959 satisfied congressional critics who thought the preemption doctrine announced by the Court in 1956 intruded upon state sovereignty.

[102]101 Cong. Rec. 143 (1955).

[103]Id. at 31 [H.R. 3], 142.

[104]H. Rept. No. 2576, 84th Cong., 2d Sess. (1956); S. Rept. No. 2117, 84th Cong., 2d Sess. (1956); S. Rept. No. 2230, 84th Cong., 2d Sess. (1956); H. Rept. No. 1878, 85th Cong., 2d Sess. (1958).

[105]104 Cong. Rec. 13844–65, 13993–4023, 14138–62 (1958).

[106]Id. at 14139–40.

[107]Id. at 14162.

[108]H. Rept. No. 422, 86th Cong., 1st Sess. (1959); 105 Cong. Rec. 11486–508, 11625–67, 11789–808 (1959).

[109]Uphaus v. Wyman, 306 U.S. 72 (1959). See also Uphaus v. Wyman, 364 U.S. 388 (1960).

Guarding Legislative Prerogatives

On occasion there have been direct confrontations to prevent courts from deciding issues considered within the institutional prerogatives of Congress. An example occurred in 1970 when the House Committee on Internal Security released a report on "Limited Survey of Honoraria Given Guest Speakers for Engagements at Colleges and Universities." The report included the names of leftist or antiwar speakers and the amounts they received. The ACLU obtained a copy of the galleys and asked for an injunction. District Judge Gesell ruled that the report served no legislative purpose and was issued solely for the sake of exposure or intimidation. He ordered the Public Printer and the Superintendent of Documents not to print the report "or any portion, restatement or facsimile thereof," with the possible exception of placing the report in the *Congressional Record*.[110] Gesell claimed that "the authority of a congressional committee to publish and distribute a report at public expense is not unlimited but is subject to judicial review in the light of the circumstances presented."[111]

On December 14, 1970, the House of Representatives passed a resolution that told the courts, in essence, to step back. During the course of the debate, it was explained that it was not the practice of the House to print committee reports in the *Congressional Record*.[112] Moreover, Judge Gesell's order "runs afoul not only of the speech and debate clause—article I, section 6—of the Constitution, but obstructs the execution of other constitutional commitments to the House as well, including article I, section 5, which authorizes each House to determine the rules of its proceedings, and requires each House to publish its proceedings."[113]

The resolution stated that the new committee report was a "restatement" of the previous one and ordered the Public Printer and the Superintendent of Documents to print and distribute it. With an eye toward Judge Gesell and others who might stand in the way, the resolution provided that all persons "are further advised, ordered,

[110]Hentoff v. Ichord, 318 F.Supp 1175, 1183 (D.D.C. 1970).
[111]Id. at 1181.
[112]116 Cong. Rec. 41358 (1970).
[113]Id.

and enjoined to refrain from molesting, intimidating, damaging, arresting, imprisoning, or punishing any person because of his participation in" publishing the report.[114] The resolution passed by a large bipartisan margin of 302 to 54.[115] The report was printed without any further interference from the judiciary.[116]

A similar confrontation occurred in 1983. The dispute began with an investigation by the House Select Committee on Aging into abuses in the sale of supplemental health insurance to the elderly. Without the knowledge of George H. Benford, an independent agent of the American Family Life Assurance Company, the committee videotaped a meeting where Benford advised two women (volunteers for the committee) of the company's cancer policy. Portions of the tapes were broadcast within a few weeks on the ABC Nightly News.

Benford filed suit, claiming that the taping and broadcasting violated his constitutional rights.[117] In 1980 a federal district court held that the committee's actions were not absolutely protected by the Speech or Debate Clause or the doctrine of official immunity.[118] The court rejected the claim that televising a portion of the taped meeting was a legitimate part of the "informing function" of Congress.[119] Early in 1983 the district court held that it had inherent power to serve a subpoena duces tecum upon the Clerk of the House, requesting certain documents related to the case.[120]

The House of Representatives responded by passing a resolution that denied the district court the documents it sought. Voting with bipartisan strength (386 to 22), the House regarded the court's subpoena as "an unwarranted and unconstitutional invasion of its congressional prerogative to determine which of its proceedings shall be made public, and in direct contravention of the constitutional protection for congressional investigative activity. . . ."[121]

The district court upped the ante by holding the Clerk of the House

[114]H. Res. 1306, 91st Cong., 2d Sess. 18 (1970).
[115]116 Cong. Rec. 41373 (1970).
[116]H. Rept. No. 1732, 91st Cong., 2d Sess. (1970).
[117]Benford v. American Broadcasting Companies, 502 F.Supp. 1148 (D. Md. 1980).
[118]Id. at 1151.
[119]Id. at 1154–55.
[120]Benford v. American Broadcasting Companies, Inc., 98 F.R.D. 40 (D. Md. 1983).
[121]129 Cong. Rec. H2450 (daily ed. April 28, 1983).

in contempt.[122] The Fourth Circuit reversed that holding and quashed the district court's subpoena for lack of proper service.[123] In 1986 the suit against the congressional defendants was dismissed.[124]

Balancing Constitutional Values

The Supreme Court's claim that it is the exclusive or at least the final interpreter of the Constitution is especially difficult to assert when it construes not merely a particular section but balances that section against another. Although there may be some legitimate grounds, such as the framer's intent, when interpreting one section of the Constitution, there are no such guidelines for balancing competing and conflicting sections. With what interpretive tools does the Court balance individual liberties against the President's claims of national security? When must the rights of a free press be subordinated to the interests of a fair trial? On what grounds should law enforcement prevail over a person's right to privacy? Answering these questions can resemble a quasi-legislative activity and invite Congress to step in and participate.

Justice Brennan once called the courts "the ultimate arbiters of all disputes concerning clashes of constitutional values,"[125] a claim that is demonstrably untrue. Resolving conflicts between constitutional values involves all branches of government. An excellent example comes from the balancing of values between law enforcement officials and the rights of a free press.

A 1978 decision by the Supreme Court involved a police search of a student newspaper, *The Stanford Daily*, which had taken photographs of a clash between demonstrators and police. A search warrant was issued to obtain the photographs and discover the identities of those who had assaulted police officers. The Supreme Court held that a state is not prevented from issuing a search warrant simply

[122]Benford v. American Broadcasting Companies, Inc., 565 F.Supp. 139 (D. Md. 1983).

[123]In re Guthrie, 733 F.2d 634 (4th Cir. 1984).

[124]For further details, see Louis Fisher, "Congress and the Fourth Amendment," 21 Ga. L. Rev. 107, 163–65 (Special Issue 1986).

[125]Gertz v. Robert Welch, Inc., 418 U.S. 323, 369 (1974) (dissenting opinion).

255

because the owner of a place is not reasonably suspected of criminal involvement.[126] In upholding the right of third-party searches, the Court invited the other two branches to participate by noting that the Fourth Amendment "does not prevent or advise against legislative or executive efforts to establish nonconstitutional protections against possible abuses of the search warrant procedure. . . ."[127]

The decision was promptly denounced by newspapers as a first step toward a police state. Although Congress could not pass legislation to weaken the Fourth Amendment, it could act to strengthen its protection.[128] The Senate Committee on the Judiciary concluded that "the search warrant procedure in itself does not sufficiently protect the press and other innocent third parties and that legislation is called for."[129] Legislation was drafted "to strike a careful balance between the first amendment right to free expression and the fourth amendment. . . ."[130] Congress passed legislation in 1980 to place limits on newsroom searches. With certain exceptions, it required the use of a subpoena instead of a search warrant to obtain documentary materials from those who disseminate newspapers, books, broadcasts, or other similar forms of public communication.[131] The "dialogue" between Congress and the Supreme Court on constitutional matters is captured nicely in these remarks by Congressman Robert Kastenmeier, who managed the bill on the House floor:

> Mr. Speaker, sometimes a longstanding principle of constitutional jurisprudence is thrown into doubt by a decision of the Supreme Court which—while it may answer a narrow question based on specific facts—leaves Government officials and members of the public in doubt as to how to interpret the law. When this occurs it is often best for Congress to step in to fill the void, rather than to await the results of many years of potential litigation which will again redefine the principle. This is the case with respect to the matter before us today—legislation to redefine a portion of the law of search and seizure in response to

[126]Zurcher v. Stanford Daily, 436 U.S. 547, 560 (1978).
[127]Id. at 567.
[128]S. Rept. No. 874, 96th Cong., 2d Sess. 4 (1980).
[129]Id.
[130]126 Cong. Rec. 21271 (1980). Statement by Senator Strom Thurmond.
[131]94 Stat. 1879 (1980).

the Supreme Court's decison in Zurcher v. Stanford Daily in 1978.[132]

The "subpoena-first" policy adopted by Congress offers several advantages to newspapers. A subpoena involves a court hearing where the newspaper can state its case, whereas search warrants are issued without any possibility of influence by a newspaper. Moreover, a subpoena allows the newspaper to produce the specific document requested, rather than having police officers enter the premises of a newsroom and disrupt operations while searching through filing cabinets, desks, and wastepaper baskets.

This interaction between Congress and the Supreme Court involved an intricate dance, both sides pretending that constitutional matters are reserved to the courts with only nonconstitutional matters left to Congress and the President. The Court had invited legislative or executive efforts to establish "nonconstitutional protections against possible abuses of the search warrant procedure."[133] Congressman George Danielson advised his colleagues in the House of Representatives that "we are not here dealing with a question of constitutionality."[134] The Court had decided that the use of a warrant to search newsrooms was constitutional. Danielson said that "if these activities are not unconstitutional, we are here, by this law, diminishing the availability of the search warrant to be used in connection with the enforcement of our criminal laws."[135] Henry Hyde, Republican of Illinois, added that the legislation "is not designed to make a sweeping change in constitutional law regarding the probable cause standard contained in the fourth amendment."[136] Yet Congress performed the identical task attempted by the Court—balancing the Fourth Amendment against other interests—and reached a strikingly different conclusion.

A second example of a congressional-judicial dialogue involves the privacy rights of bank depositors. In 1972 agents from the Treasury Department's Alcohol, Tobacco, and Firearms Bureau presented grand jury subpoenas to two banks in which a suspect maintained accounts. Without advising the depositor that subpoenas had been served, the

[132]126 Cong. Rec. 26562 (1980).
[133]Zurcher v. Stanford Daily, 436 U.S. at 567.
[134]126 Cong. Rec. 26564 (1980).
[135]Id.
[136]Id. at 26567.

banks supplied the government with microfilms of checks, deposit slips, and other records. The Supreme Court held that a Fourth Amendment interest could not be vindicated in court by challenging such a subpoena. The Court treated the materials as business records of a bank, not private papers of a person.[137]

Congress responded by passing the Right to Financial Privacy Act of 1978.[138] Congressman Charles Whalen explained that the primary purpose of the statute was to prevent warrantless government searches of bank and credit records that reveal the nature of one's private affairs. The Government should not have access "except with the knowledge of the subject individual or else with the supervision of the courts."[139] Although the statute has a "privacy" theme in its title, the right to be free of unreasonable searches and seizures appears as a fundamental constitutional principle. Said Congressman Edward Pattison: "it is our belief that the framers of the Constitution intended to provide protection for all individual records. At the time the fourth amendment to the Constitution was drafted, however, almost all personal records were kept at home."[140] He pointed out that twentieth-century financial records are held increasingly by banks and other financial institutions. Congressman John Rousselot remarked about the responsibility of Congress to redress the shortcomings of the Court's decision: "Another standing to challenge the release of information in a court of law is provided for in section 1110, which, as a practical matter, reverses the holding in the Miller case."[141] In essence, certain safeguards to Fourth Amendment rights that were unavailable because of the Supreme Court's decision were now secured by congressional action.

In the course of its lawmaking process, it is inevitable for Congress to balance and resolve conflicting constitutional values. Much of its work is final in character, for there is no guarantee that the statute will ever be tested in court or, if tested, overturned by the judiciary. Consider the Classified Information Procedures Act of 1980. In national-security cases, it is common for criminal defendants to threaten to disclose classified information as part of their defense strategy.

[137]United States v. Miller, 425 U.S. 435, 438 (1976).
[138]92 Stat. 3617 (1978).
[139]124 Cong. Rec. 33310 (1978).
[140]Id. at 33835.
[141]Id. at 33836.

This tactic, called "graymail," is often successful in forcing the government to abandon the prosecution. In balancing the rights of a defendant against the needs of the government, Congress passed legislation to authorize federal courts to issue a "protective order" to prevent the disclosure of any classified information revealed by the United States to the defendant. During debate on the bill in the House, Congressman Don Edwards described the multiple constitutional values at stake: "important sixth amendment rights of confrontation and compulsory process were closely entwined with virtually every aspect of this bill. But the proper balance between the needs of national security and constitutional guarantees was struck by the Intelligence Committee."[142]

Similarly, when Congress passed legislation in 1982 to protect the identity of intelligence sources, it had to juggle a number of constitutional values. It wanted to place criminal penalties on those who expose intelligence agents, but without threatening the right of a journalist to reveal the name of an agent in the course of a news report. As Senator John Chafee explained, the purpose of the legislation was to meet "this dual standard of protecting freedom of the press and freedom of speech and, at the same time, protecting the lives of our agents."[143]

Constitutional versus Statutory Interpretation

It is the practice of courts not to pass on the constitutionality of a statute if it can be construed solely on statutory grounds.[144] Justice Brandeis described a series of rules under which the Supreme Court "has avoided passing upon a large part of all the constitutional questions pressed upon it for decision."[145] When the validity of a congressional statute is questioned, "and even if a serious doubt of constitutionality is raised," the Court will first determine whether the statute can be construed to avoid the constitutional question.[146] "It is well

---

[142]126 Cong. Rec. 26504 (1980); 94 Stat. 2025 (1980).
[143]126 Cong. Rec. 28062 (1980); 96 Stat. 122 (1982).
[144]United States v. Clark, 445 U.S. 23, 27 (1980).
[145]Ashwander v. TVA, 297 U.S. 288, 346 (1936) (Brandeis, J., concurring).
[146]Id. at 348 (citing Crowell v. Benson, 285 U.S. 22, 62 [1932]).

settled that if a case may be decided on either statutory or constitutional grounds, [the] Court, for sound jurisprudential reasons, will inquire first into the statutory question."[147]

This judicial choice allows the courts to dispose of issues on statutory grounds in the midst of obvious constitutional questions. Instead of deciding constitutional doctrine, the judiciary enters into a dialogue with the other branches concerning the intent of prior statutes. When the Court limits its holding to statutory construction, it may sustain a statute partly because Congress took into account previous rulings by the Court decided on constitutional grounds. Through this process, constitutional reasoning becomes imbedded in statutory construction. In a concurrence to one of these cases, Justice White criticized the Court for a "thinly disguised" effort to avoid constitutional questions.[148] Illustrations can be drawn from cases involving state immunity, municipal immunity, the right to travel, religious freedom, and fugitives from justice.

The constitutional principle of federalism is clearly present in Section 1983 suits, which make state officials liable when they deprive individuals "of any rights, privileges, or immunities secured by the [Federal] Constitution and laws."[149] This statute was enacted in 1871 to enforce the Fourteenth Amendment. It is characteristic of the Court to decide Section 1983 suits by determining the intent of the 1871 statute, rather than make judgments about the constitutional validity of federal statutes that might narrow the sovereign immunity of states.[150]

Cases involving the immunity of municipal government are also decided on statutory grounds, giving Congress the ultimate control in determining the extent of immunity. Initially the Court held that city or municipal officials were immune from Section 1983 suits.[151] Partly under pressure of congressional statutes that authorized attorney's fees for the prevailing parties in civil rights suits, the Court reversed field in 1978 and allowed municipal employees to be sued

[147]Harris v. McRae, 448 U.S. 297, 306–7 (1980).
[148]Lowe v. SEC, 472 U.S. 181, 226 (1985).
[149]42 U.S.C. § 1983 (1982).
[150]Wilson v. Garcia, 471 U.S. 261 (1985). See Harry A. Blackmun, "Section 1983 and Federal Protection of Individual Rights—will the Statute Remain Alive or Fade Away?," 60 N.Y.U. Rev. 1 (1985).
[151]Monroe v. Pape, 365 U.S. 167 (1961).

for their official actions.[152] Bills have been introduced in Congress to limit municipal liability under the civil rights statute, but no final action has been taken.[153]

Congress did take action on another area of municipal liability, and here too the issue was resolved on statutory grounds by the courts. A decision by the Supreme Court in 1982 left some municipalities exposed to treble damages under the Antitrust Act.[154] In response to more than one hundred antitrust suits against cities, counties, and townships, Congress passed legislation in 1984 to shield municipalities from antitrust actions. Courts in the future can enjoin cities and villages from carrying out anticompetitive practices, but may not award monetary damages.[155]

A similar pattern emerges with the cases involving the right to travel. Claiming both constitutional and statutory authority, Presidents and their administrations use the control over passports and visas to restrict travel by foreigners to this country and by Americans to other countries. Administrations advance a number of foreign policy and national security justifications, whereas opponents of restraints on foreign travel raise First Amendment issues of access to information and right of association. Although constitutional issues are sometimes addressed,[156] the Supreme Court generally decides these cases on statutory grounds. This keeps the door fully open for participation by Congress and the President in shaping the law on the right to travel.[157] Decisions on the right to travel sometimes turn on departmental regulations and congressional silence.[158]

The Supreme Court's decision in *Goldman* v. *Weinberger* (1986) offers a recent example of the overlap between constitutional and statutory questions. By a 5 to 4 vote, the Supreme Court upheld an Air Force regulation that prohibited an orthodox Jew and ordained rabbi

[152]Monell v. New York City Dept. of Social Services, 436 U.S. 658, 698–99 (1978). See also Owen v. City of Independence, 445 U.S. 622 (1980) and Maine v. Thiboutot, 448 U.S. 1 (1980).

[153]See 126 Cong. Rec. 25292–95 (1980) and 127 Cong. Rec. 3209–12 (1981).

[154]Community Communications Co. v. Boulder, 455 U.S. 40 (1982).

[155]98 Stat. 2750 (1984).

[156]Aptheker v. United States, 378 U.S. 500 (1964).

[157]Kent v. Dulles, 357 U.S. 116 (1958); Dayton v. Dulles, 357 U.S. 144 (1958); Zemel v. Rusk, 381 U.S. 1 (1965); Regan v. Wald, 468 U.S. 222 (1984). For recent legislation, see 92 Stat. 971, § 124 (1978), 22 U.S.C. § 211a (1982) and 92 Stat. 993, § 707(b), 8 U.S.C. § 1185(a) (1982).

[158]Haig v. Agee, 453 U.S. 280 (1981).

from wearing his yarmulke (skullcap) indoors while on duty. The regulation provided that authorized headgear could be worn out of doors but that indoors, with the exception of armed security police in the performance of their duties, headgear may not be worn. Although the constitutional issue of religious freedom was present, the Court deferred to the Air Force's judgment that obedience, discipline, and unity were important and overriding values. The First Amendment, said the Court, did not prohibit the Air Force from applying its regulations "even though their effect is to restrict the wearing of the headgear required by his religious beliefs."[159]

In concurring with the majority's opinion, Justices Stevens, White, and Powell noted that the blanket prohibition in the regulation permitted the Air Force to avoid difficult line-drawing between a yarmulke, on the one hand, and the wearing of a turban by a Sikh or dreadlocks by a Rastafarian, on the other. The Court may well have anticipated that if such distinctions are to be drawn, raising delicate social questions, they should be done by a lawmaking body like Congress and not by agencies or the courts.

In his dissent, Justice Brennan remarked that the response of the Court "is to abdicate its role as principal expositor of the Constitution and protector of individual liberties in favor of credulous deference to unsupported assertions of military necessity."[160] Yet there is another expositor of the Constitution and protector of individual liberties: Congress. Within weeks of the decision, legislation was introduced to change the Air Force regulation to permit the wearing of unobtrusive headgear.[161] The House of Representatives adopted a provision stating that service members could wear religious apparel so long as it was "neat and conservative" and did not interfere with military duties.[162] The provision was dropped in conference committee. In 1987, the House again adopted language to permit the wearing of yarmulkes and other conservative apparel. Congressman Stephen Solarz supported the amendment with this reasoning:

[159]Goldman v. Weinberger, 106 S.Ct. 1310, 1314 (1986).

[160]Id. at 1316.

[161]132 Cong. Rec. S3785–86 (daily ed. April 8, 1986); 132 Cong. Rec. E1032 (daily ed. April 8, 1986); 132 Cong. Rec. S4007 (daily ed. April 9, 1986).

[162]H. Rept. No. 718, 99th Cong., 2d Sess. 200, 487–88 (1986). The Senate tabled an amendment by Senator Frank Lautenberg to permit members of the armed forces to wear religious apparel; 132 Cong. Rec. S10697–704 (daily ed. August 7, 1986).

Finally, let me say that there is a need for this amendment only because 2 years ago [one year] the Supreme Court in a 5–4 decision upheld the right of the Air Force to deny someone the right to wear a yarmulke. If that case came up today it would be a 5-to-4 decision in favor of the right to wear a yarmulke, because Justice Burger, who voted against the right to wear a yarmulke, has left, and Justice Scalia, who voted at the appellate division for the right to wear a yarmulke is now on the Court. There is a 5-to-4 majority in the Court in favor of this right now, but there is no need to wait several years for litigation to work its way up to the Supreme Court.[163]

In actual fact, Scalia was not part of the three-judge panel.[164] The point is not whether Scalia's appointment to the Supreme Court would reverse a 5-to-4 decision. Instead, the issue is whether Congress wants to follow the Court's example and defer to military judgment. If Congress wants to direct the Defense Department to alter its regulations on the wearing of religious apparel while in uniform, it is fully within its power to do so. The Senate also adopted legislation in 1987 to permit the wearing of religious apparel while in uniform. Under the language enacted into law, the Secretary of Defense may prohibit the wearing of an item of religious apparel if he determines that it would interfere with the performance of military duties or determines that the item is not "neat and conservative."[165]

The Constitution in Article IV, Section 2, provides that fugitives from justice shall be delivered up to the "State" having jurisdiction over the crime. Under a strict construction, this language would not justify the handing over of an accused to Puerto Rico, which is not a state. However, in 1987 the Supreme Court unanimously reached precisely that result by relying not on the constitutional language but rather on the implementing statute of 1793, which used the word "territories" (a category that Puerto Rico meets).[166] With this bootstrap, statutory language assumed constitutional significance.

[163]133 Cong. Rec. H3342 (daily ed. May 8, 1987).
[164]Goldman v. Secretary of Defense, 734 F.2d 1531 (D.C. Cir. 1984). The panel consisted of Judges Swygert, Mikva, and Edwards.
[165]P.L. 100–180, § 508 (1987). See 133 Cong. Rec. S12791–801 (daily ed. September 25, 1987) and H. Rept. No. 446, 100th Cong., 1st Sess. 71–72, 638–39 (1987).
[166]Puerto Rico v. Branstad, 107 S.Ct. 2802, 2809 (1987); 1 Stat. 302, § 3 (1793).

Procedural Rules versus Constitutional Interpretation

Many decisions handed down by the courts are presented as "rules" of criminal procedure, even when constitutional questions are present. When courts make these announcements, as with the exclusionary rule or the *Miranda* rule, they invite Congress to become involved in the continuous process of defining the content of individual liberties. Congress is allowed a coordinate role, as is the executive branch, because changes are being made in the Federal Rules of Criminal Procedure.

One of the most controversial areas of constitutional law concerns the "exclusionary rule," which is the general doctrine for excluding illegally obtained evidence from trial. To the extent that the exclusion of evidence is treated as a rule of evidence rather than a purely constitutional question, Congress plays a substantial part in shaping the rule.

Throughout the nineteenth century, it was the practice of state courts to admit pertinent evidence even if law enforcement officers had acted illegally. Courts did not take notice of how documents or articles were seized. Judges considered only the competence of the evidence, not the methods used to obtain it.[167] The exclusionary rule at the federal level dates from 1914 when the Supreme Court ruled unanimously that papers illegally seized by federal officers may not be introduced in court as evidence.[168]

The opportunity for Congress to shape the exclusionary rule was evident in the wiretapping case of *Olmstead* v. *United States* (1928). Prohibition agents had used wiretaps in nearby streets and in the basement of large buildings to monitor and intercept the telephone calls of bootleggers. In a bitterly divided 5-to-4 decision, Chief Justice Taft reasoned that there was no violation of the Fourth Amend-

[167]Adams v. New York, 192 U.S. 585, 595 (1904).

[168]Weeks v. United States, 232 U.S. 383 (1914). See also Boyd v. United States, 116 U.S. 616 (1886), in which the Supreme Court held that the admission into evidence of an invoice was erroneous because of Fourth and Fifth Amendment violations.

ment because the taps did not enter the premises. Hence, there was neither "search" nor "seizure."[169]

Taft's decision provoked some of the most scathing dissents ever delivered by Supreme Court Justices, particularly those penned by Holmes and Brandeis. Taft acknowledged that his opinion was not the last word on the subject. In a letter to his brother, he conceded that "Congress can change the rule if it sees fit. It will be of interest to see whether Congress will do it."[170] In personal correspondence, Justice Van Devanter advised Taft not to say anything that might encourage Congress to pass legislation to exclude evidence:

Personally I seriously doubt the propriety of making any concessions respecting the need for legislation restraining the use of evidence of the kind considered in the wiretapping cases. To my mind there is no need for such legislation: nor is there any sound basis for making a legislative distinction in this regard between different classes of crime.[171]

The Court's opinion in *Olmstead* clearly indicated that any constraint on wiretapping would have to come from Congress and the Executive, not the courts. Solicitor General William Mitchell had advised the Court that if obtaining evidence by wiretapping "is deemed an objectionable governmental practice, it may be regulated or forbidden by statute, or avoided by officers of the law."[172] Taft agreed, stating in his decision that "Congress may of course protect the secrecy of telephone messages by making them, when intercepted, inadmissible in evidence in federal criminal trials, by direct legislation, and thus depart from the common law of evidence."[173]

The executive and legislative branches of the federal government spent the next few decades exploring a variety of limitations and

[169]277 U.S. 438, 457, 464–65 (1928).

[170]Letter from Chief Justice William Howard Taft to Horace D. Taft, June 12, 1928 (Library of Congress manuscript collection).

[171]Letter from Justice William Van Devanter to Chief Justice William Howard Taft, June 25, 1928 (Library of Congress manuscript collection).

[172]Brief for the United States, at 114, Olmstead v. United States, reprinted in P. Kurland and G. Casper, eds., 26 Landmark Briefs and Arguments of the Supreme Court of the United States: Constitutional Law 232 (1975).

[173]277 U.S. at 465–66.

restrictions on wiretapping. The legality of federal wiretapping was subject to four cross-cutting pressures: the Communications Act of 1934; the interpretation of that statute by the Supreme Court to prohibit information obtained by wiretapping from being introduced as trial evidence; the refusal of Congress to grant the executive branch wiretap authority; and the decision by Attorney General Robert H. Jackson and President Franklin D. Roosevelt that wiretapping could nevertheless be done in selected areas.[174] Congressional hearings were held in the 1950s and 1960s on various bills designed to limit wiretapping. No formula could be discovered that satisfied both law enforcement officials and civil libertarians.

Finally, in 1967 the Supreme Court overturned *Olmstead* and declared electronic surveillance a violation of the Fourth Amendment.[175] In response to this decision, Congress passed legislation in 1968 requiring law enforcement officers to obtain a warrant before placing taps on phones or installing bugs (concealed microphones).[176] Judicial activity after 1968 has consisted primarily of statutory construction of this law rather than constitutional interpretation. A number of cases have scrutinized the government's compliance with the wiretap statute.[177] The wiretap statute also provided for the exclusion of evidence "in any trial, hearing, or other proceeding in or before any court, grand jury, department, officer, agency, regulatory body, legislative committee, or other authority of the United States, a State, or a political subdivision thereof" if the disclosure of that information violates the statute.[178]

Judicial-congressional dialogues on the exclusionary rule carry over into other areas of criminal law that mix constitutional law and procedural rules. In the celebrated case of *Jencks* v. *United States* (1957), the Supreme Court held that defendants were entitled to have access

[174]Louis Fisher, "Congress and the Fourth Amendment," 21 Ga. L. Rev. 107, 127–32 (Special Issue 1986); Nardone v. United States, 308 U.S. 338 (1939); Weiss v. United States, 308 U.S. 321 (1939).

[175]Katz v. United States, 389 U.S. 347 (1967). See also Berger v. New York, 388 U.S. 41 (1967).

[176]82 Stat. 197, 211–25 (1968).

[177]Scott v. United States, 436 U.S. 128 (1978); United States v. New York Tel. Co., 434 U.S. 159 (1977); United States v. Donovan, 429 U.S. 413 (1977); United States v. Chavez, 416 U.S. 562 (1974); United States v. Giordano, 416 U.S. 505 (1974); United States v. Kahn, 415 U.S. 143 (1974).

[178]82 Stat. 216 (1968); 18 U.S.C. § 2515 (1982).

to government files bearing on their trial.[179] On the basis of statements by two informers for the Federal Bureau of Investigation (FBI), the government had prosecuted Clinton Jencks for failing to state that he was a member of the Communist Party. He asked that the FBI reports be turned over to the trial judge for examination to determine whether they had value in impeaching the statements of the two informers. The Supreme Court went beyond Jencks's request by ordering the government to produce for his inspection all FBI reports "touching the events and activities" at issue in the trial.[180] The Court specifically rejected the option of producing government documents to the trial judge for his determination of relevancy and materiality.[181]

In their concurrence, Justices Burton and Harlan believed that Jencks was only entitled to have the records submitted to the trial judge.[182] In a dissent, Justice Clark agreed that the documents should be delivered only to the trial judge. In a remarkable statement, he incited Congress to act: "Unless the Congress changes the rule announced by the Court today, those intelligence agencies of our Government engaged in law enforcement may as well close up shop, for the Court has opened their files to the criminal and thus afforded him a Roman holiday for rummaging through confidential information as well as vital national secrets."[183]

The Court announced its decision on June 3, 1957. Both houses of Congress quickly held hearings and reported remedial legislation. The "Jencks Bill" (after much redrafting) passed the Senate by voice vote on August 26 and passed the House on August 27 by a vote of 351 to 17. The conference report was adopted with huge majorities: 74 to 2 in the Senate and 315 to 0 in the House. The bill became law on September 2. The statute provides that in any federal criminal prosecution, no statement or report in the possession of the government "which was made by a Government witness or prospective Government witness (other than the defendant) to an agent of the Government shall be the subject of subpena, discovery, or inspection unless said witness has testified on direct examination in the trial of the

[179]353 U.S. 657 (1957).
[180]Id. at 668.
[181]Id. at 669.
[182]Id. at 678.
[183]Id. at 681–82.

case." If a witness testifies, statements may be delivered to the defendant for examination and use unless the United States claims that the statement contains irrelevant matter, in which case the statement shall be inspected by the court in camera. The judge may excise irrelevant portions of the statement before submitting it to the defendant.[184]

Members of Congress wanted to overturn other decisions from the 1950s and 1960s affecting the rights of criminal defendants, but it took a combination of urban riots, high crime rates, and the assassinations of Martin Luther King, Jr., and Robert F. Kennedy to create momentum for the Omnibus Crime Control and Safe Streets Act of 1968. Title II responded to three controversial decisions on criminal procedures.

The first, *Mallory* v. *United States* (1957), held that suspects must be taken before a magistrate for arraignment as quickly as possible.[185] Admissions obtained from the suspect during illegal detainment could not be used against him. The Court made room for congressional involvement by basing its decision partly on the Federal Rules of Criminal Procedure enacted by Congress.[186] The decision thus allowed Congress to enter the arena and modify those rules. Congress did so: Title II established six hours as a reasonable period before arraignment.

In the second case, *Miranda* v. *Arizona* (1966), the Court held that confessions by criminal suspects could not be used unless the suspects had been informed of their rights by law enforcement officers.[187] Whether the majority opinion was based on constitutional principles or statutory rules of evidence is unclear. The Court reviewed the history of the Fifth Amendment privilege against self-incrimination,[188] spoke of the "constitutional issue we decide in each of these cases,"[189] and stated that "the issues presented are of constitutional dimensions and must be determined by the courts."[190] But

[184]71 Stat. 595 (1957); 18 U.S.C. § 3500 (1982). See Walter Murphy, Congress and the Court 127–53 (1962).
[185]354 U.S. 449, 454 (1957).
[186]Id. at 451.
[187]384 U.S. 436, 467–79 (1966).
[188]Id. at 439–44.
[189]Id. at 445.
[190]Id. at 490.

the Court also referred to the Federal Rules of Criminal Procedure[191] and invited Congress to contribute its own handiwork.[192] Congress did so again: Title II allowed for the admissibility of confessions if voluntarily given.[193] Trial judges would determine the issue of voluntariness after taking into consideration all the circumstances surrounding the confession, including five elements identified by Congress.[194]

In the third case, *United States* v. *Wade* (1967), the Court decided that if an accused was denied the right to counsel during a police lineup, the identification would be inadmissible unless the in-court identifications had an independent source or the introduction of the evidence would be harmless error.[195] The Court stated that "legislative or other regulations, such as those developed by the local police departments, [might] eliminate the risks of abuse and unintentional suggestion at lineup proceedings," but that "neither Congress nor the Federal authorities have seen fit to provide a solution."[196] Title II provided that eyewitness testimony would be admissible as evidence in any criminal prosecution, regardless of whether the accused had an attorney present at the lineup.[197]

Thus, what appears to be constitutional interpretation by the courts is sometimes "a substructure of substantive, procedural, and remedial rules drawing their inspiration and authority from, but not required by, various constitutional provisions; in short, a constitutional common law subject to amendment, modification, or even reversal by Congress."[198] Through the slow evolution of these rules, executive and legislative debate "concerning the means of implementing new-found values may provide the Supreme Court with much needed

[191]Id. at 463.

[192]Id. at 467.

[193]18 U.S.C. § 3501(a) (1982).

[194]Id. § 3501(b).

[195]388 U.S. 218, 239–42 (1967).

[196]Id. at 239.

[197]18 U.S.C. § 3502 (1982). For the impact of §§ 3501 and 3502 on the courts, see Yale Kamisar, Wayne R. LaFave, and Jerold H. Israel, Modern Criminal Procedure 604–05, 684–85 (1980).

[198]Henry P. Monaghan, "The Supreme Court 1975 Term—Foreword: Constitutional Common Law," 89 Harv. L. Rev. 1, 2–3 (1975). See also William Cohen, "Congressional Power to Interpret Due Process and Equal Protection," 27 Stan. L. Rev. 603 (1975).

feedback as to the implications, and indeed the propriety, of its activism."[199]

Enforcement of Civil War Amendments

The Thirteenth, Fourteenth, and Fifteenth Amendments give Congress the power to enforce the amendments "by appropriate legislation." Thus the creative and constructive task of giving meaning to the Civil War amendments lies largely with Congress. Early in this century, when the Court struck down city ordinances that prohibited blacks from occupying homes in blocks controlled by whites, the Court based its ruling on both the Fourteenth Amendment and congressional statutes.[200] On some occasions, such rulings have been based primarily on congressional statutes.[201] In 1968, the Court held that Congress has authority under the Thirteenth Amendment to prohibit both state action and private action that restrict the right of blacks to purchase, lease, and use property.[202]

In 1966 the Supreme Court adopted a broad interpretation of the power to enforce the provisions of the Fourteenth Amendment. At issue in *Katzenbach* v. *Morgan* was the power of Congress to prohibit New York's requirement for literacy in English as a condition for voting. Section 4(e) of the Voting Rights Act of 1965 provided that no person who had completed the sixth grade in Puerto Rico, with the language of instruction other than English, could be denied the right to vote in any election because of an inability to read or write in English. Although important constitutional issues of federalism were at stake, the Court regarded section 4(e) as a "proper exercise" of the powers granted to Congress to enforce the Fourteenth Amendment.[203] Factfinding was a legislative, not a judicial responsibility: "It was for Congress, as the branch that made this judgment, to assess and weigh the various conflicting considerations. . . . It is not for us to review the congressional resolution of these factors. It is enough that we be able to perceive a basis upon which the Con-

[199]Monaghan, "Supreme Court," 89 Harv. L. Rev., at 45.
[200]Buchanan v. Warley, 245 U.S. 60, 78–79 (1917).
[201]Hurd v. Hodge, 334 U.S. 24 (1948).
[202]Jones v. Mayer, 392 U.S. 409 (1968).
[203]384 U.S. 641, 646 (1966).

gress might resolve the conflict as it did."[204] Even Justice Harlan, in his dissent, acknowledged that decisions on equal protection and due process "are based not on abstract logic, but on empirical foundations. To the extent 'legislative facts' are relevant to a judicial determination, Congress is well equipped to investigate them, and such determinations are of course entitled to due respect."[205]

One commentator claimed that the *Morgan* decision suggested that, "to some extent at least," the power of Congress to enforce the Fourteenth Amendment exempted that amendment "from the principle of Court-Congress relationships expressed by *Marbury* v. *Madison*, that the judiciary is the final arbiter of the meaning of the Constitution."[206] This assertion goes too far. The Court treats congressional determinations under Section 5 of the Fourteenth Amendment with respect and a substantial degree of deference, but it must still "be able to perceive a basis upon which the Congress might resolve the conflict as it did." The *Morgan* Court also noted that congressional power under Section 5 "is limited to adopting measures to enforce the guarantee of the Amendment; § 5 grants Congress no power to restrict, abrogate, or dilute these guarantees."[207] As an example of the Court drawing the line, in 1970 it ruled that the power of Congress to enforce the Fourteenth Amendment did not allow it to lower the voting age to eighteen in state elections.[208]

Although congressional use of Section 5 is subject to limitations and remains a topic of controversy, the application of the Equal Protection Clause or the Due Process Clause in the Fourteenth Amendment depends heavily on congressional factfinding and judgments. The problems of application "quite genuinely involve investigation and evaluation of facts. These are areas in which Congress has at least some claims to superior competence while the Court has none."[209]

---

[204]Id. at 653.

[205]Id. at 668. See Irving A. Gordon, "The Nature and Uses of Congressional Power Under Section Five of the Fourteenth Amendment to Overcome Decisions of the Supreme Court," 72 Nw. U. L. Rev. 656 (1977).

[206]Robert A. Burt, "Miranda and Title II: A Morganatic Marriage," 1969 Sup. Ct. Rev. 81, 84.

[207]384 U.S. at 653, 651–52 n.10 (1966).

[208]Oregon v. Mitchell, 400 U.S. 112 (1970).

[209]Archibald Cox, "The Role of Congress in Constitutional Determinations," 40 U. Cinn. L. Rev. 199, 255 (1971). Footnote omitted. For the capacity of courts to engage in factfinding, see Kenneth Karst, "Legislative Facts in Constitutional Litigation," 1960

In 1980 the Court noted: "It is fundamental that in no organ of government, state or federal, does there repose a more comprehensive remedial power than in the Congress, expressly charged by the Constitution with competence and authority to enforce equal protection guarantees."[210] If there is a collision between the immunity accorded states under the Eleventh Amendment and the power of Congress to enforce the Fourteenth Amendment, the congressional statute prevails.[211]

In 1978 the Supreme Court upheld a lower court's award of attorney's fees to be paid from state funds. The Court's ruling was based in part on the Civil Rights Attorney's Fee Awards Act, which Congress passed in 1976 to overcome a Supreme Court ruling of 1975. The Court had held that only Congress, not the judiciary, could authorize the award of attorneys' fees to the prevailing party.[212] The decision in 1978 accepted the congressional statute as a legitimate means used to enforce the Fourteenth Amendment.[213]

Congress has ample powers to enforce the provisions of the Fifteenth Amendment. The Supreme Court has deferred to congressional interpretations so long as Congress uses "any rational means to effectuate the constitutional prohibition of racial discrimination in voting."[214] Congress is "chiefly responsible" for implementing the rights created in the Fifteenth Amendment.[215] Under its enforcement powers, Congress may prohibit practices that "in and of themselves" do not violate the Fifteenth Amendment "so long as the prohibitions attacking racial discrimination in voting are 'appropriate'. . . ."[216]

Beginning in 1965, Congress passed a succession of statutes to protect the voting rights of blacks. In sustaining these laws, the Supreme Court gives broad recognition to the power of Congress to enforce

---

Sup. Ct. Rev. 75, and Dean Alfange, Jr., "The Relevance of Legislative Facts in Constitutional Law," 114 U. Pa. L. Rev. 637 (1966).

[210]Fullilove v. Klutznick, 448 U.S. 448, 483 (1980).

[211]Fitzpatrick v. Bitzer, 427 U.S. 445 (1976). Principles of federalism "that might otherwise be an obstacle to congressional authority are necessarily overridden by the power to enforce the Civil War Amendments 'by appropriate legislation.' Those Amendments were specifically designed as an expansion of federal power and an intrusion on state sovereignty." Rome v. United States, 446 U.S. 156, 179 (1980).

[212]Alyeska Pipeline Co. v. United States, 421 U.S. 240 (1975).

[213]Hutto v. Finney, 437 U.S. 678, 693–94 (1978).

[214]South Carolina v. Katzenbach, 383 U.S. 301, 324 (1966).

[215]Id. at 327.

[216]Rome v. United States, 446 U.S. at 177.

the Fifteenth Amendment. In 1980, a plurality of the Court held that states are prohibited only from *purposefully* disciminating against the voting rights of blacks. Abridgement of voting rights had to be intentional, not incidental. To be held invalid, a voting plan must be conceived for the purpose of furthering racial discrimination.[217] Congress responded by amending the Voting Rights Act in 1982 to allow plaintiffs to show discrimination solely on the effects of a voting plan. The statute incorporated language directly from an earlier opinion by the Court.[218] The debate in Congress demonstrates that members of Congress were capable of analyzing a variety of materials, including court cases, to select the means best suited to implement the Fifteenth Amendment.[219] The Court applied the statute's "results tests" to invalidate districting plans in North Carolina that had the effect of diluting the black vote whether intended by the state or not.[220] The sense of "dialogue" is heightened by the briefs filed. The Reagan administration, which had opposed the 1982 amendments, argued that a lower federal court had misinterpreted the amendments by ruling that seven of North Carolina's multimember districts impermissibly diluted the black vote. Senator Robert Dole, the Senate majority leader, joined with several other Senators and Representatives of both parties in an amicus brief to support the lower court's ruling. The Supreme Court agreed with their position and rejected the Administration's.

No single institution, including the judiciary, has the final word on constitutional questions. The courts find themselves engaged in a "continuing colloquy" with political institutions and society at large, a process in which constitutional principle is "evolved conversationally and not perfected unilaterally."[221] It is this process of give and take and mutual respect that permits the unelected Court to function in a democratic society. An open dialogue between Congress and the courts is a more fruitful avenue for constitutional interpretation than simply believing that the judiciary possesses certain superior skills.

[217]Mobile v. Bolden, 446 U.S. 55 (1980).
[218]White v. Regester, 412 U.S. 755 (1973); 96 Stat. 134, § 3 (1982).
[219]128 Cong. Rec. 14100–101, 14113–15 (1982).
[220]Thornburg v. Gingles, 106 S.Ct. 2752 (1986).
[221]Alexander M. Bickel, The Least Dangerous Branch 240, 244 (1962).

No one doubts that Congress, like the Court, can reach unconstitutional results. As Justice Brennan remarked in 1983: "Legislators, influenced by the passions and exigencies of the moment, the pressure of constituents and colleagues, and the press of business, do not always pass sober constitutional judgment on every piece of legislation they enact. . . ."[222] Yet if we count the times that Congress has been "wrong" about the Constitution and compare those lapses with the occasions when the Court has been "wrong" by its own later admissions, the results make a compelling case for legislative confidence and judicial modesty. In a recent evaluation, George Anastaplo said that "in the great crises over the past two hundred years, when Congress and the Supreme Court have differed on major issues, Congress has been correct."[223]

Congress is considered an untrustworthy guardian of constitutional liberties because of its impulsive behavior. The impulsiveness with which Congress sometimes moves in wrong directions, however, allows it just as easily to reverse course and repeal the offending statute. In 1970, for example, Congress passed two ill-considered measures that authorized law enforcement officers to break and enter private dwellings and businesses.[224] Serious doubts about the constitutionality of those bills, combined with shocking reports of federal agents breaking into the wrong homes, prompted Congress four years later to repeal both provisions.[225] Compare that performance with the twelve years it took the Court in *Mapp* v. *Ohio* to overturn the exclusionary rule case of *Wolf* v. *Colorado,* or the thirty-nine years needed for the Court in *Katz* v. *United States* to reverse the wiretap case of *Olmstead* v. *United States.*[226]

[222]Marsh v. Chambers, 463 U.S. 783, 814 (1983) (dissenting opinion).
[223]Center Magazine, November/December 1986, at 15.
[224]84 Stat. 630–31 (1970); 84 Stat. 1274 (1970).
[225]88 Stat. 1455, §§ 3, 4 (1974).
[226]Mapp v. Ohio, 367 U.S. 643 (1961), overturning Wolf v. Colorado, 338 U.S. 25 (1949); Katz v. United States, 389 U.S. 347 (1967), overturning Olmstead v. United States, 277 U.S. 438 (1928).

Conclusion

Justice Brandeis observed that "the process of trial and error, so fruitful in the physical sciences, is appropriate also in the judicial function."[1] The judiciary's record of the past two centuries supports his perception. The process is eminently one of trial and error. At times the Court will admit its errors of constitutional interpretation and reverse a previous decision. Some members of the Court have the intellectual integrity to adopt Justice Jackson's attitude: "I see no reason why I should be consciously wrong today because I was unconsciously wrong yesterday."[2] Others, under the spell of stare decisis, will stick doggedly to errors of the past. It is particularly at such times that Congress, the President, the states, and the public have a duty to pursue other alternatives or prevail upon the Court to revisit and rethink anachronous holdings.

There is no justification for deferring automatically to the judiciary because of its technical skills and political independence. Each decision by a court is subject to scrutiny and rejection by private citizens and public officials. What is "final" at one stage of our political development may be reopened at some later date, leading to revisions, fresh interpretations, and reversals of Court doctrines. Through this process of interaction among the branches, all three institutions are able to expose weaknesses, hold excesses in check, and gradually forge a consensus on constitutional issues. Also through that process, the public has an opportunity to add a legitimacy and a meaning to what might otherwise be an alien and short-lived document.

At certain moments in our constitutional history there is a compelling need for an authoritative and binding decision by the Supreme Court. The unanimous ruling in 1958, signed by each Justice, was essential in dealing with the Little Rock crisis.[3] Another unani-

[1]Burnet v. Coronado Oil & Gas Co., 285 U.S. 393, 408 (1932) (dissenting opinion).
[2]Massachusetts v. United States, 333 U.S. 611, 639–40 (1948) (dissenting opinion).
[3]Cooper v. Aaron, 358 U.S. 1 (1958).

mous decision in 1974 disposed of the confrontation between President Nixon and the judiciary regarding the Watergate tapes.[4] These moments are rare. Usually the Court makes a series of exploratory movements followed by backing and filling—a necessary and sensible policy for resolving constitutional issues that have profound political, social, and economic ramifications.

For the most part, court decisions are tentative and reversible like other political events. Court orders must be obeyed, but obedience here relates only to the orderly and expeditious administration of justice, not to the soundness or finality of a court order. Upon appeal, erroneous court orders may be reversed.[5] The fact that the judiciary has acted does not relieve members of the political branches or the public from exercising independent judgment. When a member of Congress

> says that the legislature should show all possible respect and reverence for the Supreme Court of the United States, no one can dissent. When he maintains that that great tribunal should not be made the football of mob opinion, no one can question the justice or wisdom of what he says. But when he argues, in effect, that the legislature should surrender to the courts its freedom of legislating according to its lights, while some will share his convictions and believe that he states them none too strongly, to many it will seem that he indulges in a species of judicial idolatry.[6]

The Court is not the Constitution. To accept the two as equivalent is to relinquish individual responsibility and the capacity for self-government. Constitutional determinations are not matters than can be left exclusively to the judiciary. Individuals outside the courts have their own judgments to make. Spinoza advised that "no one can willingly transfer his natural right of free reason and judgment. . . ."[7] Even with our own consent we cannot abdicate the duty to think for ourselves. What is constitutional or unconstitutional must be left for

[4]United States v. Nixon, 418 U.S. 683 (1974).
[5]Maness v. Meyers, 419 U.S. 449, 458–59 (1975).
[6]Harold M. Bowman, "Congress and the Supreme Court," 25 Pol. Sci. Q. 20, 34 (1910).
[7]The Philosophy of Spinoza 333 (Modern Library ed., 1954).

us to explore, ponder, and come to terms with. In an interview in 1982, Justice Blackmun said that it "may prove to be well in the long run that people do get disturbed and concerned and interested in what the Court does. I think on balance that this is a good thing for the country, because the Supreme Court of the United States belongs to the country. It doesn't belong to me, or to the nine of us, or to the Chief Justice. It's an instrument of government. And I try to preach the gospel that lay people, as well as lawyers, should take an interest in the Court and what it's doing."[8]

A recent article by Paul Brest makes a similar point. In urging citizen participation in constitutional decisionmaking, he said that constitutional issues "are not radically discontinuous from other political issues."[9] The ethical and moral dimensions of constitutional questions necessary spread beyond the confines of courtrooms. The problem with judicial exclusivity "concerns the role of citizens in a democratic polity. If the judges exercise a monopoly over constitutional decisionmaking, then other citizens and their representatives are excluded from participating in what are among the polity's most fundamental questions."[10]

Justice Frankfurter put the Court's work in perspective by reminding his readers that it is "important to bear in mind that this Court can only hope to set limits and point the way. It falls to the lot of legislative bodies and administrative officials to find practical solutions within the frame of our decisions."[11] At times the legislative and executive branches work within the broad contours of a judicial decision. On other occasions it is the judiciary that seeks practical solutions within the frame of congressional statutes and executive precedents.

An "activist" member of the judiciary, Earl Warren, explained the limits of the courts. In times of political stress, the courts may acquiesce to actions that we later deplore. Commenting on the Court's role in upholding the treatment of Japanese-Americans during World War II, he said: "the fact that the Court rules in a case like *Hiraba-*

---

[8]"A Justice Speaks Out: A Conversation with Harry A. Blackmun," Cable News Network, Inc., December 4, 1982, at 20.

[9]Paul Brest, "Constitutional Citizenship," 34 Cleveland St. L. Rev. 1, 10 (1986).

[10]Id. at 7.

[11]Niemotko v. Maryland, 340 U.S. 268, 275–76 (1961) (concurring opinion).

yashi that a given program is constitutional, does not necessarily answer the question whether, in a broader sense, it actually is."[12] That the courts fail to strike down a governmental action does not mean that constitutional standards have been followed. The habit of looking automatically to the courts to protect constitutional liberties is ill-advised. Warren concluded that under our political system the judiciary must play a limited role: "In our democracy it is still the Legislature and the elected Executive who have the primary responsibility for fashioning and executing policy consistent with the Constitution."[13] Even here he warned against excessive dependence on the political branches: "the day-to-day job of upholding the Constitution really lies elsewhere. It rests, realistically, on the shoulders of every citizen."[14]

The belief in judicial supremacy imposes a burden that the Court cannot carry. It sets up expectations that invite disappointment if not disaster. A President once reassured his country in an inaugural address that an issue over which the nation was seriously divided "legitimately belongs to the Supreme Court of the United States, before whom it is now pending, and will, it is understood, be speedily and finally settled." The President was James Buchanan. The case about to be decided: *Dred Scott* v. *Sandford.*

What qualifications should be placed on the "last word" doctrine? First, the fact that the Supreme Court upholds the constitutionality of a measure, as when it sustained the U.S. Bank in *McCulloch,* places no obligation on executive and legislative branches to adopt that measure in the future. Congress was free to discontinue the Bank. If it passed legislation to renew it, President Jackson was within his rights to exercise his veto. A decision by the Supreme Court did not relieve the other branches of their duty or freedom to reach independent interpretations.

Second, a decision by the Supreme Court that a certain practice is not prohibited by the Constitution, such as the use of search warrants in *Stanford Daily* or access to bank records in *Miller,* does not prevent the other branches from passing legislation to prohibit or restrict

[12]Earl Warren, "The Bill of Rights and the Military," 37 N.Y.U. L. Rev. 181, 193 (1962).
[13]Id. at 202.
[14]Id.

these practices. Rights unprotected by the courts may be secured by Congress and the President.

Third, when the Supreme Court concludes that an action has no constitutional protection in the federal courts—for example, distributing petitions in a shopping center, as in *PruneYard*—the states are not inhibited in any way from protecting these actions through their own constitutional interpretations.

Fourth, many constitutional issues are resolved through rules of evidence, statutes, customs, and accommodations—a common-law method of setting disputes. Through these techniques, institutions outside the courts play a decisive role in shaping not only constitutional values but constitutional doctrines.

Fifth, there are occasions when Supreme Court rulings strike such a discordant note in the body politic that they will be tested again and again with new variations on the same theme. Court decisions are entitled to respect, not adoration. When the Court issues its judgment we should not suspend ours. The Commerce Clause, raising such issues as child labor and economic regulation by the government, is one area in which Congress eventually prevailed over judicial roadblocks. Many other examples could be cited. These challenges and collisions help keep the constitutional dialogue open and vigorous. In the search for a reconciliation between constitutional law and self-government, we must all participate.

Judicial review fits our constitutional system because we like to fragment power. We feel safer with checks and balances, even when an unelected Court tells an elected legislature or elected President that they have overstepped. This very preference for fragmented power denies the Supreme Court an authoritative and final voice for deciding constitutional questions. We do not accept the concentration of legislative power in Congress or executive power in the President. For the same reason, we cannot permit judicial power and constitutional interpretation to reside only in the courts. We reject supremacy in all three branches because of the value placed upon freedom, discourse, democracy, and limited government.

Suggested Readings

Chapter One

BALL, HOWARD. Courts and Politics: The Federal Judicial System. Englewood Cliffs, N.J.: Prentice-Hall, 1980.

BETH, LOREN P. Politics, the Constitution, and the Supreme Court. Evanston, Ill.: Row, Peterson & Co., 1962.

CAPLAN, LINCOLN. The Tenth Justice: The Solicitor General and the Rule of Law. New York: Alfred A. Knopf, 1987.

CHAYES, ABRAM. "The Role of the Judge in Public Law Litigation," 89 Harvard Law Review 1281 (1976).

EPSTEIN, LEE. Conservatives in Court. Knoxville: University of Tennessee Press, 1985.

FISHER, LOUIS. "Social Influences on Constitutional Law," 15 Journal of Political Science 7 (1987).

GILMOUR, ROBERT J. "Agency Administration by Judiciary," 6 Southern Review of Public Administration 26 (1982).

GINGER, ANN FAGAN. "Litigation As a Form of Political Action," 9 Wayne Law Review 458 (1963).

GLAZER, NATHAN. "Should Judges Administer Social Services?," The Public Interest, No. 50 (1978).

GOLDMAN, SHELDON, and THOMAS JAHNIGE. The Federal Courts as a Political System. New York: Harper & Row, 1976.

GRIFFITH, J.A.G., The Politics of the Judiciary. London: Fontana Press, 1985.

HARRIMAN, LINDA, and JEFFREY D. STRAUSSMAN. "Do Judges Determine Budget Decisions? Federal Court Decisions in Prison Reform and State Spending for Corrections," 43 Public Administration Review 343 (1983).

HODDER-WILLIAMS, RICHARD. The Politics of the U.S. Supreme Court. London: George Allen & Unwin, 1980.

LATHAM, EARL. "The Supreme Court as a Political Institution," 31 Minnesota Law Review 205 (1947).

LIEBERMAN, JETHRO K. The Litigious Society. New York: Basic Books, 1981.

MURPHY, WALTER, and JOSEPH TANENHAUS. The Study of Public Law. New York: Random House, 1972.

MURPHY, WALTER, and C. HERMAN PRITCHETT, EDS. Courts, Judges, and Politics. New York: Random House, 1986.

281

NEIER, ARYEH. Only Judgment: The Limits of Litigation in Social Change. Middletown, Conn.: Wesleyan University Press, 1982.

O'CONNOR, KAREN, and LEE EPSTEIN. "Amicus Curiae Participation in U.S. Supreme Court Litigation: An Appraisal of Hakman's 'Folklore,' " 16 Law and Society Review 311 (1981–1982).

PELTASON, JACK. Federal Courts in the Political Process. New York: Random House, 1955.

RODELL, FRED. Nine Men: A Political History of the United States from 1790 to 1955. New York: Random House, 1955.

ROSENBLUM, VICTOR G. Law as a Political Instrument. New York: Random House, 1955.

VOSE, CLEMENT E. Caucasians Only: The Supreme Court, the NAACP, and the Restrictive Covenant Cases. Berkeley: University of California Press, 1959.

WASBY, STEPHEN L. The Supreme Court in the Federal Judicial System. New York: Holt, Rinehart and Winston, 1978.

Chapter Two

AGRESTO, JOHN. The Supreme Court and Constitutional Democracy. Ithaca, N.Y.: Cornell University Press. 1984.

ALFANGE, DEAN, JR. "On Judicial Policymaking and Constitutional Change: Another Look at the 'Original Intent' Theory of Constitutional Interpretation," 5 Hastings Constitutional Law Quarterly 603 (1978)

BERGER, RAOUL. Congress v. The Supreme Court. Cambridge: Harvard University Press, 1969.

BICKEL, ALEXANDER M. The Least Dangerous Branch. New York: Bobbs-Merrill, 1962.

BISHIN, WILLIAM R. "Judicial Review in Democratic Theory," 50 Southern California Law Review 1099 (1977).

BLACK, CHARLES L., JR. The People and the Court. New York: Macmillan, 1960.

CARR, ROBERT K. The Supreme Court and Judicial Review. New York: Farrar and Rinehart, 1942.

COMMAGER, HENRY STEELE. Majority Rule and Minority Rights. New York: Oxford University Press, 1943.

CORWIN, EDWARD S. The Doctrine of Judicial Review. Princeton, N.J.: Princeton University Press, 1914.

———. Court Over Constitution. Princeton, N.J.: Princeton University Press, 1938.

DAHL, ROBERT A. "Decision-Making in a Democracy: The Role of the Supreme Court as a National Policy-Maker," 6 Journal of Public Law 279 (1957).

FISHER, LOUIS. "Methods of Constitutional Interpretation: The Limits of Original Intent," 18 Cumberland Law Review 43 (1987–1988).

HAINES, CHARLES GROVE. The American Doctrine of Judicial Supremacy. Berkeley: University of California Press, 1932.

HENKIN, LOUIS. "Some Reflections on Current Constitutional Controversy," 109 University of Pennsylvania Law Review 637 (1961).

KURLAND, PHILIP B. Politics, the Constitution, and the Warren Court. Chicago: University of Chicago Press, 1970.

MILLER, ARTHUR S., and RONALD F. HOWELL. "The Myth of Neutrality in Constitutional Adjudication," 27 University of Chicago Law Review 661 (1960).

NELSON, WILLIAM E., "Changing Conceptions of Judicial Review: The Evolution of Constitutional Theory in the States, 1790–1860," 120 University of Pennsylvania Law Review 1166 (1972).

O'BRIEN, DAVID M. "Judicial Review and Constitutional Politics: Theory and Practice," 48 University of Chicago Law Review 1052 (1981).

POLLAK, LOUIS H. "Racial Discrimination and Judicial Integrity: A Reply to Professor Wechsler," 108 University of Pennsylvania Law Review 1 (1959).

ROSTOW, EUGENE V. The Sovereign Prerogative. New Haven, Conn.: Yale University Press, 1962.

WELLINGTON, HARRY H. "The Nature of Judicial Review," 91 Yale Law Journal 486 (1982).

WOLFE, CHRISTOPHER. The Rise of Modern Judicial Review. New York: Basic Books, 1986.

WRIGHT, J. SKELLY. "The Role of the Supreme Court in a Democratic Society—Judicial Activism or Restraint," 54 Cornell Law Review 1 (1968).

———. "Professor Bickel, and Scholarly Tradition, and the Supreme Court," 84 Harvard Law Review 769 (1971).

———. "Judicial Review and the Equal Protection Clause," 15 Harvard Civil Rights–Civil Liberties Law Review 1 (1980).

Chapter Three

ALBERT, LEE A. "Justiciability and Theories of Judicial Review: A Remote Relationship," 50 Southern California Law Review 1139 (1977).

BRILMAYER, LEA. "The Jurisprudence of Article III: Perspectives on the 'Case or Controversy' Requirement," 93 Harvard Law Review 297 (1979).

CONDON, DANIEL PATRICK. "The Generalized Grievance Restriction: Prudential Restraint or Constitutional Mandate?," 70 Georgetown Law Journal 1157 (1982).

HUGHES, GRAHAM. "Civil Disobedience and the Political Question Doctrine," 43 New York University Law Review 1 (1968).

JACKSON, R. BROOKE. "The Political Question Doctrine: Where Does It Stand After *Powell* v. *McCormack, O'Brien* v. *Brown,* and *Gilligan* v. *Morgan*?," 44 University of Colorado Law Review 477 (1973).

KATES, DON B., and WILLIAM T. BARKER. "Mootness in Judicial Proceedings: Toward a Coherent Theory," 62 California Law Review 1385 (1974).

LOGAN, DAVID A. "Standing to Sue: A Proposed Separation of Powers Analysis," 1984 Wisconsin Law Review 37.

MONAGHAN, HENRY P. "Constitutional Adjudication: The Who and When," 82 Yale Law Journal 1363 (1973).

MORRISON, ALAN B. "Rights Without Remedies: The Burger Court Takes the Federal Courts Out of the Business of Protecting Federal Rights," 30 Rutgers Law Review 841 (1977).

NICHOL, GENE R., JR. "Causation as a Standing Requirement: The Unprincipled Use of Judicial Restraint," 69 Kentucky Law Journal 185 (1980).

ORREN, KAREN. "Standing to Sue: Interest Group Conflict in the Federal Courts," 70 American Political Science Review (1976).

POST, CHARLES GORDON, JR. The Supreme Court and Political Questions. Baltimore: The Johns Hopkins Press, 1936.

RADCLIFFE, JAMES E. The Case-or-Controversy Provision. University Park: Pennsylvania State University Press, 1978.

ROSENBLUM, VICTOR G. "Justiciability and Justice: Elements of Restraint and Indifference," 15 Catholic University Law Review 141 (1966).

SCALIA, ANTONIN. "The Doctrine of Standing as an Essential Element of the Separation of Powers," 17 Suffolk University Law Review 881 (1983).

SCHARPF, FRITZ W. "Judicial Review and the Political Question: A Functional Analysis," 75 Yale Law Journal 517 (1966).

SCOTT, KENNETH E. "Standing in the Supreme Court—A Functional Analysis," 86 Harvard Law Review 645 (1973).

SEDLER, ROBERT ALLEN. "Standing and the Burger Court: An Analysis and Some Proposals for Legislative Reform" 30 Rutgers Law Review 863 (1977).

STRUM, PHILIPPA. The Supreme Court and "Political Questions." University, Alabama: University of Alabama Press, 1974.

TIGAR, MICHAEL E. "Judicial Power, the 'Political Question Doctrine,' and Foreign Relations," 17 UCLA Law Review 1135 (1970).

TUCKER, EDWIN W. "The Metamorphosis of the Standing to Sue Doctrine," 17 New York Law Forum 911 (1972).

TUSHNET, MARK V. "The Sociology of Article III: A Response to Professor Brilmayer," 93 Harvard Law Review 1698 (1980).

Chapter Four

ABRAHAM, HENRY J. Justices and Presidents: A Political History of Appointments to the Supreme Court. New York: Oxford University Press, 1974.

BALL, HOWARD. Courts and Politics: The Federal Judicial System. Englewood Cliffs, N.J.: Prentice-Hall, 1980.

BLACK, CHARLES L., JR. "A Note on Senatorial Consideration of Supreme Court Nominees," 79 Yale Law Journal 657 (1970).

CARP, ROBERT A., and C. K. ROWLAND. Policymaking and Politics in the Federal District Courts. Knoxville: University of Tennessee Press, 1983.

CHASE, HAROLD W. Federal Judges: The Appointing Process. Minneapolis: University of Minnesota, 1972.

DANELSKI, DAVID J. A Supreme Court Justice is Appointed. New York: Random House, 1964.

EARLY, STEPHEN T., JR. Constitutional Courts of the U.S. Totowa, N.J.: Littlefield, Adams & Co., 1977.

FISH, PETER GRAHAM. The Politics of Federal Judicial Administration. Princeton, N.J.: Princeton University Press, 1973.

GROSSMAN, JOEL B. Lawyers and Judges: The ABA and the Politics of Judicial Selection. New York: Wiley, 1965.

HARRIS, JOSEPH P. The Advice and Consent of the Senate. Berkeley: University of California Press, 1953.

HAYNES, EVAN. The Selection and Tenure of Judges. Newark, N.J.: National Conference of Judicial Councils, 1944.

HOWARD, J. WOODFORD, JR. Courts of Appeals in the Federal Judicial System. Princeton, N.J.: Princeton University Press, 1981.

HULBARY, WILLIAM E., and THOMAS G. WALKER, "The Supreme Court Selection Process: Presidential Motivations and Judicial Performance," 33 Western Political Quarterly 185 (1980).

KAHN, MICHAEL A. "The Politics of the Appointment Process: An Analysis of Why Learned Hand Was Never Appointed to the Supreme Court," 25 Stanford Law Review 251 (1973).

KURLAND, PHILIP B. "The Constitution and the Tenure of Federal Judges: Some Notes From History," 36 University of Chicago Law Review 665 (1969).

Suggested Readings

MASON, ALPHEUS THOMAS. "Extra-Judicial Work for Judges: The Views of Chief Justice Stone," 67 Harvard Law Review 193 (1953).

MURPHY, WALTER. "In His Own Image: Mr. Chief Justice Taft and Supreme Court Appointments," 1961 Supreme Court Review 159.

SCHMIDHAUSER, JOHN R. "The Justices of the Supreme Court: A Collective Portrait," 3 Midwest Journal of Political Science 1 (1959).

―――. Judges and Justices: The Federal Appellate Judiciary. Boston: Little, Brown, 1979.

SCIGLIANO, ROBERT. The Supreme Court and the Presidency. New York: The Free Press, 1971.

TRIBE, LAURENCE H. God Save This Honorable Court. New York: Random House, 1985.

WHEELER, RUSSELL. "Extrajudicial Activities of the Early Supreme Court," 1973 Supreme Court Review 123.

WINTERS, GLENN R., ED. Selected Readings: Judicial Selection and Tenure. Chicago: American Judicature Society, 1973.

Chapter Five

BARTH, ALAN. Prophets With Honor: Great Dissents and Great Dissenters in the Supreme Court. New York: Alfred A. Knopf, 1974.

CANNON, MARK W., and DAVID M. O'BRIEN, EDS. Views from the Bench: The Judiciary and Constitutional Politics. Chatham, N.J.: Chatham House Publishers, 1985.

CASPER, GERHARD, and RICHARD A. POSNER. The Workload of the Supreme Court. Chicago: American Bar Foundation, 1976.

FRANK, JOHN P. Marble Palace: The Supreme Court in American Life. New York: Alfred A. Knopf, 1958.

HART, HENRY M., JR. "Foreword: The Time Chart of the Justices," 73 Harvard Law Review 84 (1959).

HELLMAN, ARTHUR D. "Caseload, conflicts, and decisional capacity: Does the Supreme Court need help?," 67 Judicature 29 (1983).

HOWARD, J. WOODFORD, JR. Courts of Appeals in the Federal Judicial System. Princeton, N.J.: Princeton University Press, 1981.

MASON, ALPHEUS THOMAS. Harlan Fiske Stone: Pillar of the Law. New York: Viking Press, 1956.

MILLER, ARTHUR SELWYN, and D. S. SASTRI. "Secrecy and the Supreme Court— On the Need for Piercing the Red Velour Curtain," 22 Buffalo Law Review 799 (1973). See also accompanying comments by EUGENE GRESSMAN, JOEL B. GROSSMAN, J. WOODFORD HOWARD, JR., WALTER PROBERT, GLENDON SCHUBERT, and ROLAND YOUNG.

MURPHY, WALTER F. Elements of Judicial Strategy. Chicago: University of Chicago Press, 1964.

NEWLAND, CHESTER A. "Personal Assistants to Supreme Court Justices: The Law Clerks," 40 Oregon Law Review 299 (1961).

O'BRIEN, DAVID M. Storm Center: The Supreme Court in American Politics. New York: W. W. Norton, 1986.

PELTASON, JACK W. Federal Courts in the Political Process. New York: Random House, 1955.

PROVINE, DORIS MARIE. Case Selection in the United States Supreme Court. Chicago: University of Chicago Press, 1980.

RICHARDSON, RICHARD J., and KENNETH N. VINES. The Politics of Federal Courts: Lower Courts in the United States. Boston: Little, Brown, 1970.

ROHDE, DAVID W., and HAROLD J. SPAETH. Supreme Court Decision Making. San Francisco: W. H. Freeman and Co., 1976.

SPAETH, HAROLD J. Supreme Court Policy Making. San Francisco: W. H. Freeman and Co., 1979.

STERN, ROBERT L., and EUGENE CRESSMAN. Supreme Court Practice, 5th ed. Washington, D.C.: The Bureau of National Affairs, 1978.

ULMER, S. SIDNEY. "Bricolage and Assorted Thoughts on Working in the Papers of the Supreme Court Justices," 35 Journal of Politics 286 (1973).

WESTIN, ALAN F., ED. The Supreme Court: Views from Inside. New York: W. W. Norton, 1961.

———. An Autobiography of the Supreme Court. New York: Macmillan, 1963.

WILKINSON, J. HARVIE, III. Serving Justice: A Supreme Court Clerk's View. New York, Charterhouse, 1974.

WOODWARD, BOB, and SCOTT ARMSTRONG. The Brethren: Inside the Supreme Court. New York: Simon and Schuster, 1979.

Chapter Six

BECKER, THEODORE L., and MALCOLM M. FEELEY, EDS. The Impact of Supreme Court Decisions. New York: Oxford University Press, 1973.

BRECKENRIDGE, ADAM CARLYLE. Congress Against the Court. Lincoln: University of Nebraska Press, 1970.

BREST, PAUL. "Congress as Constitutional Decisionmaker and Its Power to Counter Judicial Doctrine," 21 Georgia Law Review 57 (Special Issue 1986).

CULP, MAURICE S. "A Survey of the Proposals to Limit or Deny the Power of Judicial Review by the Supreme Court of the United States," 4 Indiana Law Journal 386, 474 (1929).

"Efforts in the Congress to Curtail the Federal Courts: Pro & Con." Washington, D.C.: Congressional Digest, May 1982.

ELLIOTT, SHELDON D. "Court-Curbing Proposals in Congress," 33 Notre Dame Lawyer 597 (1958).

HALPER, THOMAS. "Supreme Court Responses to Congressional Threats: Strategy and Tactics," 19 Drake Law Review 292 (1970).

HANDBERG, ROGER, and HAROLD F. HILL, JR. "Court Curbing, Court Reversals, and Judicial Review: The Supreme Court Versus Congress," 14 Law & Society Review 309 (1980).

HENSCHEN, BETH. "Statutory Interpretations of the Supreme Court: Congressional Responses," 11 American Politics Quarterly 441 (1983).

JACKSON, ROBERT H. The Struggle for Judicial Supremacy. New York: Alfred A. Knopf, 1941.

LEUCHTENBURG, WILLIAM E. "The Origins of Franklin D. Roosevelt's 'Court-Packing' Plan," 1966 Supreme Court Review 347–400.

LYTLE, CLIFFORD M. "Congressional Response to Supreme Court Decisions in the Aftermath of the School Desegregation Cases," 12 Journal of Public Law 290 (1963).

MURPHY, WALTER F. Congress and the Court. Chicago: University of Chicago Press, 1962.

———. "Lower Court Checks on Supreme Court Power," 53 American Political Science Review 1017 (1959).

NAGEL, STUART S. "Court-Curbing Periods in American History," 18 Vanderbilt Law Review 925 (1965).

NICHOLS, EGBERT RAY, ED. Congress or the Supreme Court: Which Shall Rule America? New York: Noble and Noble, 1935.

Note. "Congressional Reversal of Supreme Court Decisions: 1945–1957," 71 Harvard Law Review 1324 (1958).

———. "Tension Between Judicial and Legislative Powers as Reflected in Confrontations Between Congress and the Courts," 13 Georgia Law Review 1513 (1979).

PRITCHETT, C. HERMAN. Congress Versus the Supreme Court. Minneapolis: University of Minnesota Press, 1961.

SCHMIDHAUSER, JOHN R., and LARRY L. BERG. The Supreme Court and Congress. New York: The Free Press, 1972.

STEAMER, ROBERT J. The Supreme Court in Crisis. The University of Massachusetts Press, 1971.

STUMPF, HARRY P. "Congressional Response to Supreme Court Rulings: The Interaction of Law and Politics," 14 Journal of Public Law 377 (1965).

VOSE, CLEMENT E. Constitutional Change: Amendment Politics and Supreme Court Litigation Since 1900. Lexington, Mass.: D. C. Heath, 1972.

Chapter Seven

AGRESTO, JOHN. The Supreme Court and Constitutional Democracy. Ithaca, N.Y.: Cornell University Press, 1984.

ANDREWS, WILLIAM G., ED. Coordinate Magistrates: Constitutional Law by Congress and President. New York: Van Nostrand Reinhold, 1969.

BARBER, SOTIRIOS A. On What the Constitution Means. Baltimore: Johns Hopkins Press, 1984.

BRIGHAM, JOHN. The Cult of the Court. Philadelphia: Temple University Press, 1987.

BREST, PAUL. "The Conscientious Legislator's Guide to Constitutional Interpretation," 27 Stanford Law Review 585 (1975).

BURT, ROBERT A. "Miranda and Title II: A Morganatic Marriage," 1969 Supreme Court Review 81.

CHOPER, JESSE H. Judicial Review and the National Political Process. Chicago: University of Chicago Press, 1980.

COHEN, WILLIAM. "Congressional Power to Validate Unconstitutional State Laws: A Forgotten Solution to an Old Enigma," 35 Stanford Law Review 387 (1983).

COX, ARCHIBALD. "The Role of Congress in Constitutional Determinations," 40 University of Cincinnati Law Review 199 (1971).

ELY, JOHN HART. Democracy and Distrust. Cambridge: Harvard University Press, 1980.

FISHER, LOUIS. "Congress and the Fourth Amendment," 21 Georgia Law Review 107 (Special Issue 1986).

———. "Constitutional Interpretation by Members of Congress," 63 North Carolina Law Review 707 (1985).

———. Constitutional Conflicts between Congress and the President. Princeton, N.J.: Princeton University Press, 1985.

GREENAWALT, KENT. "Constitutional Decisions and the Supreme Law," 58 University of Colorado Law Review 145 (1987).

LINDGREN, JANET S. "Beyond Cases: Reconsidering Judicial Review," 1983 Wisconsin Law Review 583.

MIKVA, ABNER J. "How Well Does Congress Support and Defend the Constitution?," 61 North Carolina Law Review 587 (1983).

MIKVA, ABNER J., and JOSEPH R. LUNDY. "The 91st Congress and the Constitution," 38 University of Chicago Law Review 449 (1971).

Suggested Readings

MONAGHAN, HENRY P. "The Supreme Court 1974 Term, Foreword: Constitutional Common Law," 89 Harvard Law Review 1 (1975).

MORGAN, DONALD G. Congress and the Constitution. Cambridge: Harvard University Press, 1966.

MURPHY, WALTER F. "Who Shall Interpret? The Quest for the Ultimate Constitutional Interpreter," 48 Review of Politics 401 (1986).

NICHOLS, EGBERT RAY, ED. Congress or the Supreme Court. Which Shall Rule America? New York: Noble and Noble, 1935.

POLLACK, SHELDON D. "Constitutional Interpretation as Political Choice," 48 University of Pittsburgh Law Review 989 (1987).

Index of Cases

General Index